First Canadian Edition

Essentials of
Business Communication
for English Language Learners

> **MARY ELLEN GUFFEY**
Professor of Business Emerita
Los Angeles Pierce College

> **RICHARD ALMONTE**
George Brown College

> **AUSRA MARIA KARKA**
Humber College

NELSON EDUCATION

NELSON / EDUCATION

Essentials of Business Communication for English Language Learners, First Canadian Edition

by Mary Ellen Guffey, Richard Almonte, and Ausra Maria Karka

Associate Vice President, Editorial Director:
Evelyn Veitch

Editor-in-Chief, Higher Education:
Anne Williams

Executive Editor:
Cara Yarzab

Acquisitions Editor:
Bram Sepers

Marketing Manager:
Shelley Collacutt Miller

Senior Developmental Editor:
Linda Sparks

Permissions Coordinator:
Karen Becker

Senior Content Production Manager:
Natalia Denesiuk Harris

Production Service:
GEX Publishing Services

Copy Editor:
Margaret Crammond

Proofreader:
GEX Publishing Services

Indexer:
GEX Publishing Services

Production Coordinator:
Ferial Suleman

Design Director:
Ken Phipps

Managing Designer:
Katherine Strain

Interior Design Modifications:
Fernanda Pisani

Cover Design:
Liz Harasymczuk

Cover Image:
© José Ortega/Images.com

Compositor:
GEX Publishing Services

Printer:
RR Donnelley

Library and Archives Canada Cataloguing in Publication Data

Guffey, Mary Ellen

   Essentials of business communication for English language learners / Mary Ellen Guffey, Richard Almonte, Ausra Maria Karka. — 1st Canadian ed.

Includes bibliographical references and index.

ISBN 978-0-17-610491-7

   1. Business writing—Textbooks. 2. English language—Business English—Textbooks. 3. Business communication—Textbooks. 4. English language—Textbooks for second language learners. I. Almonte, Richard II. Karka, Ausra Maria, 1947– III. Title.

HF5718.3.G844 2007   808'.06665
C2007-906356-X

ISBN-13: 978-0-17-610491-7
ISBN-10: 0-17-610491-7

Brief Contents

UNIT 6

Communicating for Employment 233

Contents

3 Improving Writing Techniques 42

4 Revising and Proofreading Business Messages 64

UNIT 5

Developing Speaking Skills 213

10 Communicating in Person and by Telephone 214

UNIT 6

Communicating for Employment 233

11 The Job Search, Résumés, and Cover Letters 234

12 Employment Interviews and Follow-Up Messages 264

Preface

Today's graduates come from various backgrounds and experiences, but they all have one thing in common: they enter working environments that have ever-increasing demands. Because of the growing importance of team management and greater power given to employees, they will be expected to gather data, solve problems, and make decisions independently. They will be working with global trading partners and in work teams in an increasingly diverse workplace. And they will be using sophisticated technologies to communicate.

Surprisingly, writing skills are becoming more and more important. In the past, businesspeople may have written a couple of work-related letters a month, but now they receive and send hundreds of e-mail messages weekly. Their writing skills are displayed in every message they send. To help all students—especially those for whom English may not be their first language—develop the skills they need to succeed in today's technologically enhanced workplace, we have responded with an edition of *Essentials of Business Communication* for English Language Learners.

This edition of *Essentials* has been written to address the needs of students who have English as their second language. For many of these students, the lack of skill in writing clear and correct business documents presents a barrier to their success in academic as well as professional endeavours. This edition has been modified for the English language learner in the following ways:

- Condensed chapters provide a more manageable post-secondary semester curriculum;
- Revised Grammar/Mechanics Reviews and end-of-chapter Documents for Revision reflect ESL-type errors while maintaining a thorough review of all basic grammar and mechanics for effective business writing;
- Simplified, more concrete language and vocabulary are used in text explanations, Writing Improvement Exercises, and end-of-chapter Activities and Cases; and
- Each chapter contains fewer Activities and Cases.

The English Language Learners edition maintains the streamlined, efficient approach to communication that has equipped past learners with the skills needed to be successful in their work. It is most helpful to post-secondary and adult learners—especially intermediate to advanced ESL learners—preparing themselves for a new career, planning a change in their current career, or wishing to upgrade their writing and speaking skills. Features include

- **Text/workbook format.** The convenient text/workbook format presents an all-in-one teaching–learning package that includes concepts, workbook application exercises, writing problems, and a combination handbook/reference manual. Students work with and purchase only one volume for efficient, economical instruction.

- **Comprehensive but concise coverage.** An important reason for the enormous success of *Essentials of Business Communication* is that it practises what it preaches. The First Canadian Edition for English Language Learners follows the same strategy as the original text by concentrating on essential concepts presented without wasted words.
- **Writing plans and writing improvement exercises.** Step-by-step writing plans structure the writing experience so that beginning writers get started quickly—without struggling to provide unknown details to unfamiliar cases. Many revision exercises build confidence and skills.
- **Wide coverage of communication technology.** All related chapters build technological skills by including discussions and applications involving e-mail, instant messaging, PDAs, cell phones, Web research, current software, and online employment searches.
- **Grammar/mechanics emphasis.** Each chapter features a review of the Grammar/Mechanics Handbook. Readers take a short quiz to review specific concepts, and they also proofread business documents that provide a cumulative review of all concepts previously presented.

Features That Enhance Teaching and Learning

Although *Essentials of Business Communication for English Language Learners* packs considerable information into a brief book, it covers all the critical topics of a comprehensive business communication course, and it also features many teaching–learning tools to make instruction, application, and retention easier.

- **Focus on writing skills.** Most students need a great deal of instruction and practice in developing basic and advanced writing techniques, particularly with today's increased communication by e-mail. Writing skills have returned to the forefront, since so much of today's business is done through written messages.
- **E-Mail emphasis.** *Essentials of Business Communication for English Language Learners* devotes an entire chapter to the writing of e-mail, which has become the most used communication channel in the business world.
- **Listening, speaking, and nonverbal skills.** Employers are increasingly seeking well-rounded individuals who can interact with fellow employees as well as represent the organization effectively. *Essentials of Business Communication for English Language Learners* provides professional tips for managing nonverbal cues, overcoming listening barriers, developing speaking skills, planning and participating in meetings, and making productive telephone calls.
- **Coverage of report writing.** Chapter 9 develops functional report-writing skills by providing detailed instruction in the preparation of four types of commonly used informal reports. For quick comprehension, all reports contain marginal notes that pinpoint writing strategies.
- **Employment communication skills.** Successful résumés, cover letters, and other employment documents are among the most important topics in a good business communication course. This edition provides the most realistic and up-to-date résumés in the field. The models show chronological, functional, combination, and computer-friendly résumés.

- **Employment interviewing.** *Essentials of Business Communication for English Language Learners* devotes an entire chapter to effective interviewing techniques, including a discussion of screening interviews and hiring interviews. Chapter 12 also teaches techniques for fighting fear, answering questions, and following up.
- **Models comparing effective and ineffective documents.** To facilitate speedy recognition of good and bad writing techniques and strategies, *Essentials of Business Communication for English Language Learners* presents many before-and-after documents. Marginal notes spotlight targeted strategies and effective writing. We hope that instructors turn this before-and-after technique into effective pedagogy whereby all their students' written assignments undergo the scrutiny of an editing and revising process before being handed in as final products.
- **Variety in end-of-chapter activities.** An amazing array of review questions, critical-thinking questions, writing improvement exercises, revision exercises, activities, and realistic case problems holds students' attention and helps them apply chapter concepts meaningfully.
- **Diagnostic test.** An optional grammar/mechanics diagnostic test helps students and instructors systematically determine specific student writing weaknesses. Students may be directed to the Grammar/Mechanics Handbook for remediation.
- **Grammar/Mechanics Handbook.** The comprehensive Grammar/Mechanics Handbook provides a thorough review of English grammar, punctuation, capitalization style, and number usage. Its self-teaching exercises may be used for classroom instruction or for supplementary assignments. The handbook also serves as a convenient reference throughout the course and afterwards.

Unparalleled Instructor Support

The English Language Learners' edition of *Essentials of Business Communication* continues to set the standard for business communication support. Classroom success is easy to achieve with the many practical ancillary items that supplement Guffey textbooks. No other author matches her level of support.

The following time-saving ancillaries and resources accompany *Essentials of Business Communication for English Language Learners*:

- **Instructor's Manual with Test Banks.** The IM supplies general suggestions for teaching business communication and lesson plans and test banks for each chapter. In addition to ideas for course organization and evaluation, the IM provides many supplementary lectures on relevant topics not covered in the text.
- **Canadian Web Site for Students and Instructors.** This complete learning environment is available at <**www.guffeyessentialsell1e.nelson.com**>. Students will find book-specific learning tools such as chapter quizzes and learning objectives as well as general resources such as study tips and career resources. Instructors will find additional teaching aids; they should contact their Nelson sales representative for more information.

Acknowledgments

Essentials of Business Communication for English Language Learners includes many of the constructive suggestions and timely advice provided by professional communicators and educators across Canada. These dedicated reviewers include Joan Barnet, Douglas College; Joan Dundas, Brock University; Jura Eskus, Sheridan College; John Iveson, Sheridan College; Laura Lush, University of Toronto; Alan Orr, Humber College; and Patricia Raymond, University of Toronto.

A new edition like this would not be possible without the development team at Nelson. Special thanks go to Linda Sparks, Natalia Denesiuk Harris, Shelley Collacutt Miller, Bram Sepers, and Cara Yarzab. Thanks also go to the copy editor, Margaret Crammond.

Finally, this new ESL edition includes valuable input from the ESL team of colleagues at the Humber Institute of Technology and Advanced Learning in Toronto. Many thanks to Professor Linda Maloney, ESL Coordinator at Humber, as well as Professors Beverley Allix, Patricia Burke, and Barbara Danbrook.

—Mary Ellen Guffey
Richard Almonte
Ausra Karka

Communication
Foundations

Chapter 1
**Today's Communication
Challenges**

Today's Communication Challenges

We live in a time of unbridled change. Computers are taking us in bold directions never foreseen—in business, communication and society.... For years, companies have been told that their future lies in product innovation [but] tomorrow's winners will be those firms that become innovators in how they do business—not in what they make or sell.[1]

Rick Spence, Profit *magazine*

LEARNING OBJECTIVES

1. Understand the importance of becoming an effective business communicator in today's changing workplace.
2. Examine the process of communication.
3. Discuss how to become an effective listener.
4. Analyze nonverbal communication and explain techniques for improving nonverbal communication skills.
5. Explain how culture affects communication and describe methods for improving cross-cultural communication.
6. Identify specific techniques that improve effective communication among various workplace audiences.

Becoming an Effective Business Communicator

✔ Quick Check

The information revolution has made communication skills extremely important.

People with different backgrounds bring varied views to decision making. As Rick Spence implies in his *Profit* article, improving important processes like decision making and communication will lead to business success in the future. Businesses must rely on their employees' ability to work with many groups of people who are located across international borders. The more effectively employees work together, the more successful their company is. In this age of information, career success depends on good communication, a skill that is made more challenging by tremendous changes in technology, the workforce, work environments, and the globalization of business.

Through e-mail, instant messaging, and other technology-based communication channels, business communicators today are doing more writing than ever before. Their writing is also having a more immediate impact. This book focuses on developing business writing skills. But you will also learn to improve your listening, nonverbal, and speaking skills.

While you are born with the ability to acquire language and to listen, effective business communication skills are learned. Good communicators are not born; they are made. Your ability to thrive in the dynamic and demanding contemporary world of work will depend on many factors, some of which you cannot control. One factor that you do control, however, is how well you communicate.

The goal of this book is to teach you basic business communication skills, such as how to write an effective e-mail, memo, or letter and how to make a presentation. Anyone can learn these skills with the help of effective instructional materials and good model documents, all of which you'll find in this book. You also need practice—with meaningful feedback. You need someone such as your instructor to tell you how to modify your responses so that you can improve. We've designed this book to provide you with everything necessary to make you a successful business communicator in today's dynamic workplace.

Once you've had a couple of years of business experience, you will look back on this course and this textbook as the most important in your entire postsecondary education. To get started, this first chapter presents an overview. You'll take a look at (1) the changing workplace, (2) the communication process, (3) listening, (4) nonverbal communication, (5) culture and communication, and (6) workplace diversity. The remainder of the book is devoted to developing specific writing and speaking skills.

✔ **Quick Check**

Because communication skills are learned, you control how well you communicate.

✔ **Quick Check**

This book and this course might well be the most important in your postsecondary education.

Succeeding in the Changing World of Work

The entire world of work is changing quickly. Changes are happening in the kind of work you'll do, the tools you'll use, the form of management you'll work under, the environment in which you'll work, the people with whom you'll interact. Many of the changes involve processing and communicating information. Therefore, the most successful people in this new world of work will be those with highly developed communication skills. The following business trends illustrate the importance of excellent communication skills.

✔ **Quick Check**

Trends in the new world of work emphasize the importance of communication skills.

- **Creative communication technologies.** E-mail, instant messaging, the Web, mobile technologies, audio- and videoconferencing—all of these technologies mean that you will be communicating more often and more rapidly than ever before. Your writing and speaking skills will be tested as never before.
- **Fewer levels of management.** To better compete and to reduce expenses, businesses have for years been trimming layers of management. This means you will have fewer managers. You will be making decisions and communicating them to customers, to fellow employees, and to executives.
- **More involvement in management.** Nowadays, even new employees are expected to understand and contribute to the success of the organization. Improving productivity and profitability will be everyone's job, not just management's.
- **Increased emphasis on self-directed work and project teams.** Businesses today are often run by teams of peers. You can expect to work with a team in gathering information, finding and sharing solutions, making decisions, and managing conflict. Good communication skills are extremely important in working together successfully in a team environment.
- **More global competition.** Because companies are required to move beyond local markets, you may be doing business with people from many different cultures. At the same time, because of increased immigration, you may be expected to work with people from many cultures in your local market as well as in your organization.[2] As a successful business communicator, you will want to learn about other cultures. You'll also need to develop interpersonal skills including sensitivity, flexibility, patience, and tolerance.

- **New work environments.** Mobile technologies and the desire for better work/family balance have resulted in flexible working arrangements. You may become engaged in full- or part-time telecommuting.[3] Working away from the office requires exchanging even more messages in order to stay connected.

Examining the Communication Process

As you can see, in today's workplace you can expect to be communicating more quickly, more often, and with greater numbers of people than ever before. Since good communication skills are essential to your success, we need to take a closer look at the communication process.

Just what is communication? For our purposes communication is the transmission of information and meaning from one individual or group (the sender) to another (the receiver). The crucial element in this definition is meaning. Communication has as its central objective the transmission of meaning. The process of communication is successful only when the receiver understands an idea as the sender intended it. (For background about this process, see the Communication, Culture and Media Studies website at http://www.ccms -infobase.com, and search under "Shannon-Weaver model.") This theoretical process generally involves five steps, discussed here and shown in Figure 1.1.

1. **Sender has an idea.** The idea may be influenced by the sender's mood, frame of reference, background, and culture, as well as the context of the situation. (For example, an accountant realizes income tax season is about to begin.)
2. **Sender encodes the idea in a message.** Encoding means putting the idea into words or gestures that will convey meaning. A major problem in communicating any message is that words have different meanings for different people. That's why skilled communicators try to choose familiar words with concrete meanings on which both senders and receivers agree. (For example, the accountant writes a letter asking all her clients to begin scheduling income tax appointments.)

Quick Check

Communication is the transmission of information and meaning from one individual or group to another.

Quick Check

The communication process has five steps: idea formation, message encoding, message transmission, message decoding, and feedback.

FIGURE 1.1 Communication Process
Communication barriers may cause the communication process to break down.

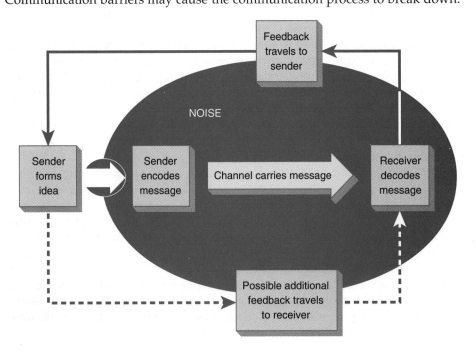

3. **Message travels over a channel.** The medium over which the message is transmitted is the channel. Messages may be sent by computer, telephone, fax, portable handheld device such as a BlackBerry, traditional mail, or website blog. Because both verbal and nonverbal messages are carried, senders must choose channels carefully. Any barrier that disrupts the transmission of a message in the communication process is called noise. Channel noise ranges from static that interrupts a telephone conversation to spelling and grammar errors in an e-mail message, to e-mails that are not sent because of firewalls. Such errors can damage the credibility of the sender. (For example, the accountant's assistant sends the letter to 125 clients via traditional mail in early January.)

4. **Receiver decodes message.** The person for whom a message is intended is the receiver. Translating the message into meaning involves decoding. Successful communication takes place only when a receiver understands the meaning intended by the sender. Such success is often hard to achieve because barriers and noise may interrupt the process. (For example, a client opens the letter, reads it, and decides to do his taxes himself this year.)

5. **Feedback travels to sender.** The response of the receiver to the sender creates feedback, a vital part of the entire communication process. Feedback helps the sender know that the message was received and understood. Senders can encourage feedback by including statements such as *Please let me know what you think as soon as possible.* Senders can further improve feedback by delivering the message at a time when receivers can respond. Senders should also provide only as much information as a receiver can handle. Receivers can improve the process by rewording the sender's message. They might say, *Thanks for your e-mail explaining the new safe procedure.* (For example, the client calls the accountant and leaves a voice-mail message thanking her for her letter but letting her know he's going to do his taxes himself this year.)

Developing Better Listening Skills

An important part of the communication process is listening. By many accounts, however, most of us are not very good listeners. Do you ever pretend to be listening when you're not? Do you know how to look attentive in class when your mind wanders far away? How about losing interest in people's messages when their ideas are boring or complex? Do you find it hard to focus on ideas when a speaker's clothing or mannerisms are unusual?

You probably answered yes to one or more of these questions because many of us have developed poor listening habits. In fact, some researchers suggest that we listen at only 25 percent efficiency. Such poor listening habits are costly in business. Workers must rewrite letters, re-ship shipments, reschedule appointments, renegotiate contracts, and restate directions.

To improve listening skills, we must first recognize barriers that prevent effective listening. Then we need to focus on specific techniques that are effective in improving listening skills.

✓ *Quick Check*

Most individuals listen at only 25 percent efficiency.

Barriers to Effective Listening

As you learned earlier, barriers and noise can interfere with the communication process. Have any of the following barriers and distractions prevented you from hearing what's said?

- **Physical barriers.** You cannot listen if you cannot hear what is being said. Physical barriers include hearing impairments, situations that carry sound poorly, and noisy surroundings. It's also difficult to listen if you're ill, tired, uncomfortable, or worried.

- **Personal barriers.** Everyone brings to the communication process a different set of cultural, ethical, and personal values. Each of us has an idea of what is right and what is important. If another person's ideas do not agree with our fixed thoughts, we tend to lose interest in his or her message and thus fail to hear.
- **Language problems.** Unfamiliar words can destroy the communication process because they lack meaning for the receiver. In addition, if a thick accent or pronunciation mistakes affect oral communication skills, listeners may be unable to understand what follows.
- **Nonverbal distractions.** Some of us find it hard to listen if a speaker is different from what we are expecting. Unusual clothing, speech mannerisms, sudden body movements, or a strange hairstyle or colour sometimes cause enough distraction to prevent us from hearing what the speaker has to say.
- **Thought speed.** Because we can process thoughts over three times faster than speakers can say them, we can become bored and allow our minds to wander.
- **Faking attention.** Most of us have learned to look as if we are listening even when we're not. Those who fake attention often find it hard to concentrate even when they want to.
- **Seeking attention.** Would you rather talk or listen? Naturally, many of us would rather talk. Since our own experiences and thoughts are most important to us, we want the attention in conversations. We sometimes don't listen carefully because we're just waiting politely for the next pause so that we can have our turn to speak.

Tips for Becoming an Active Listener

You can become a better listener by making an effort to become an active listener. This means becoming involved and taking responsibility for understanding. The following techniques will help you become an active and effective listener.

- **Stop talking.** The first step to becoming a good listener is to stop talking. Let others explain their views. Learn to concentrate on what the speaker is saying, not on your next comment.
- **Control your surroundings.** Whenever possible, remove sounds that interfere. Close windows or doors, turn off radios and noisy appliances, and move away from loud people or engines. Choose a quiet time and place for listening.
- **Accept information willingly.** Expect to learn something by listening. Strive for a positive and receptive frame of mind. If the message is complex, think of it as a mental challenge. It's hard work but good exercise to stretch and expand the limits of your mind.
- **Keep an open mind.** We all consider information through our own biases and values. For improved listening, discipline yourself to listen without prejudice. Be fair to the speaker. Hear what is really being said, not what you want to hear.
- **Listen for main points.** Concentration is stronger and satisfaction is greater when you look for and recognize the speaker's central themes.
- **Listen for nonverbal clues.** Focus both on what is spoken and what is unspoken. Listen for feelings as well as for facts.
- **Judge ideas, not appearances.** Concentrate on the content of the message, not on its delivery. Avoid being distracted by the speaker's looks, voice, or mannerisms.
- **Be patient.** Force yourself to listen to the speaker's entire argument or message before reacting. That way you may understand the speaker's reasons and logic before you jump to false conclusions.
- **Take selective notes.** For some situations thoughtful note taking may be necessary to record important facts that must be remembered later. Select only the

Quick Check

Barriers to listening may be physical, personal, verbal, or nonverbal.

Quick Check

Most North Americans speak at about 125 words per minute. The human brain can process information at least three times as fast.

Quick Check

To become an active listener, stop talking, control your surroundings, develop a positive mindset, listen for main points, and use pauses or delays to your advantage.

Quick Check

Listening actively may mean taking notes and providing feedback.

most important points so that the note-taking process does not interfere with your concentration on the speaker's total message.

- **Provide feedback.** Let the speaker know that you are listening. Nod your head and maintain eye contact. Ask questions at appropriate times. Getting involved improves the communication process for both the speaker and the listener.

Improving Your Nonverbal Communication Skills

Understanding messages often involves more than listening to spoken words. Nonverbal clues, in fact, can speak louder than words. These clues include eye contact, facial expression, body movements, space, time, distance, and appearance. All these nonverbal clues affect how a message is interpreted, or decoded, by the receiver.

Just what is nonverbal communication? It includes all unwritten and unspoken messages, whether intended or not. These silent signals have a strong effect on receivers. But understanding them is not simple. Does a downward glance indicate modesty? Fatigue? Does a constant stare reflect coldness? Dullness? Do crossed arms mean defensiveness? Withdrawal? Or do crossed arms just mean that a person is cold?

Messages are even harder to understand when the verbal and nonverbal codes do not agree. What would you think if Scott says he's not angry, but he slams the door when he leaves? Or what if Alicia assures her server that the meal is excellent, but she eats very little? The nonverbal messages in these situations speak more loudly than the words.

When verbal and nonverbal messages conflict, research shows that receivers put more faith in nonverbal clues. In one study speakers sent a positive message but shifted their eyes away as they spoke. Listeners thought the total message was negative. Moreover, they thought that looking away suggested lack of affection, lack of trust, and lack of interest.

Successful communicators recognize the power of nonverbal messages. Although it's unwise to attach specific meanings to gestures or actions, some messages given by body language are helpful in understanding the feelings and attitudes of senders.

How the Eyes, Face, and Body Send Silent Messages

Words seldom tell the whole story. Indeed, some messages are sent with no words at all. The eyes, face, and body can present a world of meaning without a single syllable being spoken.

Eye Contact. The eyes have been called the "windows of the soul." Even if they don't reveal the soul, the eyes often indicate a speaker's true feelings. Most of us cannot look another person straight in the eyes and lie. As a result, in Canada we tend to believe people who look directly at us. Longer eye contact suggests trust and admiration; brief eye contact signals fear or stress. Good eye contact enables the message sender to see if a receiver is paying attention, showing respect, responding favourably, or feeling distress. From the receiver's viewpoint, good eye contact reveals the speaker's sincerity, confidence, and truthfulness.

Facial Expression. The expression on a person's face can be almost as revealing of emotion as the eyes. Experts estimate that the human face can display over 250,000 expressions.[4] To hide their feelings, some people can control these expressions and maintain "poker faces." Most of us, however, display our emotions openly. Raising or lowering the eyebrows, squinting the eyes, swallowing

Quick Check

Nonverbal communication includes all unwritten and unspoken messages, intended or not.

Quick Check

When verbal and nonverbal messages clash, listeners tend to believe the nonverbal message.

Quick Check

The eyes are thought to be the best indicator of a speaker's true feelings.

Quick Check

Nonverbal messages often have different meanings in different cultures.

nervously, clenching the jaw, smiling broadly—these voluntary and involuntary facial expressions can add to or entirely replace verbal messages.

Posture and Gestures. A person's posture can show anything from high status and self-confidence to shyness and submissiveness. Leaning toward a speaker suggests attraction and interest; pulling away denotes fear, distrust, anxiety, or disgust. Similarly, gestures can communicate entire thoughts via simple movements. However, the meanings of these movements differ in other cultures. Unless you know local customs, they can get you into trouble. In Canada, for example, forming the thumb and forefinger in a circle means everything's OK. But in Germany and parts of South America, the gesture is rude.

How Time, Space, and Territory Send Silent Messages

In addition to nonverbal messages transmitted by your body, three external elements convey information in the communication process: time, space, and distance.

Time. How we structure and use time tells observers about our personality and attitudes. For example, if a financial planner sets aside one-hour blocks of time for client meetings, he is signalling respect for, interest in, and approval of the visitor or the topic to be discussed. If however he schedules only a 15-minute meeting, the client may feel less important.

Quick Check

People convey meaning in how they structure and organize time and how they order the space around themselves.

Space. How we order the space around us tells something about ourselves and our objectives. Whether the space is a bedroom, a classroom, an office, or a department, people reveal themselves in the design and grouping of their furniture. Generally, the more formal the arrangement, the more formal the communication. The way office furniture is arranged signals how communication is to take place. An instructor who arranges chairs informally in a circle rather than in straight rows conveys her desire for a more open exchange of ideas. A manager who creates an open office space with few dividing screens or partitions separating workers' desks seeks to encourage an open flow of communication and work among areas.

Quick Check

The distance required for comfortable social interaction is controlled by culture.

Territory. Each of us has certain areas that we feel are our own territory, whether it's a specific spot or just the space around us. Family members may have a favourite living-room chair, students who sit in a chair during their first class may return to that chair throughout the term, a cook might not want others in his or her kitchen, and more experienced employees may feel that certain work areas and tools belong to them.

We all maintain zones of privacy in which we feel comfortable. Figure 1.2 categorizes the four classic zones of social interaction among North Americans, as formulated by anthropologist Edward T. Hall.[5] Notice that North Americans are a bit cold; only intimate friends and family may stand closer than about 45 cm (1.5 ft.). If someone steps into that territory, North Americans feel uncomfortable and defensive and may step back to re-establish their space.

How Appearance Sends Silent Messages

The physical appearance of a business document, as well as the personal appearance of an individual, transmits immediate and important nonverbal messages.

Appearance of Business Documents. The way an e-mail, letter, memo, or report looks can have either a positive or a negative effect on the receiver. Sloppy e-mail messages send a nonverbal message that says you are in a big hurry or that the reader or message is not important enough for you to care. Envelopes—through their postage, stationery, and printing—can suggest routine, important,

FIGURE 1.2 Four Space Zones for Social Interaction

Zone	Distance	Uses
Intimate	0 to 45 cm (1.5 ft.)	Reserved for members of the family and other loved ones.
Personal	45 to 120 cm (1.5 to 4 ft.)	For talking with friends privately. The outer limit enables you to keep someone at arm's length.
Social	120 to 360 cm (4 to 12 ft.)	For acquaintances, fellow workers, and strangers. Close enough for eye contact yet far enough for comfort.
Public	360 cm and over (12 ft. and over)	For use in the classroom and for speeches before groups. Nonverbal signals become important as aids to communication.

or junk mail. Letters and reports can look neat, professional, well organized, and attractive—or just the opposite. In the following chapters you'll learn how to create documents that send positive nonverbal messages through their appearance, format, organization, readability, and correctness.

Appearance of People. The way you look—your clothing, grooming, and posture—sends an instant nonverbal message about you. On the basis of what they see, viewers make quick judgments about your status, credibility, personality, and potential. Because appearance is such a powerful force in business, some professionals are turning for help to image consultants. For example, at Prime Impressions in Kingston, Ontario, image consultant Catherine Bell offers corporate training in the areas of professional attire, dining protocol, and interview coaching among many others. Bell even offers a "telecoaching" service that provides training over the phone.[6]

Tips for Improving Your Nonverbal Skills

Nonverbal communication can be stronger than words in the way it influences how others see us. You can harness the power of silent messages by reviewing the following tips for improving nonverbal communication skills:

- **Establish and maintain eye contact.** Remember that in North America appropriate eye contact signals interest, attentiveness, strength, and credibility.
- **Use posture to show interest.** Encourage communication interaction by leaning forward, sitting or standing erect, and looking alert.
- **Improve your decoding skills.** Watch facial expressions and body language to understand the complete verbal and nonverbal message being communicated.
- **Search for more information.** When you see nonverbal clues that contradict verbal meanings, politely seek additional clues (*I'm not sure I understand, Please tell me more about ...*, or *Do you mean that ...*).
- **Associate with people from diverse cultures.** Learn about other cultures to widen your knowledge and tolerance of intercultural nonverbal messages.
- **Appreciate the power of appearance.** Keep in mind that the appearance of you, your business documents, and your business space sends immediate positive or negative messages to receivers.
- **Observe yourself on videotape.** Ensure that your verbal and nonverbal messages agree by taping and evaluating yourself making a presentation.
- **Enlist friends and family.** Ask them to monitor your conscious and unconscious body movements and gestures to help you become a more effective communicator.

Improving Your Nonverbal Communication Skills

Understanding the verbal and nonverbal meanings of a message is difficult even when communicators are from the same culture. But when they are from different cultures, special sensitivity and skills are necessary.

Negotiators for a Canadian company learned this lesson when they were in Japan looking for a trading partner. The Canadians were pleased after their first meeting with representatives of a major Japanese firm. The Japanese had nodded agreement throughout the meeting and had not objected to a single proposal. The next day, however, the Canadians were surprised to learn that the Japanese had rejected the entire plan. In trying to understand the nonverbal messages, the Canadians made a typical mistake. They assumed the Japanese were nodding in agreement as fellow Canadians would. In this case, however, the nods of assent indicated comprehension—not approval.

Every country has a common heritage, joint experience, and shared learning that produce its culture. These elements give members of that culture a complex system of shared values and customs. The system teaches them how to behave; it forms their reactions. Comparing North American values with those in other cultures will broaden your world-view. This comparison should also help you recognize some of the values that shape your actions and the judgments of others.

It's impossible to fully cover the many habits and beliefs of Canadian culture here, but we can look at several of the ones that, in a business context, will be especially important for you to understand.

Formality. A significant characterization of North American culture is its attitude toward formality. North Americans place less emphasis on tradition, ceremony, and social rules than do people in some other cultures. We dress casually and are soon on a first-name basis with others. Our lack of formality is often characterized by directness in our business dealings. Indirectness, we feel, wastes time, which is valuable.

Communication Style. A second important dimension of our culture is communication style. We value straightforwardness and distrust people who might have a "hidden agenda." North Americans also tend to be uncomfortable with silence and impatient with delays. Moreover, we tend to use and understand words literally.

Time Orientation. A third aspect of our culture relates to time orientation. We consider time a precious commodity to be conserved. We equate time with productivity, efficiency, and money. Keeping people waiting for business appointments wastes time and is also rude. In other cultures, time may be thought of as an unlimited and never-ending resource to be enjoyed.

Controlling Ethnocentrism and Stereotyping

The process of understanding and accepting people from other cultures is often made difficult by two barriers: ethnocentrism and stereotyping. These two barriers, however, can be overcome by developing tolerance, a powerful and effective aid to communication.

Ethnocentrism. The belief in the superiority of one's own culture is known as ethnocentrism. This attitude is found in all cultures. If you were raised in Canada, the values just described probably seem "right" to you, and you may wonder why the rest of the world doesn't function in the same sensible fashion. A Canadian

Because nonverbal clues can mean more than spoken words, learn to use nonverbal communication positively.

Verbal and nonverbal meanings are even more difficult to interpret when people are from different cultures.

North Americans tend to be direct and to understand words literally.

Quick Check

North Americans equate time with productivity, efficiency, and money.

Quick Check

Ethnocentrism is the belief in the superiority of one's own culture and group.

Quick Check

A stereotype is an oversimplified behavioural pattern applied to entire groups.

businessperson in a foreign country might be upset at time spent over coffee or other social rituals before any "real" business is done. In many cultures, however, personal relationships must be established and nurtured before earnest talks may proceed.

Ethnocentrism causes us to judge others by our own values. We expect others to react as we would, and they expect us to behave as they would. Misunderstandings naturally result. A Canadian who wants to set a deadline for completion of a deal may be considered "pushy" overseas. Similarly, a foreign businessperson who prefers a handshake to a written contract is seen as naive and possibly untrustworthy by a Canadian. These ethnocentric reactions can be reduced through knowledge of other cultures and development of flexible, tolerant attitudes.

Stereotypes. Our perceptions of other cultures sometimes cause us to form stereotypes about groups of people. A stereotype is an attitude or behaviour applied to entire groups. For example, the Swiss are hard working, efficient, and neat; Germans are formal, reserved, and blunt; Americans are loud, friendly, and impatient; Canadians are polite, trusting, and tolerant; Asians are gracious, humble, and mysterious. These attitudes may or may not accurately describe cultural norms. But when applied to individual business communicators, such stereotypes may create misunderstandings. Look beneath surface stereotypes and labels to discover individual personal qualities.

Tolerance. Working among people from other cultures demands tolerance and flexible attitudes. As global markets expand and as our multicultural society continues to develop, tolerance becomes critical. Tolerance does not mean "putting up with" or "enduring," which is one part of its definition. Instead, tolerance is used in a broader sense. It means having sympathy for and appreciating beliefs and practices that differ from our own.

One of the best ways to develop tolerance is by practising empathy. This means trying to see the world through another's eyes. It means being nonjudgmental, recognizing things as they are rather than as they "should be." It includes the ability to accept others' contributions in solving problems in a culturally appropriate manner. When a few Canadian companies began selling machinery in China, an Asian advisor suggested that the companies rely less on legal transaction and more on creating friendships. Why? In China, the notion of friendship implies a longer-term relationship of trust and loyalty where business deals are made. Instead of insisting on what "should be" (contracts and binding agreements), these companies adopted successful approaches by looking at the challenge from another cultural point of view.[7]

Making the effort to communicate with sensitivity across cultures can be very rewarding in both your work life and your personal life. The suggestions below provide specific tips for preventing miscommunication in oral and written transactions across cultures.

 Quick Check

Developing intercultural tolerance means showing acceptance of others, being nonjudgmental, and being patient.

✔ **Quick Check**

You can improve cross-cultural oral communication by using simple English, speaking slowly, enunciating clearly, encouraging feedback, observing eye messages, accepting blame, and listening without interruption.

Tips for Minimizing Oral Miscommunication among Cross-Cultural Audiences

When you have a conversation with someone from another culture, you can reduce misunderstandings by following these tips:

- **Use simple English.** Speak in short sentences (under 15 words) with familiar, short words. Eliminate puns, specific cultural references, slang, and jargon (special business terms). Be especially alert to idiomatic expressions that can't be translated, such as *burn the midnight oil* and *under the weather*.

- **Speak slowly and enunciate clearly.** Avoid fast speech, but don't raise your voice. Pause often. Always write numbers for all to see.
- **Encourage accurate feedback.** Ask probing questions, and encourage the listener to restate what you say. Don't assume that a yes, a nod, or a smile indicates comprehension or assent.
- **Check frequently for comprehension.** Avoid waiting until you finish a long explanation to request feedback. Instead, make one point at a time, pausing to check for comprehension. Don't proceed to B until A has been grasped.
- **Observe eye messages.** Be alert to a blank expression or wandering eyes. These tell you the listener is lost.
- **Accept blame.** If a misunderstanding results, graciously accept the blame for not making your meaning clear.
- **Listen without interrupting.** Curb your desire to finish sentences or to fill out ideas for the speaker. Keep in mind that Canadian listening and speaking habits may not be familiar to other cultures.
- **Remember to smile.** Roger Axtell, international behaviour expert, calls the smile the single most understood and most useful form of communication in either personal or business transactions.
- **Follow up in writing.** After conversations or oral negotiations, confirm the results and agreements with follow-up letters or e-mails. For proposals and contracts, engage a translator to prepare copies in the local language.

Tips for Minimizing Written Miscommunication Among Cross-Cultural Audiences

When you write to someone from a different culture, you can improve your chances of being understood by following these tips:

- **Adopt local styles.** Learn how documents are formatted and how letters are addressed and developed in the intended reader's country. Use local formats and styles.
- **Consider hiring a translator.** Engage a translator if (1) your document is important, (2) your document will be distributed to many readers, or (3) you must be persuasive.
- **Use short sentences and short paragraphs.** Sentences with fewer than 15 words and paragraphs with fewer than 5 lines are most readable.
- **Avoid unclear wording.** Include relative pronouns *(that, which, who)* for clarity in introducing clauses. Stay away from contractions (especially ones such as *Here's the problem*). Avoid idioms *(once in a blue moon)*, slang *(my presentation really bombed)*, acronyms *(ASAP for as soon as possible)*, abbreviations *(DBA for doing business as)*, and jargon *(input, output, bottom line)*. Use action-specific verbs *(purchase a printer* rather than *get a printer)*.
- **Cite numbers carefully.** Use figures *(15)* instead of spelling them out *(fifteen)*. Always convert dollar figures into local currency. Avoid using figures to express the month of the year. In Canada, for example, March 5, 2009, might be written as 3/5/09, while in Europe the same date might appear as 5.3.09. For clarity, always spell out the month.

Capitalizing on Workforce Diversity

As global competition opens world markets, Canadian businesspeople will increasingly interact with customers and colleagues from around the world. At the same time, the Canadian workforce is also becoming more diverse—in race, ethnicity, age, gender, national origin, physical ability, and countless other characteristics.

No longer, say the experts, will the workplace be predominantly male or oriented toward Western cultural values alone. The majority of new entrants to the workforce are women, First Nations, new Canadians, and other visible-minority groups. The Canadian workforce is getting older as the baby-boom generation ages. By the year 2016 half of the Canadian population will be over 40 and 16 percent over 65. At the same time, the proportion of people under 15 will shrink to 19 percent from the current 25 percent.[8]

While the workforce is becoming more diverse, the structure of many businesses across Canada is also changing. As you learned earlier, workers are now organized by teams. Organizations are flatter, and employees are increasingly making decisions among themselves and being asked to manage relationships with customers, suppliers, and others along the supply chain. What does all this mean for you as a future business communicator? Simply put, your job may require you to interact with colleagues and customers from around the world. Your work environment will probably demand that you cooperate effectively with small groups of coworkers. And these coworkers may differ from you in race, ethnicity, gender, age, and other ways.

A diverse work environment has many benefits. Customers want to deal with companies that reflect their values and create products and services tailored to their needs. Organizations that hire employees with different experiences and backgrounds are better able to create the customized products these customers desire. In addition, businesses with diverse workforces suffer fewer human rights complaints, fewer union clashes, and less interpersonal conflict. That's why diversity is viewed by a growing number of companies as a critical bottom-line business strategy to improve employee relationships and to increase productivity. For some businesses, diversity also makes economic sense. As Virginia Galt reports in *The Globe and Mail*, "There is one token Canadian on Western Union's national marketing team in Canada. The rest come from China, India, Colombia, Poland, the Philippines." According to Galt, while "Western Union may be further along than most employers in diversifying its work force ... others are planning to follow suit, driven by a competitive need to expand into international markets and serve the increasingly diverse population at home."[9]

Tips for Effective Communication with Diverse Workplace Audiences

Capitalizing on workplace diversity is a challenge for most organizations and individuals. Harmony and acceptance do not happen automatically when people who are dissimilar work together. The following suggestions can help you become a more effective communicator as you enter a rapidly evolving workplace with diverse colleagues and clients.

- **Understand the value of differences.** Diversity makes an organization innovative and creative. Sameness fosters "groupthink," an absence of critical thinking sometimes found in homogeneous groups. Diversity in problem-solving groups encourages independent and creative thinking.
- **Don't expect sameness.** Gone are the days when businesses could demand that new employees or customers simply accept the existing organization's culture. Today, the value of people who bring new perspectives and ideas is recognized. But with those new ideas comes the responsibility to listen and to allow those new ideas to grow.
- **Create zero tolerance for bias and stereotypes.** Cultural patterns exist in every identity group, but applying these patterns to individuals results in stereotyping. Assuming that Canadians of African descent are good athletes or that women are poor at math fails to admit the immense differences in people in each group. Check your own use of stereotypes and labels. Don't tell sexist or

Quick Check

You can expect to be interacting with customers and colleagues who may differ from you in race, ethnicity, age, gender, national origin, physical ability, and many other characteristics.

Quick Check

Diversity programs have become an important business strategy because of the benefits to consumers, work teams, and organizations.

ethnic jokes. Avoid slang, abbreviations, and jargon that imply stereotypes. Challenge others' stereotypes politely but firmly.

- **Practise focused, thoughtful, and open-minded listening.** Much misunderstanding can be avoided by attentive listening. Listen for main points; take notes if necessary to remember important details. The most important part of listening, especially among diverse communicators, is judging ideas, not appearances or accents.

- **Invite, use, and give feedback.** As you learned earlier, a critical element in successful communication is feedback. You can encourage it by asking questions such as *Is there anything you don't understand?* When a listener or receiver responds, use that feedback to adjust your delivery of information. Does the receiver need more details? A different example? Slower delivery? As a good listener, you should also be prepared to give feedback. For example, summarize your understanding of what was said or agreed on.

- **Make fewer assumptions.** Be careful of seemingly insignificant, innocent workplace assumptions. For example, don't assume that everyone wants to observe the holidays with a Christmas party and a decorated tree. Celebrating only Christian holidays in December and January excludes those who honour Hanukkah, Chinese New Year, and Ramadan. Moreover, in workplace discussions don't assume that everyone is married or wants to be or that everyone is heterosexual. For invitations, avoid phrases such as "managers and their *wives.*" *Spouses* or *partners* is more inclusive. Valuing diversity means making fewer assumptions that everyone is like you or wants to be like you.

- **Learn about your cultural self.** Knowing your own cultural biases helps you become more objective and easier to work with. Begin to recognize the reactions and thought patterns that are automatic to you as a result of your upbringing. Become more aware of your own values and beliefs. That way you can see them at work when you are confronted by differing values.

- **Seek common ground.** Look for areas where you and others not like you can agree or share opinions. Be prepared to consider issues from many sides, all of which may be valid. Accept that there is room for different points of view. Although you can always find differences, it's much harder to find similarities. Look for common ground in shared experiences, mutual goals, and similar values. Professor Nancy Adler of McGill University offers three useful methods to help diverse individuals find their way through conflicts made more difficult by cultural differences: (1) look at the problem from all participants' points of view, (2) uncover the interpretations each side is making on the basis of their cultural values, and (3) create cultural synergy by working together on a solution that works for both sides.[10] Looking for common ground and mutual goals can help each of you reach your objectives even though you may disagree on how.

Quick Check

Successful communicators invite, use, and give feedback; make few assumptions; learn about their own cultures and other cultures; and seek common ground.

Summing Up and Looking Forward

This chapter described the importance of becoming an effective business communicator in the knowledge economy. Many of the changes in today's dynamic workplace revolve around processing and communicating information. Fewer management levels, increased emphasis on work teams, heightened global competition, and creative communication technologies are all trends that increase the need for good communication skills. To improve your skills, you should understand the communication process. Communication doesn't take place unless senders encode meaningful messages that can be decoded by receivers.

One important part of the communication process is listening. You can become a more active listener by keeping an open mind, listening for main points, using pauses wisely, judging ideas and not appearances, taking selective notes, and providing feedback.

The chapter also described ways to help you improve your nonverbal communication skills.

You learned the powerful effect that culture has on communication, and you became more aware of key cultural values. Finally, the chapter discussed ways that businesses and individuals can capitalize on workforce diversity.

The following chapters present the writing process. You will learn specific techniques to help you improve your written expression. Remember, communication skills are not inherited. They are learned.

Critical Thinking

1. Why should business students and professionals alike strive to improve their communication skills, and why is it difficult or impossible to do so without help?
2. Recall a time when you experienced a problem as a result of poor communication. What were the causes of and possible remedies for the problem?
3. How are listening skills important to employees, supervisors, and executives? Who should have the best listening skills?
4. What arguments could you give for or against the idea that body language can be understood accurately by specialists?
5. Since English is becoming the preferred language in business globally, why should Canadians bother to learn about other cultures?

Chapter Review

6. List several new trends in the workplace that affect business communicators. How might they affect you in your future career?

7. Give a brief definition of the following words:
   a. Encode

   b. Channel

   c. Decode

8. List and explain several techniques for improving your listening skills.

9. What is nonverbal communication? Give several examples.

10. Why is good eye contact important for communicators?

11. What is ethnocentrism, and how can it be reduced?

12. List and explain several suggestions to improve understanding when you are talking with people for whom English is a second language.

13. List and explain several suggestions for becoming a more effective communicator in a diverse workplace.

Activities and Cases

1.1 Getting to Know You. Since today's work and class environments often involve cooperating in teams or small groups, getting to know your fellow classmates is important. To learn something about the people in this class and to give you practice in developing your communication skills, your instructor may choose one of the following techniques.

a. For larger classes your instructor may divide the class into groups of four or five. Take one minute to introduce yourself briefly (name, major interest, hobbies, goals). Spend five minutes in the first group session. Record the first name of each individual you meet. Then informally regroup. In new groups, again spend five minutes on introductions. After three or four sessions, study your name list. How many names can you associate with faces?

b. For smaller classes your instructor may ask each student to introduce himself or herself in a two-minute oral presentation to the class. Where were you born? What are your educational goals? What are your interests?

1.2 Class Listening. Observe the listening habits of the students in one of your classes for a week. What barriers to effective listening did you observe? How many of the suggestions described in this chapter are being implemented by listeners in the class? Write a memo or an e-mail message to your instructor describing your observations. (See Chapter 5 to learn more about memos and e-mails.)

1.3 Body Language. What attitudes do the following body movements suggest to you? Do these movements always mean the same thing?

a. At a meeting with the boss, you shift back and forth in your chair.
b. During a lecture in class, you twiddle your thumbs and direct your eyes to the ceiling.
c. During a job interview, the interviewer takes off his glasses, folds them, and puts them away in his shirt pocket.
d. While waiting for your presentation to a group of supervisors, your boss clicks her pen repeatedly and looks at her watch.
e. While talking to a supervisor, your posture is bowed and you lower your eyes.
f. While in the waiting room for your job interview, you pace the floor and twist your fingers through your hair.

1.4 Soup's On. As a junior manager at Florenceville, New Brunswick–based McCain Foods Limited, you have been sent to Hong Kong to work on the development of new regional food varieties to appeal to two billion Asian consumers. The Chinese are among the highest per capita soup eaters in the world, consuming an average of one bowl a day. In the Hong Kong test kitchen, you are currently working on cabbage soup, scallop broth, and a special soup that combines watercress and duck meat. You've even tested exotic ingredients such as shark's fin and snake.[11] The supervisor of the test kitchen understands English, but sometimes her eyes glaze over when you discuss procedures with her. In your hotel room that evening, you analyze what happened that day. What could you do to improve comprehension and minimize misunderstandings?

1.5 Translating Idioms. Explain in simple English what the following idiomatic expressions mean. Assume that you are explaining them to people for whom English is a second language.

a. let the cat out of the bag
b. take the bull by the horns
c. he is a tightwad
d. putting the cart before the horse
e. to be on the road
f. lend someone a hand
g. with flying colours
h. turn over a new leaf

1.6 Communication Barriers. Your life is filled with miscommunication situations. Think of a situation that happened recently that was not effective because of some barriers.

Grammar/Mechanics Review—1

The following exercise includes a variety of verb tense errors. In the space provided, write a corrected version of each sentence. Some sentences have more than one error. Your instructor has the key for this exercise.

Example: Yesterday, 16 members of the committee *meet* in the Student Centre.
Revision: Yesterday, 16 members of the committee *met* in the Student Centre.

1. Jennifer Riddock receive a prize because she was the only graduate who had never missed a day of classes.

2. If it's not too late to register, my brother and I planning to take courses in history, management, and English.

3. In just two hours' time, I was able locate nine excellent websites contain relevant information for my report.

4. We cannot proceeding with the mailing until the list of names and addresses are verified.

5. My new automobile have antilock brakes, alloy wheels, and a GPS screen.

6. My boss' biggest computer worry is the possibility of a virus attack our computers.

7. Besides your résumé and cover letter, you must submitting a separate employment application form.

8. Elizabeth was surprise that her neighbours owned two popular restaurants in town.

9. Although the cable company promised huge savings, my wife and I now paying $20 more every month.

10. Your bill is now 90 days overdue; therefore, we are submit it to an agency for collection.

11. If you have already send your payment, please disregard this notice.

12. Of the 350 letters that were mail, only a few were return.

Grammar/Mechanics Challenge—1

Document for Revision

The following memo has many faults in grammar, spelling, punctuation, capitalization, word use, and number form. Study the guidelines in the Grammar/Mechanics Handbook to sharpen your skills. When you finish, your instructor can show you a revised version of this memo. (Approximately 20 errors)

Memo

To: Tran Nguyen

From: Rachel Stivers, Manager

Date: May 14, 2009

Subject: WORK AT HOME GUIDELINES

Since you will be complete most of your work at home for the next four month. Follow these guidelines;

1. Check your message bored daily and respond promptly. To those who are try to reach you.

2. Call the office at least twice a day to pick up any telephone messages, return these call.

3. Transmit any work you doon the computer to Jerry Jackson in Computer Services Department, he will analyze each weeks accounts and send it to the proper departments. .

4. Provide me with monthly report of your progress.

We will continue hold once-a-week staff meetings at Friday on 10 a.m. Do you think it would be possible for you to attend these meeting? The next one is Friday, May 15th.

I know you will work satisfactorily at home, Tran, following these basic guideline should helps you accomplish your work, and provide the office with adequate contact with you.

Using the Net to Boost Your Career Search

As a business communicator in today's workplace, you must be able to effectively use the Internet. When searching for information on the Web, it's far too easy to waste time and money while roaming through cyberspace. Whether you're a beginner or a surfing pro, this workshop will help you sharpen your Internet skills so that your searches are done quickly and accurately.

Getting Started

Go to http://www.learnthenet.com.
Click on "Find Information" and then on "Advanced Web Searching." Read the entire article, paying special attention to the section on Boolean logic. Then try a few Internet searches using Boolean logic; for example, search for information about jobs in Canada, jobs in your city or town or province, workplace literacy in Canada, or workplace diversity in Canada. What's the difference between a Google search that uses the search term "workplace diversity in Canada" and a search that uses Boolean logic in its search term (e.g., "workplace" "diversity" "Canada")?

Career Application

Assume that you are about to finish your program and you are now looking for a job. Today, the easiest way to search for a job is on the Web. A terrific selection of job-search websites is available to students using Nelson textbooks. At the direction of your instructor, conduct a survey of electronic job advertisements in your field. What's available? What are the salaries? What are the requirements?

Your Task

Go to http://www.workopolis.com.
This is the largest jobs website in Canada. Click on "Search Jobs." Search for a job by typing in a keyword. Now go through the following steps:

- **Study the first page.** Use your scroll bar to run up and down the page. Notice how jobs are located on the page and how they are hyperlinked to additional information.
- **Conduct another practice search.** Scroll back up to the top of the page. Click on "FastTrack" and search for a job by job category. Then try another search by "Locations." Just for fun, try a location different from your home and an unusual career choice.
- **Conduct a real search.** Now conduct a job search in your career area and in geographical areas of your choice. Select five ads and print them. If you cannot print, make notes on what you find.
- **Analyze the skills required.** How often do the ads mention communication, teamwork, and computer skills? What other tasks do the ads mention? Is a salary given? Your instructor may ask you to submit your findings and/or report to the class.

Web | **Related websites: You may also consider http://www.monster.ca for this workshop.**

Writing and Revising Skills

Writing for Business Audiences

I write for a number of different business audiences and I always consider my audience before starting. The content, tone, and level of detail varies depending on whether I'm writing to clients, financial advisors or other stakeholders.[1]

John DeGoey, *Financial Advisor, Assante Wealth Management Office Team*

LEARNING OBJECTIVES

1. Understand that business writing should be audience oriented, purposeful, and economical.
2. Identify and use the three phases of the writing process.
3. Appreciate the importance of analyzing the task and the audience for business messages.
4. Create messages that use audience benefits and cultivate a "you" view.
5. Use positive as well as inclusive language.
6. List five ways in which technology helps improve business writing.

Basics of Business Writing

Quick Check

Excellent communicators concentrate on the audience for their messages.

Quick Check

Business writing is audience-oriented, purposeful, and economical.

An Ipsos Reid study conducted among Canadian CEOs indicated that CEOs devote half of their time (49 percent) to communicating with a variety of audiences including investors, government, the media, customers, employees, and management.[2] All members of the organization, from the CEO to frontline staff, must know their audience.

Audience awareness is one of the basics of business communication, as John DeGoey indicates above. This chapter focuses on writing for business audiences. Business writing may be different from other writing you have done. High-school or college compositions and term papers may have required you to describe your feelings, display your knowledge, or prove a thesis or argument. Business writing, however, has different goals. To prepare effective business messages and oral presentations, you'll need to focus on the following descriptors:

- **Audience oriented.** You will concentrate on looking at a problem from the receiver's viewpoint instead of from your own.
- **Purposeful.** You will be writing to solve problems and give information. You will have a definite purpose in each message.

- **Economical.** You will try to present ideas clearly but concisely. Length is not rewarded.

These distinctions actually ease the writer's task. You won't be searching your imagination for creative topic ideas. You won't be stretching your ideas to make them appear longer. In business writing, longer is not better. Conciseness is what counts.

The ability to prepare concise, audience-centred, and purposeful messages does not come naturally. Very few people, especially beginners, can sit down and compose an effective letter or report without training. But following a step-by-step process, studying model messages, and practising the craft can make nearly anyone a successful business writer or speaker.

Writing Process for Business Messages and Oral Presentations

Whether you are preparing an e-mail message, a memo, a letter, or an oral presentation, the process will be easier if you follow a step-by-step plan. Our plan breaks the entire task into three separate phases: prewriting, writing, and revising, as shown in Figure 2.1.

To illustrate the writing process, let's say that you own a popular local fast-food restaurant franchise. At rush times, you've got a big problem. Customers complain about the many lines to approach the service counter. You once saw two customers nearly get into a fight over who was next in line. And customers often are so intent on looking for ways to improve their positions in line that they fail to look at the menu. Then they don't know what to order when their turn arrives. You want to convince other franchise owners that a single-line system would work better. You could telephone the owners, but you want to present a serious argument with good points that they will remember and be willing to act on when they gather for their next district meeting. You decide to write a letter that you hope will win their support.

 Quick Check

Following a step-by-step process helps beginning writers create effective messages and presentations.

 Quick Check

The writing process has three parts: prewriting, writing, and revising.

Prewriting

The first phase of the writing process prepares you to write. It involves analyzing the audience and your purpose for writing. The audience for your letter will be other franchise owners who represent a group of individuals with varying educational backgrounds. Your purpose in writing is to persuade them that a change in policy would improve customer service. You are convinced that a single-line system, such as that used in banks, would reduce wait times and make customers happier because they would not have to worry about where they are in line.

Prewriting also involves anticipating how your audience will react to your message. You're sure that some of the other owners will agree with you, but

 Quick Check

The first phase of the writing process involves analyzing and anticipating the audience and then adapting to that audience.

FIGURE 2.1 The Business Writing Process

others might fear that customers seeing a long single line might go elsewhere. In adapting your message to the audience, you try to think of the right words and the right tone that will win approval.

Writing

Quick Check

The second phase of the writing process includes researching, organizing the message, and actually writing it.

The second phase involves researching, organizing, and then composing the message. In researching information for this letter, you would probably investigate other kinds of businesses that use single lines for customers. You might check out your competitors. What are other fast-food outlets doing? You might do some telephoning to see if other franchise owners are concerned about customer lines. Before writing to the entire group, you might share ideas with a few owners to increase the number of potential solutions to the problem.

Once you have collected enough information, you would focus on organizing your letter. Should you start out by offering your solution? Or should you work up to it slowly, describing the problem, presenting your evidence, and then ending with the solution? The final step in the second phase of the writing process is actually composing the letter. Naturally, you'll do it at your computer so that you can make revisions easily.

Revising

Quick Check

The third phase of the writing process includes revising for clarity and readability, proofreading for errors, and checking for effectiveness.

The third phase of the process involves revising, proofreading, and evaluating your letter. After writing the first draft, you'll spend time revising the message for clarity, conciseness, tone, and readability. Could parts of it be rearranged to make your point more effectively? This is the time when you look for ways to improve the organization and sound of your message. Next, you'll spend time proofreading carefully to ensure correct spelling, grammar, punctuation, and format. The final phase involves evaluating your entire message to decide whether it accomplishes your goal.

Scheduling the Writing Process

Although the business writing process described above shows the three phases equally, the time you spend on each varies depending on the complexity of the task, the purpose, the audience, and your schedule. Here are some rough estimates for scheduling a project:

- Prewriting—25 percent
- Writing—25 percent
- Revising—50 percent (30 percent revising and 20 percent proofreading)

These are rough guides, yet you can see that good writers spend most of their time on the final phase of revising and proofreading. Much depends, of course, on your project, its importance, and your familiarity with it. What's critical to remember, though, is that revising is a major part of the writing process.

It may appear that you complete one phase of the business writing process and go to the next, always following the same order. Although writers perform the tasks described, the steps may be rearranged, shortened, or repeated. Some writers revise every sentence and paragraph as they go. Many find that new ideas occur after they've begun to write, causing them to back up, change the organization, and rethink their plan.

We've just taken a look at the total writing process. As you develop your business writing skills, you should expect to follow this process closely. With experience, though, you'll become like other good writers and presenters who change, shorten, and rearrange the steps as needed. But following a plan is helpful at first. The remainder of this chapter covers the first phase of the writing process. You'll learn to analyze the purpose for writing, anticipate how your audience will react, and adapt your message to the audience.

Identifying Your Purpose

As you begin to compose a message, ask yourself two important questions: (1) Why am I sending this message? and (2) What do I hope to achieve? Your responses will determine how you organize and present your information.

Your message may have primary and secondary purposes. For college work your primary purpose may be to complete the assignment; secondary purposes might be to make yourself look good and to get a good grade. The primary purposes for sending business messages are typically to inform and to persuade. A secondary purpose is to promote goodwill: you and your organization want to look good in the eyes of your audience.

> ✓ **Quick Check**
>
> The primary purpose of most business messages is to inform or to persuade; the secondary purpose is to promote goodwill.

Selecting the Best Channel

After identifying the purpose of your message, you need to select the most appropriate communication channel. Some information is most efficiently and effectively delivered orally. Other messages should be written, and still others are best delivered electronically. Whether to set up a meeting, send a message by e-mail, or write a report depends on some of the following factors:

- Importance of the message
- Amount and speed of feedback required
- Necessity of a permanent record
- Cost of the channel
- Degree of formality desired
- Best practices in your company

> ✓ **Quick Check**
>
> Choosing an appropriate channel depends on the importance of the message, the feedback required, the need for a permanent record, the cost, the formality needed, and best practices of your company.

These six factors will help you decide which of the channels shown in Figure 2.2 is most appropriate for delivering a message.

Switching to Faster Channels

Technology and competition continue to speed up the pace of business today. As a result, communicators are switching to ever-faster means of exchanging information. In the early to mid twentieth century, business messages within organizations were delivered largely by hard-copy memos. Responses would typically take a couple of days. But that's too slow for today's communicators. Cell phones, faxes, websites, e-mail, and instant messaging can deliver that information much faster than traditional channels of communication. In fact, according to business writer Don Tapscott, within some organizations and between colleagues at different organizations, instant messaging is being added to e-mail as a popular channel choice. Tapscott even names some large companies such as IBM that have abandoned e-mail in favour of instant messaging.[3] Instant messaging software alerts colleagues in distant locations that a coworker is prepared for an online exchange. Once signed in, individuals or entire groups can carry on and manage two-way discussions. Instant messaging resembles a conversation where a sender types a one- or two-sentence note followed by the receiver who types his or her response to the note. Responses appear next to the original message for both sender and receiver to see. Through instant messaging, an entire conversation can be completed online without the time delay that can occur when sending and

FIGURE 2.2 Choosing Communication Channels

Channel	Best Use
Written	
E-mail	When you wish to deliver routine or urgent messages quickly and inexpensively across time zones or borders. Appropriate for small, large, local, or dispersed audiences. Quickly becoming preferred channel, replacing hard-copy memos and many letters. Printouts provide permanent records.
Instant message	When you need to have a brief conversation with a trusted colleague or customer at a distance. The question does not need a telephone call and should be about something you are working on at that moment. Expected to overcome e-mail as the most preferred channel within organizations for exchanging routine messages.
Fax	When your message must cross time zones or international boundaries, when a written record or speed is important.
Memo	When you want a written record to explain policies clearly, discuss procedures, or collect information within an organization.
Letter	When you need a written record of correspondence with customers, the government, suppliers, or others outside an organization.
Report or proposal	When you are delivering considerable data internally or externally.
Spoken	
Telephone	When you need to deliver or gather information quickly, when nonverbal cues are unimportant, and when you cannot meet in person.
Voice-mail message	When you wish to leave important or routine information that the receiver can respond to when convenient.
Face-to-face conversation	When you want to be persuasive, deliver bad news, or share a personal message.
Face-to-face group meeting	When group decisions are important. Inefficient for merely distributing information.
Video- or teleconference	When group consensus and interaction are important but members are geographically dispersed.

responding to e-mail. A few years ago, *The Globe and Mail* reported that instant messaging would soon surpass e-mail as the primary way in which people interact electronically. While this prediction has not yet come true, experts such as Tapscott signal that instant messaging is certainly a force to consider, especially because it is already so much a part of many young people's personal lives.[4]

Within many organizations, hard-copy memos are still written, especially for messages that require persuasion, permanence, or formality. But the channel of choice for corporate communicators today is clearly e-mail. It's fast, cheap, and easy. Thus, fewer hard-copy memos are being written. Fewer letters are also being written. Interestingly, the fact that fewer memos and letters are being written does not make knowing how to write one less important. In fact, it makes it more important because beginner business communicators often assume business e-mails can be as informal as their personal e-mails. However, business e-mails should be nearly as structured as memos and letters have always been.

Whether your channel choice is e-mail, a hard-copy memo, or a report, you'll be a more effective writer if you spend sufficient time in the prewriting phase.

Anticipating the Audience

A good writer anticipates the audience for each message: What is the reader like? How will the reader react to the message? Although you can't always know exactly who the reader is, you can imagine some characteristics of the reader. Even writers of direct-mail sales letters have a general idea of the audience they wish to target. Picturing a typical reader is important in guiding what you write. By profiling your audience and shaping a message to respond to that profile, you are more likely to achieve your communication goals.

Profiling the Audience

Visualizing your audience is an important step in the writing process. The questions in Figure 2.3 will help you profile your audience. How much time you devote to answering these questions depends on your message and its context. An analytical report that you compose for management or an oral presentation before a big group would, of course, require knowledge of your audience. On the other hand, an e-mail message to a coworker or a letter to a familiar supplier might require only a few moments of planning. No matter how short your message, though, spend some time thinking about the audience so that you can adjust your words appropriately for your readers or listeners. "The most often unasked question in business and professional communication," claims a writing expert, "is as simple as it is important: *Have I thought enough about my audience?*"[5]

 Quick Check

By profiling your audience before you write, you can identify the appropriate tone, language, and channel.

 Quick Check

After profiling the audience, you can decide whether the receiver will be neutral, positive, or hostile toward your message.

FIGURE 2.3 Asking the Right Questions to Profile Your Audience

Primary Audience

Who is my primary reader or listener?
What is my personal and professional relationship with that person?
What position does the individual hold in the organization?
How much does that person know about the subject?
What do I know about that person's education, beliefs, culture, and attitudes?
Should I expect a neutral, positive, or negative response to my message?

Secondary Audience

Who might see or hear this message in addition to the primary audience?
How do these people differ from the primary audience?

Analyzing the Purpose for Writing and the Audience

Responding to the Profile

Profiling your audience helps you make decisions about shaping the message. You'll discover what kind of language is appropriate, whether you're free to use specialized technical terms, whether you should explain everything, and so on. You'll decide whether your tone should be formal or informal, and you'll select the most desirable channel. Imagining whether the receiver is likely to be neutral, positive, or negative will help you determine how to organize your message.

Another advantage of profiling your audience is considering the possibility of a secondary audience. For instance, you might write a report that persuades your boss to launch a website for customers. Your boss is the primary reader, and he is familiar with many of the details of your project. But he will need to get approval from his boss, and that person is probably unfamiliar with the project details. Because your report will be passed along to secondary readers, it must include more background information and more extensive explanations than you included for the primary reader, your boss. Analyzing the task and anticipating the audience assists you in adapting your message so that it will accomplish what you intend.

Adapting to the Task and Audience

After analyzing your purpose and understanding your audience, you must convey your purpose to that audience. Adaptation is the process of creating a message that suits your audience.

One important aspect of adaptation is tone. Tone, conveyed largely by the words in a message, determines how a receiver feels upon reading or hearing it. Skilled communicators create a positive tone in their messages by using a number of adaptive techniques, some of which are unconscious. These include highlighting audience benefits, maintaining a polite "you" attitude, sounding conversational, and using inclusive language. Additional techniques include using positive expression and using plain language with familiar words.

Audience Benefits

Quick Check

Writers improve the tone of a message by using reader benefits, a polite "you" attitude, and inclusive language.

Quick Check

The most successful messages focus on the audience.

Smart communicators know that the chance of success of any message is greatly improved by pointing out reader benefits. Readers need to see how the message affects and benefits them personally.

It is human nature for individuals to be most concerned with matters that relate directly to themselves. This is a necessary condition of existence. If we weren't interested in attending to our own needs, we could not survive.

Adapting your message to the receiver's needs means putting yourself in that person's shoes. This skill is known as empathy. Think about how a receiver will decode a message. Try to give something to the receiver, solve the receiver's problems, save the receiver money, or just understand the feelings and position of that person. Which of the following messages is more appealing to the audience?

Sender focus	So that we can update our shareholder records, we ask that the enclosed card be returned.
Reader focus	So that you may promptly receive dividend cheques and information related to your shares, please return the enclosed card.
Sender focus	Our warranty becomes effective only when we receive an owner's registration.
Reader focus	Your warranty begins working for you as soon as you return your owner's registration.
Sender focus	We offer evening language courses that we know are excellent.

Reader focus	The sooner you enroll in our evening language courses, the sooner the rewards will be yours.
Sender focus	Our safety policy forbids us to rent equipment to anyone who does not know how to use the equipment.
Reader focus	For your safety, you must show ability to use the equipment that you rent from us.

Polite "You" View

Notice how many of the previous audience-focused messages included the word *you*. In concentrating on receiver benefits, skilled communicators naturally develop the "you" view. They emphasize second-person pronouns *(you, your)* instead of first-person pronouns *(I, we, my, our)*. Whether your goal is to inform, persuade, or promote goodwill, the most attention-getting words you can use are *you* and *your*. Compare the following examples.

"I/We" View	I have scheduled your vacation to begin May 1.
"You" View	You may begin your vacation May 1.
"I/We" View	We have shipped your order by courier, and we are sure it will arrive in time for the sales promotion January 15.
"You" View	Your order will be delivered by courier in time for your sales promotion January 15.
"I/We" View	As a financial planner, I care about my clients' well-being.
"You" View	Your well-being is the most important consideration for financial planners like me.

To see if you're really concentrating on the reader, try using the "empathy index." In one of your messages, count all the second-person references; then count all the first-person references. Your empathy index is low if the words *I* and *we* appear more often than *you* and *your*.

Positive Language

The clarity and tone of a message are improved if you use positive rather than negative language. Positive language generally gives more information than negative language. Moreover, positive messages are uplifting and pleasant to read. Positive wording tells what is and what can be done rather than what isn't and what can't be done. For example, *Your order cannot be shipped by January 10* is not nearly as informative as *Your order will be shipped January 20*. Notice in the following examples how you can revise the negative tone to reflect a more positive impression.

Negative	We are unable to send your shipment until we receive proof of your payment.
Positive	We will send your shipment as soon as we receive your payment.
Negative	We are sorry that we must reject your application for credit at this time.
Positive	At this time we can serve you on a cash basis only.
Negative	If you fail the exam, you will not qualify.
Positive	You'll qualify if you pass the exam.

Inclusive Language

A business writer who is alert and caring will strive to create messages that include rather than exclude people. Words, phrases, and images that indicate stereotypes reinforce mistaken beliefs about certain groups or individuals. Referring to a letter carrier as a *mailman*, for example, reinforces the stereotype

✔ **Quick Check**

Because receivers are most interested in themselves, emphasize *you* whenever possible.

✔ **Quick Check**

Emphasize *you* but don't eliminate all *I* and *we* statements.

✔ **Quick Check**

Strive for conversational expression, but also remember to be professional.

✔ **Quick Check**

Positive language creates goodwill.

✔ **Quick Check**

Sensitive communicators avoid language that excludes people.

that mail delivery is carried out only by men. This stereotype creates a barrier for women who want to be letter carriers and can exclude them from a career delivering mail. By using inclusive language such as *letter carrier*, we show we are aware that a person who delivers the mail could be either a woman or a man.

Stereotypes also show bias in our communication. Women, First Nations, people with disabilities, and visible minorities have traditionally been most affected by the negative effects of stereotyping. Biased language not only affects communication but also alienates or excludes others. All of your written, oral, electronic, and visual communication should be inclusive, unbiased, and fair for all individuals and groups.

When creating your messages, identify or address people first as individuals; then mention the group to which they belong only if that information is relevant. Job titles should describe the role rather than who is best to assume the role. Using terms such as *manager, sales clerk*, or *flight attendant* suggests that anyone can be considered an appropriate candidate for these roles.

Some words have been called sexist because they seem to exclude women or refer to women in ways the sender would not use to refer to a man. Notice the use of the masculine pronouns *he* and *his* in the following sentences:

> If a physician is needed, he will be called.
> Every homeowner must read his insurance policy carefully.

These sentences illustrate an age-old grammatical rule called "common gender." When a speaker or writer did not know the gender (sex) of an individual, masculine pronouns (such as *he* or *his*) were used. Masculine pronouns were understood to indicate both men and women. Today, however, writers and speakers replace common-gender pronouns with inclusive expressions. You can use any of four alternatives.

Sexist	Every lawyer has ten minutes for his summation.
Alternative 1	All lawyers have ten minutes for their summations. (Use a plural noun and plural pronoun.)
Alternative 2	Lawyers have ten minutes for summations. (Omit the pronoun entirely.)
Alternative 3	Every lawyer has ten minutes for a summation. (Use an article instead of a pronoun.)
Alternative 4	Every lawyer has ten minutes for his or her summation. (Use both a masculine and a feminine pronoun.)

Note that the last alternative, which includes a masculine and a feminine pronoun, is wordy. Don't use it too frequently.

Other words are considered sexist because they suggest stereotypes. For example, the nouns *fireman* and *mailman* suggest that only men hold these positions. Use neutral job titles or functions. Consider the following: *firefighter, letter carrier, salesperson, flight attendant, department head, committee chair*, and *technician*.

Some word constructions are considered sexist because they make assumptions about gender, such as *women's intuition, ladylike*, and *his better half*, or they describe women in ways that a man would not be described in the same situation, such as *an assertive man* or *a loud* (or *shrill*) *woman*.

Technology Improves Your Business Writing

Most business communicators use technology to improve their writing efforts. Computers and software provide powerful tools that make the entire process easier and more professional. Here are five ways to improve written documents, oral presentations, and webpages.

1. **Collecting information electronically.** Much of the world's information is now available by computer. Through a library's online databases, you can locate many full-text articles from magazines, newspapers, and government publications. Massive amounts of information are available from the Internet, CD-ROMs, and online services. Through specialized library online databases such as ABI-INFORM and CBCA Reference, you can have at your fingertips the latest business, legal, scientific, and scholarly information.

2. **Using templates.** One of the most useful and time-saving features of today's word-processing software for the business writer is templates. As Figure 2.4 demonstrates, templates are pre-formatted documents to which business writers simply add content. Any time you open up a new document in Microsoft Word, for example, on the right-hand side of your document you will see the option to choose a template. Typical templates include memos, letters, résumés, and reports. For the purposes of your business communication course, you should always choose a "professional" template, such as Word's Professional Letter template. Templates save time for business writers because instead of memorizing the various parts of a letter (e.g., how many spaces from the top the date and address should be placed), they can now concentrate on the more important things, such as making sure grammar and style are perfected. Knowing the parts of a letter is important (please see Appendix A); however, most of us don't have time to think about these features every time we sit down to write. In many large companies, templates have been customized for that company's needs, and few people write letters "from scratch" anymore.

3. **Improving correctness and precision.** Word-processing programs today catch and correct spelling and typographical errors. Most popular word-processing programs today also provide grammar checkers that are very much improved over earlier versions. They now detect many errors in capitalization, word use (such as *it's/its*), double negatives, verb use, subject–verb agreement, sentence structure, number agreement, number style, and other writing faults. However, grammar programs don't actually correct the errors they detect. You must know how to do that. Similarly, spell checkers don't catch all misspelled words.

4. **Adding graphics for emphasis.** Your letters, memos, and reports may be improved by the addition of graphs and artwork to illustrate data. You can import charts, diagrams, and illustrations created in database, spreadsheet, and graphics programs. Moreover, ready-made pictures, called clip art, can be used to symbolize or illustrate ideas.

FIGURE 2.4 Microsoft Templates That Outline and Organize Ideas

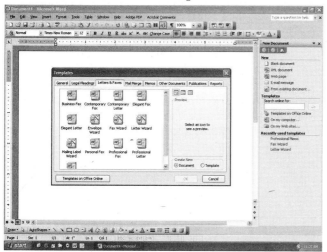

5. **Designing and producing professional-looking documents, presentations, and webpages.** Most popular word-processing programs today include a large selection of fonts (for different character sizes and styles), italics, boldface, symbols, and styling techniques to aid you in producing consistent formatting and professional-looking results. Moreover, today's presentation software, such as Microsoft's PowerPoint, enables you to include animated slide effects, colour, sound, pictures, and even movies in your talks for management or customers. Web document builders also help you design and construct webpages. These tools can be used effectively to help you reinforce your message and help your audience understand and remember your message.

Summing Up and Looking Forward

In this chapter you learned that good business writing is audience centred, purposeful, and economical. To achieve these results, business communicators typically follow a step-by-step writing process. This process includes three phases: prewriting, writing, and revising. In the prewriting phase, communicators analyze the task and the audience. They select an appropriate channel to deliver the message, and they consider ways to adapt their message to the task and the audience. Effective techniques include audience benefits, the "you" view, positive ideas, and inclusive language. Today's computer software provides wonderful assistance for business communicators. Technological tools help you collect information, put content into templates, improve correctness and precision, add graphics, and design professional-looking documents and presentations.

The next chapter continues to examine the writing process and presents additional techniques to help you become a better writer.

Critical Thinking

1. If computer software is increasingly able to detect writing errors, can business communicators stop studying writing techniques? Why?

Chapter Review

2. Name three ways in which business writing differs from other writing.

3. List the three phases of the business writing process and summarize what happens in each phase. Which phase requires the most time?

4. What five factors are important in selecting an appropriate channel to deliver a message?

5. How does understanding the audience help a business communicator prepare a message?

6. Give an example of an audience benefit.

7. Give an example of positive language in business writing.

8. List five examples of sexist pronouns and nouns.

9. Name several ways your computer can help you improve written documents.

Writing Improvement Exercises

Selecting Communication Channels. Using Figure 2.2 (p. 26), suggest the best communication channels for the following messages. Assume that all channels shown are available. Be prepared to explain your choices.

10. As department manager, you wish to inform four members about a training session scheduled for three weeks from now.

11. As assistant to the vice-president, you are to investigate the possibility of developing work placement programs with several nearby colleges and universities.

12. You wish to send price quotes for a number of your products in response to a request from a potential customer in Taiwan.

13. You must respond to a notice from the Canada Revenue Agency insisting that you did not pay the correct amount for last quarter's employee remittance.

14. As a manager, you must inform an employee that continued lateness is putting her job at risk.

15. You need to know whether Davinder in Publications can produce a special pamphlet for you within two days.

Audience Benefits and the "You" View. Revise the following sentences to emphasize the benefits to the reader and the "you" view.

16. To prevent us from possibly losing large sums of money, our bank now requires verification of any large cheque presented for immediate payment.

17. We take pride in announcing daily flights to Singapore.

18. I give my permission for you to attend the two-day workshop.

19. We're asking all employees to complete the enclosed questionnaire so that we may develop a master schedule for summer vacations.

20. I think my background and my education match the description of the manager trainee position you advertised.

21. We are offering an in-house training program for employees who want to improve their writing skills.

22. We have approved your application for credit, and the account may be used immediately.

23. We are pleased to announce that we have selected you to join our trainee program.

24. We will reimburse you for all travel expenses.

Positive Expression. Revise the following statements to make them more positive.

25. If you fail the examination, you will not qualify.

26. We can't process your application because you didn't provide your social insurance number.

   We ~~cdh~~ process your app if you provide your SIN.
   Your app. will be process as soon as you provide us you SIN

27. Construction cannot begin until the building plans are approved.

   Construction will begin when the building plans are approved

28. Customers are not eligible for the 10 percent discount unless they show their membership cards.

   Customers are eligible for the 10% disc. if they show their membership cards

Inclusive Language. Revise the following sentences to eliminate terms that are considered sexist or that suggest stereotypes.

29. Any applicant for the position of fireman must submit a medical report signed by his physician.

30. Every employee is entitled to see his personnel file.
    Every " " " their personnel file

31. At most hospitals in the area, a nurse must provide her own uniform.
    their

32. Representing the community are a businessman, a lady attorney, and a female doctor.

33. A salesman would have to use all his skills to sell those condos.
    his/her or their

34. Every doctor is provided with a parking spot for his car.
    his/her

Grammar/Mechanics Review—2

The following sentences contain errors in verb use. Below each sentence write a corrected version. Some sentences have more than one error.

1. In the evening, each of the female nurses are escorted to her car.

2. He receive the highest score, although it's hard to understand how he done it.

3. Yesterday, the manager asked Hilary to working four hours on Saturday morning.

4. Working out at the gym and to jog twenty miles a week is how she stay fit.

5. Three types of costs must be consider for proper inventory control.

6. If I was in his position, I would fill out the questionnaire immediately so that I would qualify for the prize.

7. Our team's day-to-day operations include setting goals, improving customer service, manufacture quality products, and hit sales targets.

8. If I had saw the shipper's bill, I would have pay it immediately.

9. Almost all candidates asks about three items: salary, hours, and benefits.

10. Many of Pizzarama's restaurants makes deliveries; the others concentrates on walk-in customers.

11. Everything except labour is cover in this five-year warranty.

12. The employer felt that the applicant should have be give an interview.

Correct the grammar and style errors in the following document. (Approximately 20 errors).

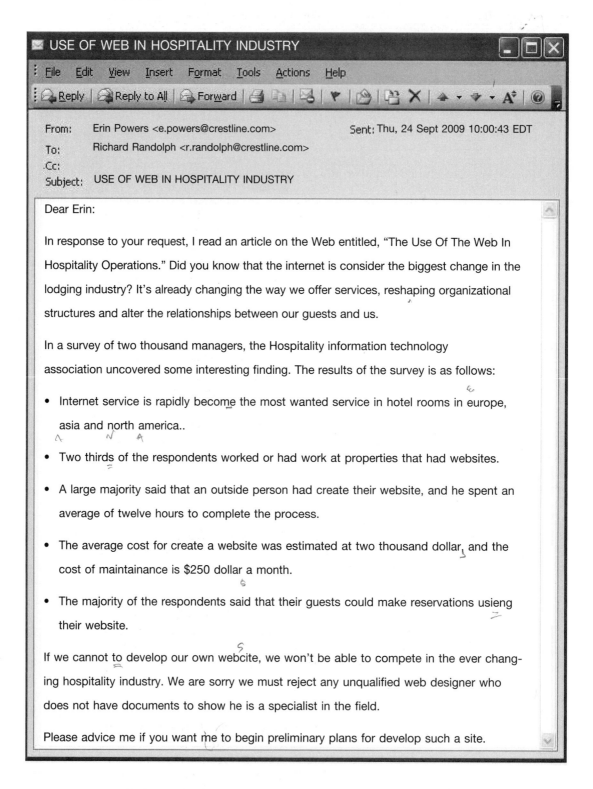

USE OF WEB IN HOSPITALITY INDUSTRY

File   Edit   View   Insert   Format   Tools   Actions   Help

Reply | Reply to All | Forward

From: Erin Powers <e.powers@crestline.com>   Sent: Thu, 24 Sept 2009 10:00:43 EDT

To: Richard Randolph <r.randolph@crestline.com>

Cc:

Subject: USE OF WEB IN HOSPITALITY INDUSTRY

Dear Erin:

In response to your request, I read an article on the Web entitled, "The Use Of The Web In Hospitality Operations." Did you know that the internet is consider the biggest change in the lodging industry? It's already changing the way we offer services, reshaping organizational structures and alter the relationships between our guests and us.

In a survey of two thousand managers, the Hospitality information technology association uncovered some interesting finding. The results of the survey is as follows:

• Internet service is rapidly become the most wanted service in hotel rooms in europe, asia and north america..

• Two thirds of the respondents worked or had work at properties that had websites.

• A large majority said that an outside person had create their website, and he spent an average of twelve hours to complete the process.

• The average cost for create a website was estimated at two thousand dollar, and the cost of maintainance is $250 dollar a month.

• The majority of the respondents said that their guests could make reservations usieng their website.

If we cannot to develop our own webcite, we won't be able to compete in the ever changing hospitality industry. We are sorry we must reject any unqualified web designer who does not have documents to show he is a specialist in the field.

Please advice me if you want me to begin preliminary plans for develop such a site.

Sharpening Your Skills for Critical Thinking, Problem Solving, and Decision Making

Gone are the days when management expected workers to follow the leader blindly and do only what they were told. Today, you'll be expected to think critically. You'll be solving problems and making decisions. Much of this book is devoted to helping you solve problems and communicate those decisions to management, fellow workers, clients, governments, and the public. Faced with a problem or an issue, most of us do a lot of worrying before making a decision. All that worrying can become directed thinking by channelling it into the following procedure.

1. Identify and clarify the problem. Your first task is to recognize that a problem exists. Some problems are big and unmistakable, such as failure of a courier service to get packages to customers on time. Other problems may be continuing annoyances, such as regularly running out of toner for an office copy machine. The first step in reaching a solution is pinpointing the problem area.

2. Gather information. Learn more about the problem situation. Look for possible causes and solutions. This step may mean checking files, calling suppliers, or brainstorming with fellow workers. For example, the courier service would investigate the tracking systems of the airlines carrying its packages to determine what is going wrong.

3. Evaluate the evidence. Where did the information come from? Does it represent various points of view? What biases could be expected from each source? How accurate is the information gathered? Is it fact or opinion? For example, it is a fact that packages are missing; it is an opinion that they are merely lost and will turn up eventually.

4. Consider alternatives and implications. Draw conclusions from the gathered evidence and pose solutions. Then weight the advantages and disadvantages of each alternative. What are the costs, benefits, and consequences? What are the obstacles, and how can they be handled? Most important, what solution best serves your goals and those of your organization? Here's where your creativity is especially important.

5. Choose and implement the best alternative. Select an alternative and put it into action. Then, follow through on your decision by monitoring the results of implementing your plan. The courier company decided to give its unhappy customers free delivery service to make up for the lost packages and downtime. Be sure to continue monitoring and adjusting the solution to ensure its effectiveness over time.

Career Application

Let's return to the fast-food franchise problem (discussed earlier in this chapter) in which some franchise owners are unhappy with the multiple lines for service. Customers don't seem to know where to stand to be next in line. People become upset when aggressive customers cut in line, and other customers spend so much time protecting their places in line that they fail to study the menu. Then they don't know what to order when they approach the counter. As a franchise owner, you would like to find a solution to this problem. Any changes in procedures, however, must be aproved by all the franchise owners in a district. That means you'll have to get a majority to agree. You know that management feels that the multi-line system accommodates higher volumes of customers more quickly than a single-line system. Moreover, the problem of perception is important. What happens when customers walk into a restaurant and see a long, single line? Do they stay to learn how fast the line is moving?

Your Task

- Individually or with a team, use the critical thinking steps outlined here. Begin by clarifying the problem.
- Where could you gather information to help you solve this problem? Would it be wise to see what your competitors are doing? How do banks handle customer lines? Airlines? Sports events?
- Evaluate your findings and consider alternatives. What are the pros and cons of each alternative?
- Choose the best alternative. Present your recommendation to your class and give your reasons for choosing it.

Web **Related website: Visit the Canadian Franchise Association's website at http://www.cfa.ca to learn the recommended ethical requirements of franchisers and franchisees in Canada. Do the opinions of franchisees really count?**

Improving Writing Techniques

Write with your target audience in mind. Ask yourself what information your audience requires and ensure you present the key messages in a clear and concise way. People don't take time to read lots of jargon and flowery words.[1]

Shelly Chagnon, *Publicist, Rogers Television*

LEARNING OBJECTIVES

1. Contrast formal and informal methods of researching data and generating ideas for messages.
2. Specify how to organize information into outlines.
3. Compare direct and indirect patterns for organizing ideas.
4. Distinguish components of complete and effective sentences.
5. Emphasize important ideas and de-emphasize unimportant ones.
6. Use active voice, passive voice, and parallelism effectively in messages.
7. Develop sentence unity by avoiding imprecise writing, mixed constructions, and misplaced modifiers.
8. Identify strategies for achieving paragraph coherence and composing the first draft of a message.

Writing naturally, as Shelly Chagnon advises, may seem easy. But it's not. It takes instruction and practice. This chapter presents additional writing tips that make your communication not only natural but also effective.

Figure 3.1 reviews the entire writing process. In Chapter 2, we focused on the prewriting stage. This chapter addresses the second stage, which includes researching, organizing, and composing.

Researching

No smart businessperson would begin writing a message before collecting the needed information. We call this collection process research. For simple documents, the process of research can be quite informal. Research is necessary before beginning to write because the information you collect helps shape the message. Discovering significant information after a message is completed

FIGURE 3.1 The Writing Process

often means starting over and reorganizing. To avoid frustration and inaccurate messages, collect information that answers this primary question:

- What does the receiver need to know about this topic?

When the message involves action, search for answers to secondary questions:

- What is the receiver to do?
- How is the receiver to do it?
- When must the receiver do it?
- What will happen if the receiver doesn't do it?

Whenever your communication problem requires more information than you have in your head or at your fingertips, you must conduct research. This research may be formal or informal.

Formal Research Methods

Long reports and complex business problems generally require some use of formal research methods. Let's say you are a market specialist for a major soft drink manufacturer, and your boss asks you to evaluate the impact on cola sales of generic ("no name") soft drinks. Or let's assume you must write a term paper for a college class. Both tasks require more data than you have in your head or at your fingertips. To conduct formal research, you could do the following:

- **Search manually.** You'll find helpful background and supplementary information through manual searching of resources in public and college libraries. These traditional sources include books and newspaper, magazine, and journal articles. Other sources are encyclopedias, reference books, handbooks, dictionaries, directories, and almanacs.
- **Search electronically.** Much of the printed material just described is now contained in searchable databases available through the Internet. College and public libraries subscribe to retrieval services that permit you to access most periodical literature. You can also find a vast amount of information, though not always of the best quality, by searching the Web.
- **Go to the source.** For firsthand information, go directly to the source. For the cola sales report, for example, you could find out what consumers really think by conducting interviews or surveys, by putting together questionnaires, or by organizing focus groups.
- **Conduct scientific experiments.** Instead of merely asking for the target audience's opinion, scientific researchers present choices with controlled variables. Let's say, for example, that the brand-name cola manufacturer wants to determine at what price and under what circumstances consumers would switch from the brand name to a generic brand. The results of such experimentation would provide valuable data for managerial decision making.

Because formal research techniques are particularly necessary for reports, you'll study them more extensively in Chapter 9.

✔ Quick Check

The second stage of the writing process involves research, which means collecting the necessary information to prepare a message.

✔ Quick Check

Formal research may include searching libraries and electronic databases or investigating primary sources.

✔ Quick Check

Good sources of primary information are interviews, surveys, questionnaires, and focus groups.

Researching

Informal Research and Idea Generation

Most routine tasks—such as composing e-mails, memos, letters, informational reports, and oral presentations—require data that you can collect informally. Here are some techniques for collecting informal data and for generating ideas:

- **Search company files.** If you are responding to an inquiry, you often can find the answer by investigating your company's files or by consulting colleagues.
- **Talk with your boss.** Get information from the individual making the assignment. What does that person know about the topic? What sources would he or she suggest?
- **Interview the target audience.** Consider talking with individuals at whom the message is aimed. They can provide information that tells you what they want to know and how you should shape your remarks.
- **Conduct an informal survey.** Gather unscientific but helpful information via questionnaires or telephone surveys. In preparing a memo report predicting the success of a proposed fitness centre, for example, circulate a questionnaire asking for employee reactions.
- **Brainstorm for ideas.** Alone or with others, discuss ideas for the writing task at hand and record at least a dozen ideas without judging them. Small groups are especially fruitful in brainstorming because people spin ideas off one another.

Organizing Data

Outlining

Quick Check

A simple way to organize data is an outline.

In developing simple messages, most writers need to organize their ideas—especially if the project is complex—into a hierarchy, such as an outline. The beauty of preparing an outline is that it gives you a chance to organize your thoughts before you start to choose specific words and sentences. Figure 3.2 shows a format for an outline.

FIGURE 3.2 Sample Outline

Awards Ceremony Costs

I. Venue
   A. Rentals
      1. Microphone
      2. Screen projector
      3. Tablecloths
   B. Extra staff
      1. Security guard
      2. Set-up, clean-up staff
II. Food
   A. Pre-awards
      1. Nonalcoholic beverages
      2. Appetizers
   B. Post-awards
      1. Alcohol
      2. Dinner
      3. Dessert
III. Awards
   A. Certificates
   B. Cash prizes

Tips for Writing Outlines

- **Define the main topic in the title.**
- **Divide the topic into major components, preferably three to five.**
- **Break the components into subpoints.**
- **Use details, illustrations, and evidence to support subpoints.**
- **Don't put a single item under a major component if you have only one subpoint; integrate it with the main item above it or reorganize.**
- **Strive to make each component exclusive (no overlapping).**

The Direct Pattern

After preparing an outline, you will need to decide where in the message you will place the main idea. Placing the main idea at the beginning of the message is called the direct pattern. In the direct pattern, the main idea comes first, followed by details, explanation, or evidence. Placing the main idea later in the message (after the details, explanation, or evidence) is called the indirect pattern. The pattern you select is determined by how you expect the audience to react to the message, as shown in Figure 3.3.

In preparing to write any message, you need to anticipate the audience's reaction to your ideas and frame your message accordingly. When you expect the reader to be pleased, mildly interested, or, at worst, neutral—use the direct pattern. That is, put your main point—the purpose of your message—in the first or second sentence. Compare the direct and indirect patterns in the following memo openings. Notice how long it takes to get to the main idea in the indirect opening.

Indirect opening Bombardier is seeking to improve the process of producing its annual company awards ceremony. The Marketing Department, which is in charge of the event, has been refining last year's plan, especially regarding rental costs and food and beverage costs.

Direct opening The Marketing Department at Bombardier suggests cutting costs for the annual awards ceremony by changing the way we order food and the way we handle rentals.

Explanations and details should follow the direct opening. What's important is getting to the main idea quickly. This direct method, also called *frontloading,* has at least three advantages:

- **Saves the reader time.** Many businesspeople can devote only a few moments to each message. Messages that take too long to get to the point may lose their readers along the way.

FIGURE 3.3 Audience Response Determines Pattern of Organization

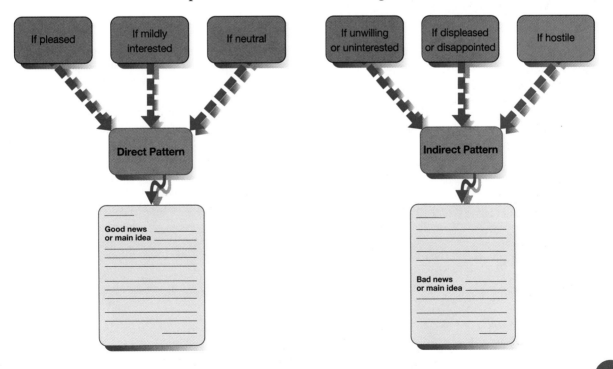

The direct pattern works best with audiences that are likely to be open to your message.

- **Sets a proper frame of mind.** Without a clear opening, the reader may be thinking, "Why am I being told this?"
- **Prevents frustration.** Readers forced to struggle through too much text before reaching the main idea become frustrated. They dislike the writer. Poorly organized messages create a negative impression of the writer.

This direct strategy works best with audiences that will likely be open to—or at least will not likely disagree with—what you have to say. Typical business messages that follow the direct pattern include routine requests and responses, orders and acknowledgments, non-sensitive memos, e-mails, informational reports, and informational oral presentations. All these tasks have one element in common: none has a sensitive subject that will upset the reader.

The Indirect Pattern

The indirect pattern works best when the audience may be uninterested, unwilling, displeased, or even hostile.

When you expect the audience to be uninterested, unwilling, displeased, or perhaps even angry, the indirect pattern is more appropriate. In this pattern, you don't reveal the main idea until after you have offered explanation and evidence. This approach works well with three kinds of messages: (1) bad news, (2) ideas that require persuasion, and (3) sensitive news, especially when being transmitted to superiors. The indirect pattern has these benefits:

- **Respects the feelings of the audience.** Bad news is often painful, but the pain can be lessened when the receiver is prepared for it.
- **Encourages more complete attention.** Messages that may upset the reader are more likely to be read when the main idea is delayed. Beginning immediately with a piece of bad news or a persuasive request, for example, may cause the receiver to stop reading or listening.
- **Minimizes a negative reaction.** A reader's overall reaction to a negative message is generally improved if the news is delivered gently.

Typical business messages that could be developed indirectly include letters and memos that refuse requests, deny claims, and disapprove credit. Persuasive requests, sales letters, sensitive messages, and some reports and oral presentations also benefit from the indirect strategy. You'll learn more about how to use the indirect pattern in Chapters 7 and 8.

In summary, business messages may be organized directly, with the main idea first, or indirectly, with the main idea delayed. Although these two patterns cover many communication problems, every business transaction is distinct. Some messages are mixed: part good news, part bad; part goodwill, part persuasion. In upcoming chapters you'll practise applying the direct and indirect patterns in typical situations. Then, you'll have the skills and confidence to evaluate communication problems and vary these patterns depending on your goals.

Effective Sentences

After deciding how to organize your message, you are ready to begin composing it. As you create your first draft, you'll be working at the sentence level of composition. Although you've used sentences all your life, you may be unaware of how they can be shaped and arranged to express your ideas most effectively. First, let's review some basic sentence elements.

Complete sentences have subjects and verbs and make sense.

SUBJECT VERB

This report is clear and concise.

Clauses and phrases, the building blocks of sentences, are related groups of words. Phrases have no subject or verb. Clauses have a subject and verb.

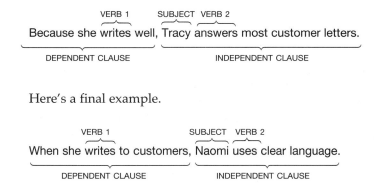

Clauses can be divided into two groups: independent and dependent. Independent clauses are grammatically complete, while dependent clauses depend for their meaning on independent clauses. In the example below, the clause beginning with *Because* does not make sense by itself, while the clause beginning with *Tracy* does make sense by itself.

VERB 1   SUBJECT VERB 2

Because she writes well, Tracy answers most customer letters.

DEPENDENT CLAUSE   INDEPENDENT CLAUSE

Here's a final example.

VERB 1   SUBJECT VERB 2

When she writes to customers, Naomi uses clear language.

DEPENDENT CLAUSE   INDEPENDENT CLAUSE

By learning to distinguish phrases, independent clauses, and dependent clauses, you'll be able to punctuate sentences correctly and avoid three basic sentence faults: the fragment, the run-on sentence, and the comma splice.

Sentence Fragment

One of the most serious errors a writer can make is punctuating a fragment as if it were a complete sentence. A fragment is a broken-off part of a sentence that is missing either a subject or a verb.

Fragments are broken-off parts of sentences and should not be punctuated as sentences.

Fragment	Because all business letters must be clear. Good writing skills are critical.
Revision	Because all business letters must be clear, good writing skills are critical.
Fragment	The interviewer requested a writing sample. Since the candidate had trouble communicating well.
Revision	The interviewer requested a writing sample since the candidate had trouble communicating well.

Fragments can often be identified by the words that introduce them—words such as *although, as, because, even, except, for example, if, instead of, since, so, such as, that, which,* and *when.* These words introduce dependent clauses. Make sure such clauses always connect to independent clauses.

Run-On (Fused) Sentence

A sentence with two independent clauses must be joined by a coordinating conjunction (*and, or, nor, but*) or by a semicolon (;). Without a conjunction or a semicolon, the result is a run-on sentence.

When two independent clauses are run together without punctuation or a coordinating conjunction, a run-on (fused) sentence results.

| **Run-on** | Most job seekers present a printed résumé some use websites as electronic portfolios. |

Revision 1	Most job seekers present a printed résumé, but some use websites as electronic portfolios.
Revision 2	Most job seekers present a printed résumé; some use websites as electronic portfolios.

Comma-Splice Sentence

A comma splice results when a writer joins two independent clauses with a comma. A comma is too weak to hold independent clauses together. Independent clauses should be joined with a coordinating conjunction (*and, or, nor, but, so, yet*) or a conjunctive adverb (*however, consequently, therefore,* and others). Notice that clauses joined by coordinating conjunctions require only a comma. Clauses joined by a coordinating adverb, however, require a semicolon. Here are three ways to fix a comma splice:

Comma splice	Some employees responded by e-mail, others picked up the telephone.
Revision 1	Some employees responded by e-mail, and others picked up the telephone.
Revision 2	Some employees responded by e-mail; however, others picked up the telephone.
Revision 3	Some employees responded by e-mail; others picked up the telephone.

Sentence Length

Because your goal is to communicate clearly, limit your sentences to 20 or fewer words. Nicholas Russell, a writer, editor, and lecturer in Victoria, B.C., has said, "If your lead sentence is more than 20 words long, it had better be damn good!"[2] Thus, in composing your sentences, think about the relationship between sentence length and comprehension:

Sentence Length	Comprehension Rate
8 words	100%
15 words	90%
19 words	80%
28 words	50%

Instead of grouping clauses with *and, but,* and *however,* break some of your sentences into separate segments. Business readers want to grasp ideas immediately. They can do that best when thoughts are separated into short sentences. On the other hand, too many short sentences will sound unprofessional and may bore or even annoy the reader. Strive for a balance between longer sentences and shorter ones.

Emphasis

When you emphasize your main ideas, you show their importance or intensity. For example, if you are talking with someone, you can emphasize your main ideas by saying them loudly or by repeating them slowly. You could hit the table if you want to show real emphasis. Another way you could signal the relative importance of an idea is by raising your eyebrows or by shaking your head or whispering in a low voice. But when you write, you must rely on other means to tell your readers which ideas are more important than others. Emphasis in writing can be achieved in two ways: through mechanics or through style.

Emphasis through Mechanics

To emphasize an idea, a writer may use any of the following devices:

Underlining	<u>Underlining</u> draws the eye to a word.
Italics and boldface	Using *italics* or **boldface** gives special meaning and emphasis.
Font changes	Changing from a large font to a smaller font or to a different font provides interest and emphasis.
All cap	Printing words in ALL CAPS is like shouting them.
Dashes	Using dashes—sparingly—can be effective in capturing attention.
Tabulation	Listing items vertically makes them stand out: 1. First item 2. Second item 3. Third item

Other means of achieving mechanical emphasis include the arrangement of space, colour, lines, boxes, columns, titles, headings, and subheadings. Today's software and colour printers provide a wide choice of options for emphasizing ideas.

✓ Quick Check

You can emphasize an idea mechanically by using underlining, italics, boldface, font changes, all caps, dashes, and tabulation.

Emphasis through Style

Often, a writer chooses words carefully and constructs sentences skillfully to emphasize main ideas and de-emphasize minor or negative ideas. Here are four suggestions for emphasizing ideas through style.

- **Use vivid words.** Vivid words allow the reader to picture ideas clearly.

General	A business uses personal selling techniques.
Vivid	Avon uses face-to-face selling techniques.
General	A customer said that he wanted the contract returned soon.
Vivid	Mr. LeClerc insisted that the contract be returned by July 1.

✓ Quick Check

You can emphasize ideas stylistically by using vivid words, labelling the main idea, and positioning the main idea strategically.

- **Place the important idea in a simple sentence or in an independent clause.** Don't minimize the effect of the idea by making it share the attention with other words and clauses.

Emphatic	You are the first trainee whom we have hired for this program. (Use a simple sentence for emphasis.)
Emphatic	Although we considered many candidates, you are the first trainee whom we have hired for this program. (Independent clause contains main idea.)
Not Emphatic	Although you are the first trainee whom we have hired for this program, we had many candidates and expect to expand the program in the future. (Main idea is lost in a dependent clause.)

De-emphasize. To de-emphasize an idea, such as bad news, try one of the following stylistic devices:

- **Use general words.**

Vivid	Our records indicate that you were recently fired.
General	Our records indicate that your employment status has changed recently.

✓ Quick Check

You can de-emphasize ideas through word choice and placement.

- **Place the bad news in a dependent clause connected to an independent clause with something positive.** In sentences with dependent clauses, the main emphasis is always on the independent clause.

Emphasizes bad news	We cannot issue you credit at this time, but we do have a plan that will allow you to fill your immediate needs on a cash basis.
De-emphasizes bad news	We have a plan that will allow you to fill your immediate needs on a cash basis since we cannot issue credit at this time.

Active and Passive Voice

In sentences with active-voice verbs, the subject is the doer of the action. In passive-voice sentences, the subject is acted upon.

Active verb	Mr. Wong completed the tax return before the April 30 deadline. (The subject, *Mr. Wong*, is the doer of the action.)
Passive verb	The tax return was completed before the April 30 deadline. (The subject, *tax return*, is acted upon.)

Quick Check

Active-voice sentences are direct and easy to understand.

In the first sentence, the active-voice verb emphasizes *Mr. Wong*. In the second sentence, the passive-voice verb emphasizes *tax return*. In sentences with passive-voice verbs, the one who performs the action may be stated or left out. In business writing, and in personal contacts, some situations demand tact and sensitivity. Instead of using a direct approach with active verbs, we may prefer the indirectness that passive verbs allow. Rather than making a blunt announcement with an active verb (*Gunnar broke the computer*), we can soften the sentence with a passive construction (*The computer was broken*).

Here's a summary of the best use of active- and passive-voice verbs:

Quick Check

Although active-voice verbs are preferred in business writing, passive-voice verbs perform useful functions.

- **Use the active voice for most business writing.** It clearly tells what the action is and who is performing that action.
- **Use the passive voice to emphasize an action or the receiver of the action.** *You have been selected to represent us.*
- **Use the passive voice to de-emphasize negative news.** *Your watch has not been repaired.*
- **Use the passive voice to conceal the one who is doing the action.** *A major error was made in the estimate.*

How can you tell if a verb is active or passive? Identify the subject of the sentence and decide whether the subject is doing the acting or being acted upon. For example, in the sentence *An appointment was made for January 1*, the subject is *appointment*. The subject is being acted upon; therefore, the verb *(was made)* is passive. Another clue in identifying passive-voice verbs is that they generally include a *to be* helping verb, such as *is, are, was, were, being,* or *been*.

Parallelism

Parallelism is a writing technique that creates balanced writing and makes sentences easy to read and understand. To get parallel construction, use similar structures to express similar ideas. For example, the words *computing, coding, recording,* and *storing* are parallel because they all end in *-ing*. The list *computing, coding,* *recording, and storage* is not balanced because the last item, *storage,* does not match the rest of the list. Try to match nouns with nouns, verbs with verbs, and clauses with clauses. Avoid mixing active-voice verbs with passive-voice verbs. Your goal is to keep the wording balanced when you are expressing similar ideas.

Quick Check

Balanced wording helps the reader anticipate and comprehend your meaning.

Lacks parallelism	The market for goods includes manufacturers, contractors, wholesalers, and those concerned with the retail function.
Revision	The market for goods includes manufacturers, contractors, wholesalers, and retailers. (Parallel construction matches nouns.)
Lacks parallelism	Our primary goals are to increase productivity, reduce costs, and the improvement of product quality.
Revision	Our primary goals are to increase productivity, reduce costs, and improve product quality. (Parallel construction matches verbs.)
Lacks parallelism	We are scheduled to meet in Toronto on January 5, we are meeting in Montreal on the 15th of March, and in Burlington on June 3.
Revision	We are scheduled to meet in Toronto on January 5, in Montreal on March 15, and in Burlington on June 3. (Parallel construction matches phrases.)
Lacks parallelism	Mrs. Chorney audits all accounts; accounts are submitted by Mr. Faheem.
Revision	Mrs. Chorney audits all accounts; Mr. Faheem submits the accounts. (Parallel construction matches active-voice verbs in balanced clauses.)

In presenting lists of data, whether horizontally or vertically, be certain to express all the items in parallel form.

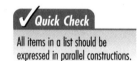
Quick Check

All items in a list should be expressed in parallel constructions.

Parallelism in vertical list	Three primary objectives of advertising are as follows:
	1. Increase the frequency of product use.
	2. Introduce complementary products.
	3. Enhance the corporate image.

Paragraph Coherence

A paragraph is a group of sentences with a controlling idea; this idea is often, but not always, stated at the beginning of the paragraph. Effective paragraphs are coherent; that is, they hold together. Coherence is achieved through effective organization, use of pronouns, and use of transitional expressions.

- **Use of pronouns.** Pronouns such as *this, that, they, these,* and *those* help coherence by connecting the thoughts in one sentence to the thoughts in a previous sentence. To make sure that the pronoun reference is clear, consider joining the pronoun with the word to which it refers.

Pronoun alone	Grania and Sinead wrote the report together. *They* make a good team.
Pronoun with repeated word	Xerox has a four-point program to assist suppliers. *This program* includes written specifications for production materials and components.

Be very careful, though, in using pronouns. An unclear pronoun can be annoying. That's because the reader doesn't know exactly to what the pronoun refers.

Faulty	When company profits increased, employees were given either a cash payment or company stock. *This* became a real encouragement to employees. (Is *This* the cash or the stock or both?)
Revision	When company profits increased, employees were given either a cash payment or company stock. *This profit-sharing plan* became a real incentive to employees.

- **Use of transitional expressions.** One of the most effective ways to achieve paragraph coherence is through the use of transitional expressions. These expressions act as road signs: they indicate where the message is headed, and they help the reader predict what is coming. Here are some of the most effective transitional expressions. They are grouped according to use.

Time Association	Contrast	Illustration
before, after	although	for example
first, second	but	in this way
meanwhile	however	
next	instead	
until	nevertheless	
when, whenever	on the other hand	

Cause, Effect	Additional Idea
consequently	furthermore
for this reason	in addition
hence	likewise
therefore	moreover

Paragraph Length

Although no rule regulates the length of paragraphs, business writers recognize the value of short paragraphs. Paragraphs with eight or fewer printed lines look inviting and readable. Long, solid chunks of print appear difficult. If a topic can't be covered in eight or fewer printed lines (not sentences), consider breaking it into smaller segments.

Composing the First Draft

Once you've researched your topic, organized the data, and selected a pattern of organization, you're ready to begin composing. To avoid "writer's block," organize your ideas and make a plan. Composition is also easier if you have a quiet environment in which to concentrate. Businesspeople with messages to compose often set aside a given time and do not allow calls, visitors, or other interruptions. This is a good technique for students as well.

As you begin composing, keep in mind that you are writing the first draft, not the final copy. Experts suggest that you write quickly (sprint writing). As you take up each idea, imagine that you are talking to the reader. If you can't think of the right word, insert a substitute or type "find perfect word later."[3] Sprint writing works especially well for those composing on a computer because it's simple to make changes at any point of the composition process. If you are handwriting the first draft, double-space so that you have room for changes.

This chapter explained the second phase of the writing process, including researching, organizing, and composing. Before beginning a message, every writer collects data, either formally or informally. For most simple messages, writers look in their company's files, talk with their boss, interview the target audience, or possibly conduct an informal survey. Information for a message is then organized into a list or an outline. Depending on the expected reaction of the receiver, the message can be organized directly (for positive reactions) or indirectly (for negative reactions or when persuasion is necessary).

In composing the first draft, writers must be sure that sentences are complete. Emphasis can be achieved through mechanics (underlining, italics, font changes, all caps, and so forth) or through style (using vivid words, identifying the main idea, and positioning the important ideas). Important writing techniques include skillful use of active- and passive-voice verbs, developing parallelism, and achieving unity. Coherent paragraphs result from proper organization of ideas, proper use of pronouns, and use of transitional expressions.

In the next chapter, you'll learn helpful techniques for the third phase of the writing process, which includes revising and proofreading.

Critical Thinking

1. Why is audience analysis so important in choosing the direct or indirect pattern of organization for a business message?
2. In what ways do you imagine that writing on the job differs from the writing you do in your academic studies?
3. Why are short sentences and short paragraphs appropriate for business communication?

Chapter Review

4. What three steps are included in the second phase of the writing process?

5. Distinguish between formal and informal methods of researching data for a business message.

6. What is frontloading, and what are its advantages?

7. When is the indirect method appropriate, and what are the benefits of using it?

8. List five techniques for achieving emphasis through mechanics.

9. List four techniques for achieving emphasis through style.

10. What is parallelism? Give an original example.

11. List two techniques for developing paragraph coherence.

Writing Improvement Exercises

Revising Sentences. Revise the following sentences. Identify whether the mistake is a sentence fragment, run-on sentence, or comma splice. *Comma splice*

12. When a company wants an effective employee. It checks résumés very carefully. *Comma*

13. The shipment was sent on April 30 it arrived three days later.

14. Although Tim Hortons is the country's number one doughnut chain. Robin's Donuts is popular in western Canada.

15. About half of Swiss Chalet's outlets make deliveries, the others concentrate on walk-in customers.

Emphasis. For each of the following sentences, circle (a) or (b). Be prepared to explain your choice.

16. Which is more emphatic?
    a. We need a faster, more efficient distribution system.
    b. We need a better distribution system.

17. Which is more emphatic?
    a. Increased advertising would improve sales.
    (b.) Adding $50,000 in advertising would double our sales.
18. Which is less emphatic?
    (a.) Lily Takahashi said that her financial status had worsened.
    b. Lily Takahashi said that she had lost her job and owed $2000.
19. Which sentence de-emphasizes the credit refusal?
    a. We are unable to give you credit at this time, but we will reconsider your application later.
    (b.) Although we welcome your cash business, we are unable to offer you credit at this time; but we will be happy to reconsider your application later.
20. Which is more emphatic?
    a. Three departments are involved: (1) Legal, (2) Accounting, and (3) Distribution.
    (b.) Three departments are involved:
        1. Legal
        2. Accounting
        3. Distribution

Active-Voice Verbs. Business writing is more forceful if it uses active-voice verbs. Revise the following sentences so that the verbs are in the active voice. Put the emphasis on the doer of the action. Add subjects if necessary.

Example: The computers were turned on each day at 7:00 a.m.
Revision: Kamal turned on the computers each day at 7:00 a.m.

21. The real-estate contract was submitted before June 1.

22. New spices and cooking techniques were tried by Sunny's Restaurant to improve its hamburgers.

23. Large sums of money were earned by employees who enrolled early in our stock option plan.

24. Many supplies were ordered by the manager for the new business.
    The manager ordered many supplies for the new business

25. Items are delivered by Purolator every day including Sunday.
    Purolator delivered items everyday including sunday.

Passive-Voice Verbs. When indirectness or tact is required, use passive-voice verbs. Revise the following sentences so that they are in the passive voice.

Example: Sade did not submit the accounting statement on time.
Revision: The accounting statement was not submitted on time.

26. Andreas made an error in the report.
    An error was made in the report

27. We cannot ship your order for 10 monitors until June 15.
    The order for 10 monitors cannot be ship until June 15

Writing Improvement Exercises

28. The government issued a warning about the use of this pesticide over 15 months ago.

29. We will notify you immediately if we make any changes in your travel arrangements.

30. We cannot allow a cash refund unless you provide a receipt.

Parallelism. Revise the following sentences so that their parts are balanced.

31. (*Hint*: Match verbs.) Some of our priorities include linking employee salaries to performance, keeping administrative costs down, the expansion of computer use, and the improvement of performance review skills of supervisors.

32. (*Hint*: Match active voice of verbs.) Yin Huang, of the Red River office, will now supervise our Western Division, and the Eastern Division will be supervised by our Ottawa office manager, David Ali. *The Western Division will be supervise by Yin Huang of the Red River office and the Eastern division will be supervise by off manger David ali of Ottawa*

33. If you have decided to cancel our service, please cut your credit card in half, and ~~the card pieces should be~~ returned to us. *the pieces*

34. We need more laboratory space, additional personnel is required, and we also need ~~much~~ more capital.

35. *Leasing* ~~To lease~~ a car is more expensive than buying one.

36. To use the copier, insert your account card, the paper trays must be loaded, indicate the number of copies needed, and your original sheet should be inserted through the feeder.

Coherence. Revise the following paragraphs to improve coherence. Be aware that the transitional expressions and key words selected depend largely on the emphasis desired. Many possible revisions exist.

Example: Computer style checkers rank somewhere between artificial intelligence and artificial ignorance. Style checkers are like clever children: smart but not wise. Business writers should be cautious. They should be aware of the usefulness of style checkers. They should know their limitations.

Revision: Computer style checkers rank somewhere between artificial intelligence and artificial ignorance. *For example*, they are like clever children: smart but not wise. *For this reason*, business writers should be cautious. *Although* they should be aware of the usefulness of these software programs, business writers should also know the programs' limitations.

37. Our computerized file includes all customer data. It provides space for name, address, and other vital information. It has an area for comments. The area for comments comes in handy. It requires more time and careful keyboarding, though.

38. No one likes to make poor products. We began checking recurring problems. Employees make a special effort to be more careful in doing their work right the first time. It doesn't have to be returned to them for corrections.

Grammar/Mechanics Review—3

The following sentences contain errors in comma splices, sentence fragments, run-ons, and parallelism. Some sentences have more than one error. Below each sentence, write a corrected version. Check with your instructor for the solutions.

1. Although most of our capital is tied up in equipment. We expect to purchase two vans in February.

2. During the fall, Elisa will be registering for classes, working part-time, and to volunteer at the local hospital.

3. A list of restaurants is included in the brochure please check for those with dinners costing less than six dollars.

4. We hire only experienced programmers, however, we occasionally consider well-trained individuals who lack experience.

5. All houses have to be inspected for termite damage, for water damage, and a check for cracked kitchen tiles should also be done.

6. Three employees are absent today. Max, Gabrielle, and Tyler.

7. Every classified employee is eligible for new health benefits. Including all certified employees and members of management.

8. The four announcements from our Human Resources Department surprised management the new employees were from outside the organization.

9. We expect to raise over two thousand dollars. During a four-week campaign.

10. All homeowners are upset over the following changes: the latest increase in property taxes, the switch to once-a-week garbage pickup, and the mail will not be delivered on Saturdays.

11. Nick Foster is a writer for *Channel Business* e-zine, he quoted a mathematician as saying "On average, people are average."

12. If the president and manager agree that next year's sales campaign should emphasize customer service. Then we can proceed.

13. Nicola is more of a team player than Nabil. Which explains her recent promotion.

14. We trust that the New Year will be profitable for you, and that you will also have success.

15. Microsoft says that the company makes computing more accessible for every one. Because they offer new ideas, new products, and services that are new.

Document for Revision 1

The following memo has many faults in grammar, spelling, punctuation, and capitalization. Study the guidelines in the Grammar/Mechanics Handbook to sharpen your skills. Rewrite the document, making corrections. When you finish, your instructor can show you the revised version of this memo.

Title Guaranty Co.

Memo

To:	Jamal Warner, Vice President
From:	Roxanne Crosley, Manager, Payroll
Date:	July 24, 2009
Subject:	Departmental Error

Last month the accounting department changed it's computer program for payroll processing. When this computer change was done, some of the stored information was not transfered to the new information database, therefore, several errors occured in employee paycheques (1) health benefits were not deducted (2) RSP deductions were not made and (3) we made several errors in Federal withholding calculations.

Every one of the employees affected have been contacted and this error has been explained. My staff and I has been working overtime to replace all the missing data. So that corrections can be made by the August 31st payroll run.

To prevent such an error in the future, I decided to take charge. I have started a rigorous new verification system. This new system will definitely prevent this event from reoccurring.

While active voice is preferred in the direct pattern, for grammar practice, revise the following memo by changing all active-voice verbs (underlined) to the passive voice.

Memo

To: Field Supervisor

From: Mary Ho, Senior Supervisor

Date: March 6, 2009

Subject: Improving Working Relations with Community Volunteers

---

Our management team <u>conducted</u> a meeting yesterday to discuss the situation with our volunteers. The following suggestions should help you work more effectively with your community volunteers:

- <u>Check</u> all flyers so that no information is missing.

- <u>Send</u> event announcements at least six weeks before the occasion.

- <u>Avoid</u> using jargon with individuals who may not understand.

- <u>Show</u> volunteers how much we appreciate them by praising their contributions.

- <u>Maintain</u> a courteous attitude with community volunteers.

The field supervisors <u>will meet</u> all volunteers next week during our annual meeting. <u>Give</u> all suggestions to me by March 9, so I can prepare the agenda for the meeting. Please <u>contact</u> me at Ext. 4745 if you have any questions. Our president, Mr. Tom Streit, <u>will present</u> each of you with this year's report about our progress.

Using Ethical Tools to Help You Do the Right Thing

In your career you will face times when you are torn by conflicting loyalties. Should you tell the truth and risk your job? Should you be loyal to your friends even if it means bending the rules? Should you be tactful or totally honest? Is it your duty to help your company make a profit, or should you be socially responsible?

Being ethical, according to the experts, means doing the right thing given the circumstances. Each set of circumstances requires analyzing issues, evaluating choices, and acting responsibly. Resolving ethical issues is never easy, but the task can be made less difficult if you know how to identify key issues. The following questions may be helpful.

- **Is the action you are considering legal?** No matter who asks you to do it or how important you feel the result will be, avoid anything that is forbidden by law. For example, giving payment to a buyer for a large order is illegal. Even if you suspect that others in your field do it, and even if you know that without the reward you will lose the sale, it is still wrong.
- **How would you see the problem if you were on the opposite side?** Look at all sides of an issue. Consider the issue of mandatory drug testing among employees. From management's viewpoint such testing could stop drug abuse and improve job performance. From the employees' viewpoint mandatory testing reflects a lack of trust of employees and is an invasion of privacy. By looking at both sides of an issue, you can arrive at a more balanced solution.
- **What are the alternative solutions?** Consider all other options. Would the other choice be more ethical? Under the circumstances, is the other choice possible? Can another solution be applied with a minimum of interruption and with a high degree of probable success?
- **Can you discuss the problem with someone whose opinion you value?** Suppose you feel ethically bound to report accurate information to a client— even though your boss has ordered you not to do so. Talking about your problem with a coworker or with a colleague in your field might give you helpful insights and lead to other possible choices.
- **How would you feel if your family, friends, employer, or coworkers learned of your action?** If the thought of revealing your action publicly produces fear, your choice is probably not a wise one. Whatever the short-term gain might be, it is not worth losing the faith of your friends or the confidence of your customers.

Career Application

After six months of job hunting, you land a job with Company X, but it's in a city 700 kilometres from your home. A week after starting work, you receive a job offer from Company Y that would increase your salary by 10 percent and would move you to a location closer to your home. You want very much to leave Company X to accept Company Y's offer. However, you are troubled because Company X has begun to train you. You feel particularly guilty because many nice people have made a special effort to welcome you and get you started in your new position.

Your Task

- In teams or individually, decide on an action to take. Begin by asking whether the action you are considering is legal.
- Look at the problem from Company X's perspective. How much harm would be done by your leaving? What will Company X lose if you leave?
- What are other solutions? Is it entirely a money issue? Would you be happy with a higher salary at Company X?
- Can you discuss the problem with someone whose opinion you value? Should you consult someone at Company X? Your family? Friends?
- How would you feel if your family, friends, employer, or coworkers learned of your action?
- Present your decision in a class discussion or in a memo to your instructor. Support your decision with your reasons.

Web **Related website: Visit the Canadian Centre for Ethics & Corporate Policy site at http://www.ethicscentre.ca.**

Revising and Proofreading Business Messages

CHAPTER

The importance of the written word in business—whether in an e-mail, proposal, or promotional piece—cannot be underestimated. It is often what a client sees first, and it becomes a living, tangible reflection of the company itself. Grammatical slip-ups can suggest to a client a lack of professionalism and inattention to detail. Believe me, it's and its can negatively impact a company's bottom line, and even jeopardize its position and branding in the marketplace.[1]

Stephanie Mikelbrencis, *Director of Marketing, Brock Solutions*

LEARNING OBJECTIVES

1. Understand the third part of the writing process, revision.
2. Revise messages to achieve concise wording by eliminating long lead-ins.
3. Revise messages to eliminate redundancies.
4. Revise messages to use jargon sparingly and avoid slang and clichés.
5. Revise messages to include concrete nouns and vivid adjectives.
6. Describe effective techniques for proofreading routine and complex documents.

Understanding the Process of Revision

The best business writing is clear, vigorous, and free of errors. In this chapter you'll concentrate on techniques to achieve those qualities. These techniques are the third part of the writing process, which centres on revising and proofreading. Revising means improving the content and sentence structure of your message. It may include adding to, cutting, and changing what you've written. Proofreading involves correcting the grammar, spelling, punctuation, format, and mechanics of your messages.

Both revising and proofreading require a little practice to develop your skills. That's what you will be learning in this chapter. Take a look at Figure 4.1. Notice how the revised version of the paragraph is clearer, more concise, and more vigorous because a lot of extra words that were not adding to the message were removed. Major ideas stand out when they are not hidden among unnecessary words.

 Quick Check

The third phase of the writing process includes revision, proofreading, and evaluating.

FIGURE 4.1 Revising for Conciseness

~~This is just a short note to inform you that,~~ as you requested, I have ~~made an~~
examined
~~examination~~ of several of our competitors' websites. Attached is a summary

of my findings ~~of my investigation.~~ I was ~~really~~ most interested in ~~making a comparison~~
comparing
~~of the~~ navigational ~~graphics or~~ cues that ~~were used to~~ guide visitors through the sites.

Since
~~In view of the fact that~~ we will be building our own website ~~in the near future,~~ I was
soon

~~extremely~~ intrigued by the organization, ~~kind of~~ content, and navigation at each ~~and~~

~~every~~ site I visited.

Rarely is the first or even the second version of a message satisfactory. The revision stage is your chance to make sure your message says what you mean. It's also your chance to present a good image of yourself.

Many professional writers compose the first draft quickly without worrying about language, precision, or correctness. Then they revise and polish extensively. Other writers prefer to revise as they go—particularly for shorter business documents. Whether you revise as you go or do it when you finish a document, you'll want to focus on concise wording. Such a focus includes eliminating long lead-ins and repetitious and redundant words. You'll also decide whether to include jargon, slang, and clichés. And you'll be looking for precise words that say exactly what you mean.

Quick Check
Some communicators write the first draft quickly; others revise and polish as they go.

Concise Wording

In business, time is money. Translated into writing, this saying means that concise messages save reading time and, thus, money. In addition, messages that are written directly and efficiently are easier to read and understand. As you revise, look for shorter ways to say what you mean. Examine every sentence you write. Could the thought be expressed in fewer words? Notice how the following wordy expressions could be said more concisely.

Quick Check
Main points are easier to understand in concise messages.

Wordy	Concise	Wordy	Concise
at a later date	later	in the near future	soon
at this point in time	now	due to the fact that	because, since
in addition to the above	also	in view of the fact that	because
are of the opinion that	believe, think that	feel free to	please
at the present time	now, currently	for the period of	for
in the amount of	for	until such time as	until

Quick Check
A wordy phrase can often be reduced to a single word.

Quick Check
Replace wordy prepositional phrases with adverbs whenever possible.

Long Lead-Ins

Delete unnecessary introductory words and phrases. The main idea of the sentence often follows the words *that* or *because*.

Quick Check

Avoid long lead-ins that delay the reader from reaching the main point of the sentence.

Wordy	*I am sending you this announcement to let you all know that* the office will be closed Monday.
Concise	The office will be closed Monday.
Wordy	*You will be interested to learn that* you can now be served at our website.
Concise	You can now be served at our website.
Wordy	*I am writing this letter because* Dr. Rahib Peshwar suggested that your organization was hiring trainees.
Concise	Dr. Rahib Peshwar suggested that your organization was hiring trainees.

Redundant Words

Repetition of words to achieve emphasis or effective transition is an important writing technique discussed in the previous chapter. However, the needless repetition of words whose meanings are clearly implied by other words is a writing fault called *redundancy.* For example, in the expression *advance warning,* the word *advance* is redundant and should be omitted, since *warning* implies an action that happens in advance. Learn to avoid redundant expressions such as the following:

absolutely essential	*grateful* thanks
adequate *enough*	*mutual* cooperation
advance warning	*necessary* prerequisite
basic fundamentals	*new* beginning
big *in size*	*past* history
combined *together*	reason *why*
continue *on*	red *in colour*
each *and every*	refer *back*
exactly identical	repeat *again*
few *in number*	*true* facts
final outcome	

Jargon

Except in certain special situations, you should avoid jargon and unnecessary technical terms. Jargon is special terminology that is peculiar to a particular activity or profession. For example, geologists speak knowingly of *exfoliation, calcareous ooze,* and *siliceous particles.* Engineers are familiar with phrases such as *infrared processing flags, output latches,* and *movable symbology.* Telecommunication experts use such words and phrases as *protocol, mode,* and *asynchronous transmission.* Business professionals are especially prone to using jargon, with words and phrases such as *leverage, ramp up, in the pipeline, cascade, pushback,* and *bullish* or *bearish* being just a few of the many you may find in the business section of the newspaper or in your local office.

Every field has its own special vocabulary. Using that vocabulary within the field is acceptable and even necessary for accurate, efficient communication. Don't use specialized terms, however, if you sense that your reader or listener may misunderstand them.

Slang

Slang is composed of informal words with excessively changed meanings. Slang words quickly go out of fashion because they are no longer appealing when everyone begins to understand them. Consider the following excerpt from an e-mail sent by a ski resort company president to his executive team: "Well, *guys,* the results of our customer survey are in, and what I'm hearing is *totally awesome.* Most of our customers are *crazy about the goods,* and I just want to congratulate all my *peeps* on a job well done!"

The meaning here is considerably hidden—and dated—by the use of slang. Good communicators, of course, aim at clarity and avoid unintelligible slang.

Clichés

Clichés are expressions that have become exhausted by overuse. These expressions lack not only freshness but also clarity. These are often idiomatic expressions specific to a particular language. Some have no meaning for people who are new to the culture. Some examples of clichés you should avoid in business writing include the following:

Clichés are dull and sometimes ambiguous.

- His argument *hit the nail on the head.* (was precise)
- After months of excuses we decided to *grab the bull by the horns.* (make a decision and go with it)
- She passed the test *with flying colours.* (she did well)
- José *made a killing* (was successful) in the stock market, so he bought a new car.

Other examples of clichés to avoid are *first and foremost, last but not least, quick as a flash,* and *easier said than done.*

Precise Verbs

Effective writing creates meaningful images in the mind of the reader. Such writing is marked by concrete and descriptive words. Ineffective writing is often dulled by boring, abstract, and generalized words. The most direct way to improve lifeless writing is to use precise verbs. Precise verbs describe action in a way that is understandable for the reader. These verbs deliver the force of the sentence. Select verbs that will help the reader see exactly what is happening.

General	Our salesperson will *contact* you next week.
Precise	Our salesperson will *(telephone, fax, e-mail, visit)* you next week.
General	The CEO *said* that we should contribute.
Precise	The CEO *(urged, pleaded, demanded)* that we contribute.
General	We must *consider* this problem.
Precise	We must *(clarify, remedy, rectify)* this problem.

Concrete Nouns

Nouns name persons, places, and things. Abstract nouns name concepts that can be difficult to imagine, such as *automation, function, justice, institution, integrity, form, judgment,* and *environment.* Concrete nouns name objects that are more easily imagined, such as *desk, car,* and *light bulb.* Nouns describing a given object can range from the very abstract to the very concrete—for example, *object, motor vehicle, car, sedan, Toyota.* All of these words or phrases can be used to describe a Toyota sedan. However, a reader would have difficulty envisioning a Toyota sedan when given just the word *object* or even *motor vehicle* or *car.*

In business writing, help your reader "see" what you mean by using concrete language.

Concrete nouns help readers visualize the meanings of words.

General	a *change* in our budget
Concrete	a *10 percent reduction* in our budget

General	*that company's product*
Concrete	*Motorola's cell phone*

General	a *person* telephoned
Concrete	*Mrs. Tomei, the administrative assistant*, telephoned

General	we *improved* the assembly line
Concrete	we *installed 26 advanced Unimate robots* on the assembly line

Vivid Adjectives

Quick Check

A thesaurus (on your computer or in a book) helps you select precise words and increase your vocabulary.

Including highly descriptive, dynamic adjectives makes writing more vivid and concrete. Be careful, though, neither to overuse them nor to lose objectivity in selecting them.

General	The report was on time.
Vivid	The *detailed 12-page* report was submitted on time.

General	Clayton needs a better truck.
Vivid	Clayton needs a *rugged, four-wheel-drive Dodge* truck.

General	We enjoyed the movie.
Vivid	We enjoyed the *entertaining* and *interesting* movie.

Too much	We enjoyed the *gutsy, exciting, captivating, and thoroughly marvellous* movie.

The Process of Proofreading

Once you have the message in its final form, it's time to proofread. Don't proofread earlier because you may waste time checking items that are eventually changed or omitted.

What to Watch For in Proofreading

Careful proofreaders check for problems in these areas:

Quick Check

Good proofreaders check spelling, grammar, punctuation, names, numbers, format, and consistency.

- **Spelling.** Now's the time to consult the dictionary. Is *recommend* spelled with one or two *c*'s? Do you mean *affect* or *effect*? Use your computer spell checker, but don't rely on it. See the Communication Workshop at the end of this chapter to learn more about the benefits and hazards of computer spell checkers.
- **Grammar.** Locate sentence subjects. Do their verbs agree with them? Do pronouns agree with their antecedents? Review the principles in the Grammar/Mechanics Handbook if necessary. The Communication Workshop discusses grammar checkers more extensively, but we recommend not using them until you've mastered grammar, mechanics, and punctuation on your own.
- **Punctuation.** Make sure that introductory clauses are followed by commas. In compound sentences put commas before coordinating conjunctions (*and, or, but, nor*). Double-check your use of semicolons and colons.

- **Names and numbers.** Compare all names and numbers with their sources, because inaccuracies are not immediately visible. Especially verify the spelling of the names of individuals receiving the message. Most of us immediately dislike someone who misspells our name.
- **Format.** Be sure that letters, printed memos, and reports are balanced on the page. Compare their parts and format with those of standard documents shown in Appendix A. If you indent paragraphs, be certain that all are indented.
- **Consistency.** Make sure all words are spelled and formatted the same way throughout your document. For example, spelling *cheque* the Canadian way three times and then twice the American way *(check)* confuses the reader.

How to Proofread Routine Documents

Most routine messages, including e-mails, require proofreading. Use the down arrow to reveal one line at a time, focusing your attention at the bottom of the screen. Read carefully for faults such as omitted or doubled words.

For routine messages such as printed letters or memos, a safer proofreading method is reading from a printed copy. You're more likely to find errors and to observe the tone. Your words convey status. In fact, recent research shows that lower-status employees tend to write longer, wordier e-mails, while higher-status employees write short messages, often with poor grammar and spelling. It is generally only the higher-status employees who can get away with poor grammar and spelling.[2] Use standard proofreading marks, shown in Figure 4.2, to indicate changes.

Routine documents need proofreading.

FIGURE 4.2   Proofreading Marks

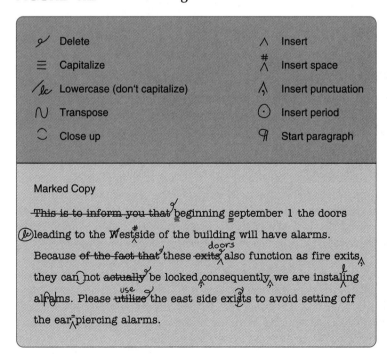

Proofreaders use these standard marks to indicate revisions.

How to Proofread Complex Documents

Long, complex, or important documents demand more careful proofreading using the following techniques:

- Print a copy, preferably double-spaced, and set it aside for some time. You'll be more alert after a breather.
- Allow adequate time to proofread carefully. A common excuse for sloppy proofreading is lack of time.
- Be prepared to find errors. One student confessed, "I can find other people's errors, but I can't seem to locate my own." Psychologically, we don't expect to find errors, and we don't want to find them. You can overcome this obstacle by anticipating errors and congratulating, not criticizing, yourself each time you find one.
- Read the message at least twice—once for word meanings and once for grammar/mechanics. For very long documents (book chapters and long articles or reports), read a third time to check consistency in formatting.
- Reduce your reading speed. Concentrate on individual words rather than ideas.
- For documents that must be perfect, have someone read the message aloud. Spell names and difficult words, note capitalization, and read punctuation.
- Use standard proofreading marks, shown in Figure 4.2, to indicate changes. A more complete list of proofreading marks appears in Appendix B.

Quick Check

For both routine and complex documents, it's best to proofread from a printed copy, not from a computer screen.

Your word-processing program may include a style or grammar checker. These programs generally analyze aspects of your writing style, including readability level and use of passive voice, unoriginal expressions, split infinitives (I want *to* always *have* a job), and wordy expressions. Most programs use sophisticated technology (and a lot of computer memory) to identify significant errors. In addition to finding spelling and typographical errors, grammar checkers can find subject–verb non-agreement, word misuse, spacing irregularities, punctuation problems, and many other faults. But they won't find everything, as you will see in the Communication Workshop at the end of this chapter. While grammar and spell checkers can help you a great deal, you are the final proofreader.

Summing Up and Looking Forward

Revision is the most important part of the writing process. To revise for clarity and conciseness, look for wordy phrases that can be shortened (such as *at this point in time*). Watch for repetitious words and redundancies *(combined together)*. Use jargon only when it is clear to receivers, and avoid slang and clichés altogether. The best writing includes precise verbs, concrete nouns, and vivid adjectives. After revising a message, you're ready for the last step in the writing process: proofreading. Watch for irregularities in spelling, grammar, punctuation, names and numbers, and format. Although routine messages may be proofread on the screen, you will have better results if you proofread from a printed copy. Complex documents should be printed, put away for a while, and then proofread several times.

In Chapters 2, 3, and 4 you've studied the writing and revision process. You've also learned many practical techniques for becoming an effective business communicator. Now it's time for you to put these techniques to work. Chapter 5 introduces you to writing e-mails and memos, the most frequently used forms of communication for most businesspeople. Later chapters present letters and reports.

Critical Thinking

1. "A real writer can sit down at a computer and create a perfect document the first time." Do you agree or disagree? Why?
2. Because clichés are familiar and have been used for long periods of time, do they help clarify writing?
3. If your boss writes in a flowery, formal tone and relies on outdated expressions, should you follow that style also?

Chapter Review

4. How is revising different from proofreading?

5. Why is conciseness especially important in business?

6. What is a long lead-in? Give an original example.

7. What is a redundancy? Give an example.

8. What is jargon? When can it be used? Give some examples from your field.

9. Should you proofread when you are writing or after you finish? Why?

10. What six areas should you especially pay attention to when you proofread?

Wordiness. Revise the following sentences to eliminate wordy phrases and long lead-ins.

Example: This is to notify you that at a later date we may be able to submit the report.

Revision: We may be able to submit the report later.

11. In the event that the response is at all favourable, we will in all probability start our website in the month of January.

    We will probably start our website in the [month] of January.

12. This is to advise you that beginning April 1, all charges made after that date will be charged to your new credit card number.

    All charges made after April 1 will be charged to your new credit card number.

13. In view of the fact that our sales are increasing slowly, we must secure a loan in the amount of $50,000.

    Because our sales are slow, we must secure a loan in the amount of $50 000

14. This is to let you know that you should feel free to use your credit card to purchase household items for a period of 60 days.

    You are free to use your credit card to purchase household items for a period of 60 days

Redundancies, Jargon, Slang, Clichés. Revise the following sentences to eliminate redundancies, jargon, slang, clichés, and any other wordiness.

Example: Last but not least, Tobias collected together as much support material as possible to avoid getting burned in cash losses or bottom-line profits.

Revision: Finally, Tobias collected as much support material as possible to avoid losing cash or profits.

15. First and foremost, we plan to get a hot new training program.

16. The members of the committee decided that the committee should meet at 11 a.m. in the morning.

17. If you will refer back to the contract, you will find specific instructions to prevent anyone from blowing the budget.

18. This memorandum serves as an advance warning that all books and magazines borrowed from the library must be taken back to the library by June 1.

19. In view of the fact that our last presentation failed, we are at this point in time convinced that we must include only the most absolutely essential selling points this time.

Precise Verbs. Revise these sentences, centring the action in the verbs.

Example: Ms. Tulita gave an appraisal of the website.
Revision: Ms. Tulita appraised the website.

20. The webmaster *made a description* of the project.

21. Can you *bring about a change in* our company travel policy?

22. Web-based customer service *will produce the effect of reduction in* overall costs.

23. In writing this proposal, we must *make application of* new government regulations.

24. An investigator *made a determination of* the fire damages.

25. We hope to *have production of* our new line of products by January.

26. The duty of the comptroller is *verification of* departmental budgets.

27. Please *make a correction in* my account to reflect my late payment.

Vivid Words. Revise the following sentences to include vivid and concrete language. Add appropriate words.

Example: They said it was a long way off.
Revision: Management officials announced that the hiring of new employees would not take place for two years.

28. Our new copier is fast.

    The Company's new copier works faster than the old copier.

29. An employee from that company notified us about the change in date.

30. Please contact them soon.

31. They said that the movie was good.

    People said the movie Up was good.

32. The report was weak.

    The 5 page report was made poorly.

Grammar/Mechanics Review—4

The following sentences contain errors in the use of verbs and pronouns. Pay special attention to eliminating wordiness. Below each sentence write a corrected version. A sentence may contain more than one error.

Example: Inasmuch as our sales have drop $50,000, the new manager and me are now aware of our competition.

Revision: Because our sales have **dropped** $50,000, the new manager and **I** are now aware of our competition.

1. This is to inform you that for a period of two weeks, Mr. Dias and myself must place a restriction on parking.

2. John and her made a plan to keep all customers' names and addresses in a database.

3. Three laptop problems have been solve: weight, size, and power consumption.

4. In view of the fact that the envelope was address to Manuel and I, him and me should receive the free gift.

5. In response to your e-mail message of the 15th of July, your shipment was send July 9.

6. The bonus will be give to anyone who has their work completed by September.

7. Although I'm sure it was him who send the e-mail message, the chief executive officer don't seem to care.

8. I am writing this e-mail to let you know that the meeting with the manager and we employees is May 15th.

9. The company's main office is in Toronto; however, most shipments comes from Montreal.

10. If your looking for a laptop that is small in size, try the Datapro 505 model.

11. We expect every one of our employees to submit their reports by November 2.

12. To improve you're language skills, you should applying the rules of grammar.

13. To improve company morale, our Human Resources Department made a distribution of free concert tickets to all their staff.

14. Each department must submit their suggestions to Donald, Jay, and myself.

15. Dr. Erek M. Sheps, along with several salespeople, are attend the conference in Vancouver.

Grammar/Mechanics Challenge—4

Document for Revision

The following e-mail has many problems, including grammar errors, faulty punctuation, conversational language, wordiness, and long lead-ins. Use standard proofreading marks (see Appendix B) to correct the errors. Study the guidelines in the Grammar/Mechanics Handbook to sharpen your skills. When you finish, your instructor may show you the revised version of this letter.

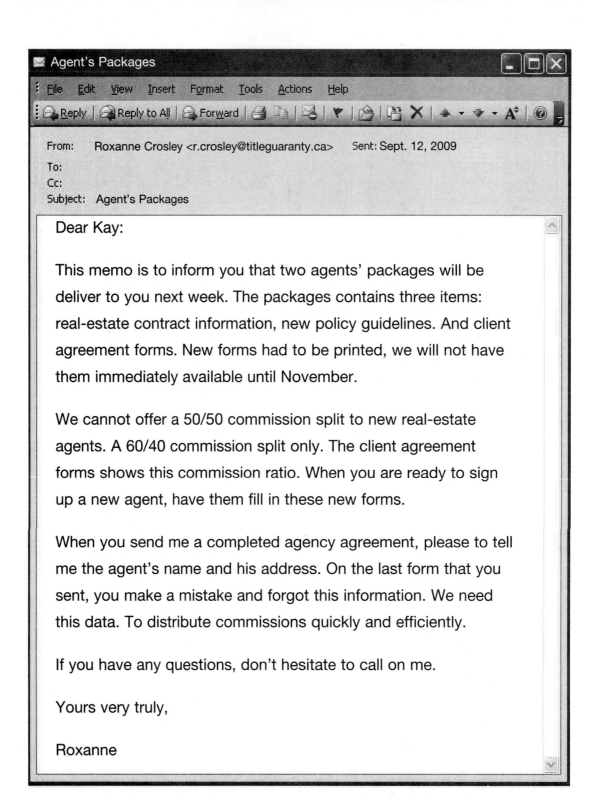

Agent's Packages

File   Edit   View   Insert   Format   Tools   Actions   Help

Reply   Reply to All   Forward

From: Roxanne Crosley <r.crosley@titleguaranty.ca>   Sent: Sept. 12, 2009
To:
Cc:
Subject: Agent's Packages

Dear Kay:

This memo is to inform you that two agents' packages will be deliver to you next week. The packages contains three items: real-estate contract information, new policy guidelines. And client agreement forms. New forms had to be printed, we will not have them immediately available until November.

We cannot offer a 50/50 commission split to new real-estate agents. A 60/40 commission split only. The client agreement forms shows this commission ratio. When you are ready to sign up a new agent, have them fill in these new forms.

When you send me a completed agency agreement, please to tell me the agent's name and his address. On the last form that you sent, you make a mistake and forgot this information. We need this data. To distribute commissions quickly and efficiently.

If you have any questions, don't hesitate to call on me.

Yours very truly,

Roxanne

Grammar and Spell Checkers

Nearly all word-processing programs now include grammar and spell checkers to help writers with their proofreading tasks.

Grammar Checkers

When first introduced, grammar and style checkers were not too helpful. They were limited in scope, awkward to use, and identified many questionable "errors." But today's grammar checkers detect a considerable number of legitimate writing lapses. Microsoft Word finds faults in word use (such as *there*, *their*) capitalization, punctuation, subject–verb agreement, sentence structure, singular and plural endings, repeated words, wordy expressions, gender-specific expressions, and many other problems.

How does a grammar checker work? Let's say you typed the sentence *The office and its equipment is for sale*. You would see a wavy green line appear under *is*. When you point your cursor at "Tools" in the tool bar and click on "Spelling and Grammar," a box opens up. It identifies the subject-verb agreement error and suggests the verb *are* as a correction. When you click on "Change," the error is corrected.

Spell Checkers

Spell checkers compare your typed words with those in the computer's memory. Microsoft Word uses a wavy red line to underline misspelled words as you type them. Although some writers dismiss spell checkers as an annoyance, most of us are only too happy to have our typos and misspelled words detected. What's annoying is that spell checkers don't find all the problems. In the following poem, for example, only two problems were detected (*your* and *it's*).

I have a spell checkers
    That came with my PC.
It plainly marks four my review
    Mistakes I cannot sea.
I've run this poem threw it,
    I'm sure your pleased too no.
Its letter perfect in it's weigh
    My checker tolled me sew.
              —Anonymous

The lesson to be learned here is that you can't rely totally on any spell checker. Homonyms—words that sound the same but are spelled differently—may not be highlighted because the spell checker doesn't know what meaning you have in mind. That's why you're wise to print out important messages and proofread them word by word.

Career Application

Your boss, Serena Simkus, is developing a training program on word processing. She wants you to analyze the effectiveness of your computer's grammar and spell checkers. Your brief report will become part of a presentation to new employees.

Your Task

- You decide to try out your software with a set of test sentences. At a computer that has grammar- and spell-checking software, type the following four sentences, including all the errors. Print the sentences.
    1. Is the companys office located on riverside drive in new york city.
    2. The manger adviced her to make a consciensous effort to improve.
    3. There house and it's furniture was allready sold before they moved to saskatoon.
    4. My friend and me was going to apply for the job in june but we were to late.
- For each sentence, underline the errors the software identified. Then circle the errors that the software missed. (A word may contain only one error.) Total your underlines and circles. Make notes on the kinds of errors identified and the kinds missed. *Tip:* You should find 20 errors.
- On the basis of your findings, as well as some Internet and library research into the pros and cons of grammar and spelling checkers, how would you rate the usefulness of your computer's grammar and spell checkers? What are the strengths and weaknesses?
- What advice would you give to employees about relying on these programs for proofreading?
- Stage an in-class debate on the topic "Resolved: Grammar and spell checkers should not be relied upon by business writers."
- Depending on your own opinion, write a memo to your boss, Serena Simkus, suggesting what kind of policy she should adopt on the use of grammar and spell checkers.

Web

Related website: Check out the following documents from the University of Minnesota and Blogos for a sampling of opinions on the efficacy and ethics of grammar- and spell-checking software:
http://writing.umn.edu/docs/home/write@uFall_2001.pdf and
http://www.multilingualblog.com/index.php/weblog/the_ethics_of_grammar_checkers.

Chapter 4 Revising and Proofreading Business Messages

Corresponding at Work

5 E-Mails and Memos

E-mail isn't just the message you write, it's also a powerful way to distribute information. It's a cost-efficient way for people with colleagues and clients in far locations to stay in immediate contact. For example, last week instead of sending by mail a 40-page contract to one of my overseas clients, I just e-mailed it, and she got it immediately.[1]

Peter Schneider, *Lawyer, Gowling Lafleur Henderson LLP*

LEARNING OBJECTIVES

1. Explain the importance of communication within an organization (internal).
2. Analyze the writing process of e-mails and memos.
3. Describe how to use e-mail effectively and safely.
4. Explain and demonstrate a writing plan for e-mails and memos.
5. Demonstrate several ways to use listing techniques and graphic highlighting.
6. Write e-mails and memos that inform.
7. Write e-mails and memos that request.
8. Write e-mails and memos that respond.

The Importance of Internal Communication

Electronic mail has become an important tool in reducing barriers created by size and distance. Employees can almost instantly communicate with each other whether they are working in separate rooms, in separate buildings, or on separate continents. As Peter Schneider states above, e-mail is an excellent channel of communication. E-mails provide the ability to send attachments. In fact, e-mail is becoming so popular that more traditional channels of communication such as the telephone and fax are becoming less widely used.

The growing demand for information means increasing use of e-mail. Until the early 1990s, hard-copy memos were the most common channel for exchanging internal communication within an organization. Now, however, e-mail is the favoured medium.

Canadians log more time online than users in any other country. We spend an average of 15 hours per month online using the Internet and sending e-mail.[2] Businesspeople are writing more messages than ever before and using e-mail to

✔ Quick Check

Businesspeople are writing more messages than ever before.

distribute those messages more often. E-mails and memos require preparation because they may travel farther than you expect. A new market researcher in Calgary, for example, was eager to please her boss. When asked to report on the progress of her project, she quickly e-mailed a summary of her work. It contained many grammatical mistakes. Later that week a vice-president asked her boss about the project. Her boss forwarded the market researcher's hurried e-mail memo. Unfortunately, the result was a poor impression of the new employee.

Developing skill in writing e-mails and memos brings you two important benefits:

1. Well-written documents are likely to achieve their goals.
2. Such documents enhance your image within the organization.

Individuals identified as competent, professional writers are noticed and rewarded; most often, they are the ones promoted into management positions.

This chapter concentrates on routine e-mails and memos. You'll study the writing process as well as how to organize and format messages that inform, request, and respond. These basic messages follow the direct strategy because their topics are not sensitive and require little persuasion.

The Writing Process

Careful e-mail and memo writing takes time—especially at first. By following a plan and practising your skill, however, you can speed up your efforts and greatly improve the product. The effort you make to improve your communication skills can be profitable. Often, your speaking and writing skills determine how much influence you'll have in your organization. To make the best impression and to write the most effective messages, follow the three-phase writing process.

Phase 1: Analyze, Anticipate, and Adapt

Ask yourself three important questions:

*   **Do I really need to write this memo or e-mail?** A phone call or a quick visit to a nearby coworker might be more effective—and save the time and expense of a written message. On the other hand, some written messages are needed to provide a permanent record.
*   **Do I write a hard-copy memo or send an e-mail?** Learn about your organization's preferred method. Not using the preferred method might signal a degree of importance that you may not intend. Consider as well that an important message sent as e-mail could become lost among the many funny and unimportant e-mails people receive during a typical work day.
*   **Why am I writing?** What do you hope to achieve by writing? Deciding your goals for writing will help you recognize what the important points are and where to place them.
*   **How will the reader react?** Imagine the reader and the effect your message will have. Consider ways to shape the message to benefit the reader.

Phase 2: Research, Organize, and Compose

Gather and review any information you may have on your subject, such as previous messages, meeting minutes, or other notes you may keep in a work file. Make an outline of the points you wish to cover. If you are responding to a message, you can write your notes on the document you are answering. For e-mails, consider printing the message and adding notes to the printed copy.

Phase 3: Revise, Proofread, and Evaluate

- **Revise for clarity.** Imagine you are the reader. Are the ideas clear? Do they need more explanation? If the e-mail is forwarded to others, will those readers need further explanation? Consider having a colleague review your message if it is an important one.
- **Proofread for correctness.** Are the sentences grammatically correct and punctuated properly? Did you overlook any typos or misspelled words?
- **Plan for feedback.** How will you know if this message is successful? You can improve feedback by asking yourself questions such as *Do these suggestions meet our needs? Have I concluded my message by requesting feedback?*

Developing a Writing Plan for E-Mails and Memos

In this book, you will be shown a number of writing plans for different messages. These plans provide a skeleton; they are the "bones" of a message. Writers provide the "flesh." Good writers provide details and link their ideas with transitions to create fluent and meaningful messages. However, a writing plan helps you get started and gives you ideas about what to include. At first, you will probably rely on these plans. As you progress, they will become less important. Later in the book, no plans are provided.

Here is a general writing plan for a routine or good-news e-mail or memo.

 Writing Plan for Routine E-Mails and Memos

- **Subject line.** Summarize contents.
- **Opening.** State the main idea.
- **Body.** Provide background information and explain the main idea.
- **Closing.** Request action, summarize message, or present closing thought.

Writing the Subject Line

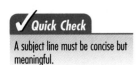

Quick Check

A subject line must be concise but meaningful.

Probably the most important part of an e-mail or memo is the subject line. It should summarize the central idea and provide quick identification. It is usually written in an abbreviated style, often without articles (*a, an, the*). It does not need to be a complete sentence, and it does not end with a period. Use capitals as you would for a title of a book or a film. Do not capitalize articles, coordinate conjunctions, or prepositions fewer than four letters. E-mail subject lines are particularly important, since meaningless ones may cause readers to delete a message without ever opening it. Good subject lines, such as the following, are specific, eye-catching, and "talking" (that is, they contain a verb form):

Subject: Funding Sources for Youth Health and Safety Internship Program
Subject: Recommendations to Improve Network Security
Subject: Staff Meeting to Discuss Summer Vacation Schedules

Opening with the Main Idea

Most memos and e-mails cover routine, non-sensitive information that can be handled in a straightforward manner. Begin by stating the main idea—the reason for your memo—immediately. Even though the purpose of a memo or e-mail is summarized in the subject line, that purpose should be restated in the first sentence. Some readers skip the subject line and plunge right into the first sentence. Notice how the following indirect memo openers can be improved by providing the main idea first.

Indirect Opening

This is to inform you that for the past six months we have been examining four changes in our benefits package as part of our negotiation package under a contract that expires soon.

As you may know, employees in the Document Production department have been complaining about eye fatigue as a result of the overhead fluorescent lighting in their centre.

Direct Opening

Please review the following four changes in our benefits package and let us know your preference by January 1.

To improve lighting in the Document Production department, I recommend that we purchase high-intensity desk lamps.

Explaining Clearly in the Body

In the body of the message, explain the main idea. If you are providing information, group similar information together (see Fig. 5.1). If you are asking for information, arrange your questions in logical order (see Fig. 5.2). When a considerable amount of information is involved, use a separate paragraph for each topic. Use effective transitions (such as *however, therefore, in addition*) between paragraphs.

Design your data for easy comprehension by using bulleted lists, headings, and tables. You'll learn more about writing lists shortly. All these techniques make readers understand important points quickly. Compare the following two versions of the same message. Notice how the graphic devices of bullets, columns, headings, and white space make the main points easier to comprehend.

> ✔ **Quick Check**
>
> Organize the message logically, keeping similar information grouped together.

Hard-to-Read Paragraph

Effective immediately are the following air travel guidelines. Between now and December 31, only account executives may take company-approved trips. These individuals will be allowed to take a maximum of two trips per year, and they are to travel economy class or discount airline only.

Improved with Graphic Highlighting

The following air travel guidelines are effective immediately:

- Who may travel: Account executives only
- How many trips: A maximum of two trips yearly
- By when: Between now and December 31
- Which air class: Economy or discount airline only

> ✔ **Quick Check**
>
> Graphic highlighting (bullets, numbered lists, headings) makes information easier to read and review.

In addition to highlighting important information, pay attention to the tone of your message. Although memos are generally informal, they should also be professional. Remember that e-mail messages are not telephone conversations. Don't be overly casual, joking, or blunt. Do attempt to establish a conversational tone by using occasional contractions (*won't, didn't, couldn't*) and personal pronouns (*I, me, we*).

Closing the Message

Generally, end an e-mail or memo with (1) action information, dates, or deadlines; (2) a summary of the message; or (3) a closing thought. The closing is where readers look for deadlines and action language. An effective e-mail or memo closing might be *Please submit your report by June 1. We need to review your recommendations before our July planning session.*

> ✔ **Quick Check**
>
> The end of an e-mail or memo should include action information (such as a deadline), a summarizing statement, or a closing thought.

In more complex messages, a summary of main points may be a suitable closing. If no action request is made, and a closing summary is unnecessary, you might end with a simple concluding thought (*I'm happy to provide answers to your questions* or *This project sounds like a good idea*). Although you needn't close messages to coworkers with goodwill statements such as those found in letters to customers or clients, some closing thought is often necessary to prevent a feeling of a sudden end to the message.

Closings can show gratitude or encourage feedback with remarks such as *Thanks for your help on this project* or *Do you have any suggestions on this proposal?* Other closings look forward to what's next, such as *How would you like to proceed?* Avoid boring expressions, such as *Please let me know if I may be of further assistance.*

Whenever possible, the closing paragraph of a request should have an end date. An end date sets a deadline for the requested action and gives a reason for this action to be completed by the deadline. Such end-dating allows the reader to plan a course of action to ensure completion by the date given. Giving a reason adds credibility to a deadline.

Please submit your order by December 1. We need to know the number of labels required for mailing the year-end reports January 15.

Putting It All Together

The memo shown in Figure 5.1 is the first draft of a message Cynthia Chomsky wrote to her team leader. Although it contains solid information, the first version is so wordy and poorly organized that the reader has trouble understanding its significance. Cynthia's revised message opens directly. Both the subject line and the first sentence explain the purpose for writing. Notice how much easier the revised version is to read. Bullets and boldfaced headings emphasize the actions necessary to solve the database problems. Notice, too, that the revised version ends with a deadline and refers to the next action to be taken.

Formatting E-Mails

Although e-mail formatting style is still developing, all messages contain *To, From, Date,* and *Subject* lines.

Because e-mail is an ongoing communication channel, the way it is formatted and used is still not fixed. On the other hand, formatting memos has become much easier because of software templates. Whereas students used to learn how to create memos from scratch (see Appendix A for details), today students are just as often encouraged to choose a template in their word-processing program (e.g., Microsoft Word's Professional Memo template) and begin filling in their content. At work, people are usually encouraged to use a company memo template. While memo formatting is standard and rarely varies, e-mail users and authorities, for instance, do not always agree on salutations and closings. The following suggestions can guide you in formatting most e-mail messages, but always check with your organization to observe its practices.

Guide Words.
- Following the guide word *To,* some writers insert just the recipient's e-mail address, such as *pwyatt@accountpro.com.* Other writers prefer to include the receiver's full name plus the e-mail address, as shown in Figure 5.2 on page 86. By including full names in the *To* and *From* slots, both receivers and senders are better able to identify the message.
- The order of *Date, To, From, Subject,* and other guide words varies depending on your e-mail program and whether you are sending or receiving the message. Most e-mail programs automatically add the current date after *Date.*

FIGURE 5.1 Revising a Draft Memo

Before

TO: Susan Hsu

This is in response to your recent inquiry about our customer database. Your message of May 9 said that you wanted to know how to deal with the database problems.

I can tell you that the biggest problem is that it contains a lot of outdated information, including customers who haven't purchased anything in five or more years. Another problem is that the old database cannot be used with the new Access database, used by our mailing service. Therefore, it is difficult to merge files.

I think I can solve both problems, however, by starting a new database. This would be the place where we put the names of all new customers. And we would have it entered into the Access database. The problem with outdated information could be solved by finding out if the customers in our old database wish to continue receiving our newsletter and product announcements. Finally, we would re-key the names of all active customers into the new database.

Fails to reveal purpose quickly and concisely

Does not help reader see the two problems or the three recommendations

Forgets to conclude with next action and end date

After

Design Source

Memo

To: Susan Hsu, Team Leader

From: Cynthia Chomsky, Marketing Associate

CC:

Date: May 15, 2009

Re: IMPROVING OUR CUSTOMER DATABASE

As you requested, here are my recommendations for improving our customer database. The database has two major problems. First, it contains many names of individuals who have not made purchases in five or more years. Second, the format cannot be used with the new Access database used by our mailing service. The following procedures, however, should solve both problems:

- **Start a new database.** Effective immediately, enter the names of all new customers in a new Access database.

- **Determine the status of customers in our old database.** Send out a mailing asking whether recipients wish to continue receiving our newsletter and product announcements.

- **Re-key the names of active customers in the new database.** Enter the names of all responding customers in our new database so that we have only one active database.

These changes will enable you, as team leader, to request mailings that go only to active customers. Please respond by May 20 with suggestions or other alternatives I could review. I will then investigate costs.

Subject line summarizes and identifies purpose

Opening states purpose concisely

Body organizes main points for readability

Closing mentions key benefit, provides deadline, and looks forward to next action

FIGURE 5.2 Typical E-Mail Request Message

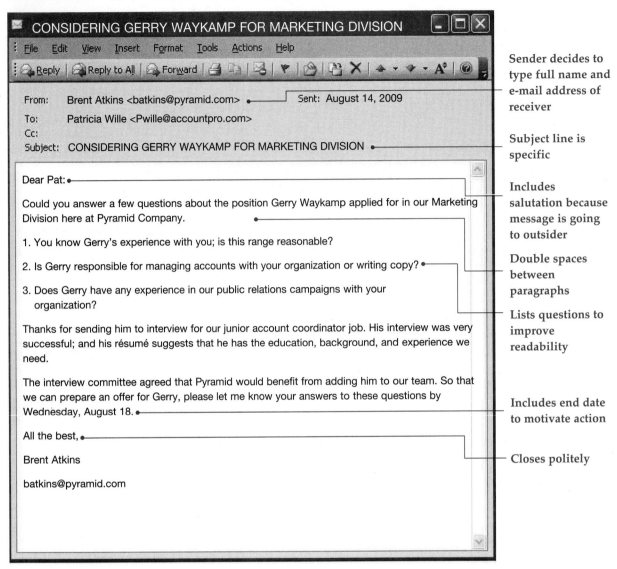

CONSIDERING GERRY WAYKAMP FOR MARKETING DIVISION

File Edit View Insert Format Tools Actions Help

Reply | Reply to All | Forward

From: Brent Atkins <batkins@pyramid.com>   Sent: August 14, 2009

To: Patricia Wille <Pwille@accountpro.com>

Cc:

Subject: CONSIDERING GERRY WAYKAMP FOR MARKETING DIVISION

Dear Pat:

Could you answer a few questions about the position Gerry Waykamp applied for in our Marketing Division here at Pyramid Company.

1. You know Gerry's experience with you; is this range reasonable?

2. Is Gerry responsible for managing accounts with your organization or writing copy?

3. Does Gerry have any experience in our public relations campaigns with your organization?

Thanks for sending him to interview for our junior account coordinator job. His interview was very successful; and his résumé suggests that he has the education, background, and experience we need.

The interview committee agreed that Pyramid would benefit from adding him to our team. So that we can prepare an offer for Gerry, please let me know your answers to these questions by Wednesday, August 18.

All the best,

Brent Atkins

batkins@pyramid.com

Annotations:
- Sender decides to type full name and e-mail address of receiver
- Subject line is specific
- Includes salutation because message is going to outsider
- Double spaces between paragraphs
- Lists questions to improve readability
- Includes end date to motivate action
- Closes politely

Tips for Formatting E-Mail

- After *To*, type the receiver's e-mail address. If you include the receiver's name, enclose the address in angle brackets <like this>.
- After *From*, type your name and e-mail address, if your program does not insert it automatically.
- After *Subject*, provide a specific description of your message.
- Insert the addresses of anyone receiving carbon or blind copies.
- Include a salutation (such as *Dear Pat, Hi Pat, Greetings*) or weave the receiver's name into the first line. Some writers omit a salutation.
- Set your line length for no more than 80 characters. If you expect your message to be forwarded, set it for 60 characters.
- Use word wrap rather than pressing Enter at line ends.
- Double-space between paragraphs.
- Do not type in all caps or in all lower-case letters.
- Include a complimentary close, your name, and (if you wish) your address.

- On the *Cc* line (which stands for *carbon* or *courtesy copy*) you can type the address of anyone who is to receive a copy of the message. Remember to send copies only to those people directly involved with the message. Most e-mail programs also include a line for *Bcc* (*blind carbon copy*); this sends a copy without the addressee's (receiver's) knowledge. Many writers today use *Bcc* for the names and addresses of a list of receivers, a technique that avoids revealing the addresses to the entire group.
- On the *Subject* line, identify the subject of the memo. Be sure to include enough information to be clear.

Salutation.

- Many e-mail writers omit a salutation because they consider the message a memo. In the past, hard-copy memos were sent only to company insiders, and salutations were omitted. However, when e-mail messages travel to outsiders, omitting a salutation seems unfriendly. Because the message is more like a letter, a salutation is appropriate (such as *Dear Jake*; *Hi Jake*; *Greetings*; or just *Jake*). Including a salutation is also a visual cue to where the message begins. Many messages are transmitted or forwarded with such long headers that finding the beginning of the message can be difficult. A salutation helps, as shown in Figure 5.2. Other writers do not use a salutation; instead, they use the name of the receiver in the first sentence.

Quick Check

Salutations may be omitted in messages to close colleagues, but they are generally used in messages to others.

Body.

- Type the body of a business e-mail with upper- and lowercase characters— never in all uppercase or all lowercase characters.
- Cover just one topic, and try to keep the total message as concise as possible. To assist you, many e-mail programs have basic text-editing features, such as cut, copy, paste, and word wrap. Avoid boldface and italics unless you know the recipient's computer can display them. Often, boldface and italics can create a string of control characters that may cause chaos on the receiver's computer.
- Finally, any time you have more than two points to make, get into the habit of using graphic highlighting (bullets, numbering, extra spaces). Graphic highlighting helps to distinguish between your points and makes your e-mail easier on the reader's eyes.

Closing Lines.

- Writers of e-mail messages sent within organizations may omit closings and even skip their names at the end of messages. They can omit these items because receivers recognize them from identification in the opening lines. But for outside messages, a writer might include a closing such as *Cheers* or *Best* or *Regards* followed by the writer's name and e-mail address (because some systems do not transmit your address automatically). If the recipient is unlikely to know you, it's wise to include your title and organization. Experienced e-mail users include a signature block containing their contact information.

Quick Check

Closing lines (or a signature block) should name the writer and provide sufficient information for identification.

Smart E-Mail Practices

The huge growth of e-mail is unstoppable. In 2000, the Internet handled about 10 billion e-mails a day. Estimates indicate e-mail use has now reached 35 billion per day.[3] Statistics Canada reports that 60 percent of Canadians use a computer in their job with the majority (78 percent) using one daily. A full 54 percent of those workers used their computer for Internet access and e-mail.[4] Suddenly, companies find that e-mail has become a very important means of internal communication as well as an essential link to customers and suppliers.

Quick Check

E-mail has become an essential means of communication within organizations as well as with customers and suppliers.

E-mail is increasingly used to send routine business messages. In large part, this increased popularity is due to the new personal digital assistants (PDAs—BlackBerry and PalmPilot are the best-known brands) that make it possible for people to carry their e-mail with them wherever they go. However, other channels of communication are still more effective for complex data or sensitive messages.

Getting Started. The following pointers will help you get off to a good start in using e-mail safely and effectively.

- **Compose offline.** Instead of writing messages in a hurry—or worse, mistakenly sending a half-finished message—take the time to compose offline. Consider word processing and then cutting and pasting your message to your e-mail program. This method can help you avoid losing all your writing through some technical problem or pressing the Send button before your message is complete.
- **Get the address right.** E-mail addresses can be long and complex, often including letters, numbers, dashes, and underscores. Omit one character or misread the letter *l* for the number *1*, and your message will be returned. Solution: use your electronic address book frequently and use the reply feature in your e-mail program. Most e-mail programs include the correct e-mail address from the original message in the reply message. And double-check every address that you key in manually.
- **Avoid misleading subject lines.** With many "spam" (junk e-mail) messages clogging inboxes and the fear of computer viruses that are spread by e-mail attachments, many e-mail users ignore or delete messages with unclear subject lines. Make sure your subject line is specific and helpful. Generic tags such as "HELLO" and "GREAT DEAL" may cause your message to be deleted before it is opened.

Content, Tone, and Correctness. Although e-mail seems as casual as a telephone call, it's not. A telephone call has its own set of rules, as does a letter, but neither of these sets of rules applies to e-mail. Concentrating on tone, content, and correctness will help to reduce the potential for misinterpretation of e-mail messages. As well, since e-mail also produces a permanent record, think carefully about what you say and how you say it.

- **Be concise.** Don't present unnecessary information. Many e-mail recipients read dozens or even hundreds of e-mails every day. A concise message is appreciated. Well-organized messages will hold the reader's interest even if the e-mail contains many ideas.
- **Send only appropriate information.** Because e-mail seems like a telephone call or a person-to-person conversation, writers sometimes send sensitive, secret, angry, or embarrassing messages. Information you consider appropriate, funny, or appealing may not be interpreted the same way by your audience. By sending an inappropriate message, you are also creating a permanent record that often does not go away even when deleted. Every message sent at work is a corporate communication for which both you and your employer are responsible.

- **Don't use e-mail to avoid contact.** Breaking bad news or resolving an argument through e-mail is not recommended. With e-mail, you cannot rely on nonverbal communication, active listening techniques, and other face-to-face communication methods to ensure correct understanding of emotion and meaning. Imagine being fired by e-mail or having your job performance evaluated through e-mail. It's also not a good channel for dealing with conflict with supervisors, subordinates, or others. If there's any possibility of hurt feelings, pick up the telephone or pay the person a visit.

- **Never respond when you're angry.** Always allow some time to compose yourself before responding to an upsetting message. You often come up with different and better alternatives after thinking about what was said. If possible, discuss problems in person.
- **Care about correctness.** People are still judged by their writing, whether electronic or paper-based. Sloppy e-mail messages (with missing apostrophes, poor spelling, and illogical writing) make readers work too hard. Readers quickly lose respect for writers of poor e-mails.
- **Resist humour and personal jokes.** Without the nonverbal cues conveyed by your face and your voice, humour can easily be misunderstood.

Netiquette. Although e-mail is an evolving communication channel, a number of rules of polite online interaction apply.

- **Don't automatically forward junk e-mail.** Internet jokes and other unnecessary messages such as warnings about new viruses, chain letters, or unusual fundraising campaigns are annoying and a waste of time.
- **Consider using identifying labels.** When appropriate, add one of the following labels to the subject line: "ACTION" (action required, please respond); "FYI" (for your information, no response needed); "RE" (this is a reply to another message); "URGENT" (please respond immediately). These labels should be agreed upon among employees.
- **Use capital letters only for emphasis or for titles.** Avoid writing entire messages in all caps, which seems as if you're shouting.
- **Announce attachments.** If you're sending a lengthy attachment, tell your receiver. Consider summarizing or highlighting important aspects of the attachment briefly in the e-mail. Make sure the receiver can open the attachment you send. Some file formats cannot be opened on all computers.
- **Consider asking for permission before forwarding.** For messages containing private or project-specific information, obtain approval before forwarding to others.

"Have a seat. There are 342 email messages ahead of you."

Replying to E-Mail. The following tips can save you time and frustration when answering messages.

- **Scan all messages in your inbox before replying to each individually.** Because some messages that follow may affect the way you respond, read them all first, especially all those from the same sender.
- **Don't automatically return the sender's message.** When replying, cut and paste the relevant parts. Avoid irritating your recipients by returning the entire "thread" or sequence of messages on a topic, unless the thread needs to be included to provide context for your remarks.
- **Revise the subject line if the topic changes.** When replying or continuing an e-mail exchange, revise the subject line as the topic changes.
- **Respond to messages quickly and efficiently.** Read them, then answer, delete, or file them into project-specific folders.

Personal Use. Remember that office computers are meant for work-related communication.

- **Don't use company computers for personal matters.** Unless your company specifically allows it, never use your employer's computers for personal messages, personal shopping, or entertainment.
- **Assume that all e-mail is monitored.** Employers can and do monitor e-mail.

Other Smart E-Mail Practices. Depending on your messages and audience, the following tips promote effective electronic communication.

- **Use graphic highlighting to improve readability of longer messages.** When a message is longer, help the reader with headings, bulleted lists, and perhaps an introductory summary that describes what will follow. Although these techniques lengthen a message, they shorten reading time.
- **Consider cultural differences.** When using this global tool, be especially clear and precise in your language. Remember that figurative clichés (*pull up stakes, play second fiddle*), sports references (*hit a home run, play by the rules*), and slang (*cool, stoked*) can cause confusion abroad.
- **Double-check before hitting the Send button.** Have you included everything? Avoid the necessity of sending a second message, which makes you look careless. Edit for grammar and style and re-read for fluency before sending.

Improving E-Mail and Memo Readability with Listing Techniques

Because readers of e-mail and memos are usually in a hurry, they want important information to stand out. One of the best ways to improve the readability of any message is by listing items. Since lists require fewer words than complete sentences, they can be read and understood quickly and easily. In writing lists, keep these general points in mind.

✓ Quick Check

You can improve the readability of a message by listing parallel items.

- **Make listed items parallel.** Listed items must all relate to the same topic, and they must be balanced grammatically. If one item is a single word but the next item requires a paragraph of explanation, the items are not suitable for listing.
- **Use bullets, numbers, or letters appropriately.** Numbers (1, 2, 3) and letters (a, b, c) suggest a sequence of operation; bullets merely separate.

Parallelism

Instead of This

She likes *sleeping*, *eating*, and *to work*.

We are hiring the following: *sales clerks, managers who will function as supervisors,* and *people to work in offices.*

Try This

She likes *sleeping*, *eating*, and *working*.

We are hiring the following: *sales clerks, supervising managers,* and *office personnel.*

Instructions

Instead of This

Here are the instructions for operating the copy machine. First, you insert your copy card in the slot. Then you load paper in the upper tray. Last, copies are fed through the feed tray.

Try This

Follow these steps to use the copy machine:
1. *Insert* your copy card in the slot.
2. *Load* paper in the upper tray.
3. *Feed* copies through the feed tray.

Listed Items with Headings

Instead of This

On May 16 we will be in Regina, and Dr. Susan Dillon is the speaker. On June 20, we will be in Saskatoon and Dr. Diane Minger is the speaker.

Try This

Date	City	Speaker
May 16	Regina	Dr. Susan Dillon
June 20	Saskatoon	Dr. Diane Minger

Listed Items for Emphasis within Sentences

Instead of This

To keep exercising, you should make a written commitment to yourself, set realistic goals for each day's workout, and enlist the support of a friend.

Try This

To keep exercising, you should (a) make a written commitment to yourself, (b) set realistic goals for each day's workout, and (c) enlist the support of a friend.

Bulleted Items

Instead of This

Our goal
- is to recruit intensely competitive sales reps
- is to use reps who know our products
- recruit intelligent reps who are quick to learn

Try This

Our goal is to recruit sales reps who are
- Intensely competitive
- Familiar with our products
- Intelligent and quick to learn

- **Use generally accepted punctuation.** Most writers use a colon following the introduction to most lists; however, they don't use a colon if the listed items follow a verb or a preposition (for example, *the colours are red, yellow, and blue*). Use end punctuation only after complete sentences, and capitalize the first word of items listed vertically.

You've now studied a basic plan for writing e-mails and memos, and you've learned how to highlight ideas with listing techniques. Now, you'll see how these techniques can be applied to specific situations. Most memos and e-mail messages can be divided into four groups: (1) those that *inform,* (2) those that *request,* (3) those that *respond,* and (4) those that *persuade.* In this chapter, we will be concerned with the first three groups because they use the direct strategy. The fourth group, persuasive messages, uses the indirect strategy and will be discussed in Chapter 7.

E-Mails and Memos That Inform

Memos that inform generally explain organization policies, procedures, and guidelines. As policy-making documents, these messages must be particularly clear and concise.

The e-mail shown in Figure 5.3 (p. 93) informs department managers of a change in job-hiring procedures. The ineffective version begins negatively with an explanation of what went wrong with a new hiring procedure. Instead of starting directly, this message is illogical. The new procedure is stated negatively *(Do not submit your advertisements ...)* and is hidden inside two hard-to-read paragraphs.

The effectively revised version begins directly by telling readers immediately what the e-mail is about. The next paragraph explains why the change is necessary. A list gives step-by-step procedures, thus making it easy for the reader to understand and follow the steps. The final paragraph restates the primary benefits of the new procedure and tells how more information may be obtained if necessary.

Quick Check

E-mails and memos that inform often consist of policies, procedures, and guidelines.

E-Mails and Memos That Request

Messages that make requests are most effective when they use the direct approach. The reader learns immediately what is being requested. However, if you have any reason to suspect that the reader may resist the request, then an indirect approach would probably be more successful.

Requests should be courteous and respectful, as illustrated in Figure 5.4 (p. 94). Requests should not be demanding. The tone of the following request would likely upset the reader:

Quick Check

The tone of a request message should encourage cooperation.

I want you to find out why the Davis account was not included in this report, and I want this information before you do anything else.

Requests should be written clearly so that the intent of the message is not misunderstood. What may seem clear to the writer may not always be clear to a reader. That's why it's always a good idea to have a fellow worker read an important message for clarity before it is sent out.

Notice in Figure 5.4 that the writer ends by asking that the responses be made before May 5 because the information will be used for a Management Team meeting May 8. Providing an end date helps the reader know how to plan a response so that action is completed by the date given. Expressions such as "do it whenever you can" or "complete it as soon as possible" make little impression on very slow or very busy people. It's always wise to provide a specific date for completion. Dates can be entered into calendars to serve as reminders.

FIGURE 5.3 E-mail That Informs

Before

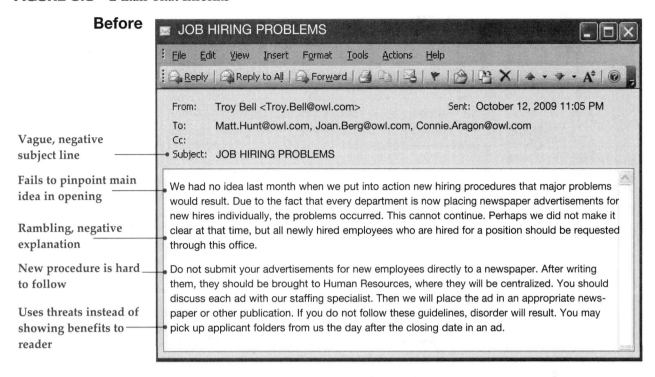

Vague, negative subject line

Fails to pinpoint main idea in opening

Rambling, negative explanation

New procedure is hard to follow

Uses threats instead of showing benefits to reader

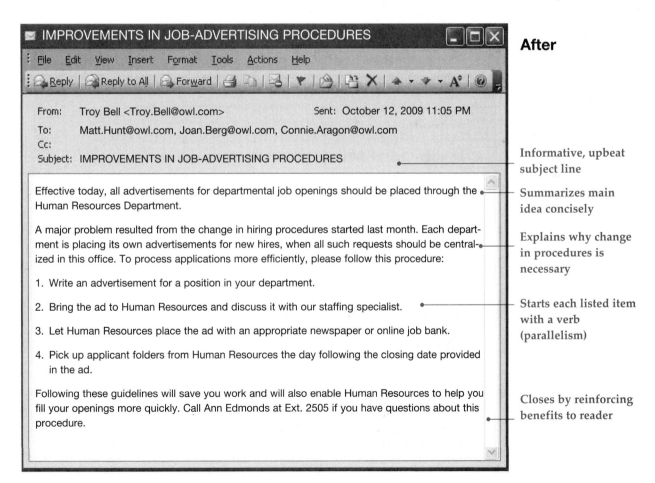

Informative, upbeat subject line

Summarizes main idea concisely

Explains why change in procedures is necessary

Starts each listed item with a verb (parallelism)

Closes by reinforcing benefits to reader

After

Writing E-Mails and Memos for Specific Situations

FIGURE 5.4 E-Mail That Requests

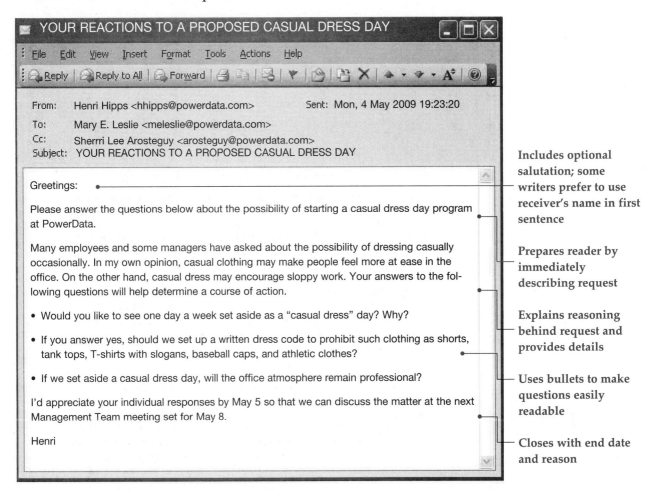

YOUR REACTIONS TO A PROPOSED CASUAL DRESS DAY	

File   Edit   View   Insert   Format   Tools   Actions   Help

Reply | Reply to All | Forward

From: Henri Hipps <hhipps@powerdata.com>   Sent: Mon, 4 May 2009 19:23:20
To: Mary E. Leslie <meleslie@powerdata.com>
Cc: Sherrri Lee Arosteguy <arosteguy@powerdata.com>
Subject: YOUR REACTIONS TO A PROPOSED CASUAL DRESS DAY

Greetings:

Please answer the questions below about the possibility of starting a casual dress day program at PowerData.

Many employees and some managers have asked about the possibility of dressing casually occasionally. In my own opinion, casual clothing may make people feel more at ease in the office. On the other hand, casual dress may encourage sloppy work. Your answers to the following questions will help determine a course of action.

• Would you like to see one day a week set aside as a "casual dress" day? Why?

• If you answer yes, should we set up a written dress code to prohibit such clothing as shorts, tank tops, T-shirts with slogans, baseball caps, and athletic clothes?

• If we set aside a casual dress day, will the office atmosphere remain professional?

I'd appreciate your individual responses by May 5 so that we can discuss the matter at the next Management Team meeting set for May 8.

Henri

Annotations:
- Includes optional salutation; some writers prefer to use receiver's name in first sentence
- Prepares reader by immediately describing request
- Explains reasoning behind request and provides details
- Uses bullets to make questions easily readable
- Closes with end date and reason

E-Mails and Memos That Respond

Much office correspondence reacts or responds to memos, e-mail messages, and other documents. When responding to a document, follow these preparatory steps:

1. Collect whatever information is necessary.
2. Organize your thoughts.
3. Make a brief outline of the points you plan to cover.

Notice in Figure 5.5 (p. 95) that Bill Leslie, manager of Legal Support Services, uses a straightforward opening in responding to his boss's request for information. He refers to her request, announces the information to follow, and identifies the date of the original message. Bill decides to answer with a standard hard-copy memo because he considers his reactions private and because he thinks that Vice-President Milowski would like to have a permanent record of each manager's reactions to take to the Management Team meeting. He also knows that he is well within the deadline set for a response.

The body of a response memo provides the information requested. Its organization generally follows the sequence of the request. In Bill's memo, he answers the questions as his boss presented them; however, he further clarifies the information by providing summarizing headings in bold type. These headings emphasize the groupings and help the reader see immediately what information is covered. The memo closes with a summary.

FIGURE 5.5 Memo That Responds

Announces main idea

Summarizes main idea and refers to previous message

Arranges responses in order of original request and uses boldface headings to emphasize and clarify groupings

Closes with reassuring remark and offer of further assistance

---

IntraData Associates
Interoffice Memo

DATE: May 4, 2009

TO: Tamara Milowski, Vice-President, Employee Relations

FROM: Bill E. Leslie, Manager, Legal Support Services *BEL*

SUBJECT: REACTIONS TO PROPOSED CASUAL DRESS DAY PROGRAM

Here are my reactions to your inquiry about a casual dress day program made in your e-mail message of May 2.

- **Establish a casual dress day?** Yes, I would like to see such a day. In my department we now have a number of employees with flex schedules. They perform part of their work at home, where they can be as casual as they wish. Employees located here in the office are a little resentful. I think a casual dress day could offer some compensation to those who come to the office daily.

- **Implement a dress code?** By all means! We definitely need a written dress code not only to establish standards but also to project a professional image of the company to our customers.

- **Ensure professional office atmosphere?** I would hope that casual dress would not make the employees have a casual work attitude as well. We must establish that professionalism is non-negotiable. For example, we can't allow two-hour lunches or entire afternoons spent gossiping instead of working. Moreover, I think we should be careful in allowing casual dress only on the designated day, once a week.

I think a casual dress program can be beneficial and improve morale. But we definitely need a dress code in place at the beginning of the program. Let me know if I may assist in implementing a casual dress day program.

Summing Up and Looking Forward

E-mails and memos are vital channels of information within business offices. They use a standardized format to request and deliver information. Because e-mail messages are increasingly a preferred channel, this chapter presented many techniques for sending safe and effective e-mail messages. You learned to apply the direct strategy in writing messages that inform, request, and respond. You also learned to use bullets, numbers, and parallel form for listing information so that main points stand out. In the next chapter, you will extend the direct strategy to writing letters that make requests and respond to requests.

1. What factors would help you decide whether to send an e-mail, write a memo, make a telephone call, leave a voice-mail message, or deliver a message in person?
2. Why are lawyers and technology experts warning companies to store, organize, and manage computer data, including e-mail, with greater care?
3. Ethical Issue: Should managers have the right to monitor the e-mail messages of employees? Why or why not? What if employees are warned that e-mail could be monitored? If a company sets up an e-mail policy, should only in-house transmissions be monitored? Only outside transmissions?

Chapter Review

4. What three questions should a writer ask before beginning an e-mail or memo?

5. Why are subject lines such as *Hello* or *Meeting* inappropriate?

6. Since e-mail messages are almost like telephone calls, why should one care about correct spelling, grammar, punctuation, and style?

7. What are the four parts of the writing plan for a routine e-mail or memo? What is included in each?

8. How can listed or graphically highlighted items improve e-mails and memos?

9. When are numbers appropriate for listing items? When are bullets appropriate?

10. What are the main kinds of business e-mails and memos? Which require a direct strategy?

Message Openers. Compare the following sets of message openers. Circle the letter of the opener that illustrates a direct opening. Be prepared to discuss the weaknesses and strengths of each.

11. A letter to a security company inquiring about costs:
    a. We are considering keeping our facility open 24 hours a day because we can increase our profitability by running three shifts a day. We need some information.
    b. Please answer the following questions about the cost of adding security guards and electronic cameras to enable 24-hour operation of our facility.

12. An e-mail message announcing a professional development program:
    a. Employees interested in improving their writing and communication skills are invited to a training program beginning October 4.
    b. For the past year we have been investigating the possibility of developing a communication skills training program for some of our employees.

13. An e-mail message announcing a study:
    a. We have noticed recently a gradual but steady decline in the number of customer chequing accounts. We are disturbed by this trend, and for this reason I am asking our Customer Relations Department to conduct a study and make recommendations regarding this important problem.
    b. Our Customer Relations Department will conduct a study and make recommendations regarding the gradual but steady decline of customer chequing accounts.

Opening Paragraphs. The following opening paragraph to a memo is wordy and indirect. After reading the paragraph, identify the main idea. Then, write an opening sentence that illustrates a more direct opening. Use a separate sheet if necessary.

14. Several staff members came to me and announced their interest in learning more about severance plans and separation policies. As most of you know, these areas of concern are increasingly important for most Human Resources professionals. A seminar entitled "Severance and Separation Benefits" is being conducted February 11. The following employees are attending the seminar: Dave Neufeld, Tayreez Mushani, and Gail Switzer.

Lists. Write lists as indicated below.

15. Use the following information to compose a single sentence that includes an introductory statement and a list with letters (a, b, c). Do not list the items vertically.

    The home page of a website should orient readers. This page should tell them what the site is about. It should also tell about the organization of the site. Finally, it should tell them how to navigate the site.

16. Use the following information to compose a bulleted vertical list with an introductory statement.

    To use the conventional in-line skate heel brake, you should do these things. First, you should move one leg slightly forward. Then the ball of your foot should be lifted. Finally, the heel should be dragged to complete the braking action.

17. Use the following information to compose a sentence containing a list.

    Your equipment lease will mature in a month. When it does, you must make a decision. Three options are available to you. If you like, you may purchase the equipment at fair market value. Or the existing lease may be extended, again at fair market value. Finally, if neither of these options is appealing, the equipment could be sent back to the leasing company.

Activities and Cases

5.1 Memo That Informs: Sky-High Printing Bills. As Patricia Isaac, director of operations for DPI, a small software company, you are disturbed about some very large printing bills you've been receiving. DPI hires outside printers to prepare software manuals, marketing brochures, and sales materials. Printing is a necessary part of your business. Although the bills seem high, a recent bill from PrintMasters is particularly suspicious.

You don't want to blame anyone, but you do want to inform all staff members that no printing bills will be paid in the future without careful inspection. In talking it over with Sylvie Marchand, your colleague, you say, "We've got to make some changes. I can't plan my budget or control costs when these outrageous printing bills keep coming in. We have to start a standardized procedure. Any ideas?" Sylvie responds, "One of the reasons that costs are so high is that some departments just don't think carefully about their printing needs before sending a job out. Maybe we should make departments write out their exact specifications and then get estimates and approvals—before they order any printing job."

You and she decide that two written estimates should be approved for any proposed printing job. You also decide that these estimates should be submitted to Sylvie for authorization. Only then can a department order any outside printing job. And this new procedure must start immediately. As Sylvie leaves, you remark, "You know, these new procedures mean that we'll probably get more competitive pricing. And they could even mean that departments will find better, more creative printing options!"

Your Task. Think through the process involved in creating a memo to the staff announcing the changes. To help you apply the principles you have learned in this chapter, read the options suggested here. Circle the most appropriate response for each question. Then compose the message as a memo addressed to all staff members or as an e-mail addressed to your instructor.

Developing the Memo

1. What is the main idea in this memo?
   a. You are outraged at the high printing bills being received lately.
   b. You can't plan budgets or control costs when these unexpected bills keep coming in.
   c. The bills from PrintMasters are particularly suspicious.
   d. A new procedure for submitting requests for outside printing jobs is being instituted immediately.
2. Which of the following would be an effective opening sentence for your memo?
   a. Sylvie Marchand and I have been concerned about the high printing bills we have received lately.
   b. Please follow the new procedures listed below in submitting requests for outside printing jobs.
   c. Very large expenditures for printing jobs have been submitted recently, some of which are quite suspicious.
   d. Henceforth, no employee may send out a printing job without prior written approval.
3. What should the body of the memo do?
   a. Explain why the new procedure is necessary and how to follow it
   b. Recount the highlights of your conversation with Sylvie
   c. Identify the bills of the most offending printers, particularly PrintMasters
   d. Identify the departments and employees who have been responsible for most of the high costs
4. In explaining the new procedure, you will probably want to list each step. Which of the following statements illustrates the best way to list a step?
   a. Submission of all written estimates should be made to Sylvie Marchand.
   b. Written estimates should be submitted to Sylvie Marchand.
   c. Submit written estimates to Sylvie Marchand.
   d. Sylvie Marchand will expect all written estimates to be submitted to her.
5. Which of the following might be an effective closing for your memo?
   a. These procedures are effective immediately. Thank you for your cooperation in this matter.
   b. Following these new procedures, which are effective immediately, will result in more competitive pricing and perhaps may even provide you with new creative printing options. If you have any questions, call Sylvie Marchand at Ext. 556.
   c. These procedures are effective immediately. By the way, don't forget to send me your ideas for equipping the new fitness centre.
   d. If I may be of assistance to you in any way, do not hesitate to call on me.

5.2 E-Mail That Requests: Making the Best of Temporary Workers Hired by Your Company. Analyze the following poorly written e-mail. List its faults in the space provided. Outline an appropriate plan for an e-mail that requests. Revise the subject line. Then, on a separate sheet or as an e-mail message, write an improved version.

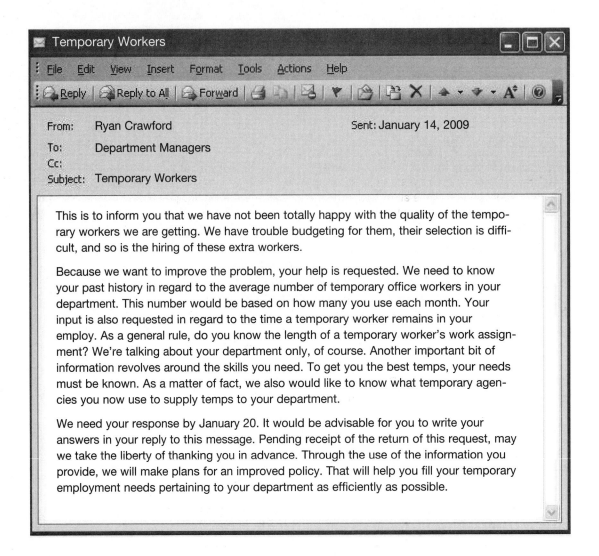

Temporary Workers

File Edit View Insert Format Tools Actions Help

Reply | Reply to All | Forward

From: Ryan Crawford   Sent: January 14, 2009
To: Department Managers
Cc:
Subject: Temporary Workers

This is to inform you that we have not been totally happy with the quality of the temporary workers we are getting. We have trouble budgeting for them, their selection is difficult, and so is the hiring of these extra workers.

Because we want to improve the problem, your help is requested. We need to know your past history in regard to the average number of temporary office workers in your department. This number would be based on how many you use each month. Your input is also requested in regard to the time a temporary worker remains in your employ. As a general rule, do you know the length of a temporary worker's work assignment? We're talking about your department only, of course. Another important bit of information revolves around the skills you need. To get you the best temps, your needs must be known. As a matter of fact, we also would like to know what temporary agencies you now use to supply temps to your department.

We need your response by January 20. It would be advisable for you to write your answers in your reply to this message. Pending receipt of the return of this request, may we take the liberty of thanking you in advance. Through the use of the information you provide, we will make plans for an improved policy. That will help you fill your temporary employment needs pertaining to your department as efficiently as possible.

1. List at least five faults in this e-mail.

2. Outline a general writing plan for this e-mail.
   Subject line:

   Opening:

   Body:

   Closing:

5.3 Memo That Informs: Time Management Tips. Read the following poorly written memo, analyze its faults, outline a general writing plan, and then revise the memo. Write a more effective subject line for your revised version.

DATE: Nov. 13, 2009

TO: Staff Members

FROM: Phil Kleeson, Manager

SUBJECT: Suggestions

Recently I had the pleasure of attending an excellent time management seminar in which we managers were told about some interesting strategies for managing the huge amount of information from which we all suffer. Since many of you have been complaining about all the time you spend on e-mail and voice mail, I thought I would send you some of the best pointers we were given. These might help you increase your productivity and decrease your frustration.

When it comes to e-mail, follow these steps. You should start by glancing through all incoming mail quickly and separating the messages you need to answer immediately, as well as determining which messages can wait and which ones can be deleted. Generally, you can do this by checking subject lines and the names of senders. To cut down on the amount of time you spend on your e-mail, you should check e-mail messages only once or twice each day and at specific times so that you develop a routine. This simple practice can save you a lot of wasted time. Another technique involves time management but also courtesy. Be sure to respond briefly to all important e-mails, even if you can say only that you are looking into a matter.

When it comes to voice mail, check it at least three times a day. This prevents "message bump"—having the same person call you several times with the same request. Another idea for saving time with voice mail is to use the functions on your telephone to skip to the end of a message or past recorded messages to the beep when you want to leave a message.

By the way, we need a volunteer to attend a conference on preventing violence in the workplace. Thank you for your cooperation.

---

1. List at least five faults in this memo.

2. Outline a general writing plan for this memo.
    Subject line:

    Opening:

    Body:

    Closing:

5.4 Memo That Informs/Requests: Dress Code Controversy. As the Vancouver-based director of Human Resources at Sensational—a leading woman's fashion chain—you have not had a good week. The national newspaper recently stated that Sensational has been reported to the Nova Scotia Human Rights Commission to defend a claim by a young woman. The young woman recently applied for a job at a Halifax Sensational location and was told in a pre-interview with a manager that "she'd never be hired if she wore her headdress to work." Citing the Commission's website claim that "It's against the law to fire an employee because he wears clothing that is required by his religion," the young woman lodged a complaint.[5] Head office in Vancouver has been trying to fix this issue ever since.

Your Task. Quickly realizing the effects the negative newspaper reporting will have, you draft a memo to all employees. The purpose of the memo is to reaffirm that Sensational abides by and supports all Canadian human rights legislation, and at the same time, that employees should not talk to any media that may ask them for comments. You realize that these two messages are somewhat contradictory (one positive, one negative), but you feel time is of the essence.

Web **Related website: Nova Scotia Human Rights Commission at http://www.gov.ns.ca/humanrights.**

5.5. Reply Memo: Someone's Going to Get Stung. The IS (Information Systems) network manager at Lionel Packaging in Peterborough, Ontario, worries that his company will have to upgrade its Internet connection because operations are much slower than in the past. Upon checking, however, he discovers that employees are surfing the Web for personal use; that is the real reason for the slowdown.

Since the company needs a good policy on using e-mail and the Internet, he assigns your team the task of investigating existing policies. Your team leader, Mary Richard, who has quite a sense of humour, says, "Developing an Internet policy is a lot like taking care of a beehive; too much activity and you can get stung, not enough and the bees do whatever they want." No one is going to like having e-mail and Internet use restricted.

Your Task. Develop a brief company policy on using e-mail and the Internet. Your team should first check websites to locate examples or models of company e-mail and Internet policies. Print any helpful material. Then meet as a group and select six to eight major topics that you think should be covered in a company policy. Write the company policy for your employer and send it by email to your team leader, Mary Richard.

5.6 Memo That Responds: What's New at Canada Post. Assume you are Maria Lopez and you work for MagicMedia, Inc., a large software manufacturer. The office manager, Rachel Wilder, asks you to seek two kinds of information from Canada Post. First, she wants to learn exactly how envelopes should be addressed according to Canada Post guidelines. Second, she wants to know the air and surface rates for sending packages to the United States. She expects to be sending plenty of parcels to a U.S. client in the spring.

Your Task. To obtain both sets of information, visit the Canada Post website. Write a one-page memo summarizing your findings.

Web **Related website: http://www.canadapost.ca.**

The following sentences contain errors in the use of adjectives and adverbs. Below each sentence, write a corrected version.

1. Of the two coffee shops—Tim Hortons and Coffee Time—which serves the best coffee?

2. The highly advertised McDonald's $1.99 hamburger promotion, which was pushed heavy by its Canadian headquarters, turned out to be disappointing.

3. Our newly-renovated office almost cost ten thousand dollars.

4. After listening careful to your advice, we only paid one month's rent in advance.

5. Please tell all employees that they're two month contract will expire in January.

6. Amir felt badly when he did not get the promotion.

7. Sony provides the most clearest explanation of how to use a video camera.

8. Maria is the nicer secretary of all secretaries in the department.

9. Most companies give a 60 day guarantee on all there products.

10. Our ten year old company has only made a small profit in the sales department.

Document for Revision

The following memo has faults in grammar, punctuation, spelling, repetition, wordiness, and other areas. Use standard proofreading marks (see Appendix B) to correct the errors. When you finish, your instructor can show you the revised version of this memo.

DATE: March 2, 2009

TO: Department Heads, Managers, and Supervisors

FROM: James Robbins, Director, Human Resources

SUBJECT: Submitting Reviews of Performance by April 15th

Please be informed that performance reviews for all you're employees are due before April 15. These appraisal are esspecially important and essential this year. Because of job changes, new technologys and because of office re-organization.

To complete your performance reviews in the most effective way, you should follow the procedures describe in our employee handbook, let me briefly explain those procedures.

1. Be sure each and every employee has a performance plan. With several main objective.

2. For each objective assess the employee on a scale of 5 (regularly goes above requirements) to 0 (does not meet requirements at all).

3. You should identify three strengths that he brings to job.

4. Name three skill that he can improve. These should relate to skills such as time management rather then to behaviours such as always be late.

5. Meet with the employee to discussing his review.

6. The completed review should be send to this office.

We look at reviews like a tool for help each worker assess his performance. And increase his output. If you would like to discuss this matter, please do not hesitate to call me.

Whose Computer or BlackBerry or PalmPilot Is It Anyway?

Many companies today provide their employees with computers and/or PDAs with Internet access. Should employees be able to use those devices for online shopping, personal messages, personal work, and listening to music or playing games?

But It's Harmless

According to a recent poll, one-third of Canadian workers have Internet access at work and four out of five of these say they log on for personal reasons, such as sending personal e-mails, checking out news or sports headlines, comparison shopping, checking investments, and making online purchases. While the poll did not determine whether this activity occurred during work or in the employee's spare time, the potential for abuse and evidence of abuse has led a growing number of employers in Canada to consider developing policies governing Internet use and also to monitor the online activities of employees.[6] To justify much of this personal activity, workers claim that doing personal online activities is performance-enhancing, because it keeps them at their desk rather than in the shopping malls or at the water cooler.

Companies Getting Involved in Checking Personal Internet Use

Employers are less happy about the increasing use of company computers for personal online activities. The growth of electronic monitoring (checking) has been significant since 1998 in both Canada and the United States. In fact, the number of companies in the United States reviewing e-mail and computer files stored on hard drives has doubled from the late 1990s.[7]

What's Reasonable?

Some companies try to enforce a "zero tolerance" policy, prohibiting any personal use of company equipment, while others allow some personal activity. In Canada under the Privacy Act and Charter of Rights and Freedoms, employees have a "reasonable expectation" of privacy in the workplace, but that expectation can be met simply by notifying employees that they are being monitored.[8] Currently many employers provide no guidelines on reasonable Internet use. Robert Lendvai, marketing director for Ottawa's Kyberpass Corporation, a maker of network security software, indicates that while Canadian corporations use the security features of his company's software, only about one in five activates the monitoring capabilities.[9]

Career Application

As an administrative assistant at Big C Technologies in Vancouver, you have just received an e-mail from your boss asking for your opinion. It seems that many employees have been shopping online; one person actually received four personal packages sent to him in one morning. Although reluctant to do so, management is considering installing monitoring software that not only tracks Internet use but also allows extensive blocking of websites, such as porn, hate, and game sites.

Your Task

- In teams or as a class, research and discuss the problem of workplace abuse of e-mail and the Internet.
- Should full personal use be allowed?
- In terms of equipment, are computers and their links to the Internet similar to office telephones?
- Should employees be allowed to access the Internet for personal use if they use their own private e-mail accounts?
- Should management be allowed to monitor all Internet use?
- Should employees be warned if e-mail is to be monitored?
- What specific reasons can you give to support an Internet checking system by management?
- What specific reasons can you give to oppose a checking system?

Decide whether you support or oppose management's checking of Internet use by employees. Explain your views in an e-mail or a memo to your boss, Roberta Everson (her address is reverson@bigc.com), or in a traditional in-class debate.

Web

Related websites: Visit the WebSpy software site at http://www.webspy.com for an inside look at Internet surveillance software. For information on Canada's privacy laws and regulations, visit the website of the Office of the Privacy Commissioner of Canada at http://www.privcom.gc.ca.

6

Routine Letters and Goodwill Messages

CHAPTER

Who cares about composing well-crafted business letters today? Didn't that mode of communication start to die in the 1980s when the fax machine began to rule our lives? Surely after the advent of sophisticated voice mail systems in the early 1990s, the mailed business letter was destined for obsolescence! If nothing else, the explosion of email users must have put this archaic form of correspondence out of its misery by now! Think again. Believe it or not, there is at least one group of people who are still impressed when they receive a well-written letter in the ordinary mail. They are called prospective clients/customers.[1]

Reg Pirie, Lead Partner, Pirie Management Consultants Inc.

LEARNING OBJECTIVES

1. Write letters requesting information and action.
2. Write letters making claims.
3. Write letters complying with requests.
4. Write letters granting claims.
5. Write letters of recommendation.
6. Write goodwill messages.

L etters that fail to get to the point or are badly written are a concern for employees and managers everywhere. For example, a bank's profits can depend on the quality of information the bank provides to its customers. Without clear, well-written messages that transmit information concisely, banks and insurance companies risk turning away current customers and losing potential customers. Messages that move slowly toward their point have little appeal for most of us. Readers want to know why a message was written and how it involves them. And they want that information up front.

Writing Everyday Business Letters

✓ Quick Check

Letters communicate with outsiders and produce a formal record.

This chapter focuses on written messages that travel outside an organization. These messages generally take the form of letters. Although, as Reg Pirie implies, business people today are writing fewer letters and more e-mail messages, you will still find many occasions when letters are required. When you need a formal record of an inquiry, response, or complaint, letters are the best communication channel.

Most business correspondence consists of routine letters. These everyday messages go to suppliers, government agencies, other businesses, and, most importantly, customers. Customer letters are given high priority because these messages encourage product feedback, project a good image of the company, and promote future business.

The content of a message and its anticipated effect on the reader determine the strategy you choose.

Like memos, letters are easiest to write when you have a plan to follow. Letters delivering bad news require an indirect approach, which you will learn about in Chapter 8. Most letters, however, carry good or neutral news. Because such letters will not produce a negative effect on their reader, they follow the direct strategy. You will recall that the main idea comes first in the direct strategy.

In this chapter, you'll learn to apply the direct strategy in writing requests for information and action. You'll also learn how to respond to such requests. Finally, you'll learn how to write typical goodwill letters.

Information and Action Requests

Many business messages are written to request information or action. The similarity of purpose in routine requests allows writers to use the following writing plan.

Writing Plan for an Information or Action Request

- **Opening**—Ask the most important question first or express a polite command.
- **Body**—Explain the request logically and courteously. Ask other questions if necessary.
- **Closing**—Request a specific action with an end date, if appropriate, and show appreciation.

Opening Directly

The most important positions in a letter are the openings and closings. Readers tend to look at them first; therefore, the writer should put the most significant statement first. The first sentence of an information request is usually a question or a polite command. Immediately tell the reader what you want. This saves the reader's time and may ensure that the message is read. A busy executive who quickly reads only the first sentence may grasp your request right away and act on it. A request that follows a lengthy explanation, on the other hand, may never be found.

A letter inquiring about hotel accommodations, shown in Figure 6.1 (p. 110), begins immediately with the most important idea. Can the hotel provide meeting rooms and accommodations for 250 people? Instead of opening with an explanation of who the writer is or how the writer happens to be writing this letter, the letter begins directly.

If several questions must be asked, you have two choices. You can ask the most important question first, as shown in Figure 6.1. An alternative opening begins with a summary statement, such as *Please answer the following questions about providing meeting rooms and accommodations for 250 people from May 25 through May 29*. Notice that the summarizing statement sounds like a question but has no question mark. That's because it's really a command disguised as a question. Rather than bluntly demanding information (*Answer the following questions*), we often soften commands by posing them as questions. Such statements, called rhetorical questions, should not be punctuated as questions because they do not require answers.

Quick Check

Readers find the openings and closings of letters most valuable.

FIGURE 6.1 Letter That Requests Information

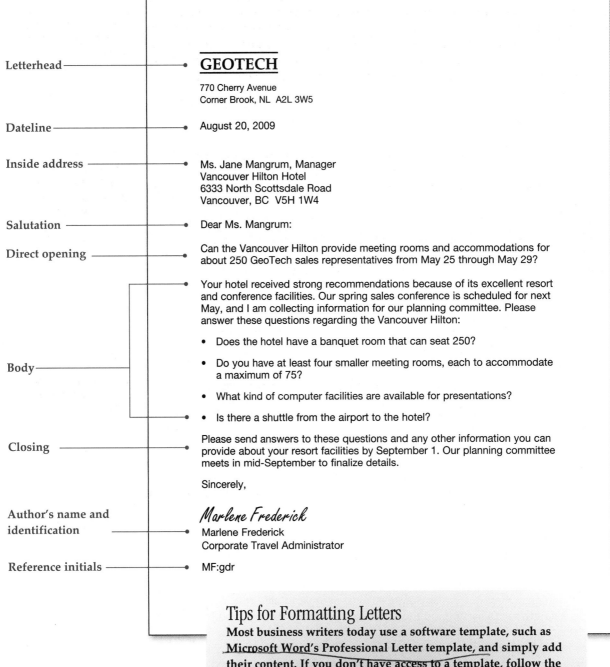

Letterhead

GEOTECH

770 Cherry Avenue
Corner Brook, NL A2L 3W5

Dateline

August 20, 2009

Inside address

Ms. Jane Mangrum, Manager
Vancouver Hilton Hotel
6333 North Scottsdale Road
Vancouver, BC V5H 1W4

Salutation

Dear Ms. Mangrum:

Direct opening

Can the Vancouver Hilton provide meeting rooms and accommodations for about 250 GeoTech sales representatives from May 25 through May 29?

Body

Your hotel received strong recommendations because of its excellent resort and conference facilities. Our spring sales conference is scheduled for next May, and I am collecting information for our planning committee. Please answer these questions regarding the Vancouver Hilton:

- Does the hotel have a banquet room that can seat 250?

- Do you have at least four smaller meeting rooms, each to accommodate a maximum of 75?

- What kind of computer facilities are available for presentations?

- Is there a shuttle from the airport to the hotel?

Closing

Please send answers to these questions and any other information you can provide about your resort facilities by September 1. Our planning committee meets in mid-September to finalize details.

Sincerely,

Marlene Frederick

Author's name and identification

Marlene Frederick
Corporate Travel Administrator

Reference initials

MF:gdr

Tips for Formatting Letters

Most business writers today use a software template, such as Microsoft Word's Professional Letter template, and simply add their content. If you don't have access to a template, follow the steps below.

- Start the date on line 13, or 1 blank line below the letterhead.
- For block style such as that used in the letter above, begin all lines at the left margin.
- For modified block style such as the style used in the letter on page 113, begin the date and closing lines at the centre.
- Leave side margins of 2.5 to 3 cm (1 to 1.5 inches), depending on the length of the letter.
- Single-space the body. Double-space between paragraphs.

Details in the Body

The body of a letter that requests information should provide necessary details and should be clear and easy to read. If you analyze your needs, organize your ideas, and arrange your request logically, you are likely to receive a meaningful answer that doesn't require a follow-up message. Whenever possible, itemize the information to improve readability. Notice that the questions in Figure 6.1 are bulleted, and they are parallel. They demonstrate an excellent use of graphic highlighting.

Quick Check

The body of a request letter may contain an explanation or a list of questions.

Closing with an Action Request

Use the final paragraph to ask for specific action, to set an end date if appropriate, and to express appreciation. As you learned in working with e-mails and memos, a request for action is most effective when an end date and a reason for that date are supplied, as shown in Figure 6.1.

Quick Check

The ending of a request letter should tell the reader what you want done and when.

It's always appropriate to end a request letter with appreciation for the action taken. However, don't fall into a cliché trap, such as *Thanking you in advance, I remain ...* or the familiar *Thank you for your cooperation*. Your appreciation will sound most sincere if you avoid mechanical, tired expressions.

Simple Claim Requests

In business many things can go wrong—promised shipments are late, goods under warranty fail, or service is disappointing. When you as a customer must write to identify or correct a "wrong" or a problem, the letter is called a *claim* (or sometimes a *complaint*). Straightforward claims are those to which you expect the receiver to agree readily. But even these claims often require a letter. While your first action may be a telephone call or a visit to submit your claim, you may not get the results you seek. Written claims are generally taken more seriously, and they also establish a record of what happened. Claims or complaints that require persuasion and usually use an indirect approach are presented in Chapter 7. In this chapter, you'll learn to apply the following writing plan for a straightforward claim that uses a direct approach.

Quick Check

Claim letters register complaints and usually seek correction of a wrong.

 Writing Plan for a Simple Claim

- **Opening**—Describe clearly the desired action.
- **Body**—Explain the nature of the claim, explain the claim is justified, and provide details regarding the action requested.
- **Closing**—End pleasantly with a goodwill statement and include end date if appropriate.

Opening with Action

If you have a legitimate claim, you can expect a positive response from a company. Smart businesses today want to hear from their customers. That's why you should open a claim letter with a clear statement of the problem or with the action you want the receiver to take. You might expect a replacement, a refund, a new order, credit to your account, correction of a billing error, free repairs, free inspection, or cancellation of an order.

Quick Check

The direct strategy is best for simple claims that require no persuasion.

When the remedy is obvious, state it immediately *(Please send us 24 colour printer cartridges to replace the 24 black ink cartridges sent in error with our order shipped January 4).* When the remedy is less obvious, you might ask for a change in policy or procedure or simply for an explanation *(Because three of our employees with confirmed reservations were refused rooms at your hotel on September 16, would you please clarify your policy regarding reservations and late arrivals).*

Explaining in the Body

In the body of a claim letter, explain the problem and justify your request. Provide the necessary details so that the difficulty can be corrected without further correspondence. Avoid becoming angry or blaming someone. Remember that the person reading your letter is seldom responsible for the problem. Instead, state the facts logically, objectively, and unemotionally; let the reader decide on the causes.

Include copies of all necessary documents such as invoices, sales receipts, catalogue descriptions, and repair records. (By the way, be sure to send copies and not your originals, which could be lost.) When service is involved, state names of individuals spoken to and dates of calls. Assume that a company honestly wants to satisfy its customers—because most do. When an alternative solution exists, describe it *(If you are unable to send 24 colour cartridges immediately, please credit our account now and notify us when they become available).*

Closing Pleasantly

Conclude a claim letter with a courteous statement that promotes goodwill and expresses a desire for continued relations. If appropriate, include an end date *(We realize that mistakes in ordering and shipping sometimes occur. Because we've enjoyed your prompt service in the past, we hope that you will be able to send us the printer cartridges by January 15).*

Finally, in making claims, act promptly. Delaying claims makes them appear less important. Delayed claims are also more difficult to verify. By taking the time to put your claim in writing, you indicate your seriousness. A written claim also starts a record of the problem, should later action be necessary. Be sure to keep a copy of your letter.

Putting It All Together

Figure 6.2 shows an angry claim letter that accomplishes little. Its tone is aggressive, and it assumes that the company intentionally overcharged the customer. Furthermore, it fails to tell the reader how to fix the problem. The revised letter softens the tone, describes the problem objectively, and provides facts and figures. Most important, it specifies exactly what the customer wants done.

Notice that the letter in Figure 6.2 is shown with the return address typed above the date. This personal business style may be used when typing on paper without a printed letterhead. Notice, too, that this letter uses modified block style. The return address, date, and closing lines start at the centre.

Information Response Letters

Often, your messages will respond favourably to requests for information or action. A customer wants information about a product. A supplier asks to arrange a meeting. Another business inquires about one of your procedures. But before responding to any inquiry, be sure to check your facts and figures carefully. Any letter written on company stationery is considered a legally binding contract. If a policy or procedure needs authorization, seek approval from a supervisor or executive before writing the letter. In complying with requests, you'll want to apply the same direct pattern you used in making requests.

FIGURE 6.2 Direct Claim Letter

Sounds angry; jumps to conclusions

Forgets that mistakes happen

Fails to suggest solution

Dear Sweet Sounds:

You call yourselves Sweet Sounds, but all I'm getting from your service is sour notes! I'm furious that you have your salespeople include unwanted service warranties to boost your sales.

When I bought my Panatronic DVD player from Sweet Sounds, Inc., in August, I specifically told the salesperson that I did NOT want a three-year service warranty. But there it is on my credit card statement this month! You people have obviously billed me for a service I did not authorize. I refuse to pay this charge.

How can you hope to stay in business with such false practices? I was expecting to return this month and look at flat-screen TVs, but I will be looking for an honest dealer this time.

Sincerely,

Brent K. Royer

After

1201 North Plum Street
Steinbach, MB R3L 2N7
September 3, 2009

Personal business letter style

Mr. Sam Lee, Customer Service
Sweet Sounds, Inc.
2003 East Street
Toronto, ON M2T 1G5

Dear Mr. Lee:

Please credit my VISA account, No. 0000-0046-2198-9421, to fix an incorrect charge of $299.

States simply and clearly what to do

On August 8 I purchased a Panatronic DVD player from the Sweet Sounds, Inc., outlet in Steinbach. Although the salesperson discussed a three-year extended warranty with me, I decided against purchasing that service for $299. However, when my credit card statement arrived this month, I noticed an extra $299 charge from Sweet Sounds, Inc.; this charge represents the warranty I declined.

Explains objectively what went wrong

Doesn't blame or accuse

Enclosed is a copy of my sales invoice along with my VISA statement on which I circled the charge. Please authorize a credit immediately and send a copy of the transaction to me at the above address.

Documents facts

I'm enjoying all the features of my DVD player and would like to be shopping at Sweet Sounds for a flat-screen TV shortly.

Uses friendly tone

Suggests continued business once problem is resolved

Sincerely,

Brent K. Royer

Brent K. Royer

Enclosure

Writing Plan for an Information Response Letter

- **Subject line**—Identify previous correspondence.
- **Opening**—Deliver the most important information first.
- **Body**—Arrange information logically, explain and clarify it, provide additional information if appropriate, and build goodwill.
- **Closing**—End pleasantly.

Subject Line Efficiency

Use the subject line to refer to previous correspondence.

An information response letter should contain a subject line which helps the reader recognize the topic immediately. Knowledgeable business communicators use a subject line to refer to earlier correspondence. Then, in the first sentence, the most important spot in a letter, they are free to emphasize the main idea. Notice in Figure 6.3 (p. 115) that the subject line identifies the subject completely.

Opening Directly

In the first sentence of an information response, deliver the information the reader wants. Avoid wordy, drawn-out openings (*I have before me your letter of February 6, in which you request information about ...*). More forceful and more efficient is an opener that answers the inquiry (*The information you wanted is as follows ...*). When agreeing to a request for action, announce the good news promptly (*I will be happy to speak to your business communication class on the topic of ...*).

Arranging Information Logically in the Body

A good way to answer questions is to number or bullet each one.

When answering a group of questions or providing considerable data, arrange the information logically and make it readable by using lists, tables, headings, bold-face, italics, or other graphic devices. When customers or prospective customers inquire about products or services, your response should do more than simply give answers. You'll also want to promote your organization and products. Be sure to present the promotional material with attention to the "you" view and to reader benefits (*You can use our standardized tests to free you from time-consuming employment screening*). You'll learn more about special techniques for developing sales and persuasive messages in Chapter 7.

Closing Pleasantly

Include a pleasant closing remark that shows your willingness to help the reader. Provide extra information if appropriate. Since everyone likes to be recognized as an individual, avoid form-letter closings such as *If we may be of further assistance ...*

Customer Claim Responses

As you learned earlier, when an organization receives a claim, it usually means that something has gone wrong. In responding to a claim, you have three goals:

- To fix the problem, if one exists
- To regain the confidence of the customer
- To promote future business and goodwill

If you decide to allow the claim, your response letter will represent good news to the reader. Use the direct strategy described in the following writing plan.

FIGURE 6.3 Information Response Letter

TRG LEGAL COUNSELLING SERVICES

930 Taylor Avenue
Regina, Saskatchewan
S4A 2Y4

February 6, 2009

Ms. Irene McKenzie, Director
Mercer Enterprises, Inc.
4980 Washington Avenue
Regina, SK S4L 4W6

Dear Ms. McKenzie:

SUBJECT: YOUR FEBRUARY 1 LETTER REQUESTING SPEAKERS FOR MEMBERS OF
         YOUR COMPANY'S MANAGEMENT COUNCIL

In response to your request, I'm happy to send you the tentative list of speakers for this
year's luncheon meetings of the management council as follows:

Date	Speaker	Topic
November 14	Dr. Linda Cooper	Performing Successful Psychologist Appraisals
January 12	Jeanette Spencer President, Spencer and Associates	Conducting Legal Job Interviews
March 13	Dr. John Hart Clearview Consultants	Managing Employee Benefits

Regarding your question about fees for the speakers, our department agreed that $300
was a reasonable sum to offer. The three speakers listed above agree to that amount.

For the last meeting in May, we have three topic possibilities to:

• Time Management for Today's Supervisors

• Effective Use of Internet and Websites

• Performing Background Checks on Prospective Employees

Please make a decision about which program you would prefer and circle that program on
the attached copy. Please respond by September 7 so I can complete the schedule
accordingly.

Sincerely,

Linda Thompson

Linda P. Thompson
Marketing Director

Enclosure

Writing Plan for Granting a Claim

• **Subject line (optional)**—Identify the previous correspondence.
• **Opening**—Agree to the request or announce the correction immediately.
  Include sales promotion if appropriate.
• **Body**—Provide details about how you will fulfill the request. Try to regain
  the customer's confidence and include sales promotion if appropriate.
• **Closing**—End positively with a forward-looking thought, express confidence
  in future business relations, and avoid referring to unpleasantness.

Quick Check

Responding to customer claims
means fixing the problem,
regaining customer confidence,
and promoting future business.

Revealing Good News in the Opening

Instead of beginning with a review of what went wrong, present the good news immediately. When Amy Hopkins responded to Electronic Warehouse's claim about a missing shipment, her first draft, shown at the top of Figure 6.4, was angry. It's clear that Electronic Warehouse had provided the wrong shipping address, and the goods were returned. But once Amy and her company decided to send a second shipment and agree with the customer's claim, she had to give up the anger and try to retain the goodwill and the business of this customer. The improved version of her letter announces that a new shipment will arrive shortly.

If you decide to agree to a customer's claim, let the receiver know immediately. Don't begin your letter with a negative statement (*We are very sorry to hear that you are having trouble with your Sno-Flake ice crusher*). This approach reminds the reader of the problem and may remind him or her about the unhappy feelings experienced when the claim was written. Instead, focus on the good news. The following openings for various letters illustrate how to begin a message with good news.

You may take your Sno-Flake ice crusher to Ben's Appliances at 310 First Street, Moose Jaw, where it will be repaired at no cost to you.

Thanks for your letter about your new Snow Crusher tires. You are certainly justified in expecting them to last more than 12,000 km.

We agree with you that the warranty on your Turbo programmable calculator Model AI 25C should be extended for six months.

The enclosed cheque for $325 demonstrates our desire to satisfy our customers and earn their confidence.

In announcing that you will grant a claim, be sure to do so without a resentful tone—even if you have doubts about whether the claim is legitimate. Once you decide to agree to the customer's request, do so happily.

Responding Positively in the Body of the Letter

In responding to claims, most organizations sincerely want to correct a problem. They want to do more than just make the customer happy. They want to stand behind their products and services; they want to do what's right.

In the body of the letter, do the following:

- Explain how you are giving a positive response to the claim.
- Seek to regain the confidence of the customer.

You might reasonably expect that a customer who has experienced difficulty with a product, with delivery, with billing, or with service has lost confidence in your organization. Rebuilding that confidence is important for future business.

How to rebuild lost confidence depends on the situation and the claim. If procedures need to be revised, explain what changes will be made. If a product has defective parts, explain how the product is being improved. If service is faulty, describe genuine efforts to improve it. Notice in Figure 6.4 that the writer promises to investigate shipping procedures to see if improvements might prevent future mishaps.

Sometimes the problem is not with the product but with the way it's being used. In other instances, customers misunderstand guarantees or unintentionally cause delivery and billing mix-ups by supplying incorrect information. Remember that logical and sincere explanations will do much to regain the confidence of unhappy customers.

Chapter 6 Routine Letters and Goodwill Messages

FIGURE 6.4 Customer Claim Response

Before

Fails to reveal good
news immediately;
blames customer

Creates ugly tone with
negative words and
sarcasm

Sounds grudging
and reluctant in
granting claim

After

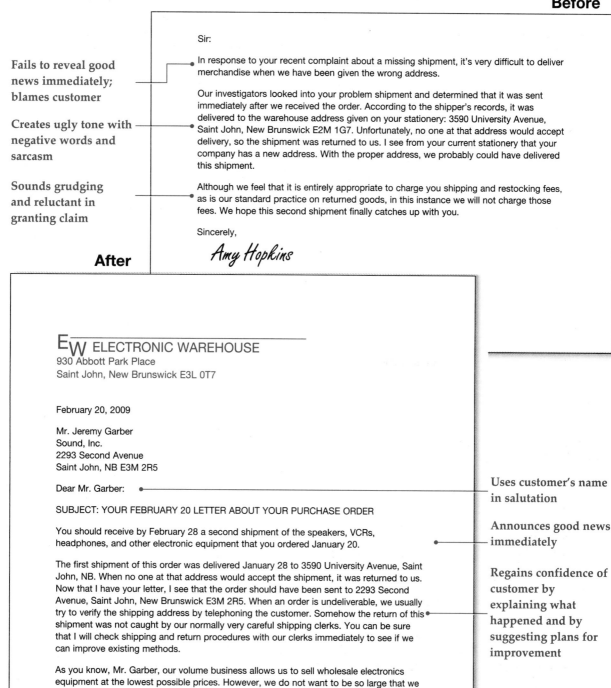

Sir:

In response to your recent complaint about a missing shipment, it's very difficult to deliver merchandise when we have been given the wrong address.

Our investigators looked into your problem shipment and determined that it was sent immediately after we received the order. According to the shipper's records, it was delivered to the warehouse address given on your stationery: 3590 University Avenue, Saint John, New Brunswick E2M 1G7. Unfortunately, no one at that address would accept delivery, so the shipment was returned to us. I see from your current stationery that your company has a new address. With the proper address, we probably could have delivered this shipment.

Although we feel that it is entirely appropriate to charge you shipping and restocking fees, as is our standard practice on returned goods, in this instance we will not charge those fees. We hope this second shipment finally catches up with you.

Sincerely,

Amy Hopkins

E_W ELECTRONIC WAREHOUSE
930 Abbott Park Place
Saint John, New Brunswick E3L 0T7

February 20, 2009

Mr. Jeremy Garber
Sound, Inc.
2293 Second Avenue
Saint John, NB E3M 2R5

Dear Mr. Garber:

SUBJECT: YOUR FEBRUARY 20 LETTER ABOUT YOUR PURCHASE ORDER

You should receive by February 28 a second shipment of the speakers, VCRs, headphones, and other electronic equipment that you ordered January 20.

The first shipment of this order was delivered January 28 to 3590 University Avenue, Saint John, NB. When no one at that address would accept the shipment, it was returned to us. Now that I have your letter, I see that the order should have been sent to 2293 Second Avenue, Saint John, New Brunswick E3M 2R5. When an order is undeliverable, we usually try to verify the shipping address by telephoning the customer. Somehow the return of this shipment was not caught by our normally very careful shipping clerks. You can be sure that I will check shipping and return procedures with our clerks immediately to see if we can improve existing methods.

As you know, Mr. Garber, our volume business allows us to sell wholesale electronics equipment at the lowest possible prices. However, we do not want to be so large that we lose touch with valued customers like you. Over the years our customers' respect has made us successful, and we hope that the prompt delivery of this shipment will earn yours.

Sincerely,

Amy Hopkins
Amy Hopkins
Distribution Manager

cc David Cole, Shipping Department

Uses customer's name
in salutation

Announces good news
immediately

Regains confidence of
customer by
explaining what
happened and by
suggesting plans for
improvement

Closes confidently
with genuine appeal
for customer's respect

In your explanation avoid emphasizing negative words such as *trouble, regret, misunderstanding, fault, defective, error, inconvenience,* and *unfortunately.* Keep your message positive and upbeat.

Deciding Whether to Apologize

Should you apologize in a claim response? Some writing experts argue that apologies remind customers of their complaints and are therefore negative. These writers avoid apologies; instead they concentrate on how they are satisfying the customer. Real letters that respond to customers' claims, however, often include apologies.[2] If you feel that your company is at fault and that an apology is an appropriate goodwill gesture, by all means include it. Be careful, though, not to admit negligence. You'll learn more about responding to negative letters in Chapter 8.

Showing Confidence in the Closing

End positively by expressing confidence that the problem has been resolved and that continued business relations will result. You might mention the product in a favourable light, suggest a new product, express your appreciation for the customer's business, or anticipate future business. It's often appropriate to refer to the desire to be of service and to satisfy customers. Notice how the following closings illustrate a positive, confident tone:

> Your Sno-Flake ice crusher will help you remain cool and refreshed this summer. For your additional summer enjoyment, consider our Smoky Joe tabletop gas grill shown in the enclosed summer catalogue. We genuinely value your business and look forward to your future orders.

Quick Check

End your letter by looking ahead positively.

> We hope that this refund cheque convinces you of our sincere desire to satisfy our customers. Our goal is to earn your confidence and continue to provide you with quality products and matchless service.

> You were most helpful in telling us about this situation and giving us an opportunity to correct it. Thank you for your cooperation.

Letter of Recommendation

Quick Check

You may write letters recommending people for awards, membership in organizations, or employment.

Letters of recommendation may be written to nominate people for awards and for membership in organizations. More frequently, though, they are written to evaluate present or former employees. The central concern in these messages is honesty. Thus, you should avoid inflating or distorting a candidate's qualifications to cover up weaknesses or to destroy the person's chances. Ethically and legally, you have a duty to the candidate as well as to other employers to describe that person truthfully and objectively. You don't, however, have to support everyone who asks. Since recommendations are generally voluntary, you can—and should—resist writing letters for individuals you can't truthfully support. Ask these people to find someone else who knows them better.

Some businesspeople today refuse to write recommendations for former employees because they fear lawsuits. Other businesspeople argue that recommendations are useless because they're always positive. Despite the general avoidance of negatives, well-written recommendations do help match candidates with jobs. Hiring companies learn more about a candidate's skills and potential. As a result, they are able to place a candidate properly. Therefore, you should learn to write such letters because you will surely be expected to do so in your future career.

For letters of recommendation, use the direct strategy as described in the following writing plan.

 Writing Plan for a Letter of Recommendation

- **Opening**—Identify the applicant, the position, and the reason for writing. State that the message is confidential. Establish your relationship with the applicant. Describe the length of employment or relationship.
- **Body**—Describe job duties. Provide specific examples of the applicant's professional and personal skills and attributes. Compare the applicant with others in his or her field.
- **Closing**—Summarize the significant attributes of the applicant. Offer an overall rating. Draw a conclusion regarding the recommendation.

Identifying the Purpose in the Opening

Begin an employment recommendation by identifying the candidate and the position sought, if it is known. State that your remarks are confidential, and suggest that you are writing at the request of the applicant. Describe your relationship with the candidate, as shown here:

> Ms. Cindy Rosales, whom your organization is considering for the position of media trainer, requested that I submit confidential information on her behalf. Ms. Rosales worked under my supervision for the past two years in our Video Training Centre.

Letters that recommend individuals for awards may open with more supportive statements, such as *I'm very pleased to nominate Robert Walsh for the Employee-of-the-Month award. For the past sixteen months, Mr. Walsh served as staff accountant in my division. During that time he distinguished himself by ...*

Describing Performance in the Body

The body of an employment recommendation should describe the applicant's job performance and potential. Employers are particularly interested in such traits as communication skills, organizational skills, people skills, ability to work with a team, ability to work independently, honesty, dependability, ambition, loyalty, and initiative. In describing these traits, be sure to back them up with evidence. One of the biggest weaknesses in letters of recommendation is that writers tend to make global, non-specific statements *(He was careful and accurate* versus *He completed eight financial statements monthly with about 99 percent accuracy)*. Employers prefer definite, task-related descriptions:

> As a training development specialist, Ms. Rosales demonstrated superior organizational and interpersonal skills. She started as a Specialist I, writing scripts for interactive video modules. After six months she was promoted to team leader. In that role she supervised five employees who wrote, produced, evaluated, revised, and installed 14 computer/videodisc training courses over a period of eighteen months.

Be especially careful to support any negative comments with verification (not *He was slower than other customer service reps* but instead *He answered 25 calls an hour, while most service reps average 40 calls an hour)*. In reporting deficiencies, be sure to describe behaviour *(Her last two reports were late and had to be rewritten by her supervisor)* rather than evaluate it *(She is unreliable and her reports are careless)*.

Evaluating in the Conclusion

In the final paragraph of a recommendation, you should offer an overall evaluation. Indicate how you would rank this person in relation to others in similar positions. Many managers add a statement indicating whether they would re-hire the applicant, given the chance. If you are strongly supportive, summarize the candidate's best qualities. In the closing you might also offer to answer questions by telephone. Such a statement, though, could suggest that the candidate has weak skills and that you will make damaging statements orally but not in print. Here's how our sample letter might close:

> Ms. Rosales is one of the most productive employees I have supervised. I would rank her in the top 10 percent of all the media specialists with whom I have worked. Were she to return to Waterloo, we would be pleased to re-hire her. If you need additional information, call me at (519) 555-3019.

General letters of recommendation, written when the candidate has no specific position in mind, often begin with the salutation TO PROSPECTIVE EMPLOYERS. More specific recommendations, to support applications to known positions, address an individual. When the addressee's name is unknown, consider using the simplified letter format, shown in Figure 6.5, which avoids a salutation.

Figure 6.5 illustrates a complete employment letter of recommendation and provides a summary of writing tips. After naming the applicant and the position sought, the letter describes the applicant's present duties. Instead of merely naming positive qualities (*He is personable, possesses superior people skills, works well with a team, is creative, and shows initiative*), these qualities are demonstrated with specific examples and details.

Writing Goodwill Messages

In expressing thanks, recognition, or sympathy, you should always do so promptly. These messages are easier to write when the situation is fresh in your mind. They also mean more to the recipient. And don't forget that a prompt thank-you note, often after an employment interview, carries the hidden message that you care and that you consider the event to be important. The writing plan for a goodwill message should include "the five Ss":

- **Selfless.** Focus the message solely on the receiver, not the sender. Don't talk about yourself; avoid such comments as *I remember when I ...*
- **Specific.** Personalize the message by mentioning specific incidents or characteristics of the receiver. Telling a colleague *Great speech* is much less effective than *Great story about RIM marketing in Washington*.
- **Sincere.** Let your words show genuine feelings. Rehearse in your mind how you would express the message to the receiver orally. Then transform that conversational language to your written message. Avoid pretentious, formal, or flowery language (*It gives me great pleasure to extend felicitations on the occasion of your firm's 20th anniversary*).
- **Spontaneous.** Keep the message fresh and enthusiastic. Avoid canned phrases (*Congratulations on your promotion, Good luck in the future*). Be direct and natural.
- **Short.** Try to accomplish your purpose in only a few sentences. What is most important is remembering an individual. Such caring does not require documentation or wordiness. Individuals and business organizations often use special note cards or stationery for brief messages.

The closing of a recommendation presents an overall ranking and may provide an offer to supply more information by telephone.

Messages that express thanks and recognition should be written promptly.

Goodwill messages are most effective when they are selfless, specific, sincere, spontaneous, and short.

FIGURE 6.5 Employment Recommendation Letter

Kelowna Health Sciences Centre

2404 Euclid Avenue   Kelowna, BC V1Y 4S3   Phone: 250 768-3434   www.khsc.bc.ca

March 2, 2009

Vice President, Human Resources
Healthcare Enterprises
1200 Riel Blvd. N.
Winnipeg, MB R3C 2X4

RECOMMENDATION OF LANCE W. OLIVER

At the request of Lance W. Oliver, I submit this confidential information in support of his application for the position of assistant director in your Human Resources Department. Mr. Oliver served under my supervision as assistant director of Patient Services at Kelowna Health Sciences Centre for the past three years.

Mr. Oliver was in charge of many customer service programs for our 770-bed hospital. A large part of his job involved monitoring and improving patient satisfaction. Because of his personable nature and superior people skills, he got along well with fellow employees, patients, and physicians. His personnel record includes a number of "spontaneous citations," given to employees caught in the act of performing excellent service.

Mr. Oliver works well with a team, as evidenced by his participation on the steering committee to develop our "Service First Every Day" program. His most significant contributions to our hospital, though, came as a result of his own creativity and initiative. He developed and implemented a patient hotline to hear complaints and resolve problems immediately. This enormously successful telephone service helped us improve our patient satisfaction rating from 7.2 last year to 8.4 this year. That's the highest rating in our history, and Mr. Oliver deserves a great deal of the credit.

We're sorry to lose Mr. Oliver, but we recognize his desire to advance his career. I am confident that his resourcefulness, intelligence, and enthusiasm will make him successful in your organization. I recommend him without reservation.

Mary E. O'Rourke

MARY E. O'ROURKE, DIRECTOR, Patient Services

MEO:rtd

Illustrates simplified letter style —

Identifies applicant and position

Supports general qualities with specific details

Summarizes main points and offers evaluation

Mentions confidentiality of message

Tells relationship to writer

Describes and interprets accomplishments

Tips for Writing Letters of Recommendation

- Identify the purpose and confidentiality of the message.
- Establish your relationship with the applicant.
- Describe the length of employment and job duties, if relevant.
- Provide specific examples of the applicant's professional and personal skills.
- Compare the applicant with others in his or her field.
- Offer an overall rating of the applicant.
- Summarize the significant attributes of the applicant.
- Draw a conclusion regarding the recommendation.

Thanks

Quick Check

Send letters of thanks to customers, hosts, and individuals who have performed kind acts.

When someone has done you a favour or when an action merits praise, you need to extend thanks or show appreciation. Letters of appreciation may be written to customers for their orders, to hosts and hostesses for their hospitality, to individuals for kindnesses performed, and especially to customers who complain. After all, complainers are actually providing you with "free consulting reports from the field." Complainers who feel that they were listened to often become the greatest promoters of an organization.[3]

Quick Check

Tell what the favour means using sincere, simple statements.

Because the receiver will be pleased to hear from you, you can open directly with the purpose of your message. The letter in Figure 6.6 thanks a speaker who addressed a group of marketing professionals. Although such thank-you notes can be quite short, this one is a little longer because the writer wants to

FIGURE 6.6 Thank-You for a Favour

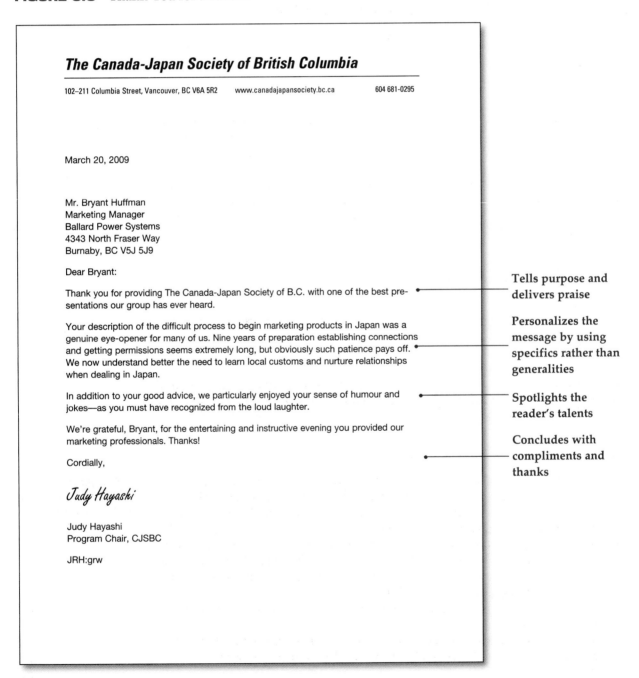

The Canada-Japan Society of British Columbia

102–211 Columbia Street, Vancouver, BC V6A 5R2   www.canadajapansociety.bc.ca   604 681-0295

March 20, 2009

Mr. Bryant Huffman
Marketing Manager
Ballard Power Systems
4343 North Fraser Way
Burnaby, BC V5J 5J9

Dear Bryant:

Thank you for providing The Canada-Japan Society of B.C. with one of the best presentations our group has ever heard. — *Tells purpose and delivers praise*

Your description of the difficult process to begin marketing products in Japan was a genuine eye-opener for many of us. Nine years of preparation establishing connections and getting permissions seems extremely long, but obviously such patience pays off. We now understand better the need to learn local customs and nurture relationships when dealing in Japan. — *Personalizes the message by using specifics rather than generalities*

In addition to your good advice, we particularly enjoyed your sense of humour and jokes—as you must have recognized from the loud laughter. — *Spotlights the reader's talents*

We're grateful, Bryant, for the entertaining and instructive evening you provided our marketing professionals. Thanks! — *Concludes with compliments and thanks*

Cordially,

Judy Hayashi

Judy Hayashi
Program Chair, CJSBC

JRH:grw

© 2001 Ted Goff

"It's a thank you letter from our office supply vendor. It used up all our fax paper."

© Ted Goff. www.tedgoff.com

lend importance to the receiver's efforts. Notice that every sentence relates to the receiver and offers enthusiastic praise. And, by using the receiver's name along with positive words, the writer makes the letter sound warm and conversational.

Written notes that show appreciation and express thanks are significant to their receivers. In expressing thanks, you generally write a short note on special notepaper or heavy card stock. The following message provides a model for expressing thanks:

> I sincerely appreciate your filling in for me last week when I was too ill to attend the planning committee meeting for the spring exhibition.

> Without your participation, much of my preparatory work would have been lost. It's comforting to know that competent and generous individuals like you are part of our team, Mark. Moreover, it's my very good fortune to be able to count you as a friend. I'm grateful to you.

Note: **Since a thank-you note as a follow-up to a job interview may be one of the most important messages you would send, please see p. 275 for interview follow-up suggestions.**

Note: **Since a thank-you note as a follow-up to a job interview may be one of the most important messages you would send, please see p. 275 for interview follow-up suggestions.**

Response

Should you respond when you receive a congratulatory note or a written pat on the back? By all means. These messages are attempts to connect personally; they are efforts to reach out, to form professional and/or personal bonds. Failing to respond to notes of congratulations and most other goodwill messages is like failing to say "You're welcome" when someone says "Thank you." Responding to such messages is simply the right thing to do. Avoid minimizing your achievements with comments that suggest you don't really deserve the praise or that the sender is exaggerating your good qualities.

Here's an example of an appropriate response to a congratulatory note:

> Thanks for your kind words regarding my award, and thanks, too, for sending me the newspaper clipping. I truly appreciate your thoughtfulness and warm wishes.

 Quick Check

Take the time to respond to any goodwill message you may receive.

In this chapter you learned to write letters that respond favourably to information requests and customer claims. You also learned to write effective responses to these letters. Finally, you learned how to write recommendation and goodwill messages. Almost all of these routine letters use the direct strategy. They open immediately with the main idea, followed by details and explanations. But not all letters will carry good news. Occasionally, you must deny requests and deliver bad news. In the next chapter, you will learn to use the indirect strategy in presenting negative news.

Critical Thinking

1. Should you include sales promotion information in a letter that responds to a claim letter from a customer? Why?
2. Why is it important to regain the confidence of a customer when you respond to a claim letter?
3. Is it appropriate for businesspeople to write goodwill messages expressing thanks or recognition to business acquaintances? Why or why not?

Chapter Review

4. Why do businesspeople still write letters when e-mail is so much faster?

5. What are the two most important positions in a letter?

6. List two ways that you could begin a request-for-information letter that asks many questions.

7. What three elements are appropriate in the closing of a request for information?

8. What is a claim letter? Give an original example.

9. What are the three goals when responding to a customer claim letter?

10. Why do some companies respond positively with nearly all claims?

11. What information should the opening in a letter of recommendation include?

12. The best goodwill messages include what five characteristics?

Writing Improvement Exercises

Letter Openers. Which of the following entries represents an effective direct opening?

13. a. Permit me to introduce myself. I am Alexa Alexander, and I represent TelCom. With the travel season approaching quickly, have you thought about upgrading your telecommunications system to meet the expected increased demand?
    b. Have you thought about upgrading your telecommunications system to meet the expected increased demand in the upcoming travel season?
14. a. Yes, the Princess Cruise Club is planning a 15-day Mediterranean cruise beginning October 20.
    b. This will acknowledge receipt of your letter of December 2 in which you ask about our Mediterranean cruise schedule.
15. a. Your letter of July 9 requesting a refund has been referred to me because Mr. Halvorson is away from the office.
    b. Your refund cheque for $175 is enclosed.
16. a. We sincerely appreciate your recent order for plywood wallboard panels.
    b. The plywood wallboard panels that you requested were shipped today by GoFast Express and should reach you by August 12.

Direct Openings. Revise the following openings so that they are more direct. Add information if necessary.

17. Hello! My name is Nalini Tomei, and I am the assistant manager of Body Trends, a fitness equipment centre in Montreal. My manager has asked me to inquire about the upright and semi-recumbent cycling machines that we saw advertised in the June issue of *Your Health* magazine. I have a number of questions.

18. Pursuant to your letter of January 15, I am writing in regard to your inquiry about whether we offer our European-style patio umbrella in colours. This unique umbrella is a very popular item and receives a number of inquiries. Its 3-metre canopy protects you when the sun is directly overhead, but it also swivels and tilts to virtually any angle for continuous sun protection all day long. It comes in two colours: off-white and forest green.

19. I am pleased to receive your inquiry regarding the possibility of my acting as a speaker at the final meeting of your business management club on April 30. The topic of online résumés interests me and is one on which I think I could impart helpful information to your members. Therefore, I am responding in the affirmative to your kind invitation.

Closing Paragraph. The following concluding paragraph to a claim letter response suffers from faults in strategy, tone, and emphasis. Revise and improve.

20. As a result of your complaint of June 2, we are sending a replacement shipment of laser printers by Excellent Express. Unfortunately, this shipment will not reach you until June 5. We hope that you will not allow this troubling incident and the resulting inconvenience and lost sales you suffered to jeopardize our future business relations. In the past we have been able to provide you with quality products and prompt service.

Activities and Cases

6.1 Information Request: Can I Do a Co-op Placement at Your Firm? You are a second-semester interior design student at Algonquin College in Ottawa. As part of your four-year applied degree program, you are required to complete a 20-week co-op term. Rather than using the services of the college's co-op office, which normally helps students find co-op positions, you've decided to find a position on your own. Being fluently bilingual, you decide you'd like to move to Montreal for your co-op term. You've narrowed down your search to one well-known design firm, Leroux + Smythe, and you have a lot of questions. For example, has the firm used co-op students before? If so, what typical tasks did the students perform? Another question you'd like answered is whether the firm can pay a salary or at least an honorarium for your 20-week placement. Also, you'd like to know what kinds of clients the firm has for its design services. Finally, you're interested in the amount of French you'll have to write and speak during your placement. You decide to write the company a letter requesting information.

1. What should you include in the opening of this information request?

2. What should the body of your letter contain?

3. How can your phrase your questions most effectively?

4. How should you close this letter?

Your Task. Using your own return address, write a personal business letter requesting information about a co-op placement to Claudette Garneau, Manager Human Resources, Leroux + Smythe, 1450 rue Maclennan, Montreal, Quebec H3X 2Y4.

Related website: Information on Algonquin College's program in interior design is available at http://extraweb.algonquincollege.com/ fulltime_programs/programOverview.aspx?id=6148X03FWO&. Information on co-op placements is available at http://www.algonquincollege.com/coop.

Web

6.2 Information Request: Meeting in Haines Junction at the Dalton Trail Lodge. Your company, Software Solutions, has just had an enormously successful two-year sales period. The CEO has asked you, as marketing manager, to arrange a special conference/retreat as a thank-you gift for all 20 engineers, product managers, and salespeople. She wants the company to host a four-day combination sales conference/vacation/retreat at some spectacular location. She suggests that you start by inquiring at the Dalton Trail Lodge in Haines Junction, Yukon. You check its website and get some good information. However, you decide to write a letter so that you can have a permanent, formal record of all the resorts you investigate. You estimate that your company will require about 20 rooms. You'll also need about three conference rooms for one and a half days. You want to know room rates, conference facilities, and outdoor activity possibilities for families. You have two times that would be possible: September 18–22 or October 4–8. You know that these are off-peak times, and you wonder if you can get a good room rate. What is the most economical way to get to Haines Junction from Software Solutions' headquarters in Prince George, B.C.? One evening you will want to host a banquet for about 140 people. The CEO wants a report from you by April 1.

Your Task. Write a well-organized information request to Dalton Trail Lodge, c/o Grayling Camp Enterprises, Box 5331, Haines Junction, Yukon Y0B 1L0.

Related website: http://www.daltontrail.com.

Web

6.3 Claim Letter: Undersized French Doors. As Julie Chen, owner of Smart Interiors, you recently completed a kitchen renovation that required made-to-order oak French doors. You ordered them by telephone on July 2 from Custom Wood, Inc. When they arrived on July 25, your carpenter gave you the bad news: the doors were cut too small. Instead of measuring a total of 3.23 square metres, the doors measured 3.13 square metres. In your carpenter's words, "No way can I stretch those doors to fit these openings!" You waited three weeks for these doors, and your clients wanted them installed immediately. Your carpenter said,

"I can rebuild this opening for you, but I'm going to have to charge you for my time." His extra charge came to $455.50.

You feel that the people at Custom Wood should reimburse you for this amount, since it was their error. In fact, you actually saved them money by not returning the doors. You decide to write to Custom Wood and enclose a copy of your carpenter's bill. You wonder whether you should also include a copy of Custom Wood's invoice, even though it does not show the exact door measurements. You are a good customer of Custom Wood, having used their quality doors and windows on many other jobs. You're confident that it will grant this claim.

Your Task. Write a claim letter to Jay Brandt, Marketing Manager, Custom Wood, Inc., 401 Main Street, Vancouver, B.C. V1L 2E6.

6.4 Claim Letter: The Real Thing. Have you ever bought a product that didn't work as promised? Have you been disappointed in service at a bank, video store, restaurant, or department store? Have you had ideas about how a company or organization could improve its image, service, or product? Remember that smart companies want to know what their customers think, especially if a product could be improved.

Your Task. Select a product or service that has disappointed you. Write a claim letter requesting a refund, replacement, explanation, or whatever seems reasonable. For claims about food products, be sure to include bar-code identification from the package, if possible. Your instructor may ask you to actually mail this letter. When you receive a response, share it with your class.

6.5 Information Response: Avoiding Employee Gifts That Are Re-gifted. A friend of yours, Megan Stowe, is an executive with a large insurance company. One day she says, "You know, I'm beginning to hate the holidays. Every year it gets harder to choose presents for our staff. Once we gave fruitcakes, which I thought were tasty and elegant, but it turns out a lot of our people re-gifted them to other people before Christmas." You say, "Well, what's your gift goal? Do you want to encourage your employees? Are you just saying thanks? Or do you want your gifts to act as a tool to keep good people on your team?" Megan responds, "I never thought of it that way. Our company doesn't really have a strategy for holiday gifts. It's just something we do every year. Do you have any ideas?"

As it turns out, you have a lot of ideas. You are an executive training coach, and you've developed a list of reasons talented people stay in organizations. Megan asks you to get in touch next week explaining some of your ideas. She thinks she will be able to use your services for this advice.

Your Task. Using your library databases and the Web, research articles and information on corporate gift giving. As a consultant, prepare a letter with a sampling of gift-giving ideas addressed to Megan Stowe, Vice President, Human Resources, London Life Insurance Company, 255 Dufferin Ave., London, Ontario N6A 4K1.

6.6 Information Response Request: Scannable Résumés. As part of your job at a Precision Shoes catalogue store, you have been asked to write a form letter to send to job applicants who inquire about your résumé-scanning techniques. The following poorly written response to an inquiry was pulled from the file.

Dear Mr. Chouxfleur:

Your letter of April 11 has been referred to me for a response. We are pleased to learn that you are considering employment here at Precision Shoes, and we look forward to receiving your résumé, should you decide to send same to us.

You ask if we scan incoming résumés. Yes, we certainly do. Actually, we use SmartTrack, an automated résumé-tracking system. SmartTrack is wonderful! You know, we sometimes receive as many as 30 résumés a day, and SmartTrack helps us sort, screen, filter, and separate the résumés. It also processes them, helps us organize them, and keeps a record of all of these résumés. Some of the résumés, however, cannot be scanned, so we have to return those—if we have time.

The reasons that résumés won't scan may surprise you. Some applicants send photocopies or faxed copies, and these can cause misreading, so don't do it. The best plan is to send an original copy. Some people use coloured paper. Big mistake! White paper (8 1/2 × 11-inch) printed on one side is the best bet. Another big problem is unusual type fonts, such as script or fancy gothic or antique fonts. They don't seem to realize that scanners do best with plain, readable fonts such as Helvetica, Arial, or Times New Roman in a 10-to-14-point size.

Other problems occur when applicants use graphics, shading, italics, underlining, horizontal and vertical lines, parentheses, and brackets. Scanners like plain résumés! Oh yes, staples can cause misreading. And folding of a résumé can also cause the scanners to foul up. To be safe, don't staple or fold, and be sure to use wide margins and a quality printer (no dot matrixes!!).

When a hiring manager within Precision Shoes decides to look for an appropriate candidate, he is told to submit keywords to describe the candidate he has in mind for his opening. We tell him (or sometimes her) to zero in on nouns and phrases that best describe what they want. Thus, my advice to you is to try to include those words that highlight your technical and professional areas of expertise.

If you do decide to submit your résumé to us, be sure you don't make any of the mistakes described herein that would cause the scanner to misread it.

Sincerely,

Your Task. As a team, discuss how this letter could be improved. Decide what information is necessary to send to potential job applicants. Search for additional information that might be helpful. Then, submit an improved version to your instructor. Although the form letter should be written so that it can be sent to anyone who inquires, address this one to Rene Chouxfleur, 629 Cathedral Street, Vancouver, B.C. V3L 2F3.

6.7 Claim Response: Undersized French Doors. As Jay Brandt, manager of Custom Wood, Inc., you have a problem. Your firm manufactures quality precut and custom-built doors and frames. You have received a letter dated August 3 from Julie Chen (described in Activity 6.3). Ms. Chen is an interior designer, and she complains that the oak French doors she recently ordered for a client were made to the wrong dimensions.

Although they were the wrong size, she kept the doors and had them installed because her clients were without outside doors. However, her carpenter charged an extra $455.50 to install them. She claims that you should reimburse her for this amount, since your company was responsible for the error. You check her July 2 order and find that the order was filled correctly. In a telephone order, Ms. Chen requested doors that measured 3.13 square metres and that's what you sent. Now she says that the doors should have been 3.23 square metres.

Your policy forbids refunds or returns on custom orders. Yet, you remember that around July 2 you had two new people working on the telephones taking orders. It's possible that they did not hear or record the measurements correctly. You don't know whether to grant this claim or refuse it. But you do know that you must look into the training of telephone order takers and be sure that they verify all custom-order measurements. It might also be a good idea to have your carpenters call a second time to confirm custom measurements.

Ms. Chen is a successful interior designer and has provided Custom Wood with a number of orders. You value her business but aren't sure how to respond. You'd like to remind her that Custom Wood has earned a reputation as a premier manufacturer of wood doors and frames. Your doors feature prime woods, meticulous craftsmanship, and award-winning designs. And the engineering is ingenious.

Your Task. Decide how to treat this claim and then respond to Julie Chen, Smart Interiors, 3282 Richmond Road, Vancouver, B.C. V5Y 2A8. You might mention that you have a new line of greenhouse windows that are available in three sizes. Include a brochure describing these windows.

6.8 Claim Response: The Real Thing. You are the receiver of the original claim letter in Activity 6.4. Decide how to respond to the original claim letter for the product or service that had disappointed the writer. Make up necessary address information or other details for an effective response to the claim letter.

6.9 Recommendation Letter: Telling It Like It Is. You are a business communication professor at a community college. Your students do a co-op semester from May to August as part of their program. In March, some of your students start asking for recommendation letters. This spring in particular there have been many such requests, and one is problematic. Jeff Brown, a second-year student, who has been in two of your classes, asks for a recommendation letter. He is applying for entry-level customer service jobs in the banking industry. You are Jeff's business communication professor, and you've got little to complain about. Jeff has been averaging an A in your two courses; his writing and speaking skills are superior; he thinks critically, solves problems in original ways, and is a good team player. Unfortunately, he's managed to demonstrate all of these strong skills and maintain his high average while continually skipping classes and arriving late for the classes he does show up to. You want to give Jeff a good recommendation, but you realize that in the work world, absenteeism and showing up late aren't treated as lightly as at college.

Your Task. Write a general letter of recommendation for Jeff Brown.

6.10 Thanks for the Favour: I Got a Job! You are Jeff Brown from Activity 6.9 above. It took you only three weeks of co-op job hunting and you landed a great job with Scotiabank. You'd like to thank your business communication professor for the recommendation letter s/he wrote you in early March. You're busy with end-of-term papers and final exams, though, so you put off writing the thank-you letter until late April, more than six weeks since the recommendation letter was written.

Your Task. Write a letter thanking your professor.

Grammar/Mechanics Review—6

The following sentences contain errors in grammar, verbs, articles, prepositions, punctuation, spelling, conjunctions, style, and usage. Below each sentence write a corrected version.

1. Every secretary's desk will be equipped with the most latest computer and printer.

2. We ordered new stationary about two months ago but I do not know where the order is at.

3. Any one of the managers are authorized to sign cheques, however for very large amounts, two signatures are required.

4. It seems like an application must be submitted before April 1st if you want to be considered for the job.

5. Both of the companies' sales now come from outside North America and the Companies expects to increase that number to 30 percent by 2010.

6. Some organizations worry that valuable company information may be stole over the internet.

7. Jennifer completed a college degree in accounting, then she took a position by Boeing corporation.

8. She had took many computer courses so Erin had numerous job opportunitys from which to chose from.

9. The number of students taking ESL courses are increasing every year.

10. A computer and softwear is use for word processing.

Document for Revision

The following fax has faults in grammar, punctuation, spelling, and wordiness. Use standard proofreading marks (see Appendix B) to correct the errors. When you finish, your instructor can show you the revised version of this fax.

January 20, 2009

FAX TRANSMISSION

Mr. Benjamin Spring

322 East Chapman St.

North Hatley, QC

Dear Mr. Spring:

SUBJECT: Your January 11 Letter Requesting Information About New All-Natural Products

We have recieved your letter of January 11 in which you inquire about our all-natural products. Needless to say, we are pleased to answer positive. Yes, our new line of freeze dried back packing foods meet the needs of older adults and young people as well. You asked number of questions, here are answers to you're questions about our products.

• Our all natural foods contains no preservatives sugars or additives. The inclosed list of dinner items tell what foods are fat-free.

• Large orders receive a discount when they're order direct with Outfitters, Inc. You can also purchase our products at Malibu Sports Center, 19605 Pacific Coast Highway Malibu CA, 90265.

• Outfitters, Inc., food products are made in our sanitary kitchens which I personally supervise. The foods are froze in a vacum process that retain freshness, texture and taste.

• Outfitters, Inc. food products is made from choice ingredients that combine good taste and quality.

• Our foods stay fresh and tasty up to 18 months.

I start Outfitters, Inc., two years ago after make custom meals for back packers who rejected typical camping food. What a pleasure it is now to share my meals with back packers like you.

I hope you'll enjoy enclosed sample meal. "Saturday Night on the Trail" is a four-coarse meal complete with fruit and elegant appetizers. Please call me at (213) 459-3342 to place an order or to ask questions about my backpacking food products.

Sincerely,

Retailer Cleans Up Its Act

For years companies have been aware of the corporate social responsibility (CSR) movement. This movement requires that companies attempt to "operate in an economically and environmentally sustainable manner, while acknowledging the interests of all ... stakeholders."[4] In a recent high-profile case in Saskatoon, a women's clothing retailer, Sensational, was picketed by local community members for "a lack of responsibility" around environmental issues. Apparently, in a bid to stand out from the competing stores in the area, the store wrapped all its customers' purchases in many layers of tissue paper, and then put this package inside a huge plastic carrying bag with the store's name printed on the side. Soon, local sidewalk garbage cans began to overflow with the unnecessary packaging offered by this retailer. A community group wrote a letter to the retailer asking that it reconsider its packaging practices, but never heard anything back. Five months later, the protest took place, and the media covered the protest. The retailer was unhappy, to say the least, about the negative media coverage.

Career Application

In class discussion, consider these questions:
- Why are companies increasingly interested in social responsibility?
- Should employees be encouraged to report suspected irresponsible behaviour of their employers?
- What are the advantages and disadvantages of detailed codes of social responsibility for companies?

Your Task

You are the assistant manager of Sensational. Your boss, the manager, asks you to research corporate social responsibility and draft a memo summary of the most important points by next week. She also implies that if she likes what she sees, she'll send it to head office in Vancouver. Using library databases and the Web, research corporate social responsibility and write a memo to your boss, Sherry Cardinal, as instructed.

Web

Related website: For a good example of a corporate social responsibility code, visit the Canadian Business for Social Responsibility (CBSR) website at http://www.cbsr.ca and look for GoodCompany Guidelines under Advisory Services.

Persuasive Messages

Persuading others to buy into your priorities is best done by looking for common interests and aligning collective goals. Provide support to those who are important to your success, and your agenda will become their agenda.[1]

Jose Ribau, *Director, Partner Negotiations & Management*
Sales Effectiveness, Branch Banking, CIBC

LEARNING OBJECTIVES

1. Use the indirect strategy to persuade.
2. Write convincing claim request letters.
3. Request favours persuasively.
4. Present new ideas in persuasive memos.
5. Analyze techniques used in sales letters.
6. Compose carefully planned sales letters.

 Quick Check

The ability to persuade is a primary factor in personal and business success.

Persuasion is the ability to make people think or do what you would like them to think or do. Developing the ability to persuade is a key factor in the success you achieve in your business messages, in your career, and in your interpersonal relations. As Jose Ribau states, persuasive individuals are highly valued in today's successful organizations. He suggests that everyone make persuasive communication skills a priority. Persuasive individuals become decision makers, managers, executives, and entrepreneurs because their ideas generally succeed. This chapter will examine techniques for presenting ideas persuasively.

Using the Indirect Pattern in Persuasive Requests

Persuasion is necessary when you expect opposition (resistance) or when ideas require preparation before they can be presented effectively. For example, asking for a favour means that you want someone to do something for nothing—or for very little. Common examples are requests for a donation of time, money, energy, a name, resources, talent, skills, or expertise. Everyone needs to ask a favour now and then. Small favours, such as asking a coworker to lock up the office for you on Friday, can be direct. Little resistance is expected. Larger favours, though, require careful planning and an indirect strategy. A busy executive is asked to serve on a committee to help disadvantaged children. A florist is asked to donate table arrangements for a charity fundraiser. A well-known author is asked to speak before a local library group. In each instance, persuasion is necessary to overcome natural resistance.

The letters in Figure 7.1 (p. 138) show two versions of a favour request. Joanne North works for an organization without funds. She hopes to persuade a well-known authority to speak before its regional conference. Such a request surely requires indirectness and persuasion, but the ineffective version begins with a direct appeal. Even worse, the reader is given an opportunity to refuse the request before the writer has a chance to present reasons for accepting. Moreover, this letter fails to convince the reader that she has anything to gain by speaking to this group. Finally, the closing suggests no specific action to help her accept, should she want to.

A favour request will probably fail if the writer does not consider its effect on the reader. In the more effective version, notice how the writer applies the indirect strategy. The opening gains the reader's attention and makes her want to read more regarding the reaction to her article. By showing how Dr. Kasdorf's interests are related to the organization's, the writer builds interest before presenting the request. The request is then followed by language that reduces resistance, showing Dr. Kasdorf how she will benefit from accepting this invitation. This successful letter concludes with a specific action closing.

A writing plan for a persuasive request is shown below:

 ## Writing Plan for a Persuasive Request

- **Gain attention** in the opening
- **Build interest** in the body
- **Reduce resistance** in the body
- **Motivate action** in the closing

The Components of an Indirect Persuasive Request

The indirect pattern described above contains separate strategies. However, in a successful persuasive message, all four come together as a unified whole. Note that the order of the four strategies is not set in stone; not every persuasive situation will require you to build interest before you reduce resistance, for example. Nevertheless, the majority of persuasive messages begin by gaining attention and end by motivating action.

Gain Attention. In the opening of the message, which is usually brief, you gain the reader's attention by one of the following strategies: describing a problem, making an unexpected statement, mentioning a reader benefit, paying the reader a compliment, or posing a stimulating question. For example, in the persuasive request letter sent by the Canadian Association of Investment Managers to a business professor to ask him to speak at a meeting, the writer might begin by paying the professor a compliment, such as *A number of our association's members have used your services in the past and praise your professionalism.*

FIGURE 7.1 Persuasive Favour Request

Before

Provides easy excuse for refusal

Sounds writer-centred instead of reader-centred

Closes negatively and fails to tell how to respond

Dear Dr. Kasdorf:

Although your research, teaching, and consulting must keep you extremely busy, we hope that your schedule will allow you to be the featured speaker at the Canadian Association of investment Managers' regional conference in Vancouver on March 23.

We are particularly interested in the article that appeared in the *Harvard Business Review*. A number of our members indicated that your topic, "Every Woman's Guide to Financial Independence," is something we should learn more about.

We have no funds to pay you, but we would like to invite you and your spouse to be our guests at the banquet following the day's sessions. We hope that you will be able to speak before our group.

Sincerely,

After

Canadian Association of Investment Managers
196 West 4th Avenue
Vancouver, BC V6R 3T4
(604) 543-8922

January 5, 2009

Professor Beverly J. Kasdorf
Thompson Rivers University
Box 3010, 900 McGill Road
Kamloops, BC V2C 5N3

Dear Dr. Kasdorf:

A number of our Association's members have used your services in the past and praise your professionalism. Your recent article on Every Woman's Guide to Financial Independence in the *Harvard Business Review* ignited a lively discussion at the last meeting of the Vancouver chapter of the Canadian Association of Investment Managers.

Many of the managers in our group are noticing a greater increase in women investors. A large majority of women want to move from "do-it-yourself" investing to working with a financial advisor or money manager to help with their financial plans. Our members are very interested in your direct, easy-to understand approach to investment strategies for women.

The members of our association have asked me to invite you to be the featured speaker March 23, when we hold our annual conference in Vancouver. About 150 financial planning specialists will attend the all-day conference at the Parkland Hotel. We would like you to speak at 2 p.m. on the topic of "Every Woman's Guide to Financial Independence."

Although an honorarium is not provided, we can offer you an opportunity to help investment managers apply your theories in solving some of their problems. You will also meet managers who might be able to supply you with data for future research into women's financial issues. In addition, the conference includes two other sessions and a banquet, to which you and a guest are invited.

Please call me at (604) 543-8922 to allow me to add your name to the program as the featured speaker before the Canadian Association of Investment Managers on March 23.

Respectfully,

Joanne North

Joanne North
Executive Assistant

Gains attention of reader by appealing to her interests

Builds interest by persuading reader that her expertise is valued

Makes direct request

Reduces resistance by softening negative aspects of request with reader benefits

Motivates specific action confidently

Build Interest. The body of the message should keep the reader's attention and persuade him or her that the request is reasonable. This section is often the longest part of the message. It includes strategies such as the use of facts and statistics, expert opinion, listing of direct benefits to the receiver, examples and specific details, as well as indirect benefits to the receiver. In the Association of Investment Managers letter, for example, the writer might have begun building interest by stating, *You may be interested to know that while 5 of our 25 members have used your services before, the other 20 members are either without a financial planner or else considering changing planners.*

Reduce Resistance. An important part of a persuasive message's body, yet one that is often left out by unsophisticated writers, is the writer putting himself or herself in the receiver's shoes and asking what kinds of problems the receiver might have with the request. For example, the association's letter writer may guess that the financial planner is a busy person with many engagements. This is her most likely reason to say "no." You should anticipate this resistance, mention it, then respond to it with a benefit. For example, the letter may read: *Even though we understand you have a busy schedule of teaching as well as daily meetings with clients, we believe an hour spent talking to us about trends in retirement planning could lead to a new client base.*

Motivate Action. Finally, no persuasive message is complete without the sender closing by telling the receiver exactly what he or she wants, and when he or she wants it. The trick in this section is to sound self-assured but not aggressive, to motivate the reader to say yes. In essence, a persuasive message should end with a specific request that is confident but not pushy. In the association letter example, the letter might end, *The club meets at 1:00 pm on the last Friday of each month, in this case the 31st. Lunch is included. We would be grateful if you responded by the end of next week confirming your acceptance of our invitation. Please call Mr. David Taylor at (613) 686-3704.*

Persuasive Claims and Complaint Messages

Let's say you buy a new car, and the transmission repeatedly requires servicing. When you finally get tired of taking it in for repair, you decide to write to the car manufacturer's district office asking that the company install a new transmission in your car. You know that your request will be resisted. You must convince the manufacturer that replacement, not repair, is needed. Routine claim letters, such as those you wrote in Chapter 6, are straightforward and direct. Persuasive claims, on the other hand, are generally more effective when they are indirect.

Use persuasion when you must change attitudes or produce action.

The organization of an effective persuasive claim or complaint message centres on the closing and the persuasion. First, decide what action you want taken to satisfy the claim. Then, decide how you can prove the worth of your claim. Plan carefully the line of reasoning you will follow in convincing the reader to take the action you request. If the claim is addressed to a business, the most effective appeals are generally to the organization's pride in its products and its services. Refer to its reputation for integrity and your confidence in it. Show why your claim is valid and why the company will be doing the right thing in granting it. Most organizations are sincere in their efforts to produce quality products that gain consumer respect.

The most successful appeals are to a company's pride in its products and services.

Although claim letters are often complaint letters, try not to be angry. Anger and emotional threats toward an organization do little to achieve the goal of a claim letter. Claims are usually referred to a customer service department. The representative answering the claim probably had nothing to do with the design,

✓ *Quick Check*

Claim letters should avoid negative and emotional words and should not attempt to lay blame.

production, delivery, or servicing of the product or service. An abusive letter may serve only to offend, thus making it hard for the representative to evaluate the claim rationally.

A writing plan for an indirect claim follows the pattern below.

Writing Plan for a Persuasive Request

- **Gain attention** in the opening by paying the receiver a compliment.
- **Build interest** in the body by explaining and justifying the claim or complaint with convincing reasons and without anger.
- **Reduce resistance** in the body by gently suggesting the responsibility of the receiver. Appeal to the receiver's sense of fairness or desire for customer satisfaction.
- **Motivate action** in the closing by explaining exactly what action you want taken and when.

Observe how the claim letter shown in Figure 7.2 illustrates the above suggestions. When AMS Limitée bought several new enhanced telephones, it discovered that they would not work when the office's fluorescent lights were on. The company's attempt to return the telephones had been refused by the retailer. Notice that the opening statement gains attention with a compliment about the product. The second paragraph builds interest by describing the problem without anger or harsh words. The letter reduces resistance by suggesting the responsibility of the manufacturer while stressing the disappointment of the writer. The final paragraph motivates action by stating exactly what action should be taken.

Persuasive Suggestions

✓ *Quick Check*

Presenting reasons first avoids early rejection of a new idea.

Within an organization the indirect strategy is useful when persuasion is needed in presenting new ideas to management or to colleagues. It's also useful in requesting action from employees and in getting acceptance for new or changed procedures. Whenever you expect resistance, use solid reasoning before the main idea. This foundation prevents the idea from being rejected too early.

You should expect new ideas to meet with resistance. It doesn't matter whether the ideas are moving downward (as in orders from management), upward (as in suggestions to management), or laterally (between coworkers). Resistance to change is natural. When asked to perform differently or to try something new, some individuals resist because they fear failure. Others resist because they feel threatened—the proposed changes may affect their status or threaten their security. Some people resist new ideas because they don't understand a proposed idea or are cautious of the person making the proposal.

Whatever the motivation, resistance to new ideas and change in procedures should be expected. You can prepare for this resistance by expecting objections, offering counterarguments, and emphasizing benefits. Don't assume that the advantages of a new idea are obvious and therefore may go unmentioned. Use concrete examples and familiar illustrations in presenting arguments.

In the e-mail shown in Figure 7.3 (p. 142), Megan Wong, supervisor, argues for the purchase of a new scanner and software. She expects the director to resist this request because the budget is already overextended. Megan's memo follows the writing plan for a persuasive request. It gains attention by describing a costly

FIGURE 7.2 Persuasive Claim

AMS *Limitée*

309 rue du la Morenie, Sherbrooke, Quebec J1H 4E6 (819) 690-3500

November 23, 2009

Customer Service
D. Gerard, Inc.
594 avenue Montmorency
Montreal, Quebec H2L 2E9

SUBJECT: CODE-A-PHONE MODEL 100S •⟶ Uses simplified letter style when name of receiver is unknown

Your Code-A-Phone Model 100S answering unit came well recommended. We liked •⟶ Gains attention with compliment
our neighbour's unit so much that we purchased 30 for different departments in our
business.

After the 30 machines were unpacked and installed, we discovered a problem. •⟶ Builds interest by describing problem calmly
Apparently our office fluorescent lighting interferes with the electronics in these units.
When the lights are on, heavy static interrupts every telephone call. When the lights are
off, the static disappears.

We can't replace the fluorescent lights; thus we tried to return the Code-A-Phones to
the place of purchase (Chauffage Saint-Laurent, 2560 Taschereau Boulevard, Brossard,
QC J4W 3J8). A salesperson inspected the units and said they could not be returned
since they were not defective and they had been used.

Because the descriptive literature and instructions for the Code-A-Phones say nothing •⟶ Reduces resistance by gently suggesting responsibility
about avoiding use in rooms with fluorescent lighting, we expected no trouble. We
were quite disappointed that this well-engineered machine—with its time/date stamp,
room monitor, and auto-dial features—failed to perform as we hoped it would. •⟶ Stresses disappointment

If you have a model with similar features that would work in our offices, give me a call. •⟶ Motivates action by stating what steps to take
Otherwise, please authorize the return of these units and refund the purchase price of
$1038 (see enclosed invoice). We're confident that a manufacturer with your reputation
for excellent products and service will want to resolve this matter quickly. •⟶ Appeals to company's desire to maintain good reputation

Reva A. Barat

Reva A. Barat, PRESIDENT

RAB:jkb
Enclosure

Tips for Making Claims

- Begin with a compliment, point of agreement, statement of the problem, or brief review of action you have taken to resolve the problem.
- Provide specific details about the problem.
- Prove that your claim is valid; explain why the receiver is responsible.
- Enclose document copies supporting your claim.
- Appeal to the receiver's fairness, ethical and legal responsibilities, and desire for customer satisfaction.
- Describe your feelings and your disappointment.
- Avoid sounding angry, emotional, or irrational.
- Close by telling exactly what you want done.

FIGURE 7.3 **Persuasive Suggestion**

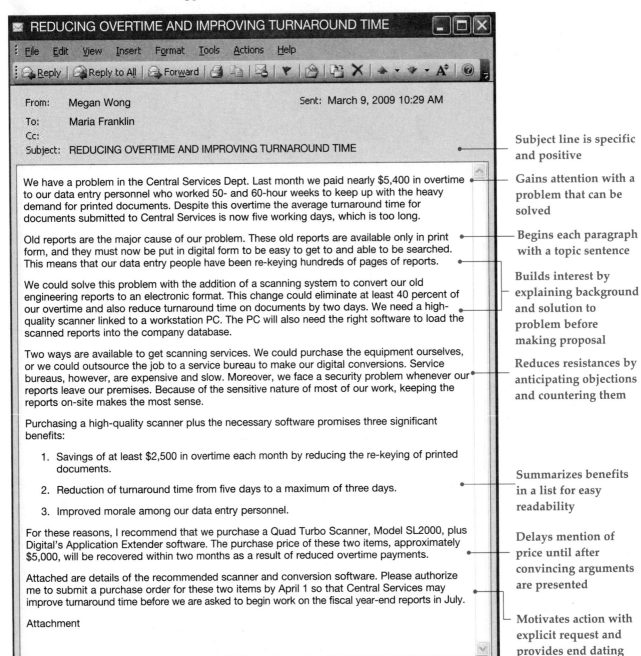

REDUCING OVERTIME AND IMPROVING TURNAROUND TIME

File   Edit   View   Insert   Format   Tools   Actions   Help

Reply   Reply to All   Forward

From: Megan Wong   Sent: March 9, 2009 10:29 AM

To: Maria Franklin

Cc:

Subject: REDUCING OVERTIME AND IMPROVING TURNAROUND TIME

We have a problem in the Central Services Dept. Last month we paid nearly $5,400 in overtime to our data entry personnel who worked 50- and 60-hour weeks to keep up with the heavy demand for printed documents. Despite this overtime the average turnaround time for documents submitted to Central Services is now five working days, which is too long.

Old reports are the major cause of our problem. These old reports are available only in print form, and they must now be put in digital form to be easy to get to and able to be searched. This means that our data entry people have been re-keying hundreds of pages of reports.

We could solve this problem with the addition of a scanning system to convert our old engineering reports to an electronic format. This change could eliminate at least 40 percent of our overtime and also reduce turnaround time on documents by two days. We need a high-quality scanner linked to a workstation PC. The PC will also need the right software to load the scanned reports into the company database.

Two ways are available to get scanning services. We could purchase the equipment ourselves, or we could outsource the job to a service bureau to make our digital conversions. Service bureaus, however, are expensive and slow. Moreover, we face a security problem whenever our reports leave our premises. Because of the sensitive nature of most of our work, keeping the reports on-site makes the most sense.

Purchasing a high-quality scanner plus the necessary software promises three significant benefits:

1. Savings of at least $2,500 in overtime each month by reducing the re-keying of printed documents.

2. Reduction of turnaround time from five days to a maximum of three days.

3. Improved morale among our data entry personnel.

For these reasons, I recommend that we purchase a Quad Turbo Scanner, Model SL2000, plus Digital's Application Extender software. The purchase price of these two items, approximately $5,000, will be recovered within two months as a result of reduced overtime payments.

Attached are details of the recommended scanner and conversion software. Please authorize me to submit a purchase order for these two items by April 1 so that Central Services may improve turnaround time before we are asked to begin work on the fiscal year-end reports in July.

Attachment

Subject line is specific and positive

Gains attention with a problem that can be solved

Begins each paragraph with a topic sentence

Builds interest by explaining background and solution to problem before making proposal

Reduces resistances by anticipating objections and countering them

Summarizes benefits in a list for easy readability

Delays mention of price until after convincing arguments are presented

Motivates action with explicit request and provides end dating

problem in which Megan knows the reader is interested. To convince the director of the need for these purchases, Megan builds interest by explaining the background and providing a possible solution to the problem. Because Megan knows that the director values short prose, she tries to focus on the main points. To further improve readability, Megan begins every paragraph with a topic sentence.

After reviewing background information and the cause of the problem, Megan brings up the request for a new scanning system. She reduces resistance by discussing it in terms of benefits to the reader and the company (eliminating 40 percent of overtime and reducing turnaround time). Megan also anticipates objections (outsourcing as an alternative) but counters this possible objection by pointing out that outsourcing is expensive, slow, and insecure. In the closing, Megan motivates action by asking for authorization to go ahead and by providing support documentation to speed the request. She also includes end-dating, which prompts the director to act by a certain date.

Sales Letters

Sales letters are usually part of direct-mail marketing efforts that many people consider "junk mail." However, advertising in Canada is growing at an annual rate of 5.5 percent, while direct marketing is growing at an annual rate of 8.8 percent. Direct marketing is an $8.48 billion industry.[2] This includes all sales letters, packets, brochures, and catalogues sent directly to consumers.

The professionals who specialize in direct-mail marketing have made a science of analyzing a market, developing an appropriate mailing list, studying the product, preparing a comprehensive presentation that appeals to the needs of the target audience, and motivating the reader to act. This carefully orchestrated presentation typically concludes with a sales letter accompanied by a brochure, a sales list, illustrations of the product, testimonials, and so forth.

We are most concerned here with the sales letter: its strategy, organization, and appeals. You'll want to learn the secrets of these messages for many reasons. Although the sales letters of large organizations are usually written by professional copywriters, many smaller companies cannot afford such specialized services. Entrepreneurs and employees of smaller businesses may be called on to write their own sales messages. For example, one recent graduate started a graphic design firm and immediately had to write a convincing letter offering her services. Another graduate went to work for a small company that installs security systems. Because of his recent diploma (other employees were unsure of their skills), he was asked to draft a sales letter outlining specific benefits for residential customers.

From a broader perspective, nearly every letter we write is a form of sales. We sell our ideas, our organizations, and ourselves. Learning the techniques of sales writing will help you be more effective in any communication that requires persuasion and promotion. Moreover, recognizing the techniques of selling will enable you to respond to such techniques more rationally. You will be a better-educated consumer of ideas, products, and services if you understand how sales appeals are made.

Analyzing the Product and the Reader

Before writing a sales letter, it's wise to study the product and the target audience so that you can emphasize features with reader appeal.

Know Your Product. To sell a product effectively, learn as much as possible about how it was created, including its design, its parts, and the process of production and distribution. Study its performance, including ease of use, efficiency, durability, and applications. Consider warranties, service, price, and special appeals. Know your own product but also that of your competitor. In this way, you can emphasize your product's strengths against the competitor's products' weaknesses.

Know the Culture. If a product is being developed and marketed for consumers in different cultures, learn as much as possible about the targeted cultures. Although companies would like to use the same products and advertising campaigns as they push into global markets, most find that using a single approach for every local market falls flat. They may think globally, but they must execute locally. In producing and selling frozen yogurt to the world, Canadian company Yogen Früz makes learning about the host country's culture a priority. For example, at the grand opening of its first franchise in Guatemala, a country with a strong religious tradition, the company ensured that a priest was on hand to bless the proceedings.[3]

Knowing the audience and adapting your message to it is important for any communication. But it's especially true for sales letters. That's why the most effective sales letters are sent to targeted audiences. Mailing lists for selected groups can be purchased or compiled. For example, the manufacturer of computer supplies would find an appropriate audience for its products in the mailing list of subscribers to a computer magazine.

Target the Audience. By using a selected mailing list, a sales letter writer is able to make certain assumptions about the readers. Readers may be expected to have similar interests, abilities, needs, income, and so forth. The sales letter can be adapted to appeal directly to this selected group. In working with a less specific audience, the letter writer can make only general assumptions and must use a catchall approach, hoping to find some appeal that motivates the reader.

The following writing plan for a sales letter attempts to overcome expected reader resistance by creating a desire for the product and by motivating the reader to act.

Writing Plan for a Sales Letter

- **Gain attention** in the opening by standing out from the competition.
- **Build interest** in the body by emphasizing a central selling point and appealing to the reader's needs.
- **Reduce resistance** in the body by creating a desire for the product and introducing price strategically.

Gaining the Reader's Attention by Standing Out from the Competition

Gaining the attention of the reader is essential in unsolicited or uninvited sales letters. In solicited sales letters, individuals have requested information; thus, attention-getting devices are less important.

Stimulating messages or unusual formats may be used to attract attention in unsolicited sales letters. These devices may be found within the body of a letter or in place of the inside address.

Offer   Your free calculator is just the beginning!
            Do you want to look ten years younger?

Product feature	Your vacations—this year and in the future—can be more rewarding thanks to an exciting new book from *Canadian Geographic*.
Inside-address opening	We Wonder, Mrs. Crain, If You Would Like to Know How to Retire in Style with a Good Investment Plan
Startling statement	Extinction is forever. That's why we need your help in preserving many of the world's endangered species.
Story	On a beautiful late spring afternoon, 25 years ago, two young men graduated from the same college. They were very much alike, these two young men ... Recently, these men returned to their college for their 25th reunion. They were still very much alike ... But there was a difference. One of the men was manager of a small department of [a manufacturing company]. The other was its president.

Other effective openings include a bargain, a proverb, a solution to a problem, a quotation from a famous person, an anecdote, and a question.

Building Interest by Appealing to the Reader and Emphasizing Central Selling Points

Persuasive appeals generally fall into two broad groups: emotional appeals and rational appeals. Emotional appeals are those associated with the senses; they include how we feel, see, taste, smell, and hear. Strategies that arouse anger, fear, pride, love, and satisfaction are emotional.

Quick Check

Emotional appeals relate to the senses; rational appeals relate to reasoning and intellect.

Rational strategies are those associated with reason and intellect; they appeal to the mind. Rational appeals include references to making money, saving money, increasing efficiency, and making the best use of resources. Generally, use rational appeals when a product is expensive, long lasting, or important to health and security. Use emotional appeals when a product is inexpensive, short lived, or nonessential.

Banks selling chequing and savings services frequently use rational appeals. They emphasize saving money in chequing fees, earning interest on accounts, receiving free personalized cheques, and saving time in opening the account. In contrast, a travel agency selling a student tour to Mexico uses an emotional strategy by describing the "sun, fun, and partying" to be enjoyed. Many successful selling campaigns combine appeals, emphasizing perhaps a rational appeal while also including an emotional appeal in a subordinated position.

Although a product may have a number of features, concentrate on just one or two of those features. Don't confuse the reader with too much information. Analyze the reader's needs and tailor your appeal directly to the reader. The letter selling a student tour to Mexico emphasized two points:

Quick Check

In sales letters, build interest by developing one or two central selling points and stressing them.

1. We see to it that you have a great time. Let's face it. By the end of the term, you've earned your vacation. The books and jobs and stress can all be shelved for a while.

2. We keep our trips affordable. Mazatlan 1A is again the lowest-priced adventure trip offered in Canada.

The writer analyzed the student audience and elected to concentrate on two appeals: (1) an emotional appeal to the senses (having a good time) and (2) a rational appeal to saving money (paying a low price).

Reducing Resistance by Creating a Desire for the Product and Introducing Price Strategically

In convincing readers to purchase a product or service, you may use a number of techniques:

✔ **Quick Check**

Reduce resistance by creating a desire for a product through reader benefit, concrete and objective language, product confidence, or testimonials.

- **Reader benefit.** Discuss product features from the reader's point of view. Show how the reader will benefit from the product:

  You'll be able to extend your summer swim season by using our new solar pool cover.

- **Concrete language.** Use concrete words instead of general or abstract language:

  Our Mexican tour provides more than just a party. Maybe you've never set eyes on a giant saguaro cactus ... or parasailed high above the Pacific Ocean ... or watched a majestic golden sunset from your own private island.

- **Objective language.** Avoid language that sounds unreasonable. Overstatements using words like *fantastic, without fail, foolproof, amazing, astounding,* and so forth do not ring true. Overblown language and preposterous claims may cause readers to reject the entire sales message.

- **Product confidence.** Build confidence in your product or service by assuring customer satisfaction. You can do this by offering a free trial, money-back guarantee, free sample, or warranty. Another way to build confidence is to associate your product with respected references or authorities:

  Our concept of economical group travel has been accepted and sponsored by three major airlines. In addition, our program has been featured in *Maclean's*, *The Toronto Star*, *The Globe and Mail*, and the *National Post*.

- **Testimonials.** The statements of satisfied customers are effective in creating a desire for the product or service:

  A student returning from one of our cruises last year said, "I've just been to paradise."

✔ **Quick Check**

Introduce price early if it is a sales feature; otherwise, delay mentioning it.

If product price is a significant sales feature, use it early in your sales letter. Otherwise, don't mention price until after you have created the reader's desire for the product. Some sales letters include no mention of price; instead, an enclosed order form shows the price. Other techniques for de-emphasizing price include the following:

- **Show the price in small units.** For instance, instead of stating the total cost of a year's subscription, state the magazine's price when calculated per issue. Or describe insurance premiums by their cost per day.

- **Show how the reader is saving money by purchasing the product.** In selling solar heating units, for example, explain how much the reader will save on heating bills.

- **Compare your prices with those of competitors.** Describe the savings to be realized when your product is purchased.

- **Make your price a bargain.** For instance, point out that the special introductory offer is one-third off the regular price. Or say that the price includes a special discount if the reader acts immediately.

- **Associate the price with reader benefits.** Note, for example, that for as little as $3 a month, you'll enjoy emergency road and towing protection, emergency trip-interruption protection, and nine other benefits.

Notice in Figure 7.4 (p. 148) how price is directly linked to customer benefits. New Western Bank opens its promotional letter by telling the reader how much money can be saved on its chequing account. This central selling feature is then emphasized throughout the letter, although other selling points are also mentioned.

Motivating Action by Stimulating the Reader to Buy

The closing of a sales letter has one very important goal: stimulating the reader to act. A number of techniques help motivate action:

- **Make the action clear.** Use specific language to tell exactly what is to be done:

   Submit your request at our website.

   Call this toll-free number.

   Send the enclosed reservation card along with your cheque.

- **Make the action easy.** Highlight the simple steps the reader needs to take:

   Just fill in your credit card number and indicate the amount of your gift. Drop the postage-paid form in the mail, and we'll handle the details.

- **Provide an offer.** Encourage the reader to act while low prices remain in effect. Offer a gift or a rebate for action:

   Now is a great time to join the Can-West Travel Club. By joining now, you'll receive a sleek and sophisticated cell phone case.

✔ **Quick Check**

Motivate action in a sales letter by telling the reader exactly what to do.

FIGURE 7.4 Sales Letter

New Western Bank

3200 Portage Avenue, Winnipeg, MB R3H 8L9

Dianne Ladd
AVP & Manager
Personal Financial Centre

April 3, 2009

Mr. Chen Xian
1045 Cuthbert Drive
Winnipeg, MB R3L 2H3

Dear Mr. Xian:

Gains attention with appealing offer

Why pay $50, $100, or even $150 a year in chequing account service charges when New Western has the right price for chequing—FREE!

Builds interest by emphasizing central selling point but also introduces other services

At New Western Bank we want your business. That's why we're offering "Totally Free Chequing." Compare the cost of your present chequing account. We know you'll like the difference. We also have six other personalized chequing plans, one of which is certain to be right for you.

Focuses on rational appeals

In addition to the best price on chequing accounts, we provide a variety of investment opportunities and two convenient credit-line programs. Once you qualify, you can use your credit line at any time without applying for a new loan each time you need money. With one of our credit-line programs, you can write a cheque for just about anything, including a vacation, home improvements, major purchases, unexpected bills, or investment opportunities.

Suggests specific reader benefits

If you have not yet heard about New Western Bank, you'll find that we have eight convenient locations to serve you.

Reduces resistance by making it easy for reader to open account

Check out the details of our services described in the enclosed pamphlets or at our website at www.newwesternbank.com. Then check us out by stopping in to open your free chequing account at one of our eight convenient locations. You can also open your account by simply filling out the enclosed postage-paid card and returning it to us.

Motivates action by offering encouragement before given date

If you open your New Western chequing account before June 15, we'll give you 200 free cheques and we'll buy back any unused cheques you have from your present chequing account. Act now to start saving money. We look forward to serving you.

Sincerely,

Dianne Ladd

Dianne Ladd
Accounts Vice-President

DL:egh
Enclosures

- **Limit the offer.** Set a specific date by which the reader must act in order to receive a gift, a rebate, benefits, low prices, or a special offer:

  Act quickly, because I'm authorized to make this special price on solar greenhouses available only until May 1.

- **Make payment easy.** Encourage the reader to send a credit card number or to return a card and be billed later.

Online Sales Letters

As consumers become more comfortable with online shopping, they will be receiving more e-mail sales letters, such as that shown in Figure 7.5 (p. 150). Chapters.indigo.ca started its online bookselling several years ago and has seen business expand significantly. To promote its online business, Chapters wrote a short e-mail message to current customers announcing its Rewards Program benefits. After defining the central selling feature, the letter presents a low-key sales pitch for Chapters' expanded product offerings.

This message illustrates some important lessons for writers of online sales messages:

✔ *Quick Check*

Consumers can expect to receive more online sales letters as e-business grows.

- **Be selective.** Send messages only to targeted, preselected customers. E-mail users detest "spam" (unsolicited sales and other messages). However, receivers are surprisingly receptive to offers specifically for them. Remember that today's customer is somebody—not anybody.
- **Make the recipient feel special.** Notice that the Chapters message begins by placing the receiver in a group of customers who "will never pay full price again." Although this message may have been seen by thousands of customers, they felt that they could become part of a special group of customers.
- **Keep the message short and conversational.** The Chapters message contains only a few short paragraphs. Because on-screen text is taxing to read, be brief. Also, try to make the message sound like casual conversation.
- **Focus on one or two central selling points.** In the Chapters sales message, the only real pitch is how easy it is to save at Chapters.
- **Provide means for being removed from mailing list.** It's polite and good business to include a statement that tells receivers how to be removed from the sender's mailing database.
- **Project sincerity.** Sending a simple, low-key message and encouraging feedback help establish a tone of sincerity in the message.

FIGURE 7.5　Online Sales Message

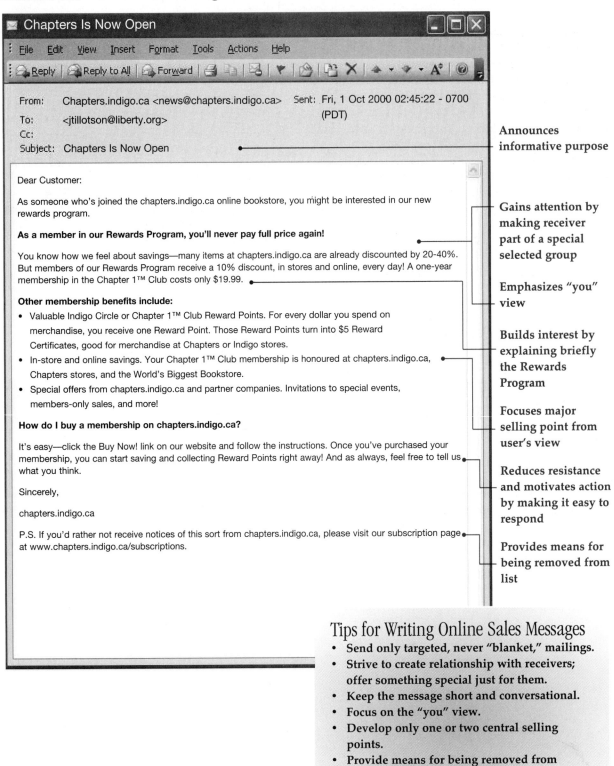

Chapters Is Now Open

File　Edit　View　Insert　Format　Tools　Actions　Help

Reply　| Reply to All　| Forward

From:　Chapters.indigo.ca <news@chapters.indigo.ca>　Sent: Fri, 1 Oct 2000 02:45:22 - 0700 (PDT)
To:　<jtillotson@liberty.org>
Cc:
Subject:　Chapters Is Now Open ●——————————————— **Announces informative purpose**

Dear Customer:

As someone who's joined the chapters.indigo.ca online bookstore, you might be interested in our new rewards program.　**Gains attention by making receiver part of a special selected group**

As a member in our Rewards Program, you'll never pay full price again!　**Emphasizes "you" view**

You know how we feel about savings—many items at chapters.indigo.ca are already discounted by 20-40%. But members of our Rewards Program receive a 10% discount, in stores and online, every day! A one-year membership in the Chapter 1™ Club costs only $19.99. ●　**Builds interest by explaining briefly the Rewards Program**

Other membership benefits include:

- Valuable Indigo Circle or Chapter 1™ Club Reward Points. For every dollar you spend on merchandise, you receive one Reward Point. Those Reward Points turn into $5 Reward Certificates, good for merchandise at Chapters or Indigo stores.
- In-store and online savings. Your Chapter 1™ Club membership is honoured at chapters.indigo.ca, Chapters stores, and the World's Biggest Bookstore. ●　**Focuses major selling point from user's view**
- Special offers from chapters.indigo.ca and partner companies. Invitations to special events, members-only sales, and more!

How do I buy a membership on chapters.indigo.ca?

It's easy—click the Buy Now! link on our website and follow the instructions. Once you've purchased your membership, you can start saving and collecting Reward Points right away! And as always, feel free to tell us what you think. ●　**Reduces resistance and motivates action by making it easy to respond**

Sincerely,

chapters.indigo.ca

P.S. If you'd rather not receive notices of this sort from chapters.indigo.ca, please visit our subscription page ● at www.chapters.indigo.ca/subscriptions.　**Provides means for being removed from list**

Tips for Writing Online Sales Messages

- Send only targeted, never "blanket," mailings.
- Strive to create relationship with receivers; offer something special just for them.
- Keep the message short and conversational.
- Focus on the "you" view.
- Develop only one or two central selling points.
- Provide means for being removed from mailing list.
- Make it easy to respond.
- Convey a tone of sincerity.

Summing Up and Looking Forward

The ability to persuade is a powerful communication tool. In this chapter, you learned to apply the indirect strategy in writing claim letters, making favour requests, writing persuasive suggestions, and writing sales letters. You also learned techniques for developing successful online sales messages. The techniques suggested here will be useful in many other contexts beyond the writing of these business documents. You will find that logical organization of arguments is also extremely effective in expressing ideas orally or any time you must overcome resistance to change.

Not all business messages are strictly persuasive. Occasionally, you must deny requests and deliver bad news. In the next chapter, you will learn to use the indirect strategy in conveying negative news.

Critical Thinking

1. Why is the ability to persuade an important trait in both business and personal relations?
2. Should a request for a favour be written directly or indirectly? Discuss.
3. Some individuals will never write a sales letter. Why is it nevertheless important for them to learn the techniques for doing so?

Chapter Review

4. In the indirect strategy, what should precede the main idea?

5. List at least four examples of persuasive favour requests.

6. What is an unsolicited sales letter? Give an example.

7. What is a solicited sales letter? Give an example.

8. List at least five ways to gain a reader's attention in the opening of a sales letter.

9. Name six writing techniques that stimulate desire for a product.

Writing Improvement Exercises

7.1 Strategies. For each of the following situations, which writing strategy would you use: direct or indirect?

10. An appeal for a contribution to Children's World, a charity
11. An announcement that in the future all dental, extended health, and life insurance benefits for employees will be reduced
12. A request to another company to verify the employment of a job applicant
13. A letter to a painting contractor demanding payment for floor tiles damaged by sloppy painters
14. A request for information about an oak desk and computer workstation
15. A letter to a grocery store asking for permission to display posters advertising a school fundraising car wash
16. A request for a refund of the cost of a computer program that does not do what its advertising claimed it would
17. A request for a refund of the cost of a hair dryer that stopped working after a month's use (the hair dryer carries a one-year warranty)
18. An invitation to a prominent author to speak before a student gathering
19. A memo to employees describing the schedule and selections of a new mobile catering service

Activities and Cases

7.2 Persuasive Claim: Exchanging Copiers. Analyze the following poorly written persuasive claim and list at least five major weaknesses. Outline an appropriate writing plan for a persuasive claim. After class discussion, your instructor may ask you to rewrite this message, fixing its weaknesses. Address your letter to International Copy Services, 1506 Fourth Street S.W., Calgary, AB T7L 2E3. Assume that you are writing on your company's letterhead. Use your word-processing software's professional letter template.

Gentlemen:

Three months ago we purchased four of your Regal Model SP-270F photocopiers, and we've had nothing but trouble ever since.

Your salesperson Jason Woo assured us that the SP-270F could easily handle our volume of 3000 copies a day. This seemed strange since the sales brochure said that the SP-270F was meant for 500 copies a day. But we believed Mr. Woo. Big mistake! Our four SP-270F copiers are down constantly; we can't go on like this. Because they're still under warranty, they eventually get repaired. But we're losing considerable business in downtime.

Your Mr. Woo has been less than helpful, so I telephoned the district manager, Heidi Berger. I suggested that we trade in our SP-270F copiers (which we got for $2500 each) for two S-55 models (at $13,500 each). However, Ms. Berger said she would have to charge 50 percent depreciation on our SP-270F copiers. What a rip-off! I think that 20 percent depreciation is more reasonable since we've had the machines only three months. Ms. Berger said she would get back to me, and I haven't heard from her since.

I'm writing to your headquarters because I have no faith in either Mr. Woo or Ms. Berger, and I need action on these machines. If you understood anything about business, you would see what a sweet deal I'm offering you. I'm willing to stick with your company and purchase a more expensive model—but I can't take such a loss on the SP-270F copiers. The SP-270F copiers are relatively new; you should be able to sell them with no trouble. And think of all the money you'll save by not having your repair technicians making constant trips to service our SP-270F copiers! Please let me hear from you immediately.

1. List at least five faults.

2. Outline a writing plan for a persuasive request.
   Opening:

   Body:

   Closing:

7.3 Persuasive Suggestion: Asking for Tuition Reimbursement. Analyze the poorly written e-mail below. List its weaknesses. If your instructor directs you to, revise it.

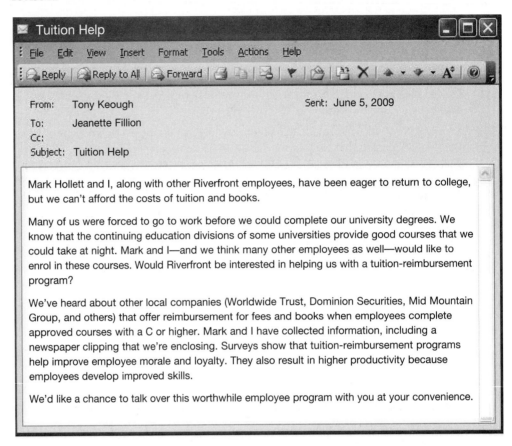

From: Tony Keough   Sent: June 5, 2009
To: Jeanette Fillion
Cc:
Subject: Tuition Help

Mark Hollett and I, along with other Riverfront employees, have been eager to return to college, but we can't afford the costs of tuition and books.

Many of us were forced to go to work before we could complete our university degrees. We know that the continuing education divisions of some universities provide good courses that we could take at night. Mark and I—and we think many other employees as well—would like to enrol in these courses. Would Riverfront be interested in helping us with a tuition-reimbursement program?

We've heard about other local companies (Worldwide Trust, Dominion Securities, Mid Mountain Group, and others) that offer reimbursement for fees and books when employees complete approved courses with a C or higher. Mark and I have collected information, including a newspaper clipping that we're enclosing. Surveys show that tuition-reimbursement programs help improve employee morale and loyalty. They also result in higher productivity because employees develop improved skills.

We'd like a chance to talk over this worthwhile employee program with you at your convenience.

1. List at least five weaknesses in this e-mail.

2. Outline a writing plan for this e-mail.
    Opening:

    Body:

    Closing:

7.4 Sales Letter: Analyzing the Pitch. Read the following sales letter and analyze its effectiveness by answering the questions listed after the letter.

Dear Friend of University of Prince Edward Island,

You are part of a special group of alumni—doctors, lawyers, bankers, managers, professors—who have a wide variety of credit cards available to them. For this reason I am inviting you to choose the superior benefits of the UPEI *Platinum Preferred* Visa credit card.

The UPEI Alumni Association has planned, together with Atlantic Bank, a superior credit card with excellent benefits, personalized customer care, and best of all, no annual fee.

Each purchase made with your UPEI *Platinum Preferred* Visa card leads directly to a contribution to the UPEI Alumni Association. This extra benefit costs nothing, but allows the Association to continue its vital work on campus and in the community.

Yours sincerely,

Margaret Simpson
Director of Alumni Relations
UPEI Alumni Association

a. What technique captures the reader's attention in the opening? Is it effective?
b. What are the central selling points?
c. Does the letter use a rational or an emotional appeal—or a combination? Explain.
d. What technique builds interest in the product? Are benefits obvious?
e. How is price handled?
f. Does the letter anticipate reader resistance and offer counterarguments?
g. What action is the reader to take? Is the action made easy? How?

Your Task. Revise the above letter, adding any improvements you think necessary based on your answers to the above questions.

7.5 Persuasive Claim: Excessive Legal Fees. You are the business manager for McConnell's, a producer of gourmet ice cream. McConnell's has 12 ice-cream shops in the Toronto area and a reputation for excellent ice cream. Your firm was approached by an independent ice-cream vendor who wanted to use McConnell's name and recipes for ice cream to be distributed through grocery stores and drugstores. As business manager, you worked with a law firm, Peretine, Valcon, and Associates, to draw up contracts regarding the use of McConnell's name and quality standards for the product.

When you received the bill from Louis Peretine, you couldn't believe it. The bill itemized 38 hours of attorney preparation, at $300 per hour, and 55 hours of paralegal assistance, at $75 per hour. The bill also showed $415 for telephone calls, which might be accurate because Mr. Peretine had to converse with McConnell's owners, who were living in Ireland at the time. However, you doubt that an experienced attorney would require 38 hours to draw up the contracts in question.

Perhaps some error was made in calculating the total hours. Moreover, you have checked with other businesses and found that excellent legal advice can be obtained for $200 per hour. McConnell's would like to continue using the services of Peretine, Valcon, and Associates for future legal business. Such future business is unlikely if an adjustment is not made on this bill.

Your Task. Write a persuasive request to Louis Peretine, Legal Counsel, Peretine, Valcon, and Associates, 2690 Whyte Avenue, Toronto, ON M2N 2E6.

7.6 Persuasive Favour Request: Inviting a Winner. As program chair of the Women in Business Association, a national group of businesswomen, you must persuade Joann R. Schulz to be the speaker at your annual conference April 14 in Toronto. Ms. Schulz was recently named Small Business Person of the Year by the Canadian Association of Independent Business.

After her 44-year-old husband died of a heart attack, Ms. Schulz threw herself into their new company and eventually transformed it from a small research company into an international manufacturer of devices for treatment of eye problems. Under her leadership, her Edmonton company grew from 3 to 75 employees in six years. It now sells more than $5 million worth of artificial lenses in 22 countries.

Although you can offer Ms. Schulz only $1000, you have heard that she is eager to encourage female entrepreneurs. You feel she might be receptive to your invitation.

Your Task. Write a letter inviting Ms. Joann R. Schulz, President, NBR Industries, 345 Selkirk Ave., Edmonton, AB T6K 4E2, to speak to your group.

7.7 Persuasive Favour Request: Helping Out a Worthy Charity. You have been a supporter of the World Partnership Walk since you were 17 years old. Five years later, you have graduated from college and are working as the office manager for a small Ottawa-based law firm, Fraser, Ahmet, and Grandpre. Last year, you were able to persuade the three partners in the firm to become local corporate sponsors for the Ottawa World Partnership Walk. This year, you'd like to be more ambitious and recruit other local law firms to make a corporate donation. This year's walk happens at a busy time: soon after the annual Terry Fox Run and just before the annual AIDS Walk Ottawa. Still, you believe the World Partnership Walk is worthy of support by area law firms.

Your Task. Write a letter that you will personalize and send to 15 small- and medium-sized Ottawa-area law firms requesting they become corporate sponsors for this year's World Partnership Walk.

Web

Related website: For more information on the World Partnership Walk, go to http://www.worldpartnershipwalk.com.

7.8 Sales Letter: Fitness at the Local Brewery. Health research shows that 33 percent of Canadians between age 20 and 64 are overweight.[4] Long-term health risks could be reduced if overweight employees shed their excess weight.

As a sales representative for Fitness Associates, you think your fitness equipment and programs could help people lose weight. With regular exercise at an on-site fitness centre, employees lose weight and improve overall health. As employee health improves, absenteeism is reduced and overall productivity increases. And employees love working out before or after work. They make the routine part of their work day, and they often have work buddies who share their fitness regimen.

Though many companies resist spending money to save money, fitness centres need not be large or expensive to be effective. Studies show that medium-sized centres coupled with motivational and training programs get the greatest success. For just $30,000, Fitness Associates will provide exercise equipment including stationary bikes, weight machines, and treadmills. Their fitness experts will design a fitness room, set up the fitness equipment, and create appropriate programs. Best of all, the one-time cost is usually offset by cost savings within one year of centre installation. For additional fees, FA can also provide fitness consultants for employee fitness assessments. FA specialists will also train employees on proper use of equipment, and they will clean and manage the facility—for an extra charge, of course.

Your Task. Write a sales letter to Ms. Kathleen Stewart, Human Resources VP, Good Times Brewing Company, 3939 Brewery Row, Moose Jaw, SK S6H 0V9. Assume you are writing on company letterhead. Ask for an appointment to meet with her. Send her a brochure detailing the products and services that Fitness Associates provides. As an incentive, offer a free fitness assessment for all employees if Good Times Brewing installs a fitness facility by December 1.

7.9 Sales Letter: Persuading an Old Friend to Switch to ACCuracy Plus. You are the owner of Software Solutions, a software consultancy based in Prince George, B.C. Recently, at a major industry trade show in Chicago, you were introduced to a new accounting software package, ACCuracy Plus. Quickly realizing its benefits, you signed a deal with the American manufacturer to become the only sales agent for the software in Canada, west of Ontario. Now that you own the right to sell the software, you have to make some sales. One day, while brainstorming possible clients, you remember your old friend from college, Tim Thom. While reading the newspaper last year, you found that Tim Thom had been promoted to VP Operations for Health & Co, a Victoria-based national retail chain selling vitamins, supplements, and natural foods. Even though you haven't seen or spoken to Tim in over eight years, you used to be good friends, and you believe a persuasive sales letter about your new software will not go unanswered. The question is, should you make a strong pitch for a sale, or should you just pitch for a get-together over lunch?

Your Task. Write a persuasive sales letter to Tim Thom, where you try to interest him in switching from his current accounting software to ACCuracy Plus.

Related websites: To build interest in ACCuracy Plus, browse the Internet for the features of its competitors such as Accpac (http://www.sageaccpac.com) and Microsoft's Dynamics (http://www.microsoft.com/dynamics/gp/default.mspx). Be careful not to plagiarize when you write your letter.

Web

Grammar/Mechanics Review—7

The following sentences contain errors in verb tenses, punctuation, and spelling. Below each sentence write a corrected version. A sentence may have more than one error.

1. Karen Armani, the job candidate we interviewed last week has written a thank-you message.

2. Carlos fixed the new computer however it is still not work very well.

3. The marketing director the sales manager and the director of personnel has to approve the budget for the next fiscal year.

4. Looking into the mirror of his new automobile Glenn put on his sunglasses, and thought that he looked very attractive.

5. Most people lists family memebers as as beneficiarys on their insurance policies.

6. The CEO arrived from Toronto Ontario on February 26, 2008 to start a new job.

7. If we sign up with a cell-phone contract many features is available free for six months

8. Maria will arrange the party but you are responsible for send the invitations.

9. Although I like the apartment $600.00 are more than I can afford paying for rent.

10. The rain forests of Indonesia have tall lush green trees and many kinds of animals.

11. Many candidates have submit applications consequently the hiring committee will spend a few months interviewing.

12. Samuel Gold the manager of Megatek told all his employees to change the new privacy policy.

13. All employees who passes the course, are entitled to have their fees refunded.

14. Please return the package to Mrs. Marie Dolton 225 Banbury Road Ottawa Ontario K2G 3A8 by July 27 2009 and send the invoice separately.

15. Tornado warnings has be posted for the residents of Windsor Barrie and Sudbury.

Grammar/Mechanics Challenge—7

Document for Revision

The following memo has faults in grammar, punctuation, spelling, redundancies and wordiness. Use standard proofreading marks (see Appendix B) to correct approximately 20 errors. When you finish, your instructor can show you the revised version of this memo.

Memo

To: Sara W. Morrisseau, Vice-President

From: Jackson Pardell, Market Research

CC:

Date: August 5, 2009

Re: ANALYSIS OF GULPIT XL

I am writing to tell you that a summery of the research of Clemence Willis and me are included with this letter. Regarding the reduced sugar sports drink being introduced by our No. 1 compititor, GulpIT. In just under a year's time, GulpIT developed new drink, it combines together a mixture of 50 percent sugar and 50 percent artificial sweetener. Apparently, GulpIT plans to spend over $8 million to introduce the new drink and to study consumers reactions to it. It will be tested on the shelves of convience stores groceries and other merchants in five cities in the Canada.

The company's spokesperson said, "The 'X' stands for excellent taste; the 'L' stands for less sugar." Intended for young adults who doesn't like the taste of sweetener but who want to control calories. The new sports drink is a mixture of sugar and diet drink. Our studies shows that similar drinks try in this country in the 1980s were unsuccessful. On the other hand, a 50-calorie low-sugar sports drink introduced in Europe two year ago was well receive, likewise in Japan a 40-calorie soda is now marketed successfully by a cola manufacturer.

However, our research and our analysis of GulpIT XL shows that Canada's consumers will be interest in a midcalorie sports drink. The Toronto Stock Exchange's response to GulpIT's announcement of it's new drink was favourable.

We are of the opinion that we should wait a few months. Before we introduce our own low-sugar sports drink.

Eight Steps to Resolving Workplace Conflicts

"No part of life is conflict free. We don't always agree with people around us—our families, friends, neighbours or the people we work with every day." Although all workplaces suffer from conflict from time to time, some people think that workplace conflict is growing.[5]

Several factors may be tied to increasing problems at work. One factor is our varied workforce. Sharing ideas that come from a variety of backgrounds, experiences, and personalities may lead to better problem solving, but it can also lead to conflict. Another factor related to increased conflict is the trend toward all employees participating in management. In the past only bosses had to resolve problems, but now more employees are making decisions and facing conflict. This is particularly true of teams. Working together involves a great deal of give and take, and conflict may result if some people feel that they are being taken advantage of. Finally, a large source of workplace problems is increasing levels of stress. Statistics Canada reports that "the highest proportion of working Canadians—more than one-third (34%)—cited too many demands or hours as the most common source of stress in the workplace." Other sources of workplace stress include "poor interpersonal relations" and "risk of accident and injury."[6]

When problems do arise in the workplace, it's important for everyone to recognize that conflict is a normal occurrence and that it won't disappear if ignored. Conflict must be confronted and resolved. Effective conflict resolution requires good listening skills, flexibility, and a willingness to change. Individuals must be willing to truly listen and seek to understand rather than immediately challenge the opponent. In many workplace conflicts, involving a third party to act as a mediator is necessary.

Although problems vary greatly, the following steps offer a good basic process for resolving conflicts.[7]

1. **Be proactive.** Arrange a time when conflicting parties are willing to have a conversation in a friendly environment.
2. **Listen to all sides.** Encourage each individual to describe the situation from his or her viewpoint.
3. **Diagnose before responding.** To promote good communication, follow this rule: No one may respond without first clearly summarizing the other person's previous remarks.
4. **Problem solve by focusing on interests.** Brainstorm together to develop many ways to meet the interests of each of the conflicting parties. Try to see each other as partners, rather than opponents, in solving the problem.
5. **Negotiate a solution.** Ensure that both parties agree to the chosen solution.
6. **Communicate the solution formally.** It is important to formalize the agreement on paper or in some other way.
7. **Implement the solution and plan follow-up communication.** Meet again on an agreed-upon date to ensure satisfactory resolution of the conflict. The deadline makes it more likely that both parties will follow through on their part of the deal.
8. **Live the solution.** Act on the solution in the workplace.

Career Application

As leader of your work team, you were recently confronted by an angry team member. Julie, a story editor on your film production team, is upset because, for the third time in as many weeks, she was forced to give up part of her weekend for work. This time it was for an awards dinner that everyone in the office tried to avoid. Julie is particularly angry with Yannick, who should have represented the team at this event. But he uttered the magic word: family. "Yannick says he has plans with his family, and it's like he gets to do anything," Julie complains to you. "I don't resent him or his devotion to his family. But I do resent it when my team constantly expects me to give up my personal time because I don't have kids. That's my choice, and I don't think I should be punished for it."[8]

Your Task

Using the principles outlined above, work out a conflict resolution plan for Julie and Yannick. Your instructor may wish to divide your class into three-person teams to role-play Julie, Yannick, and the team leader. Add any details to make a realistic scenario.

- What are the first steps in resolving this conflict?
- What arguments might each side present?
- What alternatives might be offered?
- What do you think is the best solution?
- How could it be implemented with the least friction?

Negative Messages

CHAPTER 8

Despite the fact that we sometimes have to send negative messages at work, it is important to turn the situation around and focus on lessons learned and experience gained. Just think, if not for bad news, good news would not be as good![1]

Maria Duncan, Director, Production Finance, Alliance-Atlantis Communications Inc.

Strategies for Breaking Bad News

Quick Check

If your message delivers bad news, consider using the indirect strategy.

Letters, e-mails, and memos that carry negative news can have a significant impact on a company's success. As Maria Duncan suggests, the correct way to go about writing a bad-news message is to think positively. Because bad news disappoints, irritates, and sometimes angers the receiver, such messages must be written in a way that explains the bad news but retains goodwill at the same time.

The direct strategy, which you learned to apply in earlier chapters, presents the main idea first, even when it's bad news. The direct pattern appeals to efficiency-oriented writers who don't want to waste time with efforts to soften the effects of bad news.[2] Many business writers, however, prefer to use the indirect pattern in delivering negative messages. The indirect pattern is especially appealing to writers who care about their relationships with the receivers.

Although the major focus of this chapter will be on developing the indirect pattern, you'll first learn the procedure that many business professionals follow in resolving business problems. It may surprise you. Then you'll study models of messages that use the indirect pattern to refuse requests, refuse claims, and announce bad news to customers and employees. Finally, you'll learn to identify instances in which the direct pattern may be preferable in announcing bad news.

Resolving Business Problems

In all businesses, things sometimes go wrong. Goods are not delivered, a product fails to perform as expected, service is poor, clients get incorrect invoices, or customers are misunderstood. All businesses offering products or services must sometimes deal with troublesome situations that cause unhappiness to customers and to employees. Whenever possible, these problems should be dealt with immediately and personally. One study found that a majority of business professionals resolve problems in the following manner:

- Call or see the individual involved (rather than sending an e-mail or letter).
- Describe the problem and apologize.
- Explain why the problem occurred.
- Explain what you are doing to resolve it.
- Explain how it will not happen again.
- Follow up with a letter that describes the conversation and promotes goodwill.[3]

Using the Indirect Pattern to Prepare the Reader

When sending a bad-news message that will upset or irritate the receiver, many business communicators use the indirect pattern. Revealing bad news indirectly shows sensitivity to your reader. Whereas good news can be announced quickly, bad news generally should be revealed gradually. By preparing the reader, you soften the impact. A blunt announcement of disappointing news might cause the receiver to stop reading and toss the message aside.

The indirect pattern enables you to keep the reader's attention until you have been able to explain the reasons for the bad news. The most important part of a bad-news letter is the explanation, which you'll learn about shortly. The indirect plan consists of four main parts:

The indirect pattern softens the bad news.

- Buffer opening
- Reasons given first in the body
- Bad news following in the body
- Pleasant closing

Buffering the Opening

A buffer is a device that reduces shock or pain. To buffer the pain of bad news, begin your letter with a neutral but meaningful statement that makes the reader continue reading. The buffer should be relevant and concise. Although it should not reveal the bad news immediately, it should not give a false impression that good news follows. It should provide a natural transition to the explanation that follows. The individual situation, of course, will help determine what you should put in the buffer. Here are some possibilities for opening bad-news messages.

A buffer opens a bad news letter with a neutral, concise, relevant, and upbeat statement.

- **Best news.** Start with the part of the message that has the best news. For example, in a memo that announces a new service along with a cutback in mailroom hours, you might write *To make sure that your correspondence goes out with the last pickup, we're starting a new messenger pickup service at 2:30 p.m. daily, beginning June 1.*

A good buffer may include the best news, a compliment, appreciation, facts regarding the problem, or a statement showing understanding.

- **Compliment.** Praise the receiver's accomplishments, organization, or efforts, but do so with honesty and sincerity. For instance, in a letter declining an invitation to speak, you could write *I admire The United Way for its fundraising projects in our community. Thank you for asking me to speak Friday, November 5.*
- **Appreciation.** Give thanks to the reader for doing business, for sending something, for showing confidence in your organization, for expressing feelings, or simply for providing feedback. In a letter responding to a complaint about poor service, you might say *Thank you for telling us about your experience at our hotel and for giving us a chance to look into the situation.* Avoid thanking the reader, however, for something you are about to refuse.
- **Agreement.** Make a relevant statement with which both reader and receiver can agree. A letter that rejects a loan application might read *We both realize how much your business has been affected by the U.S. ban on Canadian beef in the past few years.*
- **Facts.** Provide objective information that introduces the bad news. For example, in a memo announcing cutbacks in the hours of the employees' cafeteria, you might say *During the past five years the number of employees eating breakfast in our cafeteria has dropped from 32 percent to 12 percent.*
- **Understanding.** Show that you care about the reader. In announcing a product defect, the writer can still manage to express concern for the customer: *We know you expect superior performance from all the products you purchase from OfficeCity. That's why we're writing personally about the Excell printer cartridges you recently ordered.*

Presenting the Reasons

The most important part of a bad-news message is the section that explains why a negative decision is necessary. Without sound reasons for denying a request or refusing a claim, a letter will fail, no matter how cleverly it is organized or written. As part of your planning before writing, you analyzed the problem and decided to refuse a request for specific reasons. Before giving the bad news, try to explain those reasons. Providing an explanation reduces feelings of ill will and improves the chances that the reader will accept the bad news.

Quick Check

Bad-news messages should explain reasons before stating the negative news.

- **Being cautious in explaining.** If the reasons are not confidential or legally questionable, you can be specific: *Growers supplied us with a limited number of patio roses, and our demand this year was twice that of last year.* In refusing a speaking engagement, tell why the date is impossible: *On January 17 we have a board of directors meeting that I must attend.*
- **Giving reader benefits.** Readers are more open to bad news if in some way, even indirectly, it may help them. Readers also accept bad news better if they recognize that someone or something else benefits, such as other workers or the environment: *Although we would like to consider your application, we prefer to fill managerial positions from within.* Avoid trying to show reader benefits, though, if they appear insincere: *To improve our service to you, we're increasing our brokerage fees.*

Quick Check

Readers accept bad news more readily if they see that someone benefits.

- **Explaining company policy.** Don't use general policy statements to refuse something: *Company policy prevents us from making cash refunds* or *Proposals may be accepted from local companies only* or *Company policy requires us to promote from within.* Instead of hiding behind company policy, gently explain why the policy makes sense: *We prefer to promote from within because it rewards the loyalty of our employees. In addition, we've found that people familiar with our organization make the quickest contribution to our team effort.* By offering explanations, you demonstrate that you care about your readers and are treating them as important individuals.
- **Choosing positive words.** Because the words you use can affect a reader's response, choose carefully. Remember that the goal of the indirect pattern is to hold the reader's attention until you've had a chance to explain the reasons for

the bad news. To keep the reader in a receptive mood, avoid expressions that might cause the reader to tune out. Be sensitive to negative words such as *claim, error, failure, fault, impossible, mistaken, misunderstand, never, regret, unwilling, unfortunately,* and *violate.*

- **Showing that the matter was treated seriously and fairly.** In explaining reasons, show the reader that you've looked into the matter and are making a fair decision. Customers accept disappointing news better when they feel that their requests have been heard and that they have been treated fairly. Avoid blaming someone else (known as "passing the buck"). Such unprofessional behaviour makes the reader lose trust in you and your company.

Cushioning the Bad News

Although you can't prevent the disappointment that bad news brings, you can reduce the pain somewhat by breaking the news sensitively. Be especially thoughtful when the reader will suffer personally from the bad news. A number of techniques can lessen the impact.

- **Position the bad news.** Instead of spotlighting it, enclose the bad news between other sentences, perhaps among your reasons. Try not to let the refusal begin or end a paragraph—the reader's eye will linger on these high-visibility spots. Another technique that reduces shock is putting a painful idea in a subordinate clause: *Although another candidate was hired, we appreciate your interest in our organization and wish you every success in your job search.* Subordinate clauses often begin with words such as *although, as, because, if,* and *since.*

- **Use the passive voice.** Passive-voice verbs let you to describe an action without connecting the action to a specific person. While the active voice focuses attention on a person *(We don't give cash refunds)*, the passive voice highlights the action *(Cash refunds are not given because ...)*. Use the passive voice for the bad news. In some instances you can combine passive-voice verbs and a subordinate clause: *Although ice-cream vendors cannot be required to lower their prices, we are happy to pass along your comments for their consideration.*

- **Stress the positive.** As you learned earlier, messages are far more effective when you describe what you can do instead of what you can't do. Rather than *We will no longer accept requests for product changes after June 1,* try a more positive appeal: *We are accepting requests for product changes until June 1.*

- **Imply the refusal.** It's sometimes possible to avoid a direct statement of refusal. Often, your reasons and explanations leave no doubt that a request has been denied. Direct refusals may be unnecessary and at times cruel. In this refusal to contribute to a charity, for example, the writer never actually says no: *Because we will soon be moving into new offices, all our funds are reserved for moving and furnishings. We hope that next year we'll be able to support your worthwhile charity.* This implied refusal is effective even though the bad news is not stated. The danger of an implied refusal, of course, is that it can be so subtle that the reader misses it. Be certain that you make the bad news clear, thus preventing the need for further correspondence.

- **Suggest a compromise or an alternative.** A refusal is not so harsh—for the sender or the receiver—if a suitable compromise, substitute, or alternative is available. In denying permission to a class to visit a research facility, for instance, this writer softens the bad news by giving an alternative: *Although class tours of the entire research facility are not given due to safety and security reasons, we do offer tours of parts of the facility during our open house in the fall.*

You can further reduce the impact of the bad news by refusing to dwell on it. Present it briefly (or imply it), and move on to your closing.

Quick Check

Techniques for cushioning bad news include putting it in a strategic place, using the passive voice, emphasizing the positive, implying the refusal, and suggesting alternatives or compromises.

Closing Pleasantly

Quick Check

Closings to bad-news messages might include a forward look, an alternative, good wishes, special offers, and sales promotional information.

After explaining the bad news sensitively, close the message with a pleasant statement that encourages goodwill. The closing should be personalized and may include a forward look, an alternative, good wishes, special offers, promotional information, or an off-the-subject remark.

- **Forward look.** Anticipate future relations or business. A letter that refuses a contract proposal might read: *Thank you for your bid. We look forward to working with your talented staff when future projects demand your special skills.*
- **Alternative.** If an alternative exists, end your letter with follow-through advice. For example, in a letter rejecting a customer's demand for replacement of land-scaping plants, you might say, *We will be happy to give you a free inspection and consultation. Please call 746-8112 to arrange a date for a visit.*
- **Good wishes.** A letter rejecting a job candidate might read: *We appreciate your interest in our company. Good luck in your search to find the perfect match between your skills and job requirements.*
- **Special offers.** When customers complain—primarily about food products or small consumer items—companies often send coupons, samples, or gifts to restore confidence and to promote future business. In response to a customer's complaint about a frozen dinner, you could write *Thank you for your loyalty and for sharing in our efforts to make Green Valley frozen entrées the best they can be. We appreciate your input so much that we'd like to buy you dinner. We've enclosed a coupon to cover the cost of your next entrée.*
- **Sales promotion.** When the bad news is not upsetting or personal, references to promotional information may be appropriate: *The laptops you ordered are unusually popular because they have more plug-ins for peripheral devices than any other laptop in their price range. To help you locate additional accessories for these computers, we invite you to visit our website at www.BestEverComputers.com where our on-line catalogue provides a huge selection of peripheral devices such as stereo speakers, printers, personal digital assistants, and digital pagers.*

Avoid endings that sound shallow, insincere, or inappropriate. Don't invite further correspondence (*If you have any questions, please contact ...*), and don't repeat the bad news.

Refusing Requests

Quick Check

The indirect strategy is appropriate when refusing requests for favours, money, information, or action.

Most of us prefer to be let down gently when we're being refused something we want. That's why the indirect pattern works well when you must turn down requests for favours, money, information, action, and so forth.

The following writing plan is appropriate when you must deny a routine request or claim.

Writing Plan for Refusing Requests or Claims

- **Buffer.** Start with a neutral statement such as a compliment, appreciation, or a quick review of the facts.
- **Transition.** Include a key idea or word (such as *however*) that acts as a transition to the reasons.
- **Reasons.** Present valid reasons for the refusal, avoiding words that create a negative tone. Include sales promotion material if appropriate.
- **Bad news.** Soften the blow by de-emphasizing the bad news, using the passive voice, stressing the positive, or implying a refusal.
- **Alternative.** Suggest a compromise, alternative, or substitute if possible.
- **Closing.** Renew good feelings with a positive statement. Avoid referring to the bad news, and look forward to continued business.

Two versions of a request refusal are shown in Figure 8.1. A magazine writer requested salary information for an article she is writing, but this information could not be given out. The "Before" version is ineffective because of the following reasons:

- The memo begins with needless information that could be implied.
- The second paragraph creates a harsh tone with such negative words as *sorry, must refuse, violate,* and *liable.*
- Since the refusal goes before the explanation, the reader probably will not be in an open frame of mind to accept the reasons for refusing.
- The bad news is stressed because it is placed in a short sentence at the beginning of a paragraph. It stands out and adds more weight to the rejection already felt by the reader.
- The refusal explanation is too detailed, containing references to possible legal action. The tone at this point is threatening and overly harsh.
- Instead of offering constructive alternatives, the author throws in a self-serving comment about the high salary and commissions of his salespeople.
- Finally, the closing sounds insincere and doesn't build goodwill.

The "After" version of the memo is more effective because of the following strategies:

- The opening reflects the writer's genuine interest in the request. But it does not indicate agreement.
- The second sentence acts as a transition by introducing the words *salespeople* and *salaries,* repeated in the following paragraph.
- Reasons for refusing this request are objectively presented in an explanation that comes *before* the refusal. Notice that the refusal (*Although specific salaries and commission rates cannot be released*) is a subordinate clause in a long sentence in the middle of a paragraph.
- To further soften the blow, the letter offers an alternative. The friendly closing refers to the alternative, avoids mention of the refusal, and looks to the future.

Refusing Claims

Most businesses offering products or services will receive occasional customer claims for adjustments. Claims may also arise from employees. Most of these claims are valid, and the customer or employee receives a positive response. Even claims without warranties are sometimes granted because businesses genuinely desire to create a good public image and to maintain friendly relations with employees.

Some claims, however, cannot be approved because the customer or employee is mistaken, misinformed, unreasonable, or possibly even dishonest. Letters responding to these claims deliver bad news. And the indirect strategy breaks bad news with the least pain. It also allows the sender to explain why the claim must be refused before the reader realizes the bad news and begins resisting.

In the letter shown in Figure 8.2 (p. 171), the writer denies a customer's claim for the difference between the price the customer paid for speakers and the price she saw advertised locally (which would have resulted in a cash refund of $151). While Premier Sound Sales does match any advertised lower price, the price-matching policy applies only to exact models. This claim must be rejected because the advertisement the customer submitted shows a different, older speaker model.

The letter to Wanda Vandermark is an effective refusal of a claim because it uses the following strategies:

- The letter opens with a buffer that agrees with a statement in the customer's letter.
- It repeats the key idea of product confidence as a transition to the second paragraph.

Quick Check

In refusing requests, avoid a harsh tone or being too detailed; offer constructive alternatives whenever possible.

Quick Check

Although most customer claims are granted, occasionally some must be refused.

Quick Check

When refusing customer claims, explain objectively and do not assume that the customer is foolish or dishonest.

Refusing Claims

FIGURE 8.1 Refusing a Request

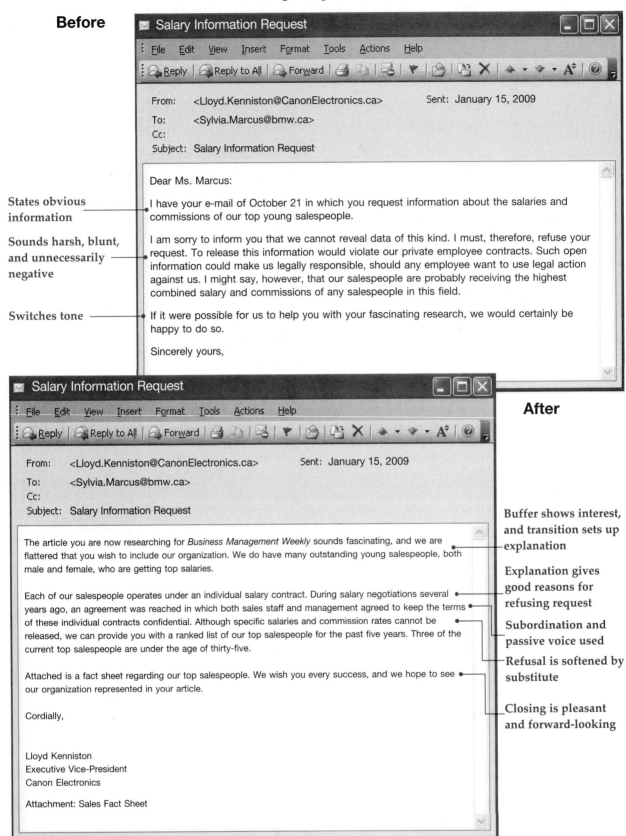

Before

States obvious information

Sounds harsh, blunt, and unnecessarily negative

Switches tone

Salary Information Request

File   Edit   View   Insert   Format   Tools   Actions   Help

Reply | Reply to All | Forward

From: <Lloyd.Kenniston@CanonElectronics.ca>   Sent: January 15, 2009
To: <Sylvia.Marcus@bmw.ca>
Cc:
Subject: Salary Information Request

Dear Ms. Marcus:

I have your e-mail of October 21 in which you request information about the salaries and commissions of our top young salespeople.

I am sorry to inform you that we cannot reveal data of this kind. I must, therefore, refuse your request. To release this information would violate our private employee contracts. Such open information could make us legally responsible, should any employee want to use legal action against us. I might say, however, that our salespeople are probably receiving the highest combined salary and commissions of any salespeople in this field.

If it were possible for us to help you with your fascinating research, we would certainly be happy to do so.

Sincerely yours,

Salary Information Request

File   Edit   View   Insert   Format   Tools   Actions   Help

Reply | Reply to All | Forward

After

From: <Lloyd.Kenniston@CanonElectronics.ca>   Sent: January 15, 2009
To: <Sylvia.Marcus@bmw.ca>
Cc:
Subject: Salary Information Request

The article you are now researching for *Business Management Weekly* sounds fascinating, and we are flattered that you wish to include our organization. We do have many outstanding young salespeople, both male and female, who are getting top salaries.

Each of our salespeople operates under an individual salary contract. During salary negotiations several years ago, an agreement was reached in which both sales staff and management agreed to keep the terms of these individual contracts confidential. Although specific salaries and commission rates cannot be released, we can provide you with a ranked list of our top salespeople for the past five years. Three of the current top salespeople are under the age of thirty-five.

Attached is a fact sheet regarding our top salespeople. We wish you every success, and we hope to see our organization represented in your article.

Cordially,

Lloyd Kenniston
Executive Vice-President
Canon Electronics

Attachment: Sales Fact Sheet

Buffer shows interest, and transition sets up explanation

Explanation gives good reasons for refusing request

Subordination and passive voice used

Refusal is softened by substitute

Closing is pleasant and forward-looking

FIGURE 8.2 Refusing a Claim

PREMIER SOUND SALES

5920 Jasper Boulevard	Fax: (780) 499-5904
Edmonton, Alberta T2C 2A6	Web: www.premiersound.ca
Telephone: (780) 499-2341	E-mail: premier1@flash.ca

May 25, 2009

Ms. Wanda Vandermark
4205 54th Avenue S.E.
Calgary, Alberta T3L 2W4

Dear Ms. Vandermark:

You're absolutely right! We take pride in selling the finest products at the lowest prices. The X Flex speakers you purchased last month are premiere concert-hall speakers. They're the only ones we present in our catalogue because they're the best. — *Begins by agreeing with receiver*

We have such confidence in our products and prices that we offer the price-matching policy you mention in your letter of May 20. That policy guarantees a refund of the price difference if you see one of your purchases offered at a lower price for 30 days after your purchase. To qualify for that refund, customers are asked to send us an advertisement or proof of the product price and model. As our catalogue states, this price-matching policy applies only to the same models. — *Explains price-matching policy*

Our X Flex AM-5 speakers sell for $749. You sent us a local advertisement showing a price of $598 for X Flex AM-4 speakers. These speakers are an older model, released more than three years ago. The AM-5 speakers you received have a wider dynamic range and smoother frequency response than the AM-4 model. Naturally, the improved model you purchased costs a little more than the older AM-4 model advertised by your local dealer. Your speakers have a new three-chamber bass module that virtually eliminates harmonic distortion. The AM-5 speakers are also 20 percent smaller than the AM-4 model. — *Without actually saying no, shows why claim can't be honoured*

You bought the finest compact speakers on the market, Ms. Vandermark. If you haven't installed them yet, you may be interested in ceiling mounts, shown in the enclosed catalogue on page 48. We value your business and invite your continued comparison shopping. — *Renews good feelings by building confidence in wisdom of purchase*

Sincerely yours,

Melanie Tang

Melanie Tang
Customer Care Specialist

Enclosure

- Next comes an explanation of the price-matching policy. The writer does not assume that the customer is not being truthful. Nor does the writer suggest that the customer is a simpleton who didn't read or understand the price-matching policy.
- The author uses a neutral explanation of the policy along with precise differences between the customer's speakers and the older ones.
- The writer also gets a chance to praise the customer's choice of speakers and confirm what a quality product they are.
- By the end of the third paragraph, it's evident to the reader that her claim is unjustified.

Notice how most of the parts of an effective claim refusal are woven together in this letter: buffer, transition, explanation, and pleasant closing. The only missing part is an alternative, which was impossible in this situation.

Announcing Bad News to Customers and Employees

Quick Check

The choice of a direct or indirect strategy depends on the expected reaction of the receiver.

In addition to resolving claims, organizations occasionally must announce bad news to customers or to their own employees. Bad news to customers might involve rate increases, reduced service, changed procedures, new locations, or technical problems. Bad news within organizations might involve declining profits, lost contracts, public relations controversies, and changes in policy.

Whether you use a direct or an indirect pattern in delivering that news depends on the expected response of the receiver. When the bad news affects customers or employees personally—such as a reduction in available overtime hours, a change in shift premium, or relocation plans—you can generally lessen its impact and promote better relations by explaining reasons before revealing the bad news.

Writing Plan for Announcing Bad News to Customers and Employees

- **Buffer.** Open with a compliment, appreciation, facts, or good news with a neutral statement on which the reader and the writer can agree.
- **Transition.** Include a key idea or word that leads from the opening to the reasons.
- **Reasons.** Explain the logic behind the bad news; use positive words and try to show reader benefits if possible.
- **Bad news.** Position the bad news so that it does not stand out. Consider implying the bad news.
- **Alternative.** Suggest a compromise, alternative, or substitute if possible.
- **Closing.** Look forward positively. Provide information about an alternative, if appropriate.

Quick Check

When announcing bad news to employees, consider starting with a neutral statement or something positive.

In many businesses today employee extended health-care plans are increasing in cost. Midland Enterprises has to announce a large increase to its employees. Figure 8.3 shows two samples of its bad-news message. The first one opens directly with the bad news. No explanation is given for why employee monthly deductions are rising. Although Midland has been absorbing the increasing costs in the past and has not charged employees, it takes no credit for this. Instead, the tone of the memo is defensive and unsatisfying to receivers.

The improved version of this bad-news memo, shown at the bottom of Figure 8.3, uses the indirect pattern. Notice that it opens with a relevant, upbeat buffer regarding extended health-care benefits—but says nothing about increasing monthly costs. For a smooth transition, the second paragraph begins with a key idea from the opening (comprehensive package). The reasons section discusses

FIGURE 8.3 Memo That Announces Bad News to Employees

MEMO TO: Staff

Beginning January 1 the monthly deduction from your paycheque for extended health benefits will be increased to $109 (up from $42 last year).

Every year extended benefits costs go up. Although we considered dropping other benefits, Midland decided that the best plan was to keep the present all inclusive package. Unfortunately, we can't do that unless we pass along some of the extra cost to you. Last year the company was forced to absorb the total increase in extended health premiums. However, such a plan this year is not possible.

We did everything possible to avoid the sharp increase in costs to you this year. A rate schedule describing the increases in payments for your family and dependents is enclosed.

Hits readers with bad news without any preparation

Does not explain why costs are rising

Fails to take credit for absorbing previous increases

Sounds defensive; fails to give reasons

After

DATE:	November 6, 2009
TO:	Fellow Employees
FROM:	Eduardo Martinez, President *EM*
SUBJECT:	MAINTAINING QUALITY BENEFITS PACKAGE

Begins with positive buffer

Extended health benefits programs have always been an important part of our commitment to employees here at Midland, Inc. We're proud that our total benefits package continues to rank among the best in our industry.

Explains why costs are rising

Such an all inclusive package does not come without cost. In the last decade, extended health premiums have risen over 50 percent among companies belonging to our group insurance plan. The costs of other insurance plans have been even higher. We're told that several factors have made the costs go up: greater number of services offered such as therapeutic massage and acupuncture, increased average age of program users, and increased support of drug purchases for program members.

Reveals bad news clearly but embeds it in paragraph

Just two years ago our monthly extended health benefits cost for each employee was $415. It rose to $469 last year. We were able to absorb that jump without increasing your contribution. But this year's hike to $539 forces us to ask you to share the increase. To maintain your current extended health benefits, you will be paying $109 a month. The enclosed rate schedule describes the cost breakdown for families and dependents.

Ends positively by stressing the company's major share of the costs

Midland continues to pay the major portion of the extended health benefit program ($430 each month). We think it's a wise investment.

Enclosure

rising costs with explanations and figures. The bad news *(you will be paying $109 a month)* is clearly presented but embedded within the paragraph.

Throughout, the writer strives to show the fairness of the company's position. The ending, which does not refer to the bad news, emphasizes how much the company is paying and what a wise investment it is. Notice that the entire memo demonstrates a kinder, gentler approach than that shown in the first draft. Of prime importance in breaking bad news to employees is providing clear, convincing reasons that explain the decision.

When to Use the Direct Pattern

Many bad-news letters are best organized indirectly, beginning with a buffer and reasons. However, the direct pattern, with the bad news first followed by the reasons and a pleasant closing, may be more effective in situations such as the following:

- **When the bad news is not damaging.** If the bad news is insignificant (such as a small increase in cost) and doesn't personally affect the receiver, then the direct strategy certainly makes sense.
- **When the receiver may otherwise overlook the bad news.** With the crush of e-mails and other communications today, many readers skim messages, looking only at the opening. If they don't find relevant material, they may discard the message. Rate increases, changes in service, new policy requirements—these critical messages may require boldness to ensure attention.
- **When organization policy suggests directness.** Some companies expect all internal messages and announcements—even bad news—to be straightforward and presented without frills.
- **When the receiver prefers directness.** Busy managers may prefer directness. Such shorter messages enable the reader to get in the proper frame of mind immediately. If you suspect that the reader prefers that the facts be presented immediately, use the direct pattern.
- **When firmness is necessary.** Messages that must show strength should not use delaying techniques. For example, the last in a series of collection letters that seek payment of overdue accounts may require a direct opener.

Figure 8.4 shows an example of a typical direct bad-news message.

✔ **Quick Check**

The direct pattern is appropriate when the bad news is not damaging, when the receiver might otherwise overlook the bad news, when the organization expects directness, when the receiver prefers directness, or when firmness is necessary.

FIGURE 8.4 **Direct Bad-News Message**

December 2009

Dear Valued Customers,

As of January 1, 2010, basic telephone service rates will be rising by 1.5 percent.

This change is taking place as a result of a recent CRTC decision, as well as for competitive reasons within the industry.

We appreciate your continued loyalty.

Toula Vassopoulos

Toula Vassopoulos
Customer Service Manager

Chapter 8 Negative Messages

Ethics and the Indirect Pattern

You may worry that the indirect pattern is unethical or manipulative because the writer deliberately delays the main idea. But consider the alternative. Breaking bad news bluntly can cause pain and hard feelings. By delaying bad news, you soften the blow somewhat, and you ensure that your reasoning will be read while the receiver is still receptive. Your motives are not to deceive the reader or to hide the news. Rather, your goal is to be a compassionate, yet effective communicator.

Quick Check

The indirect strategy is unethical only if the writer intends to deceive the reader.

The key to ethical communication lies in the motives of the sender. Unethical communicators intend to deceive. For example, Victoria's Secret, the clothing and lingerie chain, once offered free $10 gift certificates. However, when customers tried to cash the certificates, they found that they were required to make a minimum purchase of $50 worth of merchandise.[4] For this misleading, deceptive, and unethical offer, the chain paid a $100,000 fine. Although the indirect strategy provides a setting in which to announce bad news, it should not be used to avoid or misrepresent the truth.

Summing Up and Looking Forward

When faced with delivering bad news, you have a choice. You can announce it immediately, or you can delay it by presenting a buffer and reasons first. Many business communicators prefer the indirect strategy because it tends to maintain goodwill. In certain situations, however, the direct strategy is more effective in delivering bad news.

In this chapter, you learned to write follow-up bad-news messages and to apply the indirect strategy in refusing requests, denying claims, and delivering bad news to employees. This same strategy is appropriate when you make persuasive requests or when you try to sell something.

Now that you have completed your instruction in writing business e-mails, letters, and memos, you're ready to learn about writing longer business documents like proposals and reports. Chapter 9 introduces informal reports.

Critical Thinking

1. Why is the "reasons" section of a bad-news message so important?
2. Some people feel that all employee news, good or bad, should be announced directly. Do you agree or disagree? Why?

Chapter Review

3. List the six steps that many business professionals follow in resolving business problems.

4. List the four main parts of the indirect pattern for revealing bad news.

5. What is a buffer?

6. List seven possibilities for opening bad-news messages.

7. List at least five words that might affect readers negatively.

8. How can the passive voice be used effectively in bad-news messages? Provide an original example.

9. List five techniques for closing a bad-news message.

10. List three instances when bad news should be announced directly.

Writing Improvement Exercises

8.1 Subordinate Clauses. You can soften the effect of bad news by placing it in a subordinate clause that begins with *although, since,* or *because*. The focus in a sentence is on the independent clause. Instead of saying *We cannot serve you on a credit basis*, try *Since we cannot serve you on a credit basis, we invite you to take advantage of our cash discounts and sale prices*.

Chapter 8 Negative Messages

Revise the following refusals so that the bad news appears in a subordinate clause.

11. We no longer print a complete catalogue. However, we now offer all our catalogue choices at our website, which is always up-to-date.

12. We hope to have our plant remodelling completed by June. We cannot schedule tours of the bottling plant until after we finish remodelling.

13. Northern Air cannot accept responsibility for expenses caused indirectly by flight delays. However, we do recognize that this delay inconvenienced you.

8.2 Passive-Voice Verbs. Passive-voice verbs may be preferable in breaking bad news because they let you emphasize actions rather than personalities. Compare these two refusals:

Example: *Active voice:* I cannot authorize you to take three weeks of vacation in July.
Example: *Passive voice:* Three weeks of vacation in July cannot be authorized.

Revise the following refusals so that they use passive-voice instead of active-voice verbs.

14. We cannot refund cash for the items you purchased on credit.

15. I have already filled my schedule on the date you wish me to speak.

16. We do not examine patients until we have verified their health-care number.

8.3 Implied Refusals. Bad news can be de-emphasized by implying a refusal instead of stating it directly. Compare these refusals:

Example: *Direct refusal:* We cannot send you a price list nor can we sell our lawn mowers directly to customers. We sell only through dealers, and your dealer is HomeCo, Inc.
Example: *Implied refusal:* Our lawn mowers are sold only through dealers, and your dealer is HomeCo, Inc.

Revise the following refusals so that the bad news is implied.

17. We cannot give cash refunds for returned merchandise. Our policy enables us to give only store credit and only for merchandise that is returned in its original packaging and that can be re-sold.

18. I find it impossible to contribute to the fundraising campaign this year. At present all the funds of my organization are needed to lease new equipment and offices for our new branch in Richmond. I hope to be able to support this fund in the future.

19. We cannot ship our fresh fruit baskets C.O.D. Your order was not accompanied by payment, so we are not shipping it. We have it ready, though, and will rush it to its destination as soon as you call us with your credit card number.

Activities and Cases

8.4 Request Refusal: Lease Payments Cannot Be Applied to Purchase. Analyze the following letter. List its weaknesses, and then revise it.

Dear Mr. Cervello:

Unfortunately, we cannot permit you to apply the lease payments you've been making for the past ten months toward the purchase of your Sako 600 copier.

Company policy does not allow such conversion. Have you ever wondered why we can offer such low leasing and purchase prices? Converting lease payments to purchases would mean overall higher prices for our customers. Obviously, we couldn't stay in business long if we agreed to proposals such as yours.

You've had the Sako 600 copier for ten months now, Mr. Cervello, and you say that you like its versatility and reliability. Perhaps we could interest you in another Sako model, such as the Sako 400 series. It may be closer to your price range. Do give us a call.

Sincerely,

---

1. List at least five faults in this letter.

2. Outline a plan for writing a refusal to a request.

Your Task. Revise this refusal. Send your letter to Mr. Walter Cervello, Vice-President of Operations at Copiers Plus, 508 W. Inverary Road, Kingston, ON K2G 1V8. You might mention that many customers are pleased with the Sako copiers, including the Sako 400 series that has nearly as many features as the Sako 600 series. You'd like to demonstrate the Sako 400. Supply any additional information.

8.5 Customer Bad News: Retailers Unable to Deliver.[5] Who wouldn't want a new $770 digital MP3 player for $89.99? At the Future Shop website many delighted shoppers scrambled to order the bargain. Before Future Shop officials could correct the mistake, 340 of the mistakenly priced products were ordered online, representing a total of $230,000 off the original price tag.

Future Shop spared little time in correcting the problem and owning up to the mistake. The company said it would honour any single purchases but would reject bulk orders. The store immediately sent a message to the soon-to-be-disappointed bulk shoppers. The subject line made it clear a *Big Mistake!* had been made and the body of the message began with *We wish we could offer amazing deals like this every day. The price mistake on our new digital MP3 player probably went right by you, but rather than charge you such a large difference, I'm writing to alert you that this item has been removed from your recent order.*

As an assistant in the communication department at Future Shop, you saw the message that was sent to customers and tactfully suggested that the bad news might have been broken differently. Your boss says, "Okay, give it your best shot."

Your Task. Analyze the part of Future Shop's bad-news message given above. Using the principles suggested in this chapter, write an improved version. In the end, Future Shop decided to allow bulk-order customers who ordered the player at $89.99 to reorder it for 20 percent less than the retail price, depending on the number ordered. Customers were directed to a special website to reorder (make up an address). Remember that FutureShop customers are youthful and hip. Keep your message upbeat.

8.6 Request Refusal: Adieu to Cadillacs in Paris. "As I'm sure you've noticed, Cadillac has had success lately with the worldwide launch of the all-new Seville and the much-awaited launch of the Escalade," begins the GM invitation letter. This letter has been sent to many of the top automotive journalists in the country inviting them to join GM's executives on a five-day all-expenses-paid press trip to Paris. Such excursions are not unusual. Big Three automakers routinely sponsor reporters' trips to ensure favourable local coverage from the big auto shows in Paris, Frankfurt, Geneva, and Tokyo.

GM particularly wants reporters at the Paris show, where GM hopes to position Cadillac as a global luxury car manufacturer. The invitation letter, mailed in July, promises a "sneak peak at Cadillac's first major concept vehicle in nearly 10 years." But GM has only 20 spots available for the trip, and journalists have to request one of the spots. Suddenly, in late July, GM finds itself in the midst of an expensive strike. "All at once, what had seemed like a good idea is starting to look fiscally irresponsible," says J. Christopher Preuss, Cadillac spokesperson. Although exact figures are not available, some estimates are that the Paris trip could easily cost $12,000 per reporter. That's a large bill for a company facing a prolonged, damaging strike.

Your Task. As part of a group of interns working in the communications division of GM, you and your team have been asked to draft a letter to the journalists who signed up for the trip. Announce that GM must back out. About the best thing they can expect now is an invitation to the gala unveiling and champagne reception GM will sponsor in January at the annual Detroit auto show. At that time, GM will brief reporters about Cadillac's "new vision" and unveil the eye-popping Escalade. Mr. Preuss is embarrassed about cancelling the Paris trip, but he feels GM must do what is financially prudent. Prepare a draft of the letter for the signature of J. Christopher Preuss. Address the first letter to Rodney M. Olafson, *The Chronicle-Herald*, 185 Haggerty Road, Thunder Bay, ON P7E 5F6.

8.7 Claim Refusal: Wilted Landscaping. As Flora Powell, owner of Town & Country Landscaping, you must refuse the following request. Paul and Judy Alexander have asked that you replace the landscaping in the home they recently purchased in Canmore. You had landscaped that home nearly a year ago for the former owner, Mrs. Hunter, installing a sod lawn and many shrubs, trees, and flowers. It looked beautiful when you finished, but six months later, Mrs. Hunter sold the property and moved to Calgary. Four months passed before the new owners moved in. After four months of neglect and a hot, dry summer, the newly installed landscaping suffered.

You guarantee all your work and normally would replace any plants that do not survive. However, you feel that any refund should depend on proper mainte-nance by the property owner. Moreover, your guarantee is made only to the indi-vidual who contracted with you—not to subsequent owners. You would like to retain the goodwill of the new owners, since this is a wealthy neighbourhood and you hope to attract additional work here. On the other hand, you can't afford to replace the materials invested in this job. You believe that the lawn could prob-ably be fixed with deep watering and fertilizer.

Your Task. Write to Mr. and Mrs. Paul and Judy Alexander, 3318 Clearview Drive, Canmore, AB T2N 3E4, refusing their claim. You would be happy to inspect the property and offer suggestions to the Alexanders. You wonder whether the Alexanders might not have a claim against the former owner for failing to maintain the property. Clearly, however, the claim is not against you.

8.8 Claim Refusal: Evicting a Noisy Neighbour. As Robert Hsu, you must deny the request of Arman Aryai, one of the tenants in your three-storey office building. Mr. Aryai, a C.A., demands that you immediately evict a neighbouring tenant who plays loud music throughout the day, interfering with Mr. Aryai's conversations with clients and with his concentration. The noisy tenant, Bryant Haperot, seems to operate an entertainment booking agency and spends long hours in his office.

You know you can't evict Mr. Haperot immediately because of his lease. Moreover, you hesitate to do anything drastic because paying tenants are hard to find. You called your lawyer, and he said that the first thing you should do is talk to the noisy tenant or write him a letter asking him to tone it down. If this doesn't work within 30 days, you could begin the eviction process.

Your Task. Decide on a course of action. Because Mr. Aryai doesn't seem to answer his telephone, you must write him a letter. You need a permanent record of this decision anyway. Write to Arman Aryai, C.A., Suite 203, Pico Building, 1405 Bower Boulevard, Vancouver, BC V6L 1Y3. Deny his request, but tell him how you plan to resolve the problem.

8.9 Customer Bad News: Olympus Refuses Customer's Request to Repeat World Trip. Olympus Customer Service Manager Charlie Smith can't believe what he reads in a letter from Brian P. Coyle. This 27-year-old Ottawa resident actually wants Olympus to pay for a repeat round-the-world trip because his Olympus Stylus Epic camera malfunctioned and he lost 12 rolls of film!

As soon as Smith saw the letter and the returned camera, he knew what was wrong. Of the two million Stylus Epic cameras made last year, 20,000 did not work properly. A supplier squirted too much oil in the shutter mechanism, and the whole lot was recalled. In fact, Olympus spent almost $1 million to remove these cameras from store shelves. Olympus also contacted all customers who could be reached. In addition to the giant recall, the company quickly redesigned the cameras so that they would work even if they had too much oil. But somehow Coyle was not notified of the recall. When Smith checked the warranty files, he learned that this customer had not returned his warranty. Had the customer done so, he would have been notified in August, well before his trip.

Although the customer service manager is sorry for the mishap, he thinks that a request for $20,000 to replace "lost memories" is ridiculous. Olympus has never assumed any responsibility beyond replacing a camera or film. This customer, however, seems to have suffered more than a routine loss of snapshots. Therefore, Smith decides to sweeten the deal by offering to throw in a digital camera valued at $600, more than double the cost of the Stylus Epic. One of the advantages of a digital camera is that it contains an LCD panel that enables the photographer to view stored images immediately. No chance of losing memories with this digital camera!

Your Task. As the assistant to Customer Service Manager Smith, you must write a letter that refuses the demand for $20,000 but retains the customer's goodwill. Tell this customer what you will do, and be sure to explain how Olympus reacted immediately when it discovered the Stylus Epic defect. Write a sensitive refusal to Brian P. Coyle, 594 Swindon Way, Ottawa, ON K1P 5V5.

8.10 Employee Bad News: Cancelling a Holiday Season Event. In the past your office has always sponsored a holiday season party at a nice restaurant. As your company has undergone considerable downsizing and budget cuts during the past year, you know that no money is available for holiday entertaining.

Your Task. As executive vice-president, send an e-mail to Dina Gillian, office manager. Dina asked permission to make restaurant reservations for this year's holiday party. Refuse Dina's request, but offer some alternatives. How about a potluck dinner?

Grammar/Mechanics Review—8

The following sentences contain errors in grammar, punctuation, usage, and spelling. Below each sentence write a corrected version. There may be more than one error in each sentence.

1. The first report describing Canada's tobacco control laws were recently released in the following provinces Ontario Alberta and Quebec.

2. The report compiled by Statistics Canada showed adult smoking rates varied from 5 percent of the population in Alberta, to 12 percent in Quebec.

3. As expected Quebec's number of deaths related to smoking was nearly twice that of Albertans see page 8 of the report.

4. Anti-tobacco groups stressed the need for stricter regulations however the tobacco industry said the report needed more researches.

5. Statistics Canada made the following statement The comparisons might bring changes in some provinces but the report is not part of any particular policy drive.

6. Children are particularly at risk of second-hand smoke because they breathe faster than adults, they inhale more air in proportion to their body mass and their lungs are still growing and developing.

7. Smoking among high-school students is another area of study in report. Most likely to attract attention.

8. The eight provinces, with the lowest cigarette taxes, has a higher than average number of smoker.

9. The provinces of Newfoundland and British Columbia have the highest provincial tobacco taxs at $22 a pack.

10. Quebec have a nonsmoking campaign encouraging smoker who want to quit to pair up with a nonsmoking partner, both partner sign a pledge not to smoke for six weeks.

11. Walker Merryman a spokesperson for the Tobacco Institute said This report lacks research, therefore it is not useful for understanding why kids smoke.

12. Anti-tobacco supporters are ask government to support a proposal to restrict advertising, marketing, distribution, and sales of tobacco products.

13. The province of Quebec however faces the biggest problem, nearly 24 percent of it's students are daily smoker 15 to 19 years of age.

14. In 2004 the percentage of young people aged 10 to 19 who was beginning to smoke were 17 percent.

15. The government has explain that its hard to restrict smoking when the province's economy is linked so closely to gambling which is link to tobacco.

Document for Revision

The following letter has faults in grammar, spelling, and punctuation. Also, the letter does not follow effective strategies for a negative response. Analyze the letter, list its weaknesses, and revise it, adding appropriate details.

Dear Mr. Franklin:

I am writing this letter to tell you that Ms Sievers and me wish to thank you for the pleasure of allowing us to interview you last Thursday August 25 2009 in our main office. Unfortunately, we cannot offer you the position of human resources assistant. However, we were delighted to here about you're superb acedemic record and we also appreciated your interest and curiosity about the operations of the Maxwell Corporation.

As you can imagine we had many well-qualified applicants who were interest in the advertised position of human resources assistant. As you may have guessed we were particularly interested in a minority individual and could help us fill our employment equal-rights goals. Therefore, you did not fit our needs. But we enjoyed chatting and talking with you. We hired a graduate of Bloor Polytechnic University who had most of the quality that we seeked, if you know what I mean.

Although we realize that the job market is difficult at this point in time, you have our heartfelt wishes for good luck in finding exactly the job you're looking for. If you have any other or further questions please do not hesitate to contact me.

Sincerly

Etiquette 101: A Quick Course in Business Social Skills

Etiquette, civility, and sensitivity may seem out of place in today's fast-moving and competitive global economy. But lately we're seeing signs that etiquette is returning in the world of commerce and industry. More and more employers are recognizing that good manners are good for business.

Schools offering management programs often now include a short course in manners. And companies are conducting manners seminars for trainee and veteran managers. Why is politeness an important leadership tool? Because courtesy works and good manners give a positive image of an organization. People like to do business with people who show respect and treat others with courtesy.

Etiquette is more about attitude than about formal rules of behaviour. That attitude is a desire to make others feel comfortable. You might need to polish your social skills a little to be an effective businessperson today. Here are some classic tips for communicators.[6]

- Smile and greet coworkers in passing.
- Return phone calls and e-mail messages promptly.
- Share recognition for joint projects.
- Use titles for higher-ranking coworkers; avoid the use of first names unless you are asked to be less formal.
- Be on time for meetings, and don't leave early.
- Pay attention during meetings. Save portable audio machines, knitting, or "busy work" for breaks or after work.
- Contribute your fair share for office treats, gifts, or housekeeping duties.
- Pay attention to people's names so that you can remember them.
- Don't discuss sensitive topics (such as sex, religion, and politics) with people you don't know.
- Respect other people's space.
- Show interest in other people. Look at them; make eye contact. Ask questions. Laugh at others' jokes.
- Don't use social/business occasions to push for a raise, bonus, promotion, and so forth.
- Keep your hands to yourself. Some people don't like to be touched.
- Hold doors for men or women entering with you.
- Remember that "please" and "thank you" are always appropriate.

Career Application

You're part of a team of interns that is ending a two-month assignment at a large local firm. With graduation just around the corner, everyone has been looking for permanent jobs. One team member announces that he has been invited for a job interview that includes dinner. He wants to make a good impression, but he confides that he has had very few opportunities to eat at fine restaurants and he's feeling uneasy. He asks for advice.

Your Task

- What general tips of etiquette can you give regarding such things as appropriate dress, arriving at the restaurant, conversation, body language, napkins, and being introduced to people?
- What specific tips can you give regarding the use of silverware, what to order, when to begin eating, and how to eat?
- What kind of etiquette exists regarding technological gadgets such as PDAs, cell phones, and digital pagers at a formal dinner meeting?
- What should the guest do to express appreciation after a dinner meeting?
- List your suggestions and bring them to class to discuss in teams.
- Write a skit of a dinner meeting situation where your team member doesn't make a good impression. Perform the skit for your classmates, and ask them to count the number of etiquette mistakes made in the skit.

Web   **Related website:** Visit http://www.executiveplanet.com for a list of guidelines for entertaining and dining. Check out some of the recommendations for other countries while you are there. You can also read Amy Zunk's "How Rude!: PDA and Cellphone Etiquette in the New Millennium" at http://www.geek.com/pdageek/features/cybermanners.

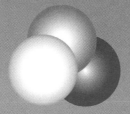

Reporting Data

Chapter 9
Informal Reports

Informal Reports

LEARNING OBJECTIVES

1. Define a report project and gather data.
2. Organize report data using effective headings.
3. Identify four kinds of informal reports and four report formats.
4. Present data objectively.
5. Write information and progress reports.
6. Write justification, recommendation, and feasibility reports.
7. Write summary reports and meeting minutes.

✓ **Quick Check**

Informal reports are relatively short (under ten pages) and are usually written in memo or letter format.

Good report writers, as Heather Jack implies, are good at simplifying facts so that anyone can understand them. Collecting information and organizing it clearly and simply into meaningful reports are skills that all successful businesspeople today require. In this age of information, reports play a significant role in helping decision makers solve problems. You can learn to write good reports by examining basic techniques and by analyzing appropriate models.

Business reports are varied and numerous; therefore, they are difficult to define. They may range from informal e-mail trip reports to formal 200-page financial forecasts. Reports may be presented orally in front of a group using presentation software (e.g., PowerPoint), or they may appear as e-mails, memos, and letters. Still others consist primarily of numerical data, such as tax reports or profit-and-loss statements. Although reports vary in length, content, format, organization, and level of formality, they all have one common purpose: they are step-by-step attempts to answer business questions and to solve business problems. In this chapter we'll concentrate on informal reports. These reports tend to be short (under ten pages); use e-mail, memo, or letter format; and are personal in tone.

Functions of Reports

Most reports can be classified into two functional categories: information reports and analytical reports.

Information Reports

Reports that present data without analysis or recommendations are primarily informational. Although writers collect and organize facts, they are not expected to analyze the facts for readers. A trip report describing an employee's visit to a conference, for example, simply presents information. Other reports that present information without analysis involve routine operations, policy statements, and procedures.

Analytical Reports

Reports that provide analysis and conclusions as well as data are analytical. If requested, writers also supply recommendations. Analysis is the process of breaking down a problem into its parts in order to understand it better and solve it. Analytical reports attempt to persuade readers to act or change their opinions. For example, a recommendation report that compares several potential locations for an employee fitness club might recommend one site, but not until after it has analyzed and discussed the alternatives. This analysis should persuade readers to accept the writer's choice.

Report Formats and Organization

How should a report look? The following four formats are frequently used.

- **Letter format** is for informal reports prepared by one organization for another. These reports are much like letters except that they are more carefully organized, using headings and lists where appropriate.
- **E-mail/memo format** is common for informal reports written for sending within an organization. These internal reports follow the conventions of e-mails and memos that you learned in Chapter 5—with the addition of headings.
- **Manuscript format** is used for longer, more complicated, and more formal reports. Printed on plain paper, with a cover, title page, executive summary, and table of contents, these reports carefully follow a specific pattern used for more formal reports. A sophisticated use of major headings (first level), subheadings (second level), and sub-subheadings (third level) characterizes this format.
- **Prepared forms or templates** are useful in reporting routine activities such as accident reports or merchandise inventories. Standardized headings on these forms save time for the writer; forms also make similar information easy to locate.

Quick Check

Informal reports may appear in four formats: letter, e-mail/memo, manuscript, or on prepared forms.

Today's reports and other business documents are far more sophisticated than typewritten documents of the past. You know how easy it is to use a computer to make your documents look as if they were professionally printed. In fact, many business reports such as corporate annual reports are not typed; they are *designed*. As a report writer, you have a wide selection of fonts and formats from which to choose, plus a number of word-processing features that will help you create attractive documents (see Figure 9.1).

Report Formats and Organization

FIGURE 9.1 Ten Tips for Designing Better Documents

Desktop publishing packages, word-processing programs, and laser printers now make it possible for you to create professional-looking documents. Ten tips for applying good sense and good design principles in "publishing" your documents are as follows:

- **Analyze your audience.** For conservative business documents, avoid overly flashy type, colours, and borders. Also consider whether your readers will be reading carefully or just browsing. Lists and headings help those readers who are in a hurry.
- **Choose an appropriate type size.** For most business memos, letters, and reports, the body text should be 10 to 12 points tall (a point is 1/72 of an inch). Larger type looks unprofessional, and smaller type is hard to read.
- **Use a consistent type font.** Although your software may provide a variety of fonts, stay with a single family of type within one document. The most popular fonts are Times New Roman, Arial, and Helvetica. For emphasis and contrast, you may vary the font size and weight with **bold,** *italic,* ***bold italic,*** and other selections.
- **Don't justify right margins.** Textbooks, novels, newspapers, magazines, and other long works are usually set with justified (even) right margins. However, for shorter works ragged-right margins are recommended because such margins add white space and help readers locate the beginnings of new lines. Slower readers find ragged-right copy easier to read.
- **Separate paragraphs and sentences appropriately.** The first line of a paragraph should be preceded by a blank line. Block format is best. To separate sentences, typists have traditionally left two spaces. This spacing is still acceptable for most business documents. If you are preparing a newsletter or brochure, however, you may wish to adopt printer's standards, leaving one space after end punctuation.
- **Design readable headlines.** Use upper- and lowercase letters for most headlines. Using all caps is generally discouraged in the text headings but should be used for memo and letter subject lines. To further improve readability, select a sans serif typeface (one without cross strokes or embellishment), such as Helvetica or Arial.
- **Strive for an attractive page layout.** In designing title pages or visual aids, provide for a balance between print and white space. Also consider placing the focal point (something that draws the reader's eye) about three lines above the centre of the page. Moreover, remember that the average reader scans a page from left to right and top to bottom in a Z pattern. Plan your visuals accordingly.
- **Limit the use of graphics and clip art.** Images created with spreadsheet or graphics programs can be imported into documents. Original drawings, photographs, and clip art can also be scanned or cut and pasted into documents. Use such images, however, only when they are well drawn, relevant, purposeful, and appropriately sized.
- **Avoid clutter.** Many beginning writers, eager to display every graphic device a program offers, produce busy, cluttered documents. Too many typefaces, ruled lines, images, and oversized headlines will overwhelm readers. Strive for simple, clean, and forceful effects.
- **Become comfortable with templates.** As mentioned in earlier chapters, word-processing software has sophisticated templates that can be used by business writers. Also, most companies have their own report templates they will want you to follow. Because not all of us can be gifted designers, a report template such as Microsoft Word's Elegant Report can save a lot of time and produce professional-looking results. Templates are not magic, though. It takes time to learn how to make them work for you. Spend some time working with one of the report templates on your word-processing software. Decide whether it makes more sense for you to use a template, to follow the examples in this book, or to make one up on your own. Your instructor may make the decision for you.

When it comes to the organization of your informal report, you have two choices. Like correspondence discussed earlier in this book, reports may be organized directly or indirectly. The choice rests on the content of your report and the expectations of your audience.

- The **direct pattern** is the most common organizational pattern for business reports. In an informational business report such as a trip report, the report opens with a short introduction, followed by the facts, and finally a summary.

Figure 9.2 shows such a direct-pattern information report. Notice that because it is an e-mail, the writer has dispensed with headings for her three sections. Many businesspeople prefer the direct pattern because it gives them the results of the report immediately. An analytical report may also be organized directly, especially when readers are supportive and familiar with the topic. In an analytical business report such as a recommendation report, the report opens with a short introduction, followed by the conclusions and recommendations, then the facts and findings, and finally the analysis and discussion.

• The **indirect pattern** is also used when writing business reports. Information reports are never indirect, but analytical reports may be. The difference between direct and indirect analytical reports is simply the placement of the conclusions and recommendations. In an indirect-pattern report, the introduction comes first, followed by the facts and findings, the analysis and discussion, and only then by the conclusions and recommendations. This pattern is helpful when readers are unfamiliar with the problem. It's also useful when readers must be persuaded or when they may be disappointed, doubtful, or not pleased about the report's findings. A side benefit of the indirect pattern is that

FIGURE 9.2 Information Report—E-Mail Format

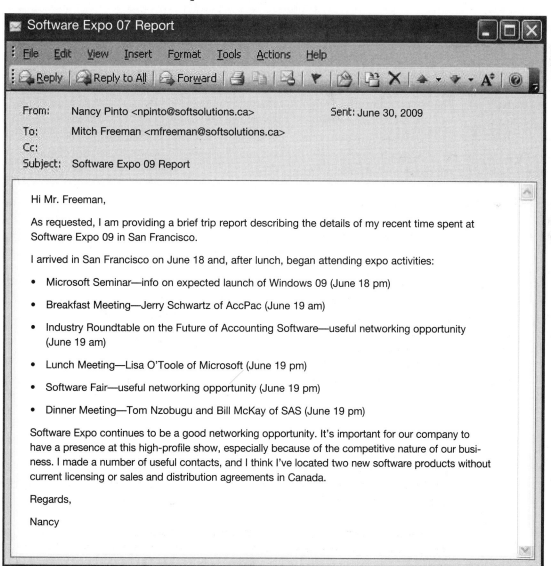

Report Formats and Organization

it reads like a novel or movie, building "suspense" toward a climax, which is resolved in the conclusions and recommendations. Figure 9.6, later in the chapter, shows an indirect-pattern analytical report.

Figure 9.3 summarizes the questions you should ask yourself about your audience before writing your report, as well as your choices for structuring your informal business report.

Guidelines for Writing Informal Reports

Your tendency in preparing a report may be to sit down and begin writing immediately. If you follow this urge, however, you will very likely have to rewrite or even start again. Reports take planning, beginning with defining the project and gathering data. The following guidelines will help you plan your project.

Defining the Project

Begin the process of report writing by defining your project. This definition should include a statement of purpose. Ask yourself: Am I writing this report to inform, analyze, solve a problem, or persuade? The answer to this question should be a clear, accurate statement identifying your purpose. In informal reports the statement of purpose may be only one sentence; that sentence usually becomes part of the introduction. Notice how the following introductory statement describes the purpose of the report:

> This report presents information regarding professional development activities by the Human Resources Department between the first of the year and the present.

FIGURE 9.3 Audience Analysis and Report Organization

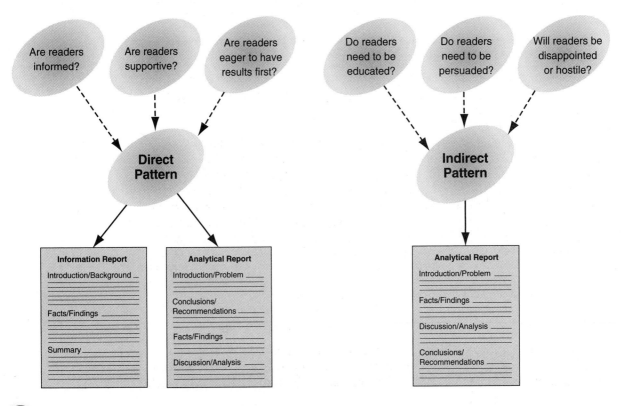

After writing a statement of purpose, analyze who will read your report. If your report is intended for your immediate supervisors, and they support your project, you need not include extensive details, historical development, definition of terms, or persuasion. Other readers, however, may require background information and persuasive strategies.

The expected audience for your report influences your writing style, research method, vocabulary, areas of emphasis, and communication strategy. Remember, too, that your audience may consist of more than one set of readers. Reports are often given to secondary readers who may need more details than the primary reader.

Gathering Data

A good report is based on solid, accurate facts. Typical sources of factual information for informal reports include (1) company records; (2) observation; (3) surveys, questionnaires, and inventories; (4) interviews; and (5) research.

Company Records. Many business-related reports begin with an analysis of company records and files. From these records you can observe past performance and methods used to solve previous problems. You can collect facts that will help determine a course of action.

Observation. Another logical source of data for many problems lies in personal observation and experience. For example, if you were writing a report on the need for additional computer equipment, you might observe how much the current equipment is being used and for what purpose.

Surveys and Questionnaires. Primary data from groups of people can be collected most efficiently and economically by using surveys and questionnaires. For example, if you were part of a committee investigating the success of a campus recycling program, you might begin by using a questionnaire to survey use of the program by students and faculty. You might also do some informal telephoning to see if departments on campus know about the program and are using it.

Interviews. Talking with individuals directly concerned with the problem produces excellent primary information. Interviews also allow for one-on-one communication, thus giving you an opportunity to explain your questions and get the most accurate information.

Electronic and Other Research. In doing secondary research information for reports, you would probably be interested in finding examples from other organizations that have experienced the same problem. You might also check out your competitors to see what they are currently doing and what they have done in the past. A good source of current and historical information is available electronically through online library databases and other online resources. From a home, office, or library computer, you can obtain access to vast amounts of information provided by governments, newspapers, magazines, and companies from all over the world. For informal reports, the most usable data will probably be found in periodicals and online resources.

Developing an Appropriate Writing Style

Like other business messages, reports can range from informal to formal, depending on their purpose, audience, and setting. Research reports from consultants to their clients tend to be rather formal. Such reports must be neutral,

Quick Check

The facts for reports are often obtained from company records, observation, surveys, interviews, and research.

authoritative, and fair. But a report to your boss describing a trip to a conference (as in Figure 9.2) would probably have informal elements. You can see the differences between formal and informal styles in Figure 9.4.

Using Headings Effectively

Headings are helpful to both the report reader and the writer. For the reader, they serve as an outline of the text, highlighting major ideas and categories. They also act as guides for locating facts and pointing the way through the text. Moreover, headings provide resting points for the mind and for the eye, breaking up large chunks of text into manageable and inviting segments. For the writer, headings force organization of the data into meaningful blocks.

Here are general tips on displaying headings effectively:

- **Consistency.** The cardinal rule of headings is that they should be similar. For example, don't use boldface headings for 80 percent of your report and underlined headings for the other 20 percent.
- **Strive for parallel construction.** Use balanced expressions such as *Visible Costs* and *Invisible Costs* rather than *Visible Costs* and *Costs That Don't Show.*
- **Use only short first- and second-level headings.** Many short business reports contain only one or two levels of headings. For such reports use first-level headings (centred, boldface) and/or second-level headings (flush left, boldface).
- **Capitalize and underline carefully.** Most writers use all capital letters (without underlines) for main titles, such as the report, chapter, and unit titles. For first- and second-level headings, they capitalize only the first letter of main words. For additional emphasis, they use a bold font.
- **Keep headings short but clear.** Try to make your headings brief but understandable. Experiment with headings that concisely tell who, what, when, where, and why.

FIGURE 9.4 Report-Writing Styles

	Informal Writing Style	**Formal Writing Style**
Use for ...	Short, routine reports Reports for familiar audiences Uncontroversial reports Most reports for company insiders	Theses Research studies Controversial or complex reports (especially to outsiders)
Effect is ...	Feeling of warmth, personal involvement, closeness	Impression of objectivity, accuracy, professionalism, fairness Distance created between writer and reader
Characteristics are ...	Use of first-person pronouns (*I, we, me, my, us, our*)	Absence of first-person pronouns; use of third-person (*the researcher, the writer*)
	Emphasis on active-voice verbs (*I conducted the study*)	Use of passive-voice verbs (*the study was conducted*)
	Shorter sentences; familiar words	Complex sentences; long words
	Occasional use of humour, metaphors	Absence of humour and figures of speech
	Occasional use of colourful speech	Reduced use of colourful adjectives and adverbs
	Acceptance of author's opinions and ideas	Elimination of "editorializing" (author's opinions, perceptions)

- **Don't enclose headings in quotation marks.** Quotation marks are appropriate only for marking quoted words or words used in a special sense, such as slang. They are unnecessary in headings.
- **Don't use headings as antecedents for pronouns such as** *this, that, these,* **and** *those.* For example, when the heading reads *Laser Printers,* don't begin the next sentence with *These are often used with desktop publishing software.*

Being Objective

Reports are convincing only when the facts and the writer are believable. You can demonstrate that you are trustworthy in a number of ways:

- **Present both sides of an issue.** Even if you favour one possibility, discuss both sides and show through logical reasoning why your position is superior. Remain neutral, letting the facts prove your point.
- **Separate fact from opinion.** Suppose a supervisor wrote *Our department works harder and gets less credit than any other department in the company.* This opinion is difficult to prove, and it makes the writer seem biased. A more convincing statement might be *Our productivity has increased 6 percent over the past year, and I'm proud of the extra effort my employees are making.* After you've made a claim or presented an important statement in a report, ask yourself: Can this fact be proved? If the answer is no, change your statement to make it sound more reasonable.
- **Be sensitive and moderate in your choice of language.** Don't exaggerate. Instead of saying *most people think,* it might be more accurate to say *some people think.* Obviously, avoid using labels and slanted expressions. Calling someone an *idiot,* a *techie,* or an *elitist* demonstrates bias. If readers suspect that a writer is prejudiced, they may discount the entire argument.
- **Cite sources.** Tell your readers where the information came from by using lead-ins to your quotations and paraphrases, and by citing your sources. If you don't do so, you are probably guilty of plagiarism. For example, in a report that reads *In a recent* Vancouver Province *article, Blake Spence, Director of Transportation, argues that the Sky Train must be expanded to cope with the influx of tourists expected during the 2010 Olympics (A17),* "Blake Spence ... argues that" is the lead-in, and "(A17)" is the page reference. Together these two elements are a citation.

Quick Check

Reports are more believable if the author is neutral, separates fact from opinion, uses moderate language, and cites sources.

Four Kinds of Informal Reports

You are about to examine four categories of informal reports frequently written in business. In many instances the boundaries of the categories overlap; distinctions are not always clear-cut. Individual situations, goals, and needs may make one report take on some characteristics of a report in another category. Still, these general categories, presented here in a brief overview, are helpful to beginning writers. The reports will be illustrated and discussed in more detail below.

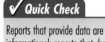
Quick Check

Reports that provide data are informational; reports that draw conclusions and make recommendations are analytical.

- **Information reports.** Reports that collect and organize information are informative. They may record routine activities such as daily, weekly, and monthly reports of sales or profits. They may investigate options, performance, or equipment. Although they provide information, they do not analyze that information nor do they give recommendations.
- **Progress reports.** Progress reports state the steps forward of routine or non-routine activities. For example, progress reports would keep management informed about a committee's preparations for a trade show 14 months from now. Such reports usually answer three questions: (1) Is the project on schedule? (2) Are changes needed? (3) What activities are next?

- **Justification/Recommendation reports.** Recommendation and justification reports are similar to information reports in that they present information; however, they offer analysis in addition to data. They attempt to solve problems by evaluating options and offering recommendations. Usually these reports revolve around a significant company decision.
- **Minutes of meetings.** A final type of informal report is "the minutes" of a meeting, a record of the proceedings and action points of a meeting. Although informal business meetings today take place without minutes being recorded, many companies, organizations, clubs, committees, and boards still require minutes to be recorded. The person who takes notes at a meeting usually turns them into the minutes, distributes them to the participants after the meeting, asks for revisions, and then files the report.

Information Reports

Quick Check

Information reports usually contain three parts: introduction, findings, and summary.

Writers of information reports provide information without drawing conclusions or making recommendations. Some information reports are highly standardized, such as police reports, hospital admittance reports, monthly sales reports, or statistical reports. Many of these are fill-in reports using prepared forms or templates for data and situations that happen on a regular basis. Other information reports are more personalized, as was illustrated in Figure 9.2 (p. 191). They often include these sections:

Introduction

The introduction to an information report may be called *Introduction* or *Background*. In this section do the following: (1) explain why you are writing, (2) describe what methods and sources were used to gather information, (3) provide any special background information that may be necessary, (4) give the purpose of the report, if known, and (5) offer a preview of your findings. In Figure 9.2 not all five of these criteria are met, nor is a heading included, because it is a short, informal information report. If you were writing an information report for a client in letter format, however, you would use the heading *Introduction* and try to fit in all five criteria.

Findings

The findings section of a report may also be called *Observations, Facts, Results,* or *Discussion.* Important points to consider in this section are organization and display. Consider one of these methods of organization: (1) chronological, (2) alphabetical, (3) topical, or (4) most important to least important. You'll notice that in Figure 9.2, the writer uses a chronological method of organization.

To display the findings effectively, number paragraphs, underline or boldface keywords, or use other graphic highlighting methods such as bullets. Be sure that words used as headings are parallel in structure. If the findings require further explanation, either include this discussion with each segment of the findings or place it in a separate section entitled *Discussion.*

Summary

A summary section is optional. If it is included, use it to summarize your findings neutrally. The information report shown in Figure 9.2 summarizes the facts laid out in bullet format, and the significance of the facts is explained.

Notice how easy this information report is to read. Short paragraphs, ample use of graphic highlighting, white space, and concise writing all contribute to improved readability.

Progress Reports

Most progress reports include these four parts:

- The purpose of the project
- A complete summary of the work already completed
- A thorough description of work currently in progress, including personnel, methods, and barriers, as well as attempts to overcome the barriers
- An estimate of future activities about the scheduled completion date, including recommendations and requests

In Figure 9.5, Maria Robinson explains the construction of a real estate company branch office. She begins with a statement summarizing the construction progress in relation to the expected completion date. She then updates the reader with a brief description of past progress. She outlines the present status of construction and concludes by describing the next steps to be taken.

> **Quick Check**
>
> Progress reports state the steps forward of routine or non-routine activities. For example, progress reports would tell management whether projects are on schedule.

Justification/Recommendation Reports

Sometimes, both managers and employees must write reports that recommend or give a reason for something, such as buying equipment, changing a procedure, hiring an employee, or investing funds. Large organizations sometimes state how these reports should be organized; they use forms with conventional headings. At other times, such reports are not standardized. For example, an employee writes a report suggesting improvements in telephone customer service because he feels strongly about it. When you are free to select an organizational plan yourself, however, let your audience and topic determine your choice of direct or indirect structure.

> **Quick Check**
>
> Justification/recommendation reports analyze a problem, discuss options, and present a recommendation, solution, or action to be taken.

For non-sensitive topics and recommendations that will be agreeable to readers, you can organize directly according to the following sequence:

- In the introduction, identify the problem or need briefly.
- Announce the recommendation, solution, or action concisely and with action verbs.
- Discuss pros, cons, and costs. Explain more fully the benefits of the recommendation or steps to be taken to solve the problem.
- Conclude with a summary specifying the recommendation and action to be taken.

Diane Andreas, an executive assistant at a large petroleum company in Calgary, Alberta, was asked to investigate ways to persuade employees to quit smoking. She gathered information about the problem and ways other companies have helped workers stop smoking. The management council needed persuasion because of the costs involved and because some of them smoke. Therefore, she used the indirect strategy by placing the alternative she thought was the strongest at the end of her report (Figure 9.6 on pages 199–200). Finally, she summarizes the findings and provides a specific recommendation.

FIGURE 9.5 **Progress Report**

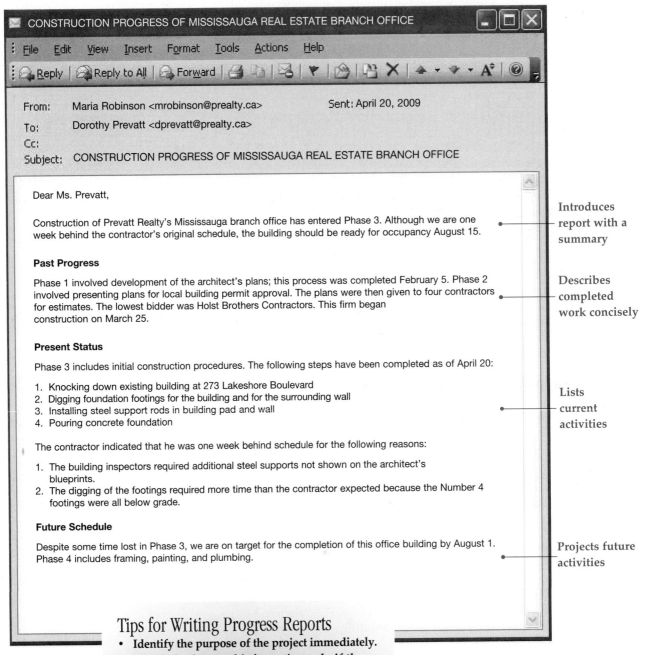

CONSTRUCTION PROGRESS OF MISSISSAUGA REAL ESTATE BRANCH OFFICE

File Edit View Insert Format Tools Actions Help

Reply Reply to All Forward

From: Maria Robinson <mrobinson@prealty.ca>   Sent: April 20, 2009

To: Dorothy Prevatt <dprevatt@prealty.ca>

Cc:

Subject: CONSTRUCTION PROGRESS OF MISSISSAUGA REAL ESTATE BRANCH OFFICE

Dear Ms. Prevatt,

Construction of Prevatt Realty's Mississauga branch office has entered Phase 3. Although we are one week behind the contractor's original schedule, the building should be ready for occupancy August 15.

Past Progress

Phase 1 involved development of the architect's plans; this process was completed February 5. Phase 2 involved presenting plans for local building permit approval. The plans were then given to four contractors for estimates. The lowest bidder was Holst Brothers Contractors. This firm began construction on March 25.

Present Status

Phase 3 includes initial construction procedures. The following steps have been completed as of April 20:

1. Knocking down existing building at 273 Lakeshore Boulevard
2. Digging foundation footings for the building and for the surrounding wall
3. Installing steel support rods in building pad and wall
4. Pouring concrete foundation

The contractor indicated that he was one week behind schedule for the following reasons:

1. The building inspectors required additional steel supports not shown on the architect's blueprints.
2. The digging of the footings required more time than the contractor expected because the Number 4 footings were all below grade.

Future Schedule

Despite some time lost in Phase 3, we are on target for the completion of this office building by August 1. Phase 4 includes framing, painting, and plumbing.

Introduces report with a summary

Describes completed work concisely

Lists current activities

Projects future activities

Tips for Writing Progress Reports

- Identify the purpose of the project immediately.
- Supply background information only if the reader must be educated.
- Describe the work completed.
- Discuss the work in progress, including personnel, activities, methods, and locations.
- Identify problems and possible remedies.
- Consider future activities.
- Close by giving the expected date of completion.

FIGURE 9.6 Justification/Recommendation Report—Memo Format

1

DATE: October 12, 2009

TO: Damon Moore, Director, Human Resources

FROM: Diane Andreas, Executive Assistant

SUBJECT: MEASURES TO HELP EMPLOYEES STOP SMOKING

At your request, I have examined measures that encourage employees to quit smoking. As company records show, approximately 23 percent of our employees still smoke, despite the antismoking and clean-air policies we adopted in 1995. To collect data for this report, I studied professional and government publications. I also inquired at companies and clinics about stop-smoking programs.

This report presents data describing the significance of the problem, three alternative solutions, and a recommendation based on my investigation.

Significance of Problem: Health Care and Productivity Losses

Employees who smoke are costly to any organization. The following statistics show the effects of smoking for workers and for organizations:

- Absenteeism is 40 to 50 percent greater among smoking employees.
- Accidents are two to three times greater among smokers.
- Bronchitis, lung and heart disease, cancer, and early death are more frequent among smokers (Johns, 2003, p. 14).

Although our clean-air policy prohibits smoking in the building, shop, and office, we have done little to encourage employees to stop smoking. Many workers still go outside to smoke at lunch and breaks. Other companies have been far more proactive in their attempts to stop employee smoking. Many companies have found that persuading employees to stop smoking was a decisive factor in reducing their supplementary health insurance premiums. Below is a discussion of three common stop-smoking measures tried by other companies, along with a projected cost factor for each.

Alternative 1: Literature and Events

The least expensive and easiest stop-smoking measure involves the distribution of literature, such as "The Ten-Step Plan" from Smokefree Enterprises and government pamphlets citing smoking dangers. Some companies have also sponsored events such as Weedless Wednesday, a one-day occasion intended to develop group spirit in spurring smokers to quit. "Studies show, however," says one expert, "that literature and company-sponsored events have little permanent effect in helping smokers quit" (Woo, 2003, p. 107).

Cost: Negligible

Annotations (left):
- Avoids revealing recommendation immediately
- Uses headings that combine function and description
- Discusses least effective alternative first

Annotations (right):
- Introduces purpose of report, tells method of data collection, and previews organization
- Documents data sources for credibility; uses APA style citing author, date, and page number in the text

Tips for Memo Reports

- Use memo format for most short (ten or fewer pages) informal reports within an organization.
- Leave side margins of 2.5 to 3 cm.
- Sign your initials on the FROM line.
- Use an informal, conversational style.
- For a receptive audience, put recommendations first.
- For an unreceptive audience, put recommendations last.

FIGURE 9.6 Continued

2

Alternative 2: Stop-Smoking Programs Outside the Workplace

Local clinics provide treatment programs in classes at their centres. Here in Calgary we have Smokers' Treatment Centre, ACC Motivation Centre, and the New-Choice Program for Stopping Smoking. These behaviour-modification stop-smoking programs are acknowledged to be more effective than literature distribution or incentive programs. However, studies of companies using off-workplace programs show that many employees fail to attend regularly and do not complete the programs.

Cost: $750 per employee, three-month individual program (New-Choice Program)
$500 per employee, three-month group sessions

Highlights costs for easy comparison

Alternative 3: Stop-Smoking Programs at the Workplace

Many clinics offer workplace programs with counsellors meeting employees in company conference rooms. These programs have the advantage of keeping a firm's employees together so that they develop a group spirit and exert pressure on each other to succeed. The most successful programs are on company premises and also on company time. Employees participating in such programs had a 72 percent greater success record than employees attending the same stop-smoking program at an outside clinic (Manley, 2002, p. 35). A disadvantage of this arrangement, of course, is lost work time—amounting to about two hours per week for three months.

Arranges alternatives so that most effective is last

Cost: $500 per employee, three-month program two hours per week release time for three months

Conclusions and Recommendation

Smokers seem to require discipline, counselling, and professional assistance in kicking the nicotine habit. Workplace stop-smoking programs, on company time, are more effective than literature, incentives, and off-workplace programs. If our goal is to reduce supplementary health care costs and lead our employees to healthful lives, we should invest in a workplace stop-smoking program with release time for smokers. Although the program temporarily reduces productivity, we can expect to recapture that loss in lower health care premiums and healthier employees.

Summarizes findings and ends with specific recommendation

Therefore, I recommend that we begin a stop-smoking treatment program on company premises with two hours per week of release time for participants for three months.

Reveals recommendation only after discussing all alternatives

3

References

Lists all references in APA style

Magazine — Johns, K. (2003, May). No smoking in your workplace. *Business Times*, 14–16.

Journal — Manley, D. (2002). Up in smoke: A case study of one company's proactive stance against smoking. *Management Review, 14*, 33–37.

Book — Woo, N. A. (2003). *The last gasp*. New York: Field Publishers.

Minutes provide a summary of what happens in a meeting. Formal, traditional minutes, illustrated in Figure 9.7, are written for large groups and government organizations. If you are the secretary of a meeting, you'll want to write minutes that do the following:

- Provide the name of the group, as well as the date, time, and place of the meeting.
- Identify the names of attendees and absentees, if appropriate.
- Describe the details of previous minutes.

FIGURE 9.7 Minutes of Meeting—Report Format

International Association of Administrative Professionals

Western Canada Division
Planning Committee Meeting
Conference Room B, Brunswick Plaza Hotel
November 4, 2009, 10 a.m.

Present: Carol Allen, Kim Jobe, LeeAnn Johnson, Barbara Leonard, Lee Schultz, Doris Williamson, Margaret Zappa

Shows attendees and absentees

Absent: Ellen Williams

The meeting was called to order by Chair Kim Jobe at 10:05 a.m. Minutes from the July 11 meeting were read and approved.

Describes disposition of previous minutes

Old Business

Summarizes discussion; does not record every word

LeeAnn Johnson and Barbara Leonard reviewed the information distributed at the last meeting about hotels being considered for the Banff conference. LeeAnn said that the Fairmont Banff Springs has plenty of conference rooms and remodelled interiors. Barbara reported that the Mount Royal Hotel also has excellent banquet facilities, adequate meeting facilities, and rooms at $112 per night.
MOTION: To recommend that IAAP hold its International Convention at the Mount Royal Hotel, July 21–24, 2010. (Allen/Leonard). PASSED 6–1.

Reports

Lee Schultz reported on convention exhibits and her desire to involve more companies and products. Discussion followed regarding how this might be accomplished.
MOTION: That IAAP office staff develop a list of possible convention exhibitors. The list should be submitted at the next meeting. (Leonard/Schultz). PASSED 7–0.

Highlights motions, showing name of person making motion and person seconding it

New Business

Summarizes new business and announcements

The chair announced three possible themes for the convention, all of which focused on technology and the changing role of administrative assistants. Doris Williamson suggested the following possible title: "Vision without Boundaries." Carol Allen suggested a communication theme. Several other possibilities were discussed. The chair appointed a subcommittee of Doris and Margaret to bring to the next committee meeting two or three concrete theme ideas.

Margaret Zappa thought that IAAP should be doing more to help members stay ahead in the changing workplace. She suggested workshops to polish skills in spreadsheet, database, presentations, and scheduling software.
MOTION: To recommend to IAAP that it investigate offering fee-based technology workshops at the national and regional conventions. (Zappa/Schultz). PASSED 5–2.

The meeting was adjourned at 11:50 by Kim Jobe.

Respectfully submitted,

Carol Allen

Carol Allen, Secretary

Shows name and signature of person recording minutes

- Record old business, new business, announcements, and reports.
- Include the precise wording of motions; record the vote and action taken.
- Conclude with the name and signature of the person recording the minutes.

Notice in Figure 9.7 that secretary Carol Allen tries to summarize discussions rather than capture every comment. However, when a motion is made, she records it exactly. She also shows in parentheses the name of the individual making the motion and the person who seconded it. By using all capital letters for "MOTION" and "PASSED," she makes these important items stand out for easy reference.

Informal minutes are usually shorter and easier to read than formal minutes. They may be formatted with three categories: summaries of topics discussed, decisions reached, and action items (showing the action item, the person responsible, and the due date).

Summing Up and Looking Forward

This chapter presented four types of informal business reports: information reports, progress reports, justification/recommendation reports, and minutes of meetings. Information reports generally provide data only. But justification/recommendation reports are more analytical in that they also evaluate the information, offer conclusions, and make recommendations. This chapter also discussed four formats for reports. Letter format is used for reports sent outside an organization; memo format is used for internal reports. More formal reports are formatted on plain paper with a manuscript design, while routine reports may be formatted on prepared forms. The chapter presented numerous model documents illustrating the many kinds of reports and their formats. Readers were also given tips for designing reports with desktop publishing programs to enhance the reports' appearance.

All of the examples in this chapter are considered relatively informal. Longer, more formal reports are necessary for major investigations and research.

Critical Thinking

1. How do business reports differ from business letters?
2. Of the reports presented in this chapter, classify those that require indirect development versus those that require direct development.
3. How are the reports that you write for your courses similar to those presented here? How are they different?

Chapter Review

4. List four kinds of informal reports. Be prepared to describe each.

5. List four formats suitable for reports. Be prepared to discuss each.

6. From the lists you made in Questions 4 and 5, select a report category and appropriate format for each of the following situations.
   a. You want to tell management about an idea you have for improving a procedure that you think will increase productivity.

   b. You just attended a meeting at which you were the only person taking notes. The person who ran the meeting sends you an e-mail asking if you could remind him of the important decisions that were made.

   c. As Engineering Department office manager, you have been asked to describe your highly regarded computer system for another department.

   d. As a police officer, you are writing a report of an arrest.

   e. At a mail-order catalogue company, your boss asks you to investigate ways to reduce the time that customers are kept waiting for service representatives to take their telephone orders. She wants your report to examine the problem and offer solutions.

7. If you were about to write the following reports, where would you gather information? Be prepared to discuss the specifics of each choice.
   a. You are a student representative on a curriculum committee. You are asked to study the course requirements in your major and make recommendations.

   b. As department manager, you must write job descriptions for several new positions you wish to establish in your department.

   c. You are proposing that management replace a photocopier in your department.

   d. You must document the progress of a 12-month advertising campaign to alter the image of a clothing manufacturer's jeans.

8. What three questions do progress reports typically address?

9. What is the purpose of a meeting minutes report?

10. Information reports generally contain what three parts?

Activities and Cases

9.1 Evaluating Headings and Titles. Evaluate the effectiveness of the following report headings and titles:

    a.   Problem

    b.   Need for Tightening Computer ID System

    c.   Annual Budget

    d.   How Direct Mail Can Deliver Profits for Your Business

    e.   Case History: Rotunda Palace Hotel Focuses on Improving Service to Customers

    f.   Solving Our Networking Problems with an Extranet

    g.   Comparing Copier Volume, Ease of Use, and Speed

    h.   Alternatives

9.2 Information Report: Canadian Tech Company Expands into Asia. You work in business development for Hydrogenics, a Mississauga, Ontario–based producer of clean energy products. Hydrogenics already has an office in Tokyo, but it wants to expand its Asian operations. Your boss has asked you to investigate the partnership opportunities available for investors in Korea and China. He gives you a tight deadline of one week, and asks for the report to be sent to him via e-mail with any attachments you think are important.

Your Task. Investigate the mechanics of opening an office and/or investing in Korea and China. Report your findings in an e-mail to Bob Khan, your boss.

9.3 Progress Report: Advancing Toward Your Educational Goal. You made an agreement with your parents (or spouse, relative, or partner) that you would submit a progress report at this time describing your progress toward your educational goal (employment, certificate, diploma, degree).

Your Task. In memo format, write a progress report that fulfills your promise to describe your progress toward your educational goals. Address your progress report to your parents, spouse, relative, or partner. In your memo (1) describe your goal; (2) summarize the work you have completed thus far; (3) discuss thoroughly the work currently in progress, including your successes and anticipated obstacles; and (4) forecast your future activities in relation to your scheduled completion date.

9.4 Recommendation Report: What Is It About Advertising? You are the CEO of a mid-size Vancouver-based advertising agency named Slam! Your company is in the enviable position of having secured the advertising contract for the 2010 Vancouver/Whistler Olympics. The problem is, you can't seem to keep your employees around long enough to ensure continuity within projects. It seems as though the advertising business is a revolving door: new college and university grads are eager to work for you, then six months later once you've trained them, they leave for more lucrative jobs at other agencies. You're too busy to figure out a solution or policy; in fact you're so busy you haven't got around to hiring a human resources manager. Instead you ask your research manager to write you a report on some possible solutions.

Your Task. As the research manager at Slam!, research and write a short e-mail recommendation report for your boss outlining some possible solutions to the "revolving door" problem. Your boss is extremely thrifty, so you'll have to be careful about how you phrase any expensive solutions.

Related website: Canada News Wire Group's recent story on this issue can be accessed at www.humanresources.about.com/od/retention, but you should also do other research on the topic of employee retention. Be careful not to plagiarize from your sources when completing this report.

Web

9.5 Justification Report: Evaluating Your Curriculum. You have been serving as a student member of a college curriculum advisory committee. The committee is expected to examine the course requirements for a degree, diploma, or certificate in your area.

Your Task. In teams of three to five, decide whether the requirements are realistic and practical. What improvements can your team suggest? Interview other students, faculty members, and employers for their suggestions. Prepare a justification report in letter or memo format to send to the dean of your college proposing your suggestions. You anticipate that the head of your faculty or department may need to be persuaded to make any changes. Consider delaying your recommendations until after you have developed a foundation of explanation and reasons.

9.6 Justification Report: Purchasing New Equipment. In your work or your training, identify equipment that needs to be purchased or replaced (computer, printer, modem, DVD, copier, digital camera, etc.). Gather information about two different models or brands.

Your Task. Write a justification report comparing the two items. Establish a context by describing the need for the equipment. Discuss the present situation, emphasizing the current deficiencies. Describe the advantages of acquiring the new equipment.

9.7 Recommendation Report: Time for a Change. Identify several problems or procedures that must be changed at your place of employment, such as poor scheduling of employees, outdated equipment, inadequate training or disappointed customers. Using the indirect pattern, write a recommendation report outlining at least three problems and suggesting ways to solve the problems. Address the memo report to your boss.

9.8 Recommendation Report: Solving a Campus Problem. In groups of three, or alone, investigate a problem on your campus such as inadequate parking, slow registration, poor class schedules, an inefficient bookstore, or course-related weaknesses. Develop a solution to the problem. Write a recommendation report to the proper campus official or to your instructor, describing the problem and offering suggestions for improvement.

9.9 Minutes: Recording the Proceedings of a Meeting. Ask your instructor to let you know when the next all-faculty or division or departmental meeting is taking place on your campus. Or, ask your student association or student council representative to let you know when the next association or council meeting is taking place. Or, next time you're at work or at your co-op job, ask your boss to let you sit in on a meeting. Volunteer to act as note-taker or secretary for this meeting.

Your Task. Record the proceedings of the meeting you attend in an informal meeting minutes report. Focus on reports presented, motions/action items, votes, and decisions reached.

9.10 Role Play: Everyone's Taking Minutes. Next time you have a group or team meeting related to one of your school assignments, videotape or audiotape one of your group or team meetings. Then, turn that meeting into a scripted skit. Perform the skit in front of your class.

Your Task. As an audience member, watch the skit discussed above. Assume you are the note-taker at the meeting. Create a minutes report for the meeting you just watched. Are there any elements of a meeting the group/team missed (e.g., motions, action statements, etc.)?

9.11 Longer Report: Solving a Problem. Choose a business or organization with which you are familiar and identify a problem or problems such as poor quality, indifferent service, absenteeism at organization meetings, uninspired cafeteria food, outdated office equipment, unresponsive management, lack of communication, underappreciated employees, wasteful procedures, or a similar problem.

Your Task. In the introductory section of the report, provide information about the company such as the history, location, staffing, and any other details to describe the company to the reader. You may use primary and/or secondary sources to develop this section. Then describe the problem(s) in detail. Assume you are to report to management (or to the leadership of an organization) about the nature and scope of the problem. Decide which kind of report to prepare (information, recommendation, justification), and choose the format. How would you gather data to lend authority to your conclusions and recommendations? Determine the exact topic and report length after consultation with your instructor.

Grammar/Mechanics Review—9

The following sentences contain errors in grammar, punctuation, spelling, and apostrophes. Below each sentence write a corrected version.

Example: Two employees schedules' were change last week.
Revision: Two employees' schedules were changed last week.

1. Last weeks appointment was cancelled by Maria the office secretary.

2. Although the meeting was first set for May 2 its been postponed until May 10.

3. If you go to the third floor you will find Mr. Franklins office.

4. Many exhibitors' at the Trade Show came from as far as Australia and Japan to promote there products.

5. One customers files have been lost, we must review our current filing system.

6. We believe that this firms service is much better then that firms.

7. Large companies are looking for ways to shrink shipping costs therefore we will revise our companys procedures for sending supplys.

8. Zoomout cameras was awarded as prizes at last months awards' ceremony.

9. Because there are so many Canadians who travel to Florida the price of hotel accommodations go up in the winter.

10. At the presidents suggestion we doubled the order and we reached our goal.

11. In Canada 68 percent of the land is wilderness, however Africas' landscape is only 28 percent wilderness.

12. This dress is her's, those scarves are our's.

13. None of the employees in our department take more than two weeks vacation.

14. As soon as the supervisor can check this weeks sales. The company will placed an order.

15. There is no Canadian football league team that plays it's home games in a domed stadium that have ever won a Grey Cup trophy.

Grammar/Mechanics Challenge—9

Document for Revision

The following progress report has faults in grammar, punctuation, spelling, number form, wordiness, and word use. Use standard proofreading marks (see Appendix B) to correct the errors. Improve the headings. When you finish, your instructor can show you the revised version of this report.

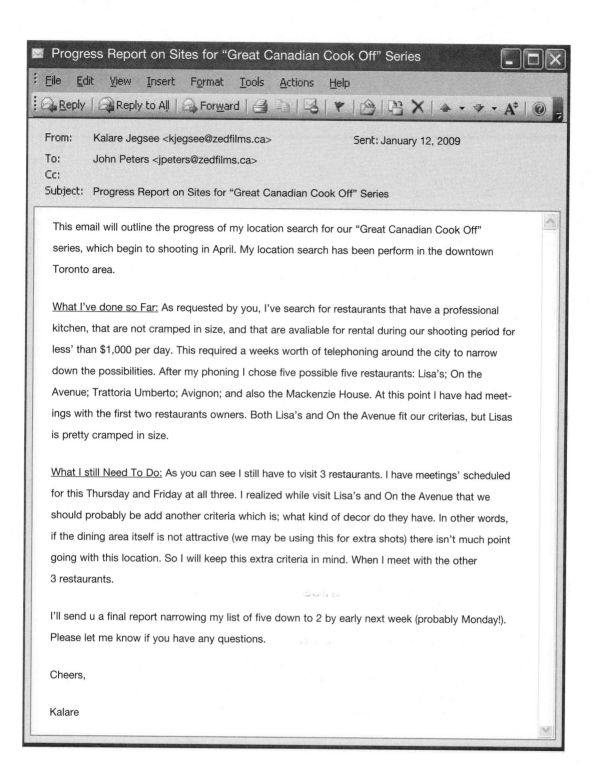

Progress Report on Sites for "Great Canadian Cook Off" Series

File   Edit   View   Insert   Format   Tools   Actions   Help

Reply | Reply to All | Forward

From: Kalare Jegsee <kjegsee@zedfilms.ca>   Sent: January 12, 2009

To: John Peters <jpeters@zedfilms.ca>

Cc:

Subject: Progress Report on Sites for "Great Canadian Cook Off" Series

This email will outline the progress of my location search for our "Great Canadian Cook Off" series, which begin to shooting in April. My location search has been perform in the downtown Toronto area.

<u>What I've done so Far:</u> As requested by you, I've search for restaurants that have a professional kitchen, that are not cramped in size, and that are avaliable for rental during our shooting period for less' than $1,000 per day. This required a weeks worth of telephoning around the city to narrow down the possibilities. After my phoning I chose five possible five restaurants: Lisa's; On the Avenue; Trattoria Umberto; Avignon; and also the Mackenzie House. At this point I have had meetings with the first two restaurants owners. Both Lisa's and On the Avenue fit our criterias, but Lisas is pretty cramped in size.

<u>What I still Need To Do:</u> As you can see I still have to visit 3 restaurants. I have meetings' scheduled for this Thursday and Friday at all three. I realized while visit Lisa's and On the Avenue that we should probably be add another criteria which is; what kind of decor do they have. In other words, if the dining area itself is not attractive (we may be using this for extra shots) there isn't much point going with this location. So I will keep this extra criteria in mind. When I meet with the other 3 restaurants.

I'll send u a final report narrowing my list of five down to 2 by early next week (probably Monday!). Please let me know if you have any questions.

Cheers,

Kalare

Laying the Groundwork for Team Writing Projects

Chances are that you can look forward to some kind of team writing in your future career. You may collaborate voluntarily (seeking advice and differing perspectives) or involuntarily (through necessity or by assignment). Working with other people can be frustrating, particularly when some team members don't produce or when conflict breaks out. Team projects, though, can be harmonious and productive when members establish ground rules at the outset and adhere to guidelines such as the following.

Preparing to Work Together. Before you discuss the project, talk about how your group will function.

- Limit the size of your team, if possible, to three or four members. Larger groups have more difficulties. An odd number is usually preferable so that ties in voting are avoided.
- Name a meeting leader (to plan and conduct meetings), a recorder (to keep a record of group decisions), and an evaluator (to determine if the group is on target and meeting its goals).
- Decide whether your team will be governed by consensus (everyone must agree, no voting) or by majority rule.
- Compare schedules of team members, and set up the best meeting times. Plan to meet often. Avoid other responsibilities during meetings.
- Discuss the value of conflict. By bringing conflict into the open and encouraging confrontation, your team can prevent personal resentment and group dysfunction. Confrontation can actually create better final documents by promoting new ideas and avoiding the tendency for group members to agree to things they normally wouldn't just to avoid conflict.
- Discuss how you will deal with members who are not producing at a level acceptable to others in the group.

Planning the Document. Once you've established ground rules, you're ready to discuss the project and resulting document. Be sure to keep a record of the decisions your team makes.

- Establish the document's specific purpose and identify the main issues involved.
- Decide on the final form of the document. What parts will it have?
- Discuss the audience(s) for the document and what appeal would help it achieve its purpose.
- Develop a work plan. Assign jobs. Set deadlines.
- Decide how the final document will be written: individuals working separately on assigned portions, one person writing the first draft, the entire group writing the complete document together, or some other method.

Collecting Information. The following suggestions help teams gather accurate information:

- Brainstorm for ideas as a group.
- Decide who will be responsible for gathering what information.
- Establish deadlines for collecting information.
- Discuss ways to ensure the accuracy of the information collected.

Organizing, Writing, and Revising. As the project progresses, your team may wish to modify some of its earlier decisions.

- Review the proposed organization of your final document, and adjust it if necessary.
- Write the first draft. If separate team members are writing segments then collecting them by e-mail, they should confirm that their e-mails have reached the receiver.
- Meet to discuss and revise the draft(s).
- If individuals are working on separate parts, appoint one person (probably the best writer) to coordinate all the parts, striving for consistent style and format.

Editing and Evaluating. Before the document is submitted, complete these steps:

- Give one person responsibility for finding and correcting grammatical and mechanical errors.
- Meet as a group to evaluate the final document. Does it fulfill its purpose and meet the needs of the audience?

Career Application

Select a report topic from this chapter. Assume that you must prepare the report as a team project. If you are working on a long report, your instructor may ask you to prepare individual progress reports as you develop your topic.

Your Task

- Form a team of three to five members.
- Prepare to work together by using the suggestions provided here.
- Plan your report by establishing its purpose, identifying the main issues, developing a work plan, and assigning tasks.
- Collect information, organize the data, and write the first draft.
- Decide how the document will be revised, edited, and evaluated.

Your instructor may assign grades not only on the final report but also on your team effectiveness and your individual contribution, as determined by fellow team members.

Developing Speaking Skills

Chapter 10
Communicating in Person and by Telephone

Communicating in Person and by Telephone

Before meeting with clients, I gather as much information as possible. The more information, the better prepared I can be to meet their needs. Preparation is key for any meeting. It's important to meet face-to-face with my clients to get to know them on a personal level. In our meetings, we work together to establish client goals, plan for future needs, and monitor client progress.[1]

Orna Spira, *Investment Advisor, CIBC Wood Gundy*

LEARNING OBJECTIVES

1. Understand how to improve face-to-face workplace communication including using your voice as a communication tool.
2. Specify procedures for positive workplace relations through conversation.
3. Review techniques for offering constructive criticism on the job, responding professionally to workplace criticism, and resolving workplace conflicts.
4. Identify ways to polish professional telephone skills, including traditional phones and cell phones.
5. List techniques for making the best use of voice mail.

✔ **Quick Check**

Strong oral communication skills can help you be hired and succeed on the job.

Oral communication skills are highly ranked by employers. Companies are looking for employees who can interact successfully with customers, work smoothly with coworkers, and provide meaningful feedback to managers. Expressing yourself well and communicating effectively with others are skills that are critical to job placement, workplace performance, career advancement, and organizational success.

Earlier in this book you studied the communication process, effective listening techniques, and nonverbal communication skills. Other chapters helped you develop good writing skills. This chapter will complete your communication skills by focusing on oral communication skills. In your business or professional career, you will be judged not only by what you say but also by the way you say it. In this chapter we'll help you become a more successful speaker when you communicate in person, by telephone, and in meetings.

Because technology provides various communication channels, you may think that face-to-face communication is no longer important in business and professional dealings. You've already learned that e-mail is now the preferred communication channel because it is faster, cheaper, and easier than telephone, mail, or fax. Yet, despite their popularity and acceptance, alternate communication technologies can't replace the richness or effectiveness of face-to-face communication.[2] Imagine that you want to tell your boss how you solved a problem. Would you settle for a one-dimensional phone call, a fax, or an e-mail when you could step into her office and explain in person?

Face-to-face conversation has many advantages. It allows you to be persuasive and expressive because you can use your voice and body language to make a point. You are less likely to be misunderstood because you can read feedback and make needed changes. In conflict resolution, you can reach a solution more efficiently and cooperate to create greater levels of mutual benefit when communicating face to face.[3] Moreover, people want to see each other to satisfy a deep human need for social interaction. For many reasons, communicating in person remains the most effective of all communication channels. In this chapter you'll explore helpful business and professional interpersonal speaking techniques, starting with viewing your voice as a communication tool.

Using Your Voice as a Communication Tool

It's been said that language provides the words, but your voice is the music that makes words meaningful.[4] You may believe that a beautiful or powerful voice is hard to achieve. After all, this is the voice you were born with, and it can't be changed. Actually, the voice is a flexible instrument. Actors hire coaches to help them get rid of or take on accents or strike a certain tone for challenging roles. For example, two of Canada's leading theatre companies, the Stratford and Shaw festivals in Ontario, both have speech coaches on staff to teach actors various accents and voice techniques. Celebrities, business executives, and everyday people consult voice and speech therapists to help them shake bad habits or help them speak so that they can be understood and not sound less intelligent than they are. Rather than consult a high-paid specialist, you can pick up useful tips for using your voice most effectively by learning how to control such elements as pronunciation, tone, pitch, volume, rate, and emphasis.

Quick Check

Like an actor, you can change your voice to make it a more powerful communication tool.

Quick Check

Proper pronunciation means saying words correctly and clearly with the accepted sounds and accented syllables.

Pronunciation. Pronunciation involves saying words correctly and clearly with the accepted sounds and accented syllables. If you practise and train to pronounce words correctly, you'll have a distinct advantage in your job. Some of the most common errors, shown in Figure 10.1, include adding or omitting vowels, omitting consonants, reversing sounds, and slurring sounds. In casual conversation with your friends, correct pronunciation is not a big deal. But on the job you want to sound intelligent, educated, and competent. If you mispronounce words or slur phrases together, you risk being misunderstood as well as giving a poor impression of yourself. How can you improve your pronunciation skills? The best way is to listen carefully to educated people, read aloud from well-written newspapers such as *The Globe and Mail* and the *National Post*, look up words in the dictionary, and avoid errors such as those in Figure 10.1.

Tone. The tone of your voice sends a nonverbal message to listeners. It identifies your personality and your mood. Some voices sound enthusiastic and friendly,

FIGURE 10.1 Pronunciation Errors to Avoid

Adding vowel sounds	*athlete* (NOT *ath-a-lete*)
	disastrous (NOT *disas-ter-ous*)
Omitting vowel sounds	*federal* (NOT *fed-ral*)
	ridiculous (NOT *ri-dic-lous*)
	generally (NOT *gen-rally*)
Substituting vowel sounds	*get* (NOT *git*)
	separate (NOT *sep-e-rate*)
Adding consonant sounds	*butter* (NOT *budder*)
	statistics (NOT *sta-stis-tics*)
	especially (NOT *ex-specially*)
Omitting consonant sounds	*library* (NOT *libery*)
	perhaps (NOT *praps*)
Confusing or distorting sounds	*ask* (NOT *aks*)
	hundred (NOT *hunderd*)
	accessory (NOT *assessory*)
Slurring sounds	*didn't you* (NOT *dint ya*)
	going to (NOT *gonna*)

giving the impression of an upbeat person who is happy to be with the listener. But voices can also sound controlling, slow-witted, angry, or childish. This doesn't mean that the speaker has that quality. It may mean that the speaker is just carrying on a family tradition or pattern learned in childhood. To check your voice tone, record your voice and listen to it critically. Is it projecting a positive quality about you?

Pitch. Effective speakers use a relaxed, controlled, well-pitched voice to attract listeners to their message. Pitch refers to sound vibration frequency; that is, it indicates the highness or lowness of a sound. In Canada, speakers and listeners prefer a variety of pitch patterns. Voices are most attractive when they rise and fall in conversational tones. Flat, monotone voices are considered boring and unimpressive. In business, communicators strive for a moderately low voice, which is thought to be pleasing and professional.

 Quick Check

Speaking in a moderately low-pitched voice at about 125 words a minute makes you sound pleasing and professional.

Volume and Rate. Volume indicates the degree of loudness or the intensity of sound. Just as you adjust the volume on your radio or television, you should adjust the volume of your speaking to the occasion and your listeners. When speaking face to face, you generally know whether you are speaking too loudly or softly by looking at your listeners. Are they straining to hear you? To judge what volume to use, listen carefully to the other person's voice. Use it as a guide for adjusting your voice. Rate refers to the pace of your speech. If you speak too slowly, listeners are bored and their attention wanders. If you speak too quickly, listeners can't understand you. Most people normally talk at about 125 words a minute. If you're the kind of speaker who speeds up when talking in front of a group of people, watch the nonverbal signs of your listeners and change your rate as needed.

Emphasis. By stressing certain words, you can change the meaning you are expressing. For example, read these sentences aloud, stressing the italicized words:

Matt said the hard drive failed again. (Matt knows what happened.)
Matt *said* the hard drive failed again. (But he may be wrong.)
Matt said the hard drive failed *again*? (Did he really say that?)

As you can see, emphasis affects the meaning of the words and the thought expressed. To make your message interesting and natural, use emphasis appropriately. You can raise your volume to sound authoritative and raise your pitch to sound disbelieving. Lowering your volume and pitch makes you sound professional or reasonable.

Promoting Positive Workplace Relations Through Conversation

In the workplace, conversations may involve giving and taking instructions, providing feedback, exchanging ideas on products and services, or chatting about such things as families and sports. Face-to-face conversation helps people work together and feel that they are part of the larger organization. There are several guidelines, starting with using correct names and titles, that promote positive workplace conversations.

Use Correct Names and Titles. Although the world seems increasingly informal, it's still wise to use titles and last names when addressing professional adults (*Mrs. Smith, Mr. Rivera*). In some organizations senior staff members will speak to junior employees on a first-name basis, but the reverse may not be encouraged. Probably the safest plan is to ask your superiors how they want to be addressed. Customers and others outside the organization should always be addressed by title and last name.

When you meet strangers, do you have trouble remembering their names? You can improve your memory if you associate the person with an object, place, colour, animal, job, adjective, or some other memory hook. For example, *computer pro Kevin, Miami Kim, silver-haired Mr. Lee, bull-dog Chris, bookkeeper Lynn, traveller Ms. Janis.* The person's name will also be more deeply printed in your memory if you use it immediately after being introduced, in later conversation, and when you part.

✔ *Quick Check*

You will be most effective in workplace conversations if you use correct names and titles, choose appropriate topics, avoid negative and judgmental remarks, and give sincere and specific praise.

Choose Appropriate Topics. In some workplace activities, such as social gatherings or interviews, you will be expected to engage in "small" talk. Be sure to stay away from controversial topics with someone you don't know very well. Avoid politics, religion, or current event items that can start heated arguments until you know the person better. To start appropriate conversations, read newspapers and listen to radio and TV shows discussing current events. Make a mental note of items that you can use in conversation, taking care to remember where you saw or heard the news items so that you can report correctly and with authority. Try not to be defensive or annoyed if others give information that upsets you.

Avoid Negative Remarks. Workplace conversations are not the place to complain about your colleagues, your friends, the organization, or your job. Your criticism of a coworker may be overheard by or repeated to the wrong person. It may be changed or twisted in the retelling and gain meanings you did not intend. Be cautious in all negative judgments. Remember, some people love to repeat statements that will stir up trouble or set off internal workplace wars.

Listen to Learn. In conversations with colleagues, subordinates, and customers, train yourself to learn something from what you are hearing. Being attentive is not only instructive but also courteous. Beyond displaying good manners, you'll probably find that your conversation partner has information that you don't have. Being receptive and listening with an open mind means not interrupting or prejudging. Let's say you very much want to be able to work at home for part of your workweek. You try to explain your ideas to your boss, but he cuts you off shortly after you start. He says, "It's out of the question; we need you here every day."

Suppose instead he says, "I have strong doubts about your telecommuting, but maybe you'll change my mind"; and he settles in to listen to your presentation. Even if your boss decides against your request, you will feel that your ideas were heard and respected.

Give Sincere and Specific Praise. A wise person once said, "Man does not live by bread alone. He needs to be buttered up once in a while." Probably nothing promotes positive workplace relationships better than sincere and specific praise. Whether the compliments and appreciation are travelling upward to management, downward to workers, or horizontally to colleagues, everyone responds well to recognition. Organizations run more smoothly and morale is higher when people feel appreciated. In your workplace conversations, look for ways to recognize good work and good people. And try to be specific. Instead of "You did a good job in leading that meeting," try something more specific, such as "Your leadership skills certainly kept that meeting short, focused, and productive."

Offering Useful Criticism on the Job

No one likes to receive criticism, and most of us don't like to give it either. But in the workplace many activities demand feedback and evaluation. How are we doing on a project? What went well? What failed? How can we improve our efforts? Today's workplace often involves team projects. As a team member, you will need to judge the work of others. In addition to working on teams, you can also expect to become a supervisor or manager one day. As such, you will need to evaluate workers below you. Good employees seek good feedback from their supervisors. They want and need timely, detailed observations about their work to support what they do well and help them overcome weak spots. But making that feedback pleasant and positive is not always easy. Depending on your situation, you may find some or all of the following suggestions helpful when you must deliver useful criticism:

- **Mentally outline your conversation.** Think carefully about what you want to achieve and what you will say. Find the right words at the right time and in the right setting.
- **Generally, use face-to-face communication.** Most helpful criticism is better delivered in person rather than in e-mail messages or memos. Personal feedback offers an opportunity for the listener to ask questions and give explanations. Occasionally, however, complex situations may require a different strategy. You might prefer to write out your opinions and deliver them by telephone or in writing. A written document allows you to organize your thoughts and include all the details. Remember, though, that written documents create permanent records—for better or worse.
- **Focus on improvement.** Instead of attacking, use language that offers other choices of behaviour. Use phrases such as "Next time, you could ..."
- **Offer to help.** Criticism is accepted more readily if you volunteer to help in removing or solving the problem.
- **Be specific.** Instead of a vague comment such as "Your work is often late," be more specific: "The contract on the Riverside job was due Thursday at 5 p.m., and you didn't hand it in until Friday." Explain how the person's performance put the entire project at risk.
- **Avoid broad generalizations.** Don't use words such as *should, never, always,* and other broad expressions as they may cause the listener to shut down.
- **Discuss the behaviour, not the person.** Instead of "You think you can come to work any time you want," focus on the behaviour: "Coming to work late means that we have to fill in with someone else until you arrive."

- **Use the word *we* rather than *you*.** "We need to meet project deadlines," is better than saying "You need to meet project deadlines." Emphasize organizational expectations rather than personal ones. Avoid sounding critical.
- **Encourage two-way communication.** Even if well-planned, criticism is still hard to deliver. It may surprise or hurt the feelings of the employee. Consider ending your message with, "It can be hard to hear this type of feedback. If you would like to share your thoughts, I'm listening."
- **Avoid anger, sarcasm, and a raised voice.** Criticism is rarely constructive when you lose your temper. Plan in advance what you will say and deliver it in low, controlled, and sincere tones.
- **Keep it private.** Offer praise in public; offer criticism in private. "Setting an example" through public criticism is never a wise management policy.

Responding Professionally to Workplace Criticism

Quick Check

Offering useful criticism is easier if you plan what you will say, focus on improvement, offer to help, be specific, discuss the behaviour and not the person, speak privately face to face, and avoid anger.

As much as we hate giving criticism, we dislike receiving it even more. Yet, the workplace requires that you not only provide it but also be able to accept it. When being criticized, you probably will feel that you are being attacked. You can't just sit back and relax. Your heart beats faster, your temperature shoots up, your face reddens, and you respond with the classic "fight or flight" syndrome. You feel that you want to instantly strike back or escape from the attacker. But focusing on your feelings keeps you from hearing the content of what is being said, and it prevents you from responding professionally. Some or all of the following suggestions will guide you in reacting positively to criticism so that you can benefit from it:

- **Listen without interrupting.** Even though you might want to protest, let the speaker finish her thought.
- **Determine the speaker's intent.** If you think the intent is positive, focus on what is being said rather than reacting to poorly chosen words.
- **Recognize what you are hearing.** Respond with a pause, a nod, or a neutral statement such as "I understand you have a concern." This buys you time. Do not disagree, counterattack, or blame, which may harden the speaker's position.
- **Paraphrase what was said.** In your own words restate objectively what you are hearing; for example, "So what you're saying is ..."
- **Ask for more information if necessary.** Clear up what is being said. Stay focused on the main idea rather than bringing up other issues.
- **Agree—if the comments are accurate.** If an apology is in order, give it. Explain what you plan to do differently. If the criticism is reasonable, the sooner you agree, the more likely you will gain respect from the other person.
- **Disagree respectfully and constructively—if you feel the comments are unfair.** After hearing the criticism, you might say, "May I tell you my viewpoint?" Or you could try to solve the problem by saying, "How can we improve this situation in a way we can both accept?" If the other person continues to criticize, say "I want to find a way to resolve your concern. When do you want to talk about it next?"
- **Look for a middle position.** Search for a middle position. Be pleasant even if you don't like the person or the situation.

Resolving Workplace Conflicts

Quick Check

If you feel you are being criticized unfairly, disagree respectfully and look for a middle position.

Conflict is a normal part of every workplace, but it is not always negative. When managed properly, conflict can improve decision making, clarify values, increase group unity, encourage creativity, decrease tensions, and reduce discontent. Unresolved conflict, however, can destroy productivity and harm morale. The following six-step procedure can help prepare you for resolving workplace conflict.

Six-Step Procedure for Dealing with Conflict. Probably the best pattern for resolving conflicts in the workplace involves cooperation and problem-solving procedures. But this method requires a certain amount of training. Fortunately, experts in the field of negotiation have developed a six-step pattern that you can try the next time you need to resolve a conflict:

1. **Listen.** To be sure you understand the problem, listen carefully. If the other person doesn't seem to be listening to you, you need to set the example and be the first to listen.
2. **Understand the other point of view.** Once you listen, it's much easier to understand the other's position. Show your understanding by asking questions and summarizing or restating. This will also verify what you think the other person means.
3. **Show a concern for the relationship.** By focusing on the problem, not the person, you can build, maintain, and even improve relationships. Show an understanding of the other person's situation and needs. Show an overall willingness to come to an agreement.
4. **Look for common ground.** Identify your interests and help the other side to identify its interests. Learn what you have in common, and look for a solution to which both sides can agree.
5. **Invent new problem-solving options.** Spend time identifying the interests of both sides. Then brainstorm to invent new ways to solve the problem. Be open to new options.
6. **Reach an agreement based on what's fair.** Seek to determine a standard of fairness that is acceptable to both sides. Then weigh the possible solutions, and choose the best option.[5]

Polishing Your Professional Telephone and Voice-Mail Skills

Quick Check

For most businesses, telephones — both traditional and wireless — are a primary contact with the outside world.

The telephone is the most universal—and, some would say, the most important—piece of equipment in offices today.[6] For many businesspeople, it is a primary contact with the outside world. Some people predicted that e-mail and faxes would "kill off phone calls."[7] In fact, the amazing expansion of wireless communication has given the telephone a new and vigorous place in our lives. Telephones are definitely here to stay. But many of us do not use them efficiently or effectively. In this chapter we'll focus on traditional telephone techniques as well as voice-mail efficiency.

Making Productive Telephone Calls

Before making a telephone call, decide whether the intended call is necessary. Could you find the information yourself? If you wait a while, would the problem resolve itself? Perhaps your message could be delivered better by some other means. One U.S. company found that telephone interruptions took up about 18 percent of staff members' workdays. Another study found that two-thirds of all calls were less important than the work they interrupted.[8] Other means of communication besides telephone calls include e-mail, memos, or calls to voice-mail systems. If a telephone call must be made, consider using the following suggestions to make it fully productive.

- **Plan a mini-agenda.** Have you ever been embarrassed when you had to make a second telephone call because you forgot an important item the first time? Before placing a call, jot down notes regarding all the topics you need to discuss. Following an agenda guarantees not only a complete call but also a quick one. You'll be less likely to wander from the business at hand while rummaging through your mind trying to remember everything.

- **Use a three-point introduction.** When placing a call, immediately (1) name the person you are calling, (2) identify yourself and your affiliation, and (3) give a brief explanation of your reason for calling. For example: "May I speak to Larry Levin? This is Hillary Dahl of Acme Ltd., and I'm seeking information about a software program called Power Presentations." This kind of introduction enables the receiving individual to respond immediately without asking further questions.

- **Be quick if you are rushed.** For business calls when your time is limited, avoid questions such as "How are you?" Instead, say, "Lisa, I knew you'd be the only one who could answer these two questions for me." Another efficient strategy is to set a "contract" with the caller: "Hi, Lisa, I have only ten minutes, but I really wanted to get back to you."

- **Be cheerful and accurate.** Let your voice show the same kind of energy that you have when you greet people in person. In your mind, try to picture the individual answering the telephone. A smile can certainly affect the tone of your voice, so smile at that person. Moreover, be accurate about what you say. "Hang on a second; I'll be right back" rarely is true. Better to say, "It may take me two or three minutes to get that information. Would you prefer to hold or have me call you back?"

- **Bring it to a close.** The responsibility for ending a call lies with the caller. This is sometimes difficult to do if the other person keeps talking. You may need to use closing language, such as "I've certainly enjoyed talking with you," "I've learned what I needed to know, and now I can proceed with my work," "Thanks for your help," or "I must go now, but may I call you again in the future if I need ...?"

- **Leave complete voice-mail messages.** Remember that there's no rush when you leave a voice-mail message. Always speak clearly. And be sure to provide a complete message, including your name, telephone number, and the time and date of your call. Always speak slowly, so the listener has time to write down your information. Explain your purpose so that the receiver can be ready with the required information when returning your call.

✓ Quick Check

You can make productive telephone calls by planning an agenda, identifying the purpose, being polite and cheerful, and being concise.

Receiving Productive Telephone Calls

You can make your telephone a productive, efficient work tool. Developing good telephone manners also reflects well on you and on your organization.

- **Identify yourself immediately.** In answering your telephone or someone else's, provide your name, title or affiliation, and, possibly, a greeting. For example, "Larry Levin, Proteus Software. How may I help you?" Force yourself to speak clearly and slowly. Remember that the caller may be unfamiliar with what you are saying and may fail to recognize slurred syllables.

- **Be responsive and helpful.** Be sympathetic to callers' needs. Instead of "I don't know," try "That's a good question; let me investigate." Instead of "We can't do that," try "That's a tough one; let's see what we can do." Avoid "No" at the beginning of a sentence. It sounds especially rude and displeasing because it suggests total rejection.

- **Be cautious when answering calls for others.** Be courteous and helpful, but don't give out confidential information. Better to say, "She's away from her desk" or "He's out of the office" than to report a colleague's exact whereabouts.

- **Take messages carefully.** Few things are as frustrating as receiving a potentially important phone message that is hard to read. Repeat the spelling of names and verify telephone numbers. Write messages clearly and record their time and date.

✓ Quick Check

You can improve your telephone reception skills by identifying yourself, acting responsive, being helpful, and taking accurate messages.

Using Cell Phones for Business

Cell phones allow you to conduct business from almost anywhere at any time. The cell phone has become a necessary part of communication in many of today's workplaces. As with many new technologies, a set of rules on usage is still evolving for cell phones. How are they best used? When is it acceptable to take calls? Where should calls be made? Most of us have experienced thoughtless and rude cell phone behaviour. To avoid offending, smart business communicators practise cell phone etiquette, as outlined in Figure 10.2. In projecting a professional image, they are careful about location, time, and volume when making cell phone calls.

Making the Best Use of Voice Mail

Voice mail links a telephone system to a computer that stores incoming messages. Some systems also provide functions that allow callers to reach any linked extension by pushing specific buttons on a touch-tone telephone. For example, a ski resort in British Columbia uses voice mail to answer routine questions that once were routed through an operator: *Welcome to Panorama. For information on accommodations, press 1; for snow conditions, press 2; for ski equipment rental, press 3,* and so forth.

Within some companies, voice mail accounts for 90 percent of all telephone messages.[9] Its popularity results from serving many functions, the most important of which is message storage. Because as many as half of all business calls require no discussion or feedback, the messaging capabilities of voice mail can mean huge savings for businesses. Incoming information is delivered without interrupting receivers and without all the niceties that most two-way conversations require. Voice-mail messages allow communicators to focus on essentials because it eliminates chatting. Voice mail also eliminates telephone tag, inaccurate message taking, and time-zone barriers. Critics complain, nevertheless, that automated systems seem cold and impersonal and are sometimes confusing and irritating.

FIGURE 10.2 Practising Courteous and Responsible Cell Phone Use

Business communicators find cell phones to be very convenient and real timesavers. But the rudeness of some users has caused many people to resent impolite and thoughtless cell phone use. Here are specific suggestions for using cell phones safely and responsibly:

- **Be courteous to those around you.** Don't force those near you to hear your business.
- **Observe wireless-free quiet areas.** Don't allow your cell phone to ring in theatres, restaurants, museums, classrooms, important meetings, and similar places. Use the cell phone's silent/vibrating option. A majority of travellers prefer that cell phone conversations *not* be held on most forms of public transportation.
- **Speak in low, conversational tones.** Microphones on cell phones are quite sensitive, thus making it unnecessary to talk loudly. Avoid "cell yell."
- **Don't interrupt a face-to-face conversation to accept a cell call.** When you are having a conversation with a business partner or customer—or anyone for that matter—it is rude to interrupt it for an incoming call.
- **Take only urgent calls.** Make full use of your cell phone's caller ID feature to screen incoming calls. Let voice mail take those calls that are not urgent.
- **Drive now, talk later.** Pull over if you must make a call. Talking while driving increases the chance of accidents fourfold, about the same as driving while intoxicated.

"Do you mind? I happen to be on the phone!"

In any event, here are some ways that you can make voice mail work more effectively for you.

- **Announce your voice mail.** If you rely on a voice-mail message system, identify it on your business stationery and cards. Then, when people call, they will be ready to leave a message.
- **Prepare a warm and informative greeting.** Make your mechanical greeting sound warm and inviting, both in tone and content. Identify yourself and your organization so that callers know they have reached the right number. Thank the caller and briefly explain that you are unavailable. Invite the caller to leave a message or, if appropriate, call back. Here's a typical voice-mail greeting: "Hi! This is Larry Levin of Proteus Software, and I appreciate your call. Please leave your name, number, and reason for calling so that I can be prepared when I return your call." Give callers an idea of when you will be unavailable, such as "I'll be out of my office until Wednesday, May 20."
- **Test your message.** Call your number and check your message. Does it sound inviting? Sincere? Understandable? Are you pleased with your tone? If not, says one consultant, have someone else, perhaps a professional, record a message for you.

Summing Up and Looking Forward

In this chapter you studied how to improve face-to-face communication in the workplace. You can use your voice as a communication tool by focusing on pronunciation, tone, pitch, volume, rate, and emphasis. In workplace conversations, you should use correct names and titles, choose appropriate topics, avoid negative remarks, listen to learn, and be willing to offer sincere and specific praise. You studied how to give and take useful criticism on the job. The chapter also presented techniques for polishing your professional telephone and voice-mail skills, including making and receiving productive telephone calls.

This chapter focused on developing speaking skills in face-to-face workplace communication. In Chapter 12 you will learn to apply these speaking skills to a very important part of your career search: the employment interview.

Critical Thinking

1. When is face-to-face communication preferred to one-dimensional channels of communication such as e-mail and fax?
2. Some people predict that new communications media will destroy old ones. Do you think e-mail, PDAs, and instant messaging will "kill off" phone calls? Why or why not?
3. Why do so many people hate voice mail when it is an efficient system for recording messages?

Chapter Review

4. Name five elements that you control in using your voice as a communication tool.

5. What topics should be avoided in workplace conversations?

6. List six techniques that you consider most important when delivering useful criticism.

7. If you are criticized at work, what are eight ways that you can respond professionally?

8. Describe the parts of a three-point introduction for a telephone call.

9. Name five ways in which callers can practise courteous and responsible cell phone use.

10. Constructive Criticism. You work for a large company that is organized in work teams. Your work team, in the company's marketing department, meets weekly for a quick half-hour meeting to review the week's activities and projects. The meetings are run by the team leader, Mandy Miller. The team leader is a position of extra responsibility with a higher salary than that of other marketing staffers. For the past three months, Mandy has been regularly missing or showing up late for meetings. No one has said anything but you. You had a conversation with Mandy in the cafeteria three weeks ago in which you stated your concerns to her in as positive a way as possible. Mandy has again started to miss meetings. You feel it's appropriate to send an e-mail to the director of the marketing department, letting him know what's been happening, that you've talked to Mandy, and that things haven't improved.

Activities and Cases

10.1 Pronunciation. You can improve your effectiveness and credibility as a speaker if you pronounce words correctly.

Your Task. In teams or in class discussion, study the following list of words. What vowel do you think is frequently omitted or mispronounced? How can you be sure of the correct pronunciation? How can you improve your own pronunciation of these words?

accurate	manufacturer
burglar	original
company	popular
disastrous	positive
eleven	responsible
entrance	separately
excellent	singular
family	terrible
federal	usually
history	variable
liability	veteran

10.2 Voice Quality. Recording your voice gives you a chance to learn how your voice sounds to others and provides an opportunity for you to improve its effectiveness. Don't be surprised if you fail to recognize your own voice.

Your Task. Record yourself reading a newspaper or magazine article.

a. If you think your voice sounds a bit high, practise speaking slightly lower.
b. If your voice is low or expressionless, practise speaking slightly louder and with more inflection.
c. Ask a colleague, teacher, or friend to provide feedback on your pronunciation, pitch, volume, rate, and professional tone.

10.3 Role Play: Delivering and Responding to Criticism. Develop your skills in handling criticism by joining with a partner to role-play critical messages you might deliver and receive on the job.

Your Task. Designate one person "A" and the other "B." A describes the kinds of critical messages she or he is likely to receive on the job and identifies who might deliver them. In Scenario 1, B takes the role of the critic and delivers the criticism in an unskilled manner. A responds using techniques described in this chapter. In Scenario 2, B again is the critic but delivers the criticism using techniques described in this chapter. A responds again. Then A and B reverse roles and repeat Scenarios 1 and 2.

10.4 Role Play: Discussing Workplace Criticism. In the workplace, criticism is often delivered thoughtlessly.

Your Task. In teams of two or three, describe a time when you were criticized by an untrained superior or colleague. What made the criticism painful? What goal do you think the critic had in mind? How did you feel? How did you respond? Considering techniques discussed in this chapter, how could the critic have improved his or her delivery? How does the delivery technique affect the way a receiver responds to criticism? Script the situation you've just discussed and present it to the rest of the class in a before-and-after scenario.

10.5 Rules for Cell Phone Use in Sales. As one of the managers of Wrigley Canada, a gum and candy company, you are alarmed at a newspaper article you just read. A stockbroker for BMO Nesbitt Burns was making calls on his cell phone while driving. His car hit and killed a motorcyclist. The brokerage firm was sued and accused of contributing to an accident by encouraging employees to use cell phones while driving. To avoid the risk of paying huge damages awarded by an emotional jury, the brokerage firm offered the victim's family a $500,000 settlement.

Your Task. Individually or in teams, write an e-mail to Wrigley sales reps outlining company suggestions (or should they be rules?) for safe cell phone use in cars. Check library databases for articles that discuss cell phone use in cars. Look for additional safety ideas. In your message to sales reps, try to suggest receiver benefits. How is safe cell phone use beneficial to the sales rep?

10.6 Role Play: Improving Telephone Skills. Acting out the roles of telephone caller and receiver is an effective technique for improving skills. To give you such practice, your instructor will divide the class into pairs.

Chapter 10 Communicating in Person and by Telephone

Your Task. Read each scenario and rehearse your role silently. Then improvise the role with your partner. After improvising a couple of times, script one of the situations and present it to the rest of the class.

PARTNER 1	**PARTNER 2**
a. You are the personnel manager of Datatronics, Inc. Call Elizabeth Franklin, office manager at Computers Plus. Inquire about a job applicant, Chelsea Chavez, who listed Ms. Franklin as a reference.	You are the receptionist for Computers Plus. The caller asks for Elizabeth Franklin, who is home sick today. You don't know when she will be able to return. Answer the call appropriately.
b. As the personnel manager of Datatronics, Inc., call Ms. Franklin again the following day to inquire about the same job applicant, Chelsea Chavez. Ms. Franklin answers today, but she talks on and on, describing the applicant in great detail. Tactfully close the conversation.	You are Ms. Franklin, office manager. Describe Chelsea Chavez, an imaginary employee. Think of someone with whom you've worked. Include many details, such as her ability to work with others, her appearance, her skills at computing, her schooling, her ambition, and so forth.
c. You are the receptionist for Tom Wing, of Wing Imports. Answer a call for Mr. Wing, who is working in another office, at ext. 134, where he will accept calls.	You are an administrative assistant for lawyer Michael Murphy. Call Tom Wing to verify a meeting date Mr. Murphy has with Mr. Wing. Use your own name in identifying yourself.
d. You are Tom Wing, owner of Wing Imports. Call your lawyer, Michael Murphy, about a legal problem. Leave a brief, incomplete message.	You are the receptionist for lawyer Michael Murphy. Mr. Murphy is skiing in Tremblant and will return in two days, but he doesn't want his clients to know where he is. Take a message.
e. As Tom Wing, call Mr. Murphy again. Leave a message that will prevent telephone tag.	As Michael Murphy's receptionist, take a message again.

10.7 Role Play: Investigating Oral Communication in Your Field. Despite the popularity of communications technologies such as PDAs, e-mail, and instant messaging that require people to write, oral communication still plays an important role in the lives of most people working in business.

Your Task. Working in teams of three or four, interview three individuals in your professional field. How is oral communication important in this profession? What are some typical oral communication tasks in a given day, week, or month? As a percentage, how much time is spent communicating orally versus in writing? Besides person-to-person discussions, telephone conversations, and meetings, can this individual name other types of oral communication used at work? Does the need for oral skills change as one advances? What suggestions can this individual make to newcomers to the field for developing good oral communication skills? Once you've completed your interviews, create a ten-minute panel discussion between an interviewer and two or three experts on oral communication. Perform the skit in front of the class and discuss it afterward.

The following sentences contain errors in grammar, punctuation, capitalization, number style, usage, and spelling. Below each sentence write a corrected version.

1. The five top food service franchisors in the country are the following, mcdonald's, subway sandwiches & salads, burger king, 7-eleven, and tim hortons.

2. Fairlee Wells Corporation and it's german partner have develop a large-sized cooker to make donuts that taste greasy but are not.

3. Although the time and temperature is set by the user the cooker adjusts itself automatically.

4. The President and Chief Executive of Fairlee Wells said, "this machine is programmed to learn.

5. We rented the 8205 sq. metre building in winnipegs business district to many small space tenants.

6. The most important tasks for managers' are planning and supervise projects.

7. Proper tools and modern equipments makes business's run smooth.

8. In Canada's political history no Prime Minister having so much influence on Canadas people then Sir John A. Macdonald.

9. Last fall, the kejimkujik national park installed bicycle paths and it created many playground for it's childrens.

10. The membership of Rogers Wireless membership has grew by nearly 2.5 million, because the company provided good customer service.

11. At the Delta residence inn in Edmonton alberta a 1 bedroom suite costs more than a single room at Torontos hilton hotel.

12. One of the most popular items offerred by many popular hotels are the free Buffet breakfasts.

13. Just between you and I do you prefer a backpacking trip to the rockies or river rafting down the snake river.

14. We had less than fifteen items but others in the grocery store line were over the limit.

15. The President, Ceo, and 3 Managers will tour our facilitys in nova scotia and newfoundland.

Document for Revision

The following report showing meeting minutes has faults in grammar, punctuation, spelling, number form, wordiness, and word use. Use standard proofreading marks (see Appendix B) to correct the errors. When you finish, your instructor can show you the revised version of this summary.

Canadian Federation of Small Business
Policy Board Committee
February 4, 2009

Present: Debra Chinnapongse, Tweet Jackson, Irene Kishita, Barry Knaggs, Kevin Poepoe, and Ralph Mason

Absent: Alex Watanabe

The meeting was call to order by Chair Kevin Poepo at 9:02 a.m. in the morning. Minutes from the January 7 meeting was read and approve.

Old Business

Debra Chinnapongse discussed the cost of the annual awards luncheon. That honours outstanding members. The ticket price does not cover all the expenses. The major expenses include: awards and free lunches for the judges, VIP guests and volunteers. CFSB cannot continue to pay for the costs of the awards luncheon. Ms. Chinnapongse reported that other associations depended on members contributions for their awards' programs.

The group decided to send a letter to board members. Asking for there contributions to support the annual awards luncheon.

Reports

Barry Knaggs reported that the media relations committee sponsor a get acquainted meeting in November. More then eighty people from various agencys attended.

The Outreach Committee reported that they have been ask to assist the Partnership for Small Business, an Ottawa-based organization, to establishing a speakers agency of Canadian small business owners. The agency would be available to speak at schools and colleges about Small business and employment.

New Business

The chair announced a planning meeting to be held in march regarding revising the business plan. Ralph Mason report that the staff had purchase 50 tickets for members, and our committee will attend the Zig Ziglar seminar in April.

Next Meeting

The next meeting of the Policy Board Committee will be held in early April at the Lord Elgin hotel, Ottawa. At that time the meeting will conclude with tour of the seaway Networks inc. offices in Kanata.

The meeting concluded at 10:25 a.m. by Keven Poepoe.

How to Deal With Difficult People at Work

Difficult people in the workplace challenge your patience and your communication skills. In your work life and in your personal life, you are often confronted by people who are negative, manipulative, uncooperative, or just plain difficult. Although everyone is irritable or indecisive at times, some people are so difficult that they require us to react with special coping skills. In his well-known book *Coping With Difficult People*, psychologist and management consultant Robert M. Bramson provides helpful advice in dealing with a number of personality types.

Bullies try to control you with force, arrogance, preaching, and anger. To cope, try the following:

* Give them time to run down; maintain eye contact.
* Don't worry about being polite; state your opinions forcefully.
* Don't argue or be sarcastic; be ready to be friendly.

Sneaks hide behind cover. They attack by teasing and making "only joking" insults. To cope, try the following:

* Refuse to be attacked indirectly. Ask questions such as, "What did you mean by your remark?" "It sounds as if you are ridiculing me. Are you?"
* Ask the group to confirm or deny the sneaker's criticism. "Does anyone else see it that way?" Get other points of view.
* Recognize the root problem and try to find a practical solution.

Exploders blow up in frustrated rage; they have an adult tantrum. To cope, try the following:

* Give them time to cool off and regain control on their own.
* If they don't stop, break into the outburst by saying, "Stop!"
* Show that you take them seriously.
* Find a way to speak to them in private.

Complainers find fault with everything. Some complaints are made directly; others are made indirectly to third parties. To cope, try the following:

* Listen attentively, even if you feel guilty or impatient.
* Recognize what they are saying and reword it to see whether you understand.
* Don't agree or apologize, even if you feel you should.
* Try to solve the problem by (a) asking specific informational questions, (b) assigning fact-finding tasks, or (c) asking for the complaint in writing.
* If all else fails, ask the complainer, "How do you want this discussion to end?"

Postponers are unable to make decisions; therefore, they are difficult to work with. To cope, try the following:

- Encourage them to tell you about conflicts or doubts that prevent the decision. Listen for clues.
- Help them solve their problems by examining the facts and proposing solutions in order, moving from most important to least important issue.
- Give support after a decision has been made.

Career Application

In most workplaces you can expect to meet one or more truly difficult people. To provide practice in dealing with such people, develop a coping plan.

Your Task

1. Describe in detail the behaviour of a person whom you find to be difficult.
2. Analyze and describe your understanding of that behaviour.
3. Review your past contact with this person. Did you get along better with this person before? What has changed?
4. Decide what coping behaviour would be appropriate.
5. Recognize what you might need to change about yourself to best carry out the most promising coping behaviour.
6. Prepare an action plan explaining what you will do and by what date.

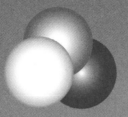

Communicating for Employment

11

CHAPTER

The Job Search, Résumés, and Cover Letters

Gone are the days when you could do a job search by showing up at an organization with your résumé. In today's competitive environment, your cover letter and résumé are the key to getting the interview. You have one fleeting moment to let the reader know what you have to offer. The wrong format or spelling and grammatical errors can quickly put you out of the running.[1]

Christine Shreves, *Human Resources Consultant, George Brown College*

LEARNING OBJECTIVES

1. Prepare for employment by knowing what strengths you have, choosing a career path, and studying traditional and electronic job search techniques.

2. Learn the differences between chronological, functional, and combination résumés.

3. Organize the parts of a résumé to produce a persuasive product.

4. Identify techniques that prepare a résumé for computer scanning, faxing, and e-mailing.

5. Write a persuasive cover letter to accompany your résumé.

This chapter provides up-to-date advice in preparing for employment, searching the job market, writing a persuasive résumé, and developing an effective cover letter.

Preparing for Employment

Quick Check

Finding a satisfying career means learning about oneself, the job market, and the employment process.

You may think that the first step in finding a job is writing a résumé, but the job search process actually begins long before you are ready to prepare your résumé. Regardless of the kind of employment you seek, you must invest time and effort getting ready. In addition to searching for career information and choosing a specific job objective, you should be studying the job market. You'll also want to understand how to use the latest Internet resources in your job search. When you have finished the preparation, you're ready to design a persuasive résumé and job application letter. These documents should be appropriate for small businesses as well as for larger organizations that may be using résumé-scanning programs. Following the steps described in this chapter will give you a master plan for landing a job you really want.

Evaluating Your Qualifications

Check your qualifications. Employers today want to know what you have to offer them. Your responses to the following questions will prepare a foundation for your résumé. Remember that employers want proof of your qualifications.

- What computer skills can I offer? (What specific software programs can I name?)
- What other skills have I acquired in school, on the job, or through activities? How can I demonstrate these skills?
- Do I work well with people? What proof can I offer? (Consider extracurricular activities, clubs, and jobs.)
- Am I a leader, a self-starter, or a manager? What evidence can I offer?
- Do I speak, write, or understand another language?
- Do I learn quickly? Am I creative? How can I demonstrate these characteristics?
- Do I communicate well in speech and in writing? How can I verify these talents?

✔ **Quick Check**

Assessing your skills and experience prepares you to write a persuasive résumé.

Choosing a Career Path

Today's job market is very different from that of a decade or two ago. The average Canadian can expect to change careers at least three times and change jobs at least seven times in a lifetime. Some of you probably have not yet settled on your first career choice; others are starting a second or perhaps third career. Although you may be changing jobs in the future, you still need to train for a specific career area now. In choosing an area, you'll make the best decisions when you can match your interests and qualifications with the requirements and rewards in specific careers. But where can you find career information? Here are some suggestions:

✔ **Quick Check**

People can expect to have eight to ten jobs in three or more different careers in a lifetime.

- **Visit your school career or counselling centre.** Most have literature, software programs, and Internet connections that allow you to investigate such fields as accounting, finance, office technology, information systems, hotel management, and so forth.
- **Search the Internet.** Many job search sites on the Web offer career planning information and resources. For example, WorkopolisCampus.com (http://www.campus.workopolis.com) helps you link to various career search resources in its "Resource Centre" link.
- **Use your library.** Many print and online resources are especially helpful. Consult the latest edition of the *Index of Occupational Titles*, the U.S. government's *Occupational Outlook Handbook* (http://www.bls.gov/oco), and "Training, Career and Worker Information" at the Government of Canada's website (http://www.jobsetc.ca) for information about career duties, qualifications, salaries, and employment trends.
- **Take a summer job, internship, or part-time position in your field.** Nothing is better than trying out a career by actually working in it or in a similar area. Many companies offer internships and temporary jobs to begin training students and to develop relationships with them. These relationships sometimes turn into permanent positions.
- **Interview someone in your chosen field.** People are usually pleased when asked to describe their careers. Inquire about needed skills, required courses, financial and other rewards, benefits, working conditions, future trends, and entry requirements.
- **Examine the classified ads.** Early in your education career, begin monitoring want ads and websites of companies in your career area. Check job availability,

✔ **Quick Check**

Career information can be obtained at school career centres and libraries, from the Internet, in classified ads, and from professional organizations.

✔ **Quick Check**

Summer and part-time jobs and internships are good opportunities to learn about different careers.

qualifications sought, duties, and salary range. Don't wait until you're about to graduate to see how the job market looks.
- **Join professional organizations in your field.** Often, these organizations offer student membership status and reduced rates. You'll get inside information on issues, career news, and possible jobs.

Using Traditional Job Search Techniques

Finding the perfect job requires an early start and a determined effort. Whether you use traditional or online job search techniques, you should be prepared to launch an aggressive campaign. And you can't start too early. Students are told early on that a degree or diploma alone doesn't guarantee a good job. They are cautioned that final grades make a difference to employers. And they are advised of the importance of experience and networking. Here are some traditional steps that job candidates take:

- **Study classified ads in local and national newspapers.** Be aware, though, that classified ads are only one small source of jobs. Nearly two-thirds, representing the "hidden" job market, are unadvertised.
- **Check announcements in publications of professional organizations.** If you do not have a student membership, ask your professors to share current copies of professional journals, newsletters, and so on. Your college library is another good source.
- **Contact companies in which you're interested, even if you know of no current opening.** Write an unsolicited letter and include your résumé. Follow up with a telephone call. Check the company's website for employment possibilities and procedures.
- **Sign up for school interviews with visiting company representatives.** Campus recruiters may open your eyes to exciting jobs and locations.
- **Ask for advice from your instructors.** They often have contacts and ideas for expanding your job search.
- **Develop your own network of contacts.** Networking still accounts for most of the jobs found by candidates. Therefore, plan to spend a large portion of your job search time developing a personal network. The Communication Workshop at the end of this chapter gives you step-by-step instructions for traditional networking as well as some ideas for online networking.

Using Electronic Job Search Techniques

The Internet is changing the nature of the job search. Increasing numbers of employers are listing their job openings at special websites that are similar to newspaper classified ads, as shown in Figure 11.1. Companies are also listing job openings at their own websites, providing a more direct connection to employment opportunities.

- **Canada's Job Bank**, a Service Canada site at http://jobbank.gc.ca/Intro_en.aspx, lists more than 46,000 jobs across the country with up to 2,000 new jobs posted every day. The service is free.
- **JobsEtc.ca**, a Government of Canada website at http://www.jobsetc.ca, offers a wealth of information including the top 15 job websites in Canada.
- **CharityVillage.com** is a website at http://www.charityvillage.com that advertises jobs in the nonprofit sector. Often overlooked by students and graduates, this site offers a wealth of opportunities in traditional business areas such as accounting, finance, customer service, and marketing, all in the nonprofit sector.

FIGURE 11.1 Results from Online Job Search

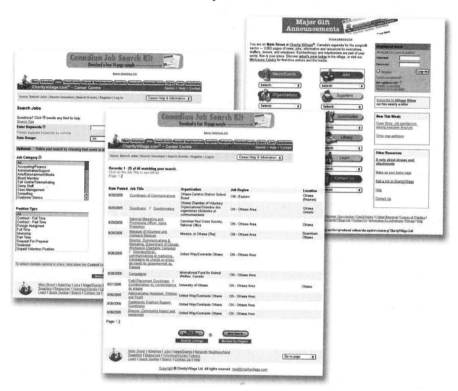

- **Workopolis.ca** is Canada's biggest job site. Use Workopolis to register and save your résumé online, build and save job searches, and track job opportunities. You can also research a company, interact with career advisors, and read employment-related newspaper articles.
- **Monster.ca** offers access to information on Canadian and international jobs. It enables company searches, arranges chat sessions on helpful topics for job seekers, and posts pages of targeted career advice.

Perhaps even better are the job openings listed at company websites. Check out your favourite companies to see what positions are open. Use your favourite search engine to search a company's website. Some companies even have online résumé forms that encourage job candidates to submit their qualifications immediately.

The Internet now has hundreds of job websites, and increasing numbers of companies offer online recruiting. In spite of these opportunities, landing a job is still much easier if you have personal contacts in a career area.

The Persuasive Résumé

After reviewing traditional and online employment market and job lead resources, you'll focus on writing a persuasive résumé. Such a résumé does more than just list your qualifications. It takes your skills and qualifications and organizes the information into a convincing advertisement that sells you for a specific job. The goal of a persuasive résumé is winning an interview. Even if you are not in the job market at this moment, preparing a résumé now has advantages. Having a current résumé makes you look well organized and professional should an unexpected employment opportunity arise. Moreover, preparing a résumé early can help you recognize weak areas and give you time to strengthen your credentials.

The Persuasive Résumé

Choosing a Résumé Style

✓ **Quick Check**

Chronological résumés focus on past employment; functional résumés focus on skills.

Your qualifications and career goal will help you choose from among three résumé styles: chronological, functional, and combination.

Chronological. Most popular with recruiters is the chronological résumé, shown in Figure 11.2. It lists work history job by job, starting with the most recent position. Such résumés quickly reveal a candidate's experience and education record. The chronological style works well for candidates who have experience in their field of employment and for those who show steady career growth. But for many students and others who lack extensive experience, the functional résumé format may be preferable.

Functional. The functional résumé, shown in Figure 11.3, focuses attention on a candidate's skills rather than on past employment. Like a chronological résumé, the functional résumé begins with the candidate's name, address, telephone number, job objective, and education. Instead of listing jobs, though, the functional résumé groups skills and accomplishments in special categories, such as *Supervisory and Management Skills* or *Retailing and Marketing Experience.* This résumé style highlights accomplishments and can de-emphasize a negative employment history. People who have changed jobs frequently or who have gaps in their employment records may prefer the functional résumé. Recent graduates with little employment experience often find the functional résumé useful.

Functional résumés are also called skill résumés. Although the functional résumé of Jon Penner shown in Figure 11.3 concentrates on skills, it does include a short employment section because recruiters expect it. Notice that Jon breaks his skills into three categories.

Combination. The combination résumé style, shown in Figure 11.4, draws on the best features of the chronological and functional résumés. This style highlights a candidate's abilities while also including a complete job history. The combination résumé is a good choice for recent graduates because it lets them profile what they can do for a prospective employer. If the writer has a specific job in mind, the items should be targeted to that job description.

Arranging the Parts

✓ **Quick Check**

Résumés should be arranged with the most important qualifications first.

Although résumés have standard parts, their arrangement and content should be carefully planned. Many job applicants today prepare individual résumés that are targeted for each company or position sought. Thanks to word processing, the task is easy.

Résumés show a candidate's most important qualifications first. To avoid a cluttered look, you must arrange the parts of your résumé with no more than six headings. No two résumés are ever exactly alike, but most writers consider the following parts.

Main Heading. Your résumé should always begin with your name, address, telephone number, and e-mail address. If possible, include a telephone number where messages may be left for you. Prospective employers tend to call the next applicant when no one answers. Adding your e-mail address makes contacting you more convenient. Avoid showing both permanent and temporary addresses; some specialists say that dual addresses immediately identify about-to-graduate college students. Keep the main heading as uncluttered and simple as possible. And don't include the word *résumé*; it's like putting the word *letter* above correspondence.

FIGURE 11.2   Chronological Résumé

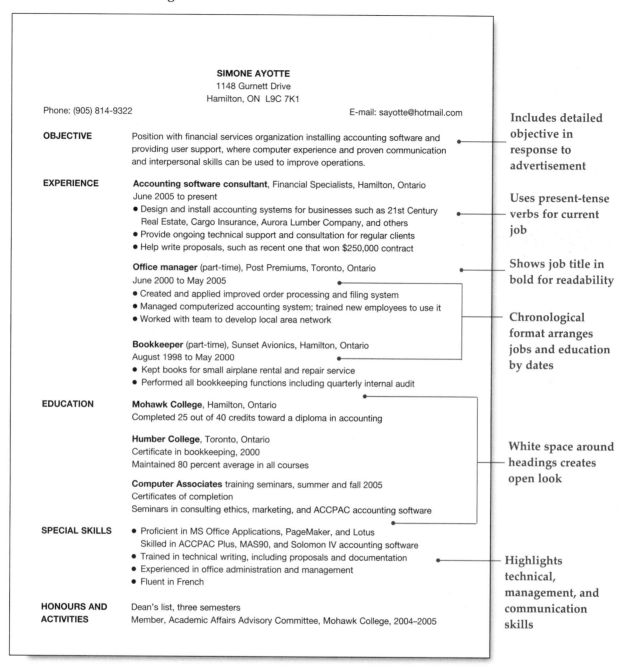

SIMONE AYOTTE
1148 Gurnett Drive
Hamilton, ON L9C 7K1

Phone: (905) 814-9322   E-mail: sayotte@hotmail.com

OBJECTIVE   Position with financial services organization installing accounting software and
                       providing user support, where computer experience and proven communication
                       and interpersonal skills can be used to improve operations.

EXPERIENCE   **Accounting software consultant**, Financial Specialists, Hamilton, Ontario
                       June 2005 to present
                       ● Design and install accounting systems for businesses such as 21st Century
                          Real Estate, Cargo Insurance, Aurora Lumber Company, and others
                       ● Provide ongoing technical support and consultation for regular clients
                       ● Help write proposals, such as recent one that won $250,000 contract

                       Office manager (part-time), Post Premiums, Toronto, Ontario
                       June 2000 to May 2005
                       ● Created and applied improved order processing and filing system
                       ● Managed computerized accounting system; trained new employees to use it
                       ● Worked with team to develop local area network

                       Bookkeeper (part-time), Sunset Avionics, Hamilton, Ontario
                       August 1998 to May 2000
                       ● Kept books for small airplane rental and repair service
                       ● Performed all bookkeeping functions including quarterly internal audit

EDUCATION   **Mohawk College**, Hamilton, Ontario
                       Completed 25 out of 40 credits toward a diploma in accounting

                       Humber College, Toronto, Ontario
                       Certificate in bookkeeping, 2000
                       Maintained 80 percent average in all courses

                       Computer Associates training seminars, summer and fall 2005
                       Certificates of completion
                       Seminars in consulting ethics, marketing, and ACCPAC accounting software

SPECIAL SKILLS   ● Proficient in MS Office Applications, PageMaker, and Lotus
                          Skilled in ACCPAC Plus, MAS90, and Solomon IV accounting software
                       ● Trained in technical writing, including proposals and documentation
                       ● Experienced in office administration and management
                       ● Fluent in French

HONOURS AND   Dean's list, three semesters
ACTIVITIES   Member, Academic Affairs Advisory Committee, Mohawk College, 2004–2005

Annotations (right margin):
- Includes detailed objective in response to advertisement
- Uses present-tense verbs for current job
- Shows job title in bold for readability
- Chronological format arranges jobs and education by dates
- White space around headings creates open look
- Highlights technical, management, and communication skills

Simone Ayotte uses a chronological résumé to highlight her work experience, most of which is related directly to the position she seeks. Although she is a recent graduate, she has experience in two part-time jobs and one full-time job. If she had wished to highlight her special skills (which is not a bad idea considering her heavy computer expertise), she could have placed the special skills section just after her objective.

FIGURE 11.3 Functional Résumé

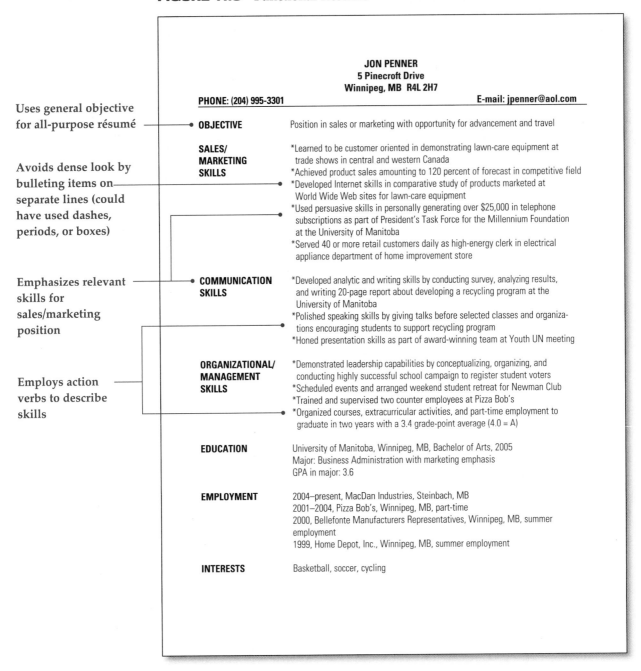

Uses general objective for all-purpose résumé

Avoids dense look by bulleting items on separate lines (could have used dashes, periods, or boxes)

Emphasizes relevant skills for sales/marketing position

Employs action verbs to describe skills

JON PENNER
5 Pinecroft Drive
Winnipeg, MB R4L 2H7

PHONE: (204) 995-3301   E-mail: jpenner@aol.com

OBJECTIVE   Position in sales or marketing with opportunity for advancement and travel

SALES/ MARKETING SKILLS
*Learned to be customer oriented in demonstrating lawn-care equipment at trade shows in central and western Canada
*Achieved product sales amounting to 120 percent of forecast in competitive field
*Developed Internet skills in comparative study of products marketed at World Wide Web sites for lawn-care equipment
*Used persuasive skills in personally generating over $25,000 in telephone subscriptions as part of President's Task Force for the Millennium Foundation at the University of Manitoba
*Served 40 or more retail customers daily as high-energy clerk in electrical appliance department of home improvement store

COMMUNICATION SKILLS
*Developed analytic and writing skills by conducting survey, analyzing results, and writing 20-page report about developing a recycling program at the University of Manitoba
*Polished speaking skills by giving talks before selected classes and organizations encouraging students to support recycling program
*Honed presentation skills as part of award-winning team at Youth UN meeting

ORGANIZATIONAL/ MANAGEMENT SKILLS
*Demonstrated leadership capabilities by conceptualizing, organizing, and conducting highly successful school campaign to register student voters
*Scheduled events and arranged weekend student retreat for Newman Club
*Trained and supervised two counter employees at Pizza Bob's
*Organized courses, extracurricular activities, and part-time employment to graduate in two years with a 3.4 grade-point average (4.0 = A)

EDUCATION
University of Manitoba, Winnipeg, MB, Bachelor of Arts, 2005
Major: Business Administration with marketing emphasis
GPA in major: 3.6

EMPLOYMENT
2004–present, MacDan Industries, Steinbach, MB
2001–2004, Pizza Bob's, Winnipeg, MB, part-time
2000, Bellefonte Manufacturers Representatives, Winnipeg, MB, summer employment
1999, Home Depot, Inc., Winnipeg, MB, summer employment

INTERESTS   Basketball, soccer, cycling

Jon Penner, a recent graduate, chose this functional format to take away attention from his lack of work experience and to highlight his potential in sales and marketing. Within each of the three major categories, he lists specific achievements, all introduced by action verbs. He has also included a number of keywords that could be helpful if his résumé is scanned. He included an employment section to satisfy recruiters.

FIGURE 11.4 Combination Résumé

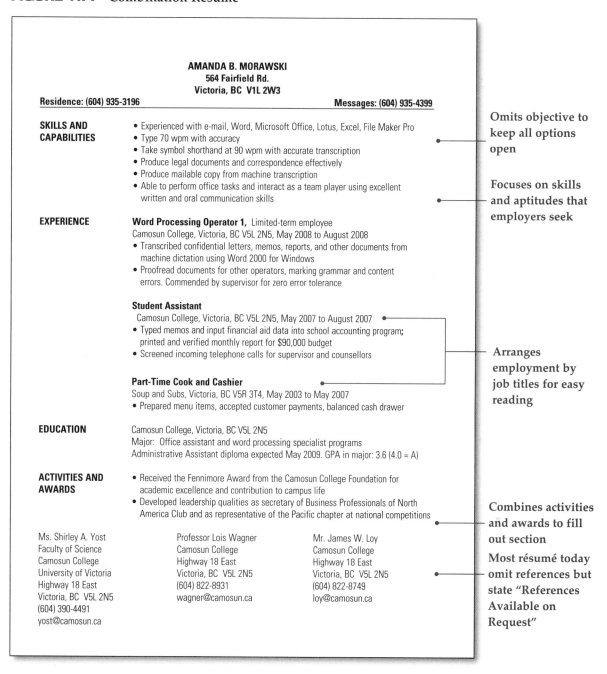

AMANDA B. MORAWSKI
564 Fairfield Rd.
Victoria, BC V1L 2W3

Residence: (604) 935-3196   Messages: (604) 935-4399

SKILLS AND CAPABILITIES
- Experienced with e-mail, Word, Microsoft Office, Lotus, Excel, File Maker Pro
- Type 70 wpm with accuracy
- Take symbol shorthand at 90 wpm with accurate transcription
- Produce legal documents and correspondence effectively
- Produce mailable copy from machine transcription
- Able to perform office tasks and interact as a team player using excellent written and oral communication skills

Omits objective to keep all options open

Focuses on skills and aptitudes that employers seek

EXPERIENCE

Word Processing Operator 1, Limited-term employee
Camosun College, Victoria, BC V5L 2N5, May 2008 to August 2008
- Transcribed confidential letters, memos, reports, and other documents from machine dictation using Word 2000 for Windows
- Proofread documents for other operators, marking grammar and content errors. Commended by supervisor for zero error tolerance

Student Assistant
Camosun College, Victoria, BC V5L 2N5, May 2007 to August 2007
- Typed memos and input financial aid data into school accounting program; printed and verified monthly report for $90,000 budget
- Screened incoming telephone calls for supervisor and counsellors

Part-Time Cook and Cashier
Soup and Subs, Victoria, BC V5R 3T4, May 2003 to May 2007
- Prepared menu items, accepted customer payments, balanced cash drawer

Arranges employment by job titles for easy reading

EDUCATION
Camosun College, Victoria, BC V5L 2N5
Major: Office assistant and word processing specialist programs
Administrative Assistant diploma expected May 2009. GPA in major: 3.6 (4.0 = A)

ACTIVITIES AND AWARDS
- Received the Fennimore Award from the Camosun College Foundation for academic excellence and contribution to campus life
- Developed leadership qualities as secretary of Business Professionals of North America Club and as representative of the Pacific chapter at national competitions

Combines activities and awards to fill out section

Most résumé today omit references but state "References Available on Request"

Ms. Shirley A. Yost
Faculty of Science
Camosun College
University of Victoria
Highway 18 East
Victoria, BC V5L 2N5
(604) 390-4491
yost@camosun.ca

Professor Lois Wagner
Camosun College
Highway 18 East
Victoria, BC V5L 2N5
(604) 822-8931
wagner@camosun.ca

Mr. James W. Loy
Camosun College
Highway 18 East
Victoria, BC V5L 2N5
(604) 822-8749
loy@camosun.ca

Because Amanda Morawski wanted to highlight her skills along with her experience, she combined the best features of functional and traditional résumés. This résumé style is becoming increasingly popular.

Career Objective. You have four choices regarding career objectives:

1. Include a career objective only when applying for a specific, targeted position. For example, the following responds to an advertised position: *Objective: To work in the health-care industry as a human resources trainee with exposure to recruiting, training, and benefits administration.*
2. Omit a career objective, especially if you are preparing an all-purpose résumé, one that will be sent to various companies.
3. Include a general statement, such as *Objective: Challenging position in urban planning* or *Job Goal: Position in sales/marketing.*
4. Omit an objective on the résumé but include it in the cover letter, where it can be tailored to a specific position.

Some consultants warn against using the term *entry-level* in your objective, as it emphasizes lack of experience.

Education. The next part on your résumé is your education—if it is more significant than your work experience. In this section you should include the name and location of schools, dates of attendance, major fields of study, and degrees, diplomas, and certificates received. Your grade average is important to future employers. One way to increase the average of your grades is to calculate it in your major courses only (for example, *A average in major*).

A list of completed courses makes dull reading: refer to courses only if you can relate them to the position sought. When relevant, include certificates earned, seminars attended, and workshops completed. If your education is incomplete, include such statements as *B.A. degree expected June 2008* or *80 units completed in 120-unit program.* Entitle this section *Education, Academic Preparation,* or *Professional Training.*

Work Experience or Employment History. Anyone seeking a job today must recognize the value of experience. When asked what advice she had for people with little experience, résumé expert Yana Parker replied, "Get some!"[2] She suggests internships, part-time jobs, or even volunteer work in your career area.

If your work experience is significant and related to the position sought, this information should appear before education. List your most recent employment first and work backward, including only those jobs that you think will help you win the targeted position. A job application form may demand a full employment history, but your résumé may be selective. (Be aware, though, that time gaps in your employment history will probably be questioned in the interview.) For each position show the following:

- Employer's name, city, and province
- Dates of employment, including month and year
- Most important job title
- Major duties, activities, accomplishments, and promotions

Describe your employment achievements concretely. Avoid general statements such as *Worked with customers.* Be more specific, with statements such as *Served 40 or more retail customers a day;* or *Successfully resolved problems about custom stationery orders.* If possible, provide a measure of your accomplishments, such as *Conducted study of equipment needs of 100 small businesses in Edmonton; Personally generated orders for sales of $90,000 annually;* or *Keyboarded all the production models for a 250-page employee procedures manual.*

In addition to technical skills, employers seek individuals with communication, management, and interpersonal capabilities. This means you'll want to select work experiences and achievements that illustrate your initiative, dependability,

Quick Check

Include a career objective for a specific, targeted position; omit an objective on a general résumé.

Quick Check

The work experience section of a résumé should list specifics and quantify achievements.

responsibility, creativity, and leadership. Employers also want people who can work in teams. Thus, include statements such as *Worked together with a task force in developing 15-page handbook for temporary workers* and *Headed student government team that conducted most successful voter registration in school history.*

Statements describing your work experience become forceful and persuasive by using action verbs, such as those listed in Figure 11.5 and illustrated in Figure 11.6.

Skills and Abilities. Recruiters want to know exactly what you can do for their companies. Therefore, list your special skills, such as *Skilled in preparing reports using MS Word.* Include your ability to use computer programs, office equipment, other languages, or sign language. Describe skills you have gained through training and experience, such as *Trained in computer accounting, including general ledger, accounts receivable, accounts payable, and payroll.*

You'll also want to highlight special abilities, such as working well under stress and learning computer programs quickly, but give details that back up your claim; for example, *learned image manipulation using Photoshop in 40 hours with little instruction.* Search for examples of your writing, speaking, management, organizational, and interpersonal skills—particularly those talents that are relevant to your targeted job.

For recent graduates, this section can be used to give recruiters evidence of your potential.

Quick Check

Highlight the skills and aptitudes that recommend you for a specific position.

Awards, Honours, and Activities. If you have three or more awards or honours, highlight them by listing them under a separate heading. If not, put them with activities. Include awards, scholarships (financial and other), fellowships, honours, recognition, commendations, and certificates. Be sure to identify items clearly; explain what the awards mean. Instead of saying *Recipient of Star award,* give more details: *Recipient of Star award, given by Red River College to outstanding graduates who combine academic excellence and extracurricular achievement.*

Also include school, community, and professional activities. Employers are interested in evidence that you are a well-rounded person. This section gives you a chance to show leadership and interpersonal skills. Use action statements. For example, instead of saying *Treasurer of business club,* explain more fully: *Collected dues, kept financial records, and paid bills while serving as treasurer of 35-member business management club.*

Quick Check

Awards, honours, and activities are appropriate for résumés; most personal information is not.

Personal Information. Today's résumés omit personal information, such as birth date and marital status. Recruiters are legally barred from asking for such information. Some job seekers do, however, include hobbies or interests (such as skiing or photography) that might grab the recruiter's attention or serve as conversation starters. You should also indicate your willingness to travel or to relocate, since many companies will be interested in that information.

References. Listing references on a résumé is favoured by some recruiters and opposed by others. Such a list takes up valuable space. Moreover, it does not normally help in getting an interview—few companies check references before the interview. Instead, they prefer that a candidate bring to the interview a list of individuals willing to discuss her or his qualifications. If you do list them, use parallel form. For example, if you show a title for one person (*Professor, Dr., Mrs.*), show titles for all. Include mailing addresses, e-mail addresses, and telephone numbers with area codes.

You should have the names of your references available when you begin your job search. Ask three to five instructors or previous employers whether they are willing to answer inquiries regarding your qualifications for employment. Be sure, however, to provide them with an opportunity to refuse. No reference is better than a negative one. Do not include personal or character references, such

Quick Check

References are unnecessary for the résumé, but they should be available for the interview.

The Persuasive Résumé

FIGURE 11.5　Action Verbs for Persuasive Résumés

Management Skills	Communication Skills	Research Skills	Technical Skills	Teaching Skills
administered	addressed	clarified	assembled	adapted
analyzed	arbitrated	collected	built	advised
consolidated	arranged	critiqued	calculated	clarified
coordinated	collaborated	diagnosed	computed	coached
delegated	composed	evaluated	designed	communicated
developed	convinced	examined	devised	coordinated
directed	developed	extracted	engineered	developed
evaluated	drafted	identified	executed	enabled
improved*	edited	inspected	fabricated	encouraged
increased	explained	interpreted	maintained	evaluated
organized	formulated	interviewed	operated	explained
oversaw	interpreted	investigated	overhauled	facilitated
planned	negotiated	organized	programmed	guided
prioritized	persuaded	summarized	remodelled	informed
recommended	promoted	surveyed	repaired	instructed
scheduled	publicized	systematized	solved	persuaded
strengthened	recruited		upgraded	set goals
supervised	translated			trained
	wrote			

*The underlined words are especially good for pointing out accomplishments.

as friends or neighbours, because recruiters rarely consult them. Companies are more interested in the opinions of objective individuals.

✓ Quick Check

Use of scanners requires job candidates to prepare computer-friendly résumés.

✓ Quick Check

Computer-friendly résumés are free of graphics and fancy fonts.

Making Your Résumé Computer-Friendly

Thus far our résumé advice has been aimed at human readers. However, the first reader of your résumé may well be a computer. Some companies now use computer programs to reduce hiring costs and make résumé information more available. The process of résumé scanning is shown in Figure 11.7.

FIGURE 11.6　Using Action Verbs to Strengthen Your Résumé

Identified weaknesses in internship program and **researched** five alternative programs.

Reduced delivery delays by an average of three days per order.

Organized holiday awards program for 1200 attendees and 140 awardees.

Created a 12-point checklist for managers to use when requesting temporary workers.

Designed five posters announcing new employee suggestion program.

Calculated shipping charges for overseas deliveries and **recommended** most economical rates.

Managed 24-station computer network linking data and employees in three departments.

Distributed and **explained** voter registration forms to over 500 prospective student voters.

Praised by top management for enthusiastic teamwork and achievement.

Received national recognition from Parks Canada for tree project.

FIGURE 11.5 Continued

Financial Skills	Creative Skills	Helping Skills	Clerical or Detail Skills	More Verbs for Accomplishments
administered	acted	assessed	approved	achieved
advised	conceptualized	assisted	catalogued	expanded
allocated	created	clarified	classified	improved
analyzed	customized	coached	collected	pioneered
appraised	designed	counselled	compiled	reduced (losses)
audited	developed	demonstrated	generated	resolved
balanced	directed	diagnosed	inspected	(problems)
budgeted	established	educated	monitored	restored
calculated	founded	expedited	operated	spearheaded
computed	illustrated	facilitated	organized	transformed
developed	initiated	familiarized	prepared	
forecasted	instituted	guided	processed	
managed	introduced	motivated	purchased	
marketed	invented	referred	recorded	
planned	originated	represented	screened	
projected	performed		specified	
researched	planned		systematized	
	revitalized		tabulated	

Source: Adapted from Yana Parker, *The Damn Good Résumé Guide* (Berkeley, CA: Ten Speed Press). Reprinted with permission.

Before you send your résumé, you should learn whether the receiver uses scanning software. One way to find out is to call any company where you plan to apply and ask if it scans résumés electronically. If you can't get a clear answer and you have even the slightest suspicion that your résumé might be read electronically, you'd be smart to prepare a plain, scannable version.

A scannable résumé must leave out many attractive features. Computers aren't impressed by good looks; they prefer résumés that are free of graphics and fancy fonts. To make a computer-friendly résumé, you'll want to apply the following suggestions about its physical appearance.

- **Avoid unusual typefaces, underlining, and italics.** Moreover, don't use boxing, shading, or other graphics to highlight text. These features don't scan well. Most applicant-tracking programs, however, can accurately read bold print, solid bullets, and asterisks.

FIGURE 11.7 What a Résumé-Scanning Program Does

Reads résumé with scanner	Identifies job categories and ranks applicants	Generates letters of rejection or interview offers	Stores information or actual résumé image for future searches

1 2 3

The Persuasive Résumé

- **Use 10-to-14-point type.** Because touching letters or unusual fonts are likely to be misread, it's safest to use a large, well-known font, such as 12-point Times New Roman or Helvetica. This may mean that your résumé will require two pages. After printing, inspect your résumé to see if any letters touch—especially in your name.
- **Use smooth white paper, black ink, and quality printing.** Avoid coloured and textured papers as well as dot-matrix printing.
- **Be sure that your name is the first line on the page.** Don't use fancy layouts, which may confuse a scanner.
- **Provide white space.** To ensure separation of words and categories, leave plenty of white space. For example, instead of using parentheses to enclose a telephone area code, insert blank spaces, such as 613 555-1212. Leave blank lines around headings.
- **Avoid double columns.** When listing job duties, skills, computer programs, and so forth, don't organize items into two- or three-column lists. As scanners read across columns and tables, they may change the order of the text.
- **Don't fold or staple your résumé.** Send it in a large envelope so that you can avoid folds. Words that appear on folds may not be scanned correctly. Avoid staples, because the indentions left after they are removed may cause pages to stick.
- **Use abbreviations carefully.** Minimize unfamiliar abbreviations, but maximize easily recognized abbreviations—especially those within your field, such as CAD or COBRA or CGA. When abbreviations are unclear, write them out in full.
- **Include your entire address and telephone number.** Be sure your résumé contains your e-mail address, as well as your street address, telephone numbers with area codes, and fax number, if available.
- **Be prepared to provide your résumé in Plain Text format.** This format offers electronic documents as text only and is immediately readable by all computer programs. It eliminates italics, bold, underlining, and unusual keyboard characters but allows you to e-mail your résumé in a format that you know will work for all computers.

Emphasizing Keywords

Quick Check

Keywords are nouns that describe specific candidate traits or job requirements.

Quick Check

A computer-friendly résumé may contain a keyword summary filled with words (usually nouns) that describe the job or candidate.

In addition to paying attention to the physical appearance of your résumé, you must also be concerned with keywords. Keywords are usually nouns that describe what an employer wants. Suppose a manager at Canadian Tire wants to hire an administrative assistant with special skills. That manager might submit the following keywords to the Canadian Tire applicant-tracking system: *Administrative Assistant, Computer Skills, MS Office, Self-Starter, Report Writing, Proofreading, Communication Skills.* The system would then search through all the résumés on file to see which ones best match the requirements.

The Royal Bank of Canada receives hundreds of résumés every year. They suggest using a keyword summary to assist recruiters who use keyword matching techniques when searching résumé databases. This list of keyword descriptors immediately follows your name and address on your résumé.[3] A keyword summary, as illustrated in the résumé in Figure 11.9 (p. 248), should contain your targeted job title and other labels, as well as previous job titles, skills, software programs, and selected jargon known in your field. It concentrates on nouns rather than on verbs or adjectives.

To construct your summary, go through your core résumé and mark all relevant nouns. Also try to imagine what eight to ten words an employer might use to describe the job you want. Then select the 25 best words for your summary. Because interpersonal traits are often requested by employers, consult Figure 11.8. You may entitle your list *Keyword Summary, Keyword Profile,* or

Keyword Index. Here's an example of a possible keyword summary for a junior accountant:

Keyword Summary
Accountant: Public. Junior. Staff. PricewaterhouseCoopers. Administration. AJ Hawkins—Accounting. Payables. Receivables. Payroll Experience. Quarterly Reports. Unemployment Reports. Communication Skills. Computer Skills. Excel. MS Office. PCs. Mainframes. Internet. Web. Networks. J. D. Edwards Software. Ability to learn software. Accurate. Dean's List. Award of Merit. Team player. Willing to travel. Relocate.

After an introductory keyword summary, your résumé should contain the standard parts discussed in this chapter. Remember that the keyword section merely helps ensure that your résumé will be selected for inspection. Then human eyes take over. Therefore, you'll want to observe the other writing tips you've learned to make your résumé attractive and forceful.

Notice that the scannable résumé in Figure 11.9 is not drastically different from the others. It does, however, include a keyword summary.

Risking Your Future with an Inflated Résumé

A résumé is expected to showcase a candidate's strengths and minimize weaknesses. For this reason, recruiters expect a certain degree of self-promotion. But some résumé writers step over the line that separates honest self-marketing from deceptive half-truths and outright lies. Distorting facts on a résumé is unethical; lying is illegal. And either practice can destroy a career.

✓ Quick Check

Deception on a résumé, even if discovered much later, can result in firing.

Applying the Final Touches

Because your résumé may be the most important document you will ever write, you should expect to revise it many times. With so much information in concentrated form and with so much depending on its outcome, your résumé demands careful polishing, proofreading, and critiquing.

As you continue revising, always be looking for ways to improve your résumé. Above all, do your best to make your résumé look professional:

✓ Quick Check

In addition to being well written, a résumé must be carefully formatted and thoroughly proofread.

- Avoid anything humorous or attempts to be witty.
- Eliminate the personal pronoun *I.*

FIGURE 11.8 Interpersonal Keywords Most Requested by Employers Using Résumé-Scanning Software*

Ability to delegate	Creative	Leadership	Self-accountable
Ability to implement	Customer-oriented	Multitasking	Self-managing
Ability to plan	Detail-minded	Open communication	Setting priorities
Ability to train	Ethical	Open-minded	Supportive
Accurate	Flexible	Oral communication	Takes initiative
Adaptable	Follow instructions	Organizational skills	Team building
Aggressive worker	Follow through	Persuasive	Team player
Analytical ability	Follow up	Problem solving	Tenacious
Assertive	High energy	Public speaking	Willing to travel
Communication skills	Industrious	Results-oriented	
Competitive	Innovative	Safety-conscious	

*Reported by Resumix, a leading producer of résumé-scanning software.
Source: Joyce Lain Kennedy and Thomas J. Morrow, *Electronic Résumé Revolution* (New York: John Wiley & Sons), 70. Reprinted by permission of John Wiley & Sons, Inc.

FIGURE 11.9 Computer-Friendly Résumé

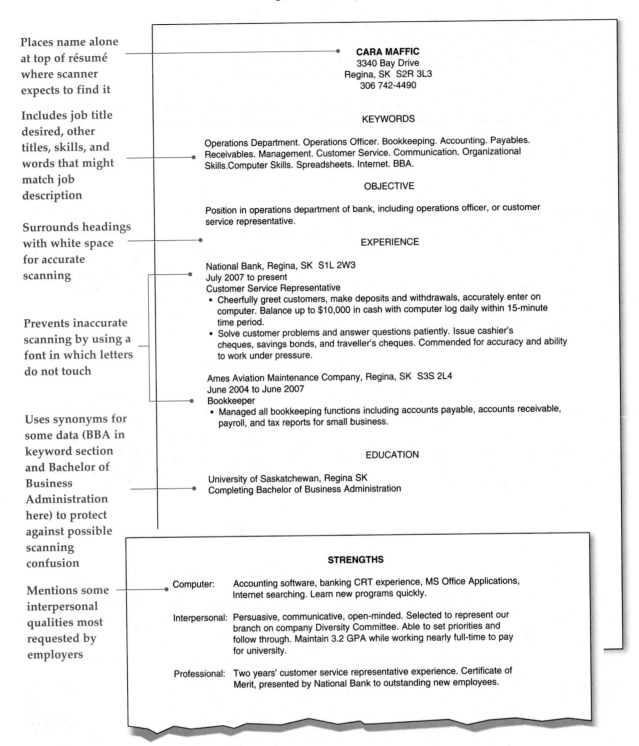

Places name alone at top of résumé where scanner expects to find it

Includes job title desired, other titles, skills, and words that might match job description

Surrounds headings with white space for accurate scanning

Prevents inaccurate scanning by using a font in which letters do not touch

Uses synonyms for some data (BBA in keyword section and Bachelor of Business Administration here) to protect against possible scanning confusion

Mentions some interpersonal qualities most requested by employers

CARA MAFFIC
3340 Bay Drive
Regina, SK S2R 3L3
306 742-4490

KEYWORDS

Operations Department. Operations Officer. Bookkeeping. Accounting. Payables. Receivables. Management. Customer Service. Communication. Organizational Skills.Computer Skills. Spreadsheets. Internet. BBA.

OBJECTIVE

Position in operations department of bank, including operations officer, or customer service representative.

EXPERIENCE

National Bank, Regina, SK S1L 2W3
July 2007 to present
Customer Service Representative
• Cheerfully greet customers, make deposits and withdrawals, accurately enter on computer. Balance up to $10,000 in cash with computer log daily within 15-minute time period.
• Solve customer problems and answer questions patiently. Issue cashier's cheques, savings bonds, and traveller's cheques. Commended for accuracy and ability to work under pressure.

Ames Aviation Maintenance Company, Regina, SK S3S 2L4
June 2004 to June 2007
Bookkeeper
• Managed all bookkeeping functions including accounts payable, accounts receivable, payroll, and tax reports for small business.

EDUCATION

University of Saskatchewan, Regina SK
Completing Bachelor of Business Administration

STRENGTHS

Computer: Accounting software, banking CRT experience, MS Office Applications, Internet searching. Learn new programs quickly.

Interpersonal: Persuasive, communicative, open-minded. Selected to represent our branch on company Diversity Committee. Able to set priorities and follow through. Maintain 3.2 GPA while working nearly full-time to pay for university.

Professional: Two years' customer service representative experience. Certificate of Merit, presented by National Bank to outstanding new employees.

Cara Maffic prepared this résumé free of graphics and fancy formatting so that it would scan well if read by a computer. Notice that she begins with a keyword summary that contains job titles, skills, qualities, and other descriptive words. She hopes that some of these keywords will match those submitted by an employer. To improve accurate scanning, she avoids italics, vertical and horizontal lines, and double columns.

- Use white, off-white, or buff-coloured heavy bond paper (24-pound) and a quality laser printer.
- Do not hire someone to write your résumé because you'll end up with either a generic or a one-time résumé. A generic résumé in today's highly competitive job market will lose out to a targeted résumé nine times out of ten.
- Try to fit your résumé on one page. However, two-page résumés are justified for people with long work histories.

After revising, proofread, proofread, and proofread again: for spelling and mechanics, for content, and for format. Then, have a knowledgeable friend or relative proofread it again.

This is one document that must be perfect.

 Quick Check

Because résumés must be perfect, they should be proofread many times.

Faxing or E-Mailing Your Résumé

In this hurried world, employers increasingly want information immediately. If you are asked to fax or e-mail your résumé, take a second look at it. The key to success is *space*. Without it, letters and characters blur. Underlines blend with the words above, and bold print may look blurred. How can you improve your chances of making a good impression when you must fax or e-mail your résumé?

Quick Check

Résumés to be faxed should have ample space between letters, be printed in 12-point or larger font, and avoid underlines.

If you are faxing your printed résumé, select a font with adequate space between each character. Thinner fonts—such as Times, Garamond, Arial, Courier, and Bookman—are clearer than thicker ones. Use a 12-point or larger font, and avoid underlines, which may look broken or choppy when faxed. To be safe, get a transmission report to ensure that all pages were transmitted satisfactorily. Finally, follow up with your polished, printed résumé.

If you are e-mailing your résumé, you should prepare a Plain Text version. It will eliminate bold, italics, underlining, tabulated indentions, and unusual characters. To prevent lines from wrapping at awkward spots, keep your line length to 65 characters or less. You can, of course, transmit a fully formatted, attractive résumé if you send it as an attachment and your receiver is using a compatible e-mail program. To avoid disappointment, attach one fully formatted résumé, one Plain Text résumé, and one cut-and-pasted résumé in the body of your e-mail.

Quick Check

Résumés that are sent by e-mail transmit best as Plain Text files without tabs or underlines, and without italic, bold, or unusual characters.

The Persuasive Cover Letter

To accompany your résumé, you'll need a persuasive cover letter. The cover letter has three purposes: (1) introducing the résumé, (2) highlighting ways your strengths will benefit the reader, and (3) obtaining an interview. In many ways your cover letter is a sales letter; it sells your talents and tries to beat the competition. It will, accordingly, include many of the persuasive techniques you learned in Chapter 7.

Quick Check

Cover letters introduce résumés, relate writer strengths to reader benefits, and seek an interview.

Regardless of its length, a cover letter should have three primary parts: (1) an opening that gets attention, (2) a body that builds interest and reduces resistance, and (3) a closing that motivates action.

Gaining Attention in the Opening

The first step in gaining the interest of your reader is addressing that individual by name. Rather than sending your letter to the "Personnel Manager" or "Human Resources Department," try to identify the name of the appropriate individual. Make it a rule to call the organization for the correct spelling and the complete address. This personal touch distinguishes your letter and demonstrates your serious interest.

Quick Check

The opening in a cover letter gets attention by addressing the receiver by name.

How you open your cover letter depends largely on whether your résumé is for a position that is solicited or unsolicited. If an employment position has been

✓ **Quick Check**

Openings for solicited jobs refer to the source of the information, the job title, and qualifications for the position.

announced and applicants are being solicited, you can use a direct approach. If you do not know whether a position is open and you are prospecting for a job, use an indirect approach. Whether direct or indirect, the opening should attract the attention of the reader. Strive for openings that are more imaginative than *Please consider this letter an application for the position of ...* or *I would like to apply for....*

Openings for Solicited Jobs. Here are some of the best techniques to open a letter of application for a job that has been announced:

- **Refer to the name of an employee in the company.** Remember that employers always hope to hire known quantities rather than complete strangers:

  Mitchell Sims, a member of your Customer Service Department, told me that DataTech is seeking an experienced customer service representative. The attached summary of my qualifications demonstrates my preparation for this position.

  At the suggestion of Ms. Claudette Guertin of your Human Resources Department, I submit my qualifications for the position of personnel assistant.

- **Refer to the source of your information precisely.** If you are answering an advertisement, include the exact position advertised and the name and date of the publication. For large organizations, it's also wise to mention the section of the newspaper where the ad appeared:

  Your advertisement in the Careers section of the June 1 *Vancouver Sun* for a junior accountant (competition 06-003) greatly appeals to me. With my accounting training and computer experience, I believe I could serve DataTech well.

  The September 10 issue of the *National Post* reports that you are seeking a mature, organized, and reliable administrative assistant (competition 06-A54) with excellent communication skills.

  Susan Butler, placement director at Carleton University, told me that DataTech has an opening for a technical writer with knowledge of Web design and graphics.

- **Refer to the job title and describe how your qualifications fit the requirements.** Human resources directors are looking for a match between an applicant's qualifications and the job needs:

  Will an honours graduate with a degree in recreation studies and two years of part-time experience organizing social activities for a retirement community qualify for your position of activity director?

  Because of my specialized training in computerized accounting at Simon Fraser University, I feel confident that I have the qualifications you described in your advertisement for an accountant trainee.

Openings for Unsolicited Jobs. If you are unsure whether a position actually exists, you may wish to use a more persuasive opening. Since your goal is to convince this person to read on, try one of the following techniques:

- **Demonstrate interest in and knowledge of the reader's business.** Show the human resources director that you have done your research and that this organization is more than a mere name to you:

  Since the Canadian Automobile Association is organizing a new information management team for its recently established group insurance division, could you use the services of a well-trained information systems graduate who seeks to become a professional underwriter?

- **Show how your special talents and background will benefit the company.** Human resources directors need to be convinced that you can do something for them:

> Could your rapidly expanding publications division use the services of an editorial assistant who offers exceptional language skills, an honours degree from Brandon University, and two years' experience in producing a school literary publication?

In applying for an advertised job, Mabel Lam wrote the solicited cover letter shown in Figure 11.10. Notice that her opening identifies the position and the newspaper completely so that the reader knows exactly what advertisement Mabel refers to. Using features on her word-processing program, Mabel designed her own letterhead that uses her name and looks like professionally printed letterhead paper.

✔ **Quick Check**

Openings for unsolicited jobs show interest in and knowledge of the company, as well as spotlighting reader benefits.

FIGURE 11.10 Solicited Cover Letter

Mabel Lam

1770 Hawthorne Place, Red Deer AB T4R 3L2 — *Uses personally designed letterhead*

May 23, 2009

Mr. William A. Caldwell
Director, Human Resources
Del Rio Enterprises
Calgary, AB T2A 3L4

— *Addresses proper person by name and title*

Dear Mr. Caldwell:

Your advertisement for an assistant product manager, appearing May 22 in Section C of the *National Post*, caught my attention because my education and training match your needs.

— *Gains attention by identifying job and exact page where ad appeared*

Your ad states that the job includes "assisting in the coordination of a wide range of marketing programs as well as analyzing sales results and tracking marketing budgets." A recent internship at Ventana Corporation introduced me to similar tasks. Assisting the marketing manager allowed me to analyze the promotion, budget, and overall sales success of two products Ventana was evaluating. My major report examined the current market, the products' life cycles, and their sales/profit return. In addition to this research, I helped formulate a product merchandising plan and answered consumers' questions at a local trade show.

— *Builds interest by relating writer's experiences to job requirements*

Intensive courses in marketing and management, as well as skills in computer spreadsheets and databases, have given me the kind of marketing and computer training that Del Rio would expect in a product manager. Moreover, my recent retail sales experience and participation in school organizations have helped me develop the kind of customer service and interpersonal skills necessary for an effective product manager.

— *Builds interest by discussing schooling*

— *Builds interest by discussing experience*

After you have examined the enclosed résumé for details of my qualifications, I would be happy to answer questions. Please call me to arrange an interview so that we may discuss how my marketing experience, computer training, and interpersonal skills could contribute to Del Rio Enterprises.

— *Refers reader to résumé*

— *Motivates action by asking for interview and repeating main qualifications*

Sincerely,

Mabel Lam

Mabel Lam

Enclosure

More challenging are unsolicited letters of application, such as Jon Penner's, shown in Figure 11.11. Because he hopes to discover or create a job, his opening must grab the reader's attention immediately. To do that, he capitalizes on company information appearing in the newspaper. Jon purposely kept his application letter short because he anticipated that a busy executive would be unwilling to read a long, detailed letter. Jon's unsolicited letter "prospects" for a job. Some job candidates feel that such letters may be even more productive than efforts to secure advertised jobs, since "prospecting" candidates face less competition. Notice that Jon's letter uses a standard return address consisting of his street, city, and the date.

FIGURE 11.11   **Unsolicited Cover Letter**

Uses standard return address format, but could have designed his own letterhead

2250 Pinecroft Drive
Winnipeg, MB R4L 2H7
May 29, 2009

Mr. Arthur P. Minsberg
Vice President, Operations
Sports World, Inc.
4907 Portage Avenue
Winnipeg, MB R2G 1L7

Dear Mr. Minsberg:

Gains attention by showing knowledge of company

Builds interest by keeping letter brief to retain reader's attention

Today's *Winnipeg Free Press* reports that your organization plans to expand its operations to include national distribution of sporting goods. You may be needing highly motivated, self-starting sales representatives and marketing managers. Here are three significant qualifications I have to offer:

- Four years of formal training in business administration, including specialized courses in sales management, retailing, marketing promotion, and consumer behaviour.

- Practical experience in demonstrating and selling consumer products, as well as successful experience in telephone marketing.

- Good communication skills and a strong interest in most areas of sports (which helped me become a sports broadcaster at the University of Manitoba radio station CLQW).

Motivates action by referring to résumé and taking initiative for follow-up

I would like to talk with you about how I can put these qualifications, and others summarized in the enclosed résumé, to work for Sports World as it develops its national sales force. Please contact me if you have any questions regarding the details of my qualification, Alternately, I'll call during the week of June 9 to discuss your company's expansion plans and the opportunity for an interview.

Sincerely yours,

Jon Penner

Jon Penner

Enclosure

Chapter 11 The Job Search, Résumés, and Cover Letters

Building Interest in the Body

Once you have captured the attention of the reader, you can use the body of the letter to build interest and reduce resistance. Keep in mind that your résumé emphasizes what you have done; your cover letter stresses what you can do for the employer. Here are some important points to consider:

✓ Quick Check

The body of a cover letter should build interest, reduce resistance, and discuss relevant personal qualities.

- Relate your remarks to a specific position. If you are responding to an advertisement, you'll want to explain how your preparation and experience fill the stated requirements. Your employment research and knowledge of your field should give you a reasonably good idea of what is expected for this position.
- Emphasize reader benefits. In other words, you should describe your strong points in relation to the needs of the employer. In one employment survey, many human resources professionals expressed the same view: "I want you to tell me what you can do for my organization. This is much more important to me than telling me what courses you took in college or what 'duties' you performed on your previous jobs."[4] Instead of *I have completed courses in business communication, report writing, and technical writing,* try this:

✓ Quick Check

Spotlighting reader benefits means matching one's personal strengths to an employer's needs.

> Courses in business communication, report writing, and technical writing have helped me develop the research and writing skills required of your technical writers.

- Choose your strongest qualifications and show how they fit the targeted job. Remember, students with little experience are better off spotlighting their education and its practical applications, as these candidates did:

> Because you seek an architect's apprentice with proven ability, I submit a drawing of mine that won second place in the Algonquin College drafting contest last year.

> Successfully transcribing over 100 letters and memos in my college transcription class gave me experience in converting the spoken word into the written word, an exacting communication skill demanded of your legal assistants.

- Discuss relevant personal qualities. Employers are looking for candidates who, among other things, are team players, take responsibility, show initiative, and learn easily.
- Refer the reader to your résumé. Do so directly or as part of another statement, as shown here:

> Please refer to the attached résumé for additional information regarding my education, experience, and references.

> As you will notice from my résumé, I will graduate in June with a bachelor's degree in business administration.

Motivating Action in the Closing

After presenting your case, you should conclude with a prompt to action. This is where you ask for an interview. If you live in a distant city, you may request an employment application or an opportunity to be interviewed by the organization's nearest representative. However, never ask for the job. To do so is considered unprofessional. In requesting an interview, suggest reader benefits or review your strongest points. Sound sincere and appreciative. Remember to make it easy for the reader to agree by supplying your telephone number and the best times to call you. And keep in mind that some human resources directors prefer that you take the initiative to call them. Here are possible endings:

✓ Quick Check

The closing of a cover letter should include a request for an interview.

> I hope this brief description of my qualifications and the additional information on my résumé indicate to you my genuine desire to put my skills in accounting to work for

you. Please call me at (416) 488-2291 before 10 a.m. or after 3 p.m. to arrange an interview.

To add to your staff an industrious, well-trained word-processing specialist with proven communication skills, call me at (604) 492-1433 to arrange an interview. I can meet with you at any time convenient to your schedule.

Next week, after you have examined the attached résumé, I will call you to discuss the possibility of arranging an interview.

Avoiding "I" Dominance

As you revise your application letter, notice how many sentences begin with *I*. Although it's impossible to talk about yourself without using *I*, you can reduce the number of sentences beginning with this pronoun by using two techniques. First, place *I* in the middle of sentences instead of dominating the opening. Instead of *I was the top salesperson in my department,* try *While working in X department, I did Y and Z, and among 15 coworkers, I received top ratings from my managers.* Incorporating *I* into the middle of sentences considerably reduces its domination.

Another technique for avoiding "I" dominance involves making activities and outcomes, not yourself, the subjects of sentences. For example, rather than *I took classes in business communication and computer applications,* say *Classes in business communication and computer applications prepared me to....* Instead of *I enjoyed helping customers,* say *Helping customers taught me to be patient under stress.*

Final Tips

Like the résumé, your cover letter must look professional and suggest quality:

- Use a traditional letter style, such as block or modified block.
- Print it on the same bond paper as your résumé.
- Proofread your application letter several times; have a friend read it for content and mechanics.

Summing Up and Looking Forward

In today's competitive job market, an employment search begins with identifying your interests, evaluating your qualifications, and choosing a career path. Finding the perfect job will mean a concentrated effort devoted to checking classified advertisements, networking, and studying online job possibilities. In applying for jobs, you'll want to submit a persuasive résumé that sells your skills and experience. Whether you choose a chronological, functional, or combination résumé style, you should tailor your qualifications to fit the position sought. If you think your résumé might be scanned, emphasize keywords and keep the format simple. A persuasive cover letter should introduce your résumé and describe how your skills and experiences match those required.

Now, if your résumé and cover letter have been successful, you'll proceed to the employment interview, one of life's most stressful experiences. The last chapter in this book provides helpful suggestions for successful interviewing and follow-up communication.

Critical Thinking

1. Some job candidates think that applying for unsolicited jobs can be more productive than applying for advertised openings. Discuss the advantages and disadvantages of letters that seek jobs.

2. *Ethical Issue:* At work, fellow employee Karl lets it slip that he did not complete the degree he claims on his résumé. You have never liked Karl, but he does satisfactory work. You are both competing for the same promotion. You are considering writing an anonymous note to the boss telling him to verify Karl's degree. Use the tools in the Ethics Workshop at the end of Chapter 3 (p. 61) to decide whether this is an ethical action.

Chapter Review

3. List at least five questions that you should ask yourself to identify your employment interests.

4. List five or more sources of career information.

5. How are most jobs likely to be found? Through the classified ads? Employment agencies? Networking? Explain.

6. What is the goal of your résumé?

7. Describe a chronological résumé and discuss its advantages.

8. Describe a functional résumé and discuss its advantages.

9. What are the disadvantages of a functional résumé?

10. When does it make sense to include a career objective on your résumé?

11. In addition to technical skills, what characteristics do employers seek?

12. List some suggestions for making a résumé easily scannable by a computer.

13. What are keywords and why are they important in résumé scanning? Give examples.

14. If you are e-mailing your résumé, why is it wise to send a text-only version?

15. What are the three purposes of a cover letter?

Writing Improvement Exercises

16. Cover Letter Opening. James Nickson has just graduated from college with a three-year diploma in accounting. With the help of his college's career centre, James has begun applying for full-time employment. Below is the opening of one of James's cover letters. Analyze the letter, identify any problems, and rewrite this section of the letter following the guidelines in this chapter.

To whom it may concern,

It was a stroke of luck to find the job advertisement in the local newspaper last week for your company. I've always wanted to work for a company like yours, and this job opening may now give me the opportunity! My name is Jim Nickson and I just graduated in Accounting from Humber College.

17. Cover Letter Body. Below is the body of James Nickson's cover letter. Analyze the letter, identify any problems, and rewrite this section of the letter following the guidelines in this chapter.

As you can see from my enclosed résumé, I am a strong student, and I am also a good team player. I think these skills would be useful to me in your company. For example, I took a course in Auditing in which I received the highest grade in the program. Finally, I have worked as a bookkeeper for the past two summers.

18. Cover Letter Closing. The closing of James Nickson's cover letter is found below. Analyze the letter, identify any problems, and rewrite this section of the letter following the guidelines in this chapter.

In closing, permit me to be blunt and say that there's nothing I'd like more than the opportunity to work for your company. I know I would be an asset to your organization. I look forward to hearing from you at your earliest convenience.

Best,

Jim Nickson

Activities and Cases

11.1 Evaluating Your Qualifications. Prepare four worksheets that list your own qualifications in the areas of employment, education, capabilities and skills, and honours and activities. Use active verbs when appropriate.

a. *Employment.* Begin with your most recent job or internship. For each position list the following information: employer; job title; dates of employment; and three to five duties, activities, or accomplishments. Highlight the duties, activities, or accomplishments related to your job goal.
b. *Education.* List degrees, certificates, diplomas, and training accomplishments. Include courses, seminars, or skills that are relevant to your job goal. Calculate your grade point average in your major.
c. *Capabilities and skills.* List all capabilities and skills that recommend you for the job you seek. Use words such as *skilled, competent, trained, experienced,* and *ability to.* Also list five or more qualities or skills necessary for a successful individual in your chosen field. Write action statements demonstrating that you possess some of these qualities; try to show evidence (*Developed teamwork skills by working with a committee of eight to produce a ...*).
d. *Awards, honours, and activities.* Explain any awards so that the reader will understand them. List school, community, and professional activities that suggest you are a well-rounded individual or possess traits relevant to your target job.

11.2 Choosing a Career Path. Visit your school library, local library, or employment centre. Select an appropriate resource such as Human Resources and Skills Development Canada's National Occupational Classification (http://www23.hrdc -drhc.gc.ca/2001/e/generic/welcome.shtml) to find a description for a position for which you could apply in two to five years. Photocopy or print the pages from the resource you chose that describe employment in the area in which you are interested. If your instructor directs, attach these copies to the cover letter you will write in Activity 11.8. Were you able to find the job that interests you? If not, where else can you find information on this job?

11.3 Searching the Job Market. Clip a job advertisement from the classified section of a newspaper or print one from a career site on the Web. Select an ad describing the kind of employment you are seeking now or plan to seek when you graduate. Save this advertisement to attach to the résumé you will write in Activity 11.7.

11.4 Posting a Résumé on the Web. Research at least three online employment sites where you could post your résumé. In an e-mail to your instructor, imagine you are providing text for the updating of your college's career centre website. Describe the procedure involved in posting résumés on these three sites in a clear set of steps, and list the advantages and disadvantages of each site.

11.5 Draft Document: Résumé. Analyze the following résumé. Discuss its strengths and weaknesses. Your instructor may ask you to revise sections of this résumé before showing you an improved version.

Winona Skudra
5349 Main Street
Saskatoon, SK S2N 0B4
Phone: (d) (306) 834-4583 (n) (306) 594-2985

Seeking to be hired at Meadow Products as an intern in Accounting

SKILLS: Accounting, Internet, Windows 98, Excel, PowerPoint, Freelance Graphics

EDUCATION

Now working on B.Comm. in Business Administration. Major, Management and Accounting; GPA is 3.5. Expect to graduate in June, 2009.

EXPERIENCE:

Assistant Accountant, 2002 to present. March and McLennan, Inc., Bookkeeping/Tax Service, Saskatoon. I keep accounting records for several small businesses accurately. I prepare 150 to 200 individual income tax returns each year. For Hill and Hill Trucking I maintain accurate and up-to-date A/R records. And I prepare payroll records for 16 employees at three firms.

Peterson Controls Inc., Saskatoon. Data Processing Internship, 2006 to present. I design and maintain spreadsheets. I prepare graphs to illustrate uptime and downtime data.

Saskatoon Curling Club. Accounts Payable Internship, 2005 to 2006. Took care of accounts payable including filing system for the club. Responsible for processing monthly adjusting entries for general ledger. Worked closely with treasurer to give the Board budget/disbursement figures regularly.

Saskatoon High School, Saskatoon. I marketed the VITA program to students and organized volunteers and supplies. Official title: Coordinator of Volunteer Income Tax Assistance Project.

COMMUNITY SERVICE: March of Dimes Drive, Central High School; All Souls Lutheran Church, coordinator for Children's Choir

---

11.6 Draft Document: Cover Letter. Analyze each section of the following cover letter written by an accounting major about to graduate.

Dear Human Resources Director:

I am writing this letter as an application for the position of staff accountant that I saw advertised in the *Saskatoon Star Phoenix.* Although I have had no paid work experience in this field, accounting has been my major in college and I think I could be an asset to your company.

For four years I have studied accounting, and I am fully trained for full-charge book-keeping as well as electronic accounting. I have completed 36 credits of college accounting and courses in business law, economics, statistics, finance, management, and marketing. In addition to my course work, during the tax season I have been a student volunteer for VITA. This is a project to help individuals in the community prepare their income tax returns, and I learned a lot from this experience. I have also received some experience in office work and working with figures when I was employed as an office assistant for Copy Quick, Inc.

I am a competent and responsible person who gets along pretty well with others. I have been a member of some college and social organizations and have even held elective office.

I feel that I have a strong foundation in accounting as a result of my course work and my experience. Along with my personal qualities and my desire to succeed, I hope that you will agree that I qualify for the position of staff accountant with your company.

Sincerely,

11.7 Résumé. Using the data you developed in Activity 11.2, write your résumé. Aim it at a full-time job, part-time position, or internship. Attach a job listing for a specific position (from Activity 11.3). Revise your résumé until it is perfect.

11.8 Cover Letter. Write an application letter introducing your résumé from Activity 11.7. Revise your application letter until it is perfect.

11.9 Unsolicited Cover Letter. As you read in this chapter, job applications are not always solicited. As part of your college education, you have no doubt come into contact with periodicals related to your field. For example, you may have read articles in *Canadian Business, Report on Business, HR Reporter, Marketing,* or any number of other magazines. In these magazines, you've come across the names of various business people, either because they were featured in an article, or else because they were quoted as experts.

Your Task. Using your college or local library, read through an issue of a business-related periodical or your local newspaper's business section. Look for a businessperson who is mentioned, quoted, or featured in that periodical. Write that person an unsolicited cover letter asking for an entry-level position or internship either for the summer or upon graduation. Make sure to revise this letter sufficiently, and hand it in to your instructor for comments before actually mailing it.

Grammar/Mechanics Review—11

The following sentences contain errors in grammar and mechanics. Below each sentence write a corrected version. There may be more than one error in each sentence.

1. Please send the softwear to me or whomever submitted the order.

2. All committe member knew the assignment, and were prepared with there reports.

3. Was any of the managers absent on the Monday for the all day meeting?

4. The canadian government has ask all companys to conserve energy.

5. Many automobile manufacturer are now produce vehicles that lower pollution.

6. The president of sony electronics is preparing a statement about new advances in Video games for childrens.

7. We are still using a 4 year old printer, however it will be inspected every year.

8. Before five p.m. we must return all 3 computers and all other equipments to our 7th Avenue office.

9. Canada post announced on July 1 that it would increase rates by 4.5%.

10. The three Cs of credit is the following, character, capacity, and capital.

11. Porter Kohl said that his Father gave him the following advice to making speeches—"Be sincere, be brief; and be seated.

12. One of the trucks built in north america are experimenting with a 1950s design for this years' production.

13. One of the quickly-printed computer book have been priced to sell at ten dollars and ninety-five cents.

14. If you will send the shipment to Elizabeth or I; it's contents will be inspected carefully.

15. The itinerary for Luke included three countrys holland france and germany.

Document for Revision

The following résumé (shortened for this exercise) has faults in grammar, punctuation, spelling, number form, verb form, wordiness, and word use. Use standard proofreading marks (see Appendix B) to correct the errors. When you finish, your instructor can show you the revised version of this résumé.

MEGAN A. Kozlov

245 Topsail Street

St. John's, Newfoundland A1B 3Z4

EDUCATION

Memorial University, St. John's, Newfoundland. Bachelor of Arts Degree expected in June 2010. Major English.

EXPERIENCE:

- Administrative Assistant. Host Systems, St. John's. 2005 too present. Responsible for enter data on Macintosh computer. I had to ensure accuracy and completeness of data that was to be enter. Another duty was maintaining a clean and well-organized office. I also served as Office Courier.

- Lechter's Housewares. Outlook Newfoundland. 2nd Asst. Mgr I managed store in absence of mgr. and asst. mgr. I open and close registers. Ballanced daily reciepts. Ordered some merchandise.. I also had to supervising two employees.

- Clerk typist. Sunshine Travel Outlook. 2002-2003. (part time) Entered travel information on IBM PC. Did personalized follow-up letters to customers questions. Was responsible for phones. I also handled all errands as courier.

STRENGTHS

Microsoft Office Applications, transcription, proofreading.

Can type 50 word/per/minute.

I am fast learner, and very accurate.

Word-perfect, Excell, InterNet

How to Use Traditional and Online Networking to Explore the Hidden Job Market

Not all jobs are advertised in classified ads or listed in job databases. The "hidden" job market, according to some estimates, accounts for as much as two-thirds of all positions available. Companies don't always announce openings publicly because it's time consuming to interview all the applicants, many of whom are not qualified. But the real reason that companies resist announcing a job is that they dislike hiring "strangers." One recruiter says that when she needs to hire, she first looks around among her friends and acquaintances. If she can't find anyone suitable, she then turns to advertising.[5] It's clear that many employers are more comfortable hiring a person they know.

The key to finding a good job, then, is changing yourself from a "stranger" into someone who is known. One way to become known is by networking. You can use either traditional methods or online resources.

Traditional Networking

- *Step 1: Develop a list.* Make a list of anyone who would be willing to talk with you about finding a job. List your friends, relatives, former employers, former coworkers, classmates from grade school and high school, college friends, members of your religious group, people in social and athletic clubs, present and former teachers, neighbours, and friends of your parents.
- *Step 2: Make contacts.* Call the people on your list or, even better, try to meet with them in person. To set up a meeting, say "Hi, Aunt Martha! I'm looking for a job and I wonder if you could help me out. When could I come over to talk about it?" During your visit, be friendly, well organized, polite, and interested in what your contact has to say. Provide a copy of your résumé, and try to keep the conversation centred on your job search area. Your goal is to get two or more referrals. In specifying your request, ask two questions: "Do you know of anyone who might have an opening for a person with my skills?" and "Do you know of anyone else who might know of someone who would?"
- *Step 3: Follow up on your referrals.* Call the people whose names are on your referral list. You might say something like, "Hello. I'm Carlos Ramos, a friend of Connie Cole. She suggested that I call and ask you for help. I'm looking for a position as a marketing trainee, and she thought you might be willing to see me and give me a few ideas." *Don't ask for a job.* During your referral interview ask how the individual got started in this line of work, what he or she likes best (or least) about the work, what career paths exist in the field, and what problems must be overcome by a newcomer. Most important, ask how a person with your background and skills might get started in the field. Send an informal thank-you note to anyone who helps you in your job search, and stay in touch with the most promising contacts. Ask whether you may call every three weeks or so during your job search.

Online Networking

As with traditional networking, the goal is to make connections with people who are advanced in their fields. Ask for their advice about finding a job. Most people like talking about themselves, and asking them about their experiences is an excellent way to begin an online correspondence that might lead to "electronic mentoring" or a letter of recommendation from an expert in the field. "Hanging out" at an online forum, discussion group, or newsgroup where industry professionals can be found is also a great way to keep tabs on the latest business trends and potential job leads.

Web

- *Web-Based Discussion Groups, Forums, and Boards.* An especially good discussion group resource for beginners is Yahoo! Groups (http://groups.yahoo.com). You may choose from groups ranging from business and finance to romance and relationships to science. If you click the "Business & Finance" listing, you will see listings for more specialized groups. Click "Employment and Work," and you will find career groups including construction, customer service, secretaries, court reporting, interior design, and so on.
- *Mailing Lists and Newsgroups.* The most relevant Internet discussions can be found on mailing lists. You can subscribe to an e-mail newsletter or discussion group at Topica (http://lists.topica.com). To post and read newsgroup (Usenet) messages, try the Google website (http://www.google.ca) and click "Groups."

Career Application

Everyone who goes out into the job market needs to develop his or her own network. Assume you are ready to change jobs or look for a permanent position. Begin developing your personal network.

Your Task

- Conduct at least one referral interview and report on it to your class.
- Join one professional mailing list. Ask your instructor to recommend an appropriate mailing list for your field.
- Take notes on discussions at your mailing list and report your reactions and findings to your class.

12 Employment Interviews and Follow-Up Messages

Nothing delights interviewers more than candidates who have done their homework. They want to know that a candidate has done a little research on the company or industry ... and understands the challenges it is facing. As a bonus, the most heartwarming candidates have actually given a little thought to the job they are applying for.[1]

Michael Stern, *President, Michael Stern Associates Inc., an executive search firm headquartered in Toronto*

LEARNING OBJECTIVES

1. Find information about specific companies.
2. Explain how to prepare for employment interviews.
3. Recognize how to control nonverbal messages and how to fight interview fears.
4. Be prepared to answer most common interview questions and know how to close an interview.
5. Itemize topics and behaviours to avoid in interviews.
6. Write follow-up letters and other employment messages.

Job interviews, for most of us, are intimidating; no one enjoys being judged and, possibly, rejected. Should you expect to be nervous about an upcoming job interview? Of course. Most people are uneasy about being examined and questioned. But think of how much more nervous you would be if you had no idea what to expect in the interview and if you were unprepared.

This chapter shows you how to prepare for interviews. You'll learn how to gather information about an employer, as well as how to reduce nervousness, control body language, and fight fear during an interview. You'll pick up tips for responding to recruiters' most common questions and learn how to cope with illegal questions and salary matters. Moreover, you'll receive tips on significant questions you can ask during an interview. Finally, you'll learn what you should do as a successful follow-up to an interview.

Hiring/Placement Interviews

Hiring/placement interviews are like a game. Trained interviewers try to uncover any negative information that will eliminate a candidate. The candidate tries to minimize faults and highlight strengths to avoid being eliminated. Like most games, the more practice you get, the better you perform because you know what to expect. Hiring/placement interviews are conducted in depth and may take many forms.

- **One-on-one interviews** are most common. You can expect to sit down with a company representative or two and talk about the job and your qualifications. If the representative is the hiring manager, questions will be specific and job related. If the representative is from the human resources department, the questions will probably be more general.
- **Chronological and group interviews** are common with companies that rule by agreement. You may face many interviewers one by one, all of whom you must listen to carefully and respond to positively. Many group interviews are conducted by teams. With team interviews, begin to think in terms of "we" instead of "I." Individual achievement is less important in group interviews than how you contributed to a team effort. Strive to stay focused, summarize important points, and ask good questions.

Investigating the Company

One of the most important steps in being successful at the interview game is gathering information about a potential employer. In learning about a company, you may uncover information that convinces you that this is not the company for you. It's always better to learn about negatives early in the process. More likely, though, the information you collect will help you adapt your application and interview responses to the organization's needs. Recruiters are impressed by candidates who have done their homework.

Quick Check

Researching an organization enlightens candidates and impresses recruiters.

Searching for Company Information

For Canadian companies that are publicly held, you can generally learn a great deal from annual reports and financial disclosure reports available at http://www.sedar.com. Company information is also available from D&B Canada (http://www.dnb.ca) and Canadian Business Resource (http://www.cbr.ca). One of the best things a job seeker can do is to get into the habit of reading the newspaper regularly. The best place to go for current information on Canadian companies is the business section of the two national newspapers, the *National Post* and *The Globe and Mail*. Your local city or town newspaper will sometimes profile local businesses. Finally, large and small companies alike also maintain their own websites, bursting with helpful information. Another way to learn about an organization is to call the receptionist or the interviewer directly. Ask what you can read to prepare for the interview. Here are some specifics to research:

Quick Check

Study company leaders, organizational strategies, finances, products, customers, competition, and advertising.

- Find out all you can about company leaders. Their goals, ambitions, and values are often adopted by the entire organization—including your interviewer.
- Investigate the business philosophy of the leaders, such as their priorities, strategies, and managerial approaches. Are you a good match with your target employer? If so, be sure to let the interviewer know that there is a connection between the employer's needs and your qualifications.
- Learn about the company's accomplishments and setbacks. This information should help you determine where you might make your best contribution.
- Study the company's finances. Are they so shaky that a takeover is imminent? If so, look elsewhere. Try to get your hands on an annual report. Many larger companies now post them on their websites.

- Examine the company's products and customers. What excites you about this company?
- Check out the competition. What are its products, strengths, and weaknesses?
- Analyze the company's advertising, including sales and marketing brochures. One candidate, a marketing major, spent a great deal of time poring over brochures from an aerospace contractor. During his initial interview, he shocked and impressed the recruiter with his knowledge of the company's guidance systems. The candidate had, in fact, relieved the interviewer of his least-favourite task—explaining the company's complicated technology.

Learning About Smaller Companies

For smaller companies and those that are not publicly owned, you'll probably have to dig a little deeper. You might start with the local library. Ask the reference librarian to help you locate information. Newspapers might contain stories or press releases with news of an organization. Visit the Better Business Bureau or Chamber of Commerce to discover whether the company has had any difficulties with other companies or consumers. Also, find out what kinds of contributions the company has made to the local community. Try your local Canada Business Service Centre for company information and annual reports.

Quick Check

The best source of inside information is company employees.

Talking with company employees is always a good idea, if you can manage it. They are probably the best source of inside information. Try to be introduced to someone who is currently employed there—but not working in the immediate area where you wish to be hired.

You know how flattered you feel when an employer knows about you and your background. That feeling works both ways. Employers are pleased when job candidates take an interest in them. Be ready to put in plenty of effort in investigating an employer because this effort really pays off at interview time.

Preparing and Practising

After you have learned about the organization, study the job description. It not only helps you write a focused résumé but also enables you to match your education, experience, and interests with the employer's position. Finding out the duties and responsibilities of the position will help you practise your best response strategies.

One of the best ways to prepare involves listing your (1) most important skills, (2) greatest areas of knowledge, (3) strongest personality traits, and (4) key accomplishments. Write this information down and practise relating these strengths to the kinds of questions frequently asked in interviews. Here are some specific tips for preparation:

- Practise, practise, practise. Recite answers to typical interview questions in a mirror, with a friend, while driving in your car, or in spare moments. Keep practising until you have the best responses down pat.
- Consider videotaping or tape-recording a practice session to see and hear how you really come across. Do you look and sound enthusiastic?
- Expect to explain problem areas on your résumé. For example, if you have little or no experience, you might emphasize your recent training and up-to-date skills. If you have gaps in your résumé, be prepared to answer questions about them positively and truthfully.
- Try to build interviewing experience with less important jobs first. You will become more confident and better able to sell your strengths with repeated interviewing exposure. Think of it as a game that requires practice.

Quick Check

Practise success stories that highlight your most strategic skills, areas of knowledge, strongest personality traits, and key accomplishments.

Sending Positive Nonverbal Messages

What comes out of your mouth and what's written on your résumé are not the only messages an interviewer receives about you. Nonverbal messages also create powerful impressions. Here are suggestions that will help you send the right nonverbal messages during interviews:

✔ Quick Check

Send positive nonverbal messages by arriving on time, being courteous, dressing professionally, greeting the interviewer confidently, controlling your body movements, making eye contact, and smiling.

- Arrive on time or a little early. If necessary, find the location on a trial run a few days before the interview so that you know where to park, how much time the drive takes, and what office to find.
- Be courteous and friendly to everyone. Remember that you are being judged not only by the interviewer but by the receptionist and anyone else who sees you before and after the interview.
- Introduce yourself to the receptionist and wait to be invited to sit.
- Dress professionally. Even if some employees in the organization dress casually, you should look qualified, competent, and successful. One young applicant complained to his girlfriend about having to wear a suit for an interview when everyone at the company dressed casually. She replied, "You don't get to wear the uniform, though, until you make the team!"
- Greet the interviewer confidently. Extend your hand, look him or her directly in the eye, and say, "I'm pleased to meet you, Mr. X. I am Z." In this culture a firm, not crushing, handshake sends a nonverbal message of poise and confidence.
- Wait for the interviewer to offer you a chair. Make small talk with upbeat comments, such as "This is a beautiful headquarters. How many employees work here?" Don't immediately begin rummaging in your briefcase for your résumé. Being at ease and unrushed suggest that you are self-confident.
- Control your body movements. Keep your hands, arms, and elbows to yourself. Don't lean on a desk. Sit erect, leaning forward slightly. Keep your feet on the floor.
- Make eye contact frequently but don't get into a staring contest. A direct eye gaze, at least in Canada, suggests interest and trustworthiness.
- Smile enough to convey a positive attitude. Have a friend give you honest feedback on whether you generally smile too much or not enough.
- Sound enthusiastic and interested—but sincere.

Fighting Fear

Expect to be nervous. It's natural. Other than public speaking, employment interviews are the most dreaded events in many people's working lives. One of the best ways to overcome fear is to know what happens in a typical interview. Figure 12.1 describes how a recruiter usually structures an interview. You can further reduce your fears by following these suggestions:

✔ Quick Check

Fight fear by practising, preparing 110 percent, breathing deeply, and knowing that you are in charge for part of the interview.

- Practise interviewing as much as you can—especially with real companies. The more times you experience the interview situation, the less nervous you will be.
- Prepare 110 percent! Know how you will answer the most frequently asked questions. Be ready with success stories. Rehearse your closing statement. One of the best ways to reduce nervousness is to know that you have done all you can to be ready for the interview.
- Take deep breaths, particularly if you feel anxious while waiting for the interviewer. Deep breathing makes you concentrate on something other than the interview and also provides much-needed oxygen.
- Remember that the interviewer isn't the only one who is getting information. You have come to learn about the job and the company. In fact, during some parts of the interview, you will be in charge. This should give you courage.

FIGURE 12.1 Steps in an Employment Interview from a Recruiter's Perspective

Step 1	Step 2	Step 3
Before interview, review candidate's résumé.	Check career objective. Look for skills; note items to pursue.	Greet candidate. Introduce self. Make candidate feel comfortable.

Step 4	Step 5	Step 6
Describe open position. Confirm candidate's interest in position.	Give brief overview of organization.	Using résumé, probe for evidence of relevant skills and traits.

Step 7	Step 8	Step 9
Solicit questions from candidate.	Close interview by promoting organization and explaining next step.	Fill out evaluation form.

Answering Questions

Quick Check

How you answer questions can be as important as the answers themselves.

Quick Check

Stay focused on the skills and traits that employers seek; don't reveal weaknesses.

The way you answer questions can be almost as important as what you say. Use the interviewer's name and title from time to time when you answer: *Ms. Lyon, I would be pleased to tell you about....* People like to hear their own names. But be sure you are pronouncing the name correctly.

Occasionally it may be necessary to clear up vague questions. Some interviewers are inexperienced and uncomfortable in the role. You may even have to ask your own question to understand what was asked: *By ... do you mean ...?*

Consider closing some of your responses with *Does that answer your question?* or *Would you like me to further explain any particular experience?*

Always aim your answers at the key characteristics interviewers seek: skill and ability, motivation, people skills, decision making skills, enthusiasm for the job, and a pleasing personality. And remember to stay focused on your strengths. Don't reveal weaknesses, even if you think they make you look human. You won't be hired for your weaknesses, only for your strengths.

Use proper English and pronounce clearly. Remember, you will definitely be judged by how well you communicate. Avoid slurred words such as *gonna* and *y'know*, as well as slangy expressions such as *yeah, like,* and *whatever.* Also eliminate verbal static *(ah, and, uhm).* As you practise for the interview, a good idea is to record answers to expected interview questions. Is your speech filled with verbal static?

You can't expect to be perfect in an employment interview. No one is. But you can increase your chances of success by avoiding certain topics and behaviours such as those described in Figure 12.2.

FIGURE 12.2 Interview Actions to Avoid

1. Don't ask for the job. It's undignified and unprofessional. Wait to see how the interview develops.

2. Don't be negative about your previous employer, supervisors, or colleagues. The tendency is for interviewers to wonder if you would speak about their companies the same way.

3. Don't be a threat to the interviewer. Avoid suggesting directly or indirectly that your goal is to become a head or supervisor, a path that might include the interviewer's job.

4. Don't be late or too early for your appointment. Arrive five minutes before you are scheduled.

5. Don't discuss strong or emotional subjects, and don't use swear words.

6. Don't highlight salary or benefits. If the interview goes well and these subjects have not been addressed, you may mention them toward the end of the interview.

7. Don't be negative about yourself or others.

8. Don't interrupt. Not only is it impolite but it also prevents you from hearing a complete question or remark.

9. Don't accept an offer until you have completed all your interviews.

All-Time Favourite Questions with Selected Answers

Employment interviews are all about questions. And most of the questions are not new. You can actually predict 90 to 95 percent of all questions that will be asked before you ever walk into an interview room.[2]

The following questions represent all-time favourites asked of recent graduates and other job seekers. You'll find get-acquainted questions, experience and accomplishment questions, future-oriented questions, and money questions. To get you thinking about how to respond, we've provided an answer or discussion for the first question in each group. As you read the remaining questions in each group, think about how you could respond most effectively.

Questions to Get Acquainted

After opening introductions, recruiters generally try to start the interviewing questioning period with personal questions that put the candidate at ease. They are also striving to gain a picture of the candidate to see if he or she will fit into the organization's culture.

1. Tell me about yourself.

Experts agree that you must keep this answer short (one to two minutes tops) but on target. Try practising this formula: "My name is _____. I have completed _____ degree

✔ Quick Check

You can anticipate 90 to 95 percent of all questions you will be asked in an interview.

✔ Quick Check

Prepare for get-acquainted questions by practising a short formula response.

with a major in _____. Recently I worked for _____ as a _____. Before that I worked for _____ as a _____. My strengths are _____ (interpersonal) and _____ (technical)." Try rehearsing your response in 30-second segments devoted to your education, your work experience, and your qualities/skills. Some candidates end with "Now that I've told you about myself, can you tell me a little more about the position?"

2. What was your area of specialization in college/university, and why did you choose it?
3. If you had it to do over again, would you choose the same major? Why?
4. Tell me about your college/university (or your major) and why you chose it.
5. Do you prefer to work by yourself or with others? Why?
6. What are your key strengths?
7. What are some things you do in your spare time? Hobbies? Sports?
8. How did you happen to apply for this job?
9. What particular qualifications do you have for this job?
10. Do you consider yourself a team player? Describe your style as a team player.

Questions About Your Experience and Accomplishments

After questions about your background and education, the interview generally becomes more specific with questions about your experience and accomplishments.

1. Why should we hire you when we have applicants with more experience or better qualifications?

✓ Quick Check

Employers will hire a candidate with less experience and fewer accomplishments if he or she can demonstrate the skills required.

In answering this question, remember that employers often hire people who present themselves well instead of others with better qualifications. Emphasize your personal strengths that could be an advantage with this employer. Are you a hard worker? How can you demonstrate it? Have you had recent training? Some people have had more years of experience but actually have less knowledge because they have done the same thing over and over. Stress your experience using the latest methods and equipment. Be sure to mention your computer training and use of the Internet. Stress that you are open to new ideas and learn quickly.

2. Tell me about your part-time jobs, internships, or other experience.
3. What were your major accomplishments in each of your past jobs?
4. Why did you change jobs?
5. What was a typical workday like?
6. What job functions did you enjoy most? Least? Why?
7. Who was the toughest boss you ever worked for and why?
8. What were your major achievements in college/university?
9. Tell me about a difficult situation in a previous work situation and how you dealt with it.

Questions About the Future

✓ Quick Check

When asked about the future, show ambition and interest in succeeding with this company.

Questions that look into the future tend to confuse some candidates, especially those who have not prepared enough. Some of these questions give you a chance to discuss your personal future goals, while others require you to think on your feet and explain how you would respond in imaginary situations.

1. Where do you expect to be five years from now?

It's a sure sign of failure to respond that you'd like to have the interviewer's job. Instead, show an interest in the current job and in making a contribution to the organization. Talk about the levels of responsibility you'd like to achieve. One employment counsellor suggests showing ambition but not committing to a specific job title. Suggest that you will have learned enough to have moved up to a position where you will continue to grow.

2. If you get this position, what would you do to be sure you fit in?
3. If your supervisor gave you an assignment and then left town for two weeks, what would you do?
4. This is a large (or small) organization. Do you think you'd like that environment?
5. If you were aware that a coworker was lying about data, what would you do?
6. If your supervisor was not satisfied with your work and you thought it was acceptable, how would you resolve the conflict?
7. Do you plan to continue your education?

Questions That Make You Uncomfortable

The following questions may make you uncomfortable, but the important thing to remember is to answer truthfully without discussing your weaknesses. As quickly as possible, change any negative response into a discussion of your strengths.

✓ **Quick Check**

Strive to change discussion of your weaknesses to topics that show your strengths.

1. What are your key weaknesses?

It's amazing how many candidates lose in the interview by answering this question poorly. Actually, you have many choices. You can present a strength as a weakness *(Some people complain that I'm a workaholic or too attentive to details)*. You can mention a corrected weakness *(I found that I really needed to learn about the Internet, so I took a course)*. You could talk about an unrelated skill *(I really need to brush up on my French)*. You can refer to a learning objective *(One of my long-term goals is to learn more about international management. Does your company have any plans to expand overseas?)*. Another possibility is to repeat your qualifications *(I have no weaknesses that affect my ability to do this job)*.

2. If you could change one thing about your personality, what would it be and why?
3. What would your former boss say about you?
4. What do you want the most from your job? Money? Security? Power?
5. How did you prepare for this interview?
6. Do you feel you achieved the best grade point average of which you were capable in your education?
7. Relate an event in which you faced an ethical dilemma. How did you react? How did you feel?
8. If your supervisor told you to do something a certain way, and you knew that way was wrong, what would you do?

"Apart from being a CEO and a job bagging bagels, what other work experience do you have?"

© Ted Goff. www.tedgoff.com

Questions About Money

Although money is a very important consideration, don't let it enter the interview process too early. Some interviewers forget to mention money at all, while others ask what you think you are worth. Here are some typical money questions.

1. How much money are you looking for?

One way to handle salary questions is to ask politely to wait until it's clear that a job will be offered to you. (I'm sure when the time comes, we'll be able to work out a fair compensation package. Right now, I'd rather focus on whether we have a match). Another possible response is to reply honestly that you can't know what to ask for until you know more about the position and the company. If you continue to be pressed for a dollar figure, give a salary range. Be sure to do research before the interview so that you know what similar jobs are paying. For example, check the full-time earnings estimates published at Job Futures (http://www.jobfutures.ca).

2. How much are you currently earning?
3. How did you finance your education?
4. How much money do you expect to earn at age _____?

For more tips on how to negotiate a salary, see the Communication Workshop at the end of this chapter.

Quick Check

Don't discuss salary until later in the interview when you know more about the job and whether it will be offered.

Questions for You to Ask

At some point in the interview, you will be asked if you have any questions. Your questions should not only help you gain information but also impress the interviewer with your thoughtfulness and interest in the position. Remember that the interview is an opportunity for you to see how you would fit with the company as well. You want a position for which your skills and personality are matched. Use this opportunity to find out whether this job is right for you.

1. What will my duties be (if not already discussed)?
2. Tell me what it's like working here in terms of the people, management practices, work loads, expected performance, and rewards.
3. Why is this position open? Did the person who held it previously leave?
4. What training programs are available from this organization? What specific training will be given for this position?
5. What are the possibilities for promotion from this position?
6. Who would be my immediate supervisor?
7. What is the organizational structure, and where does this position fit in?
8. Is travel required in this position?
9. How is job performance evaluated?
10. Assuming my work is excellent, where do you see me in five years?
11. How long do employees generally stay with this organization?
12. What are the major challenges for a person in this position?
13. What can I do to make myself more employable to you?
14. What is the salary for this position?
15. When will I hear from you regarding further action on my application?

Quick Check

Your questions should impress the interviewer but also draw out valuable information about the job.

Answering Illegal Questions

Because human rights legislation protects job applicants from discrimination, interviewers may not ask questions such as those in the following list. Nevertheless, you may face an inexperienced interviewer who does ask some of these questions. How should you react? If you find the question harmless and if you want the job, go ahead and answer. If you think that answering would damage your chance to be hired, try to prevent a direct answer with a response such as *Could you tell me how my marital status relates to the responsibilities of this position?* Or you could use the opportunity to further highlight your strengths. An older worker responding to a question about age might mention experience, fitness, knowledge, maturity, stability, or extensive business contacts. You might also wish to reconsider working for an organization that supports such procedures.

Here are some questions that you may or may not want to answer:

✔ Quick Check

You may respond to an illegal question by asking how it relates to the responsibilities of the position.

1. Are you married, divorced, separated, single, or living common-law?
2. Is your spouse subject to transfer in his/her job? Tell me about your spouse's job.
3. What is your corrected vision? (But it is legal to ask about quality of vision if visual acuity is directly related to safety or some other factor of the job.)
4. Do you have any disabilities? Do you drink or take drugs? Have you ever received psychiatric care or been hospitalized for emotional problems? Have you ever received workers' compensation? (But it is legal to ask if you have any condition that could affect your ability to do the job or if you have any condition that should be considered during selection.)
5. Have you ever been arrested? Have you ever been convicted of a crime? Do you have a criminal record? (But if bonding is a requirement of the job, it is legal to ask if you are eligible.)
6. How old are you? What is your date of birth? Can I see your birth certificate? (But it is legal to ask *Are you eligible to work under Canadian laws pertaining to age restrictions?*)
7. In what other countries do you have a current address? (But it is legal to ask *What is your current address, and how long have you lived there?*)
8. What is your maiden name? (But it is legal to ask *What is your full name?*)
9. What is your religion? How often do you attend religious services? Would you work on a specific religious holiday? Can you provide a reference from a cleric or religious leader?
10. Do you have children? What are your child-care arrangements? (But it is legal to ask *Can you work the required hours?* and *Are you available for overtime?*)
11. Where were you born? Were you born in Canada? Can you provide proof of citizenship? (But it is legal to ask *Are you legally entitled to work in Canada?*)
12. Were you involved in military service in another country? (But it is legal to ask about Canadian military service.)
13. What is your first language? Where did you receive your language training? (But it is legal to ask if you understand, read, write, and/or speak the language(s) required for the job.)
14. How much do you weigh? How tall are you?
15. What is your sexual orientation?
16. Are you under medical care? Who is your family doctor? Are you receiving therapy or counselling? (But it is legal to make offers of employment conditional on successful completion of a medical exam that is relevant to that job.)

Closing the Interview

After the recruiter tells you about the organization and after you have asked your questions, the interviewer will signal the end of the interview, usually by standing up or by expressing thanks that you came. If not addressed earlier, you should at this time find out what action will follow. Too many candidates leave the interview without knowing their status or when they will hear from the recruiter.

You may learn that your résumé will be distributed to several departments for review. If this is the case, be sure to ask when you will be contacted. When you

End the interview by thanking the interviewer, reviewing your strengths for this position, and asking what action will follow.

are ready to leave, briefly review your strengths for the position and thank the interviewer for telling you about the organization and for considering you for the position. Ask if you may leave an additional copy of your résumé or your list of references. If the recruiter says nothing about notifying you, ask, "When can I expect to hear from you?" You can follow this by saying, "If I don't hear from you by then, may I call you?"

After leaving the interview, make notes of what was said in case you are called back for a second interview. Also, note your strengths and weaknesses so that you can work to improve in future interviews. Be sure to contact your references (whom you prepared in advance with a copy of your résumé, highlighted with sales points). Finally, write a thank-you letter, which will be discussed shortly.

If you don't hear from the recruiter within five days (or at the specified time), call him or her. Practise saying something such as "I'm wondering what else I can do to convince you that I'm the right person for this job."

Follow-Up Letters and Other Employment Documents

Although the résumé and cover letter are your major tasks, other important letters and documents are often required during the employment process. You may need to make requests or write follow-up letters. Because each of these tasks reveals something about you and your communication skills, you'll want to do your best. These documents often influence company officials to extend an interview or offer a job.

Reference Request

Most employers expect job candidates at some point to submit names of individuals who are willing to discuss the candidates' qualifications. Before you list anyone as a reference, however, be sure to ask permission. Try to do this in person. Ask an instructor, for example, if he or she would be willing and has the time to act as your reference. If you detect any sign of hesitation, don't force the issue. Your goal is to find willing individuals who think well of you.

What your references need most is information about you. What should they stress to prospective employers? Let's say you're applying for a specific job that requires a letter of recommendation. Professor Degen has already agreed to be a reference for you. To get the best letter of recommendation from Professor Degen, help her out. Write a letter telling her about the position, its requirements, and the recommendation deadline. Include a copy of your résumé. You might remind her of a positive experience with you (*You said my report was well organized*) that she could use in the recommendation. Remember that references need evidence to support generalizations, as in the following letter:

Quick Check

Identify the position and company. Tell immediately why you are writing.

Quick Check

Specify the job requirements so that the reference knows what to stress in the letter.

Dear Professor Degen:

Recently I applied for the position of administrative assistant in the Human Resources Department of Host International. Because you kindly agreed to help me, I am now asking you to write a letter of recommendation to Host.

The position calls for good organizational, interpersonal, and writing skills, as well as computer experience. To help you review my skills and training, I enclose my résumé. As you may recall, I earned an A in your business communication class, and you commended my long report for its clarity and organization.

Please send your letter before July 1 in the enclosed stamped, addressed envelope. I'm grateful for your support, and I promise to let you know the results of my job search.

Application or Résumé Follow-Up

If your letter or application gets no response within a reasonable time, you may decide to send a short follow-up e-mail message such as the following. Doing so (1) reminds the human resources officer, (2) demonstrates your serious interest, and (3) allows you to highlight your qualifications or to add new information.

Dear Ms. Stritz:

Please know I am still interested in becoming an administrative support specialist with Data Tech Inc.

Since I submitted an application in May, I have completed my schooling and have been employed as a summer replacement for office workers in several downtown offices. This experience has perfected my word-processing and communication skills. It has also introduced me to a wide range of office procedures.

Please keep my application in your active file and let me know when I may put my formal training, technical skills, and practical experience to work for you.

Open by reminding the reader of your interest.

Use this opportunity to review your strengths or to add new qualifications.

Interview Follow-Up

After a job interview you should always send a brief e-mail of thanks whether that interview occurs in person or on the telephone. This courtesy sets you apart from other applicants (many of whom may not bother). Your letter also reminds the interviewer of your visit as well as suggesting your good manners and genuine enthusiasm for the job.

Follow-up e-mails are most effective if sent immediately after the interview. In your e-mail refer to the date of the interview, the exact job title for which you were interviewed, specific topics discussed, and whether the interview was on the telephone or in person. Avoid worn-out phrases, such as *Thank you for taking the time to interview me.* Be careful, too, about overusing *I*, especially to begin sentences. Most important, show that you really want the job and that you are qualified for it. Notice how the following letter conveys enthusiasm and confidence:

Dear Ms. Singh:

Talking with you Thursday, May 23, about the graphic designer position was both informative and interesting.

Thanks for describing the position in such detail. Your current project designing the annual report in four colours on a Macintosh sounds fascinating as well as quite challenging.

Now that I've learned in greater detail the specific tasks of your graphic designers, I'm more than ever convinced that my computer and creative skills can make a genuine contribution to your graphic productions. My training in design and layout using Photoshop ensures that I could be immediately productive on your staff.

You will find me an enthusiastic and hard-working member of any team effort. I'm eager to join the graphics staff at your St. John headquarters, and I look forward to hearing from you soon.

Mention the interview date and specific position.

Show appreciation, good manners, and resolve—qualities that recruiters value.

Personalize your e-mail by mentioning topics discussed in the interview.

This e-mail example can also be modified to work as a follow-up to a telephone interview. By replacing *Talking with you* with *Our telephone conversation of,* the e-mail becomes an effective response to a telephone interview.

Rejection Follow-Up

If you didn't get the job and you think it was perfect for you, don't give up. Employment consultant Patricia Windelspecht advises, "You should always respond to a rejection letter.... I've had four clients get jobs that way." In a rejection follow-up e-mail, it's okay to admit you're disappointed. Be sure to add, however, that you're still interested and will contact them again in a month in case a job opens up. Then follow through for a couple of months—but don't overdo it. "There's a fine line between being professional and persistent and being a pest," adds consultant Windelspecht.[3] Here's an example of an effective rejection follow-up e-mail:

Dear Mr. Crowston:

Although I'm disappointed that someone else was selected for your accounting position, I appreciate your promptness and courtesy in notifying me.

Because I firmly believe that I have the technical and interpersonal skills needed to work in your fast-paced environment, I hope you will keep my résumé in your active file. My desire to become a productive member of your staff remains strong.

I enjoyed our interview, and I especially appreciate the time you and Mr. Kuzina spent describing your company's expansion into international markets. To enhance my qualifications, I've enrolled in a course in International Accounting at Sheridan College.

Should you have an opening for which I am qualified, you may reach me at (905) 719-3901. In the meantime, I will call you in a month to discuss employment possibilities.

Quick Check

Emphasize your continuing interest. Express confidence in meeting the job requirements.

Quick Check

Refer to specifics of your interview. If possible, explain how you are improving your skills.

Application Form

Some organizations require job candidates to fill out job application forms instead of submitting résumés. This practice permits them to gather and store standardized data about each applicant. Here are some tips for filling out such forms:

- Carry a card summarizing the vital statistics not included on your résumé. If you are asked to fill out an application form in an employer's office, you will need a handy reference to the following data: social insurance number, graduation dates, and beginning and ending dates of all employment; salary history; full names, titles, and present work addresses of former supervisors; and full names, occupational titles, occupational addresses, and telephone numbers of persons who have agreed to serve as references.
- Look over all the questions before starting. Fill out the form neatly, printing if your handwriting is poor.
- Answer all questions. Write *Not applicable* if appropriate.
- Be prepared for a salary question. Unless you know what comparable employees are earning in the company, the best strategy is to suggest a salary range or to write *Negotiable* or *Open*.
- Ask if you may submit your résumé in addition to the application form.

Summing Up and Looking Forward

Whenever you face an interview, you must be well prepared. You can increase your chances of success and reduce your stress by knowing how interviews are typically conducted and by investigating the target company thoroughly. Practise answering typical questions, including legal and illegal ones. Consider tape-recording or videotaping a mock interview so that you can check your body language and improve your answering techniques.

Close the interview by thanking the interviewer, reviewing your main strengths for the position, and asking what the next step is. Follow up with a thank-you letter and a call back, if appropriate.

Chapter 12 Employment Interviews and Follow-Up Messages

1. Is it normal to be nervous about an employment interview? What can be done to overcome this fear?
2. What can you do to improve the first impression you make at an interview?
3. Why is it important to avoid discussing salary early in an interview?
4. Why should a job candidate write a thank-you e-mail after an interview?

Chapter Review

5. If you have sent out your résumé to many companies, what information should you keep near your telephone and why?

6. Your first interview is with a small local company. What kind of information should you seek about this company and where could you expect to find it?

7. Name at least two ways in which you can practise for the interview and receive feedback on your performance.

8. Name at least six ways you can send positive nonverbal messages.

9. Should you be honest with an interviewer when asked about your weaknesses?

10. How should you respond to questions you believe to be illegal?

11. Preparing Answers to Typical Interview Questions. You've probably already been through a number of job interviews in your life, but they may not have been formal like the interviews you will go through when you start applying for post-college jobs. Prepare a one- to two-minute answer to the following interview question, and memorize it. Then practise speaking the answer in a natural voice so that it doesn't look like you've memorized it.

Question: Tell me about yourself and your previous work experience.

12. Preparing Answers to Typical Interview Questions. Prepare a one- to two-minute answer to the following typical interview question, and memorize it. Then practise speaking the answer in a natural voice so that it doesn't look like you've memorized it.

Question: Tell me about a time in a previous job when you faced a difficulty or a criticism or a problem and how you dealt with it.
Follow-Up Question: What would you do differently if this problem happened again?

13. Preparing Answers to Typical Interview Questions. Prepare a one- to two-minute answer to the following typical interview question, and memorize it. Then practise speaking the answer in a natural voice so that it doesn't look like you've memorized it.

Question: Tell me about a former boss or coworker whom you admire a lot and why you admire him or her.

Now that you've memorized these three answers, practise interviewing a partner. As you ask each other questions, surprise each other by slightly modifying the questions so they're not exactly as printed above. This modification will force you to improvise on the spot, a valuable interviewing skill.

Activities and Cases

12.1 Researching an Organization. Select an organization where you would like to be employed. Assume you've been selected for an interview. Using resources described in this chapter, locate information about the organization's leaders and their business philosophy. Find out about the organization's accomplishments, setbacks, finances, products, customers, competition, and advertising. Prepare a summary report documenting your findings.

12.2 Building Interview Skills. Successful interviews require careful preparation and repeated practice. To be best prepared, you need to know what skills are required for your desired position. In addition to computer and communication skills, employers generally want to know whether a candidate works well with a team, accepts responsibility, solves problems, is efficient, meets deadlines, shows leadership, saves time and money, and is a hard worker.

Your Task. Consider a position for which you are eligible now or one for which you will be eligible when you complete your education. Identify the skills and traits necessary for this position. If you prepared a résumé in Chapter 11, be sure that it addresses these areas. Now prepare interview worksheets listing at least ten technical and other skills or traits you think a recruiter will want to discuss in an interview for your position.

12.3 Preparing Success Stories. You can best showcase your talents if you are ready with your own success stories that show how you have developed the skills or qualities required for your wanted position.

Your Task. Using the worksheets you prepared in Activity 12.2, prepare success stories that highlight the required skills or traits. Select three to five stories to develop into answers to potential interview questions. For example, here's a typical question: "How does your background relate to the position we have open?" A possible response: "As you know, I have just completed an intensive training program in _____. In addition, I have over three years of part-time work experience in a variety of business settings. In one position I was selected to manage a small business in the absence of the owner. I developed responsibility and customer-service skills in filling orders efficiently, resolving shipping problems, and supervising key accounts. I also organized products worth over $200,000. When the owner returned from a vacation to Florida, I was commended for increasing sales and was given a bonus in recognition of her gratitude." People relate to and remember stories. Try to shape your answers into memorable stories.

12.4 Polishing Answers to Interview Questions. Practice makes perfect in interviewing. The more often you rehearse responses to typical interview questions, the closer you are to getting the job.

Your Task. Select three questions from each of the five question categories discussed in this chapter (pp. 267–270). Write your answers to each set of questions. Try to incorporate skills and qualities required for the targeted position. Polish these answers and your delivery technique by practising in front of a mirror or with a video or audio recorder.

12.5 Knowing What to Ask. When it is your turn to ask questions during the interview process, be ready.

Your Task. Decide on three to five questions that you would like to ask during an interview. Write these questions out and practise asking them so that you sound confident and sincere.

12.6 Role Play: Practising Answering Interview Questions. One of the best ways to understand interview dynamics and to develop confidence is to role-play the parts of interviewer and candidate.

Your Task. Choose a partner from your class. Make a list of five interview questions from those presented in this chapter. In team sessions, you and your partner will role-play an actual interview. One acts as interviewer, the other as the candidate. Prior to the interview, the candidate tells the interviewer what job and company he/she is applying to. For the interview, the interviewer and candidate should dress appropriately and sit in chairs facing each other. The interviewer greets the candidate and makes him/her comfortable. The candidate gives the interviewer a copy of his/her résumé. The interviewer asks three (or more, depending on your instructor's time schedule) questions from the candidate's list. The interviewer may also ask follow-up questions if appropriate. When finished, the interviewer ends the meeting graciously. After one interview, reverse roles and repeat.

12.7 Handling Difficult Interview Questions. Although some questions are not appropriate in job interviews, many interviewers will ask them anyway—whether intentionally or unknowingly. Being prepared is important.

Your Task. How would you respond in the following scenario? Let's assume you are being interviewed at one of the top companies on your list of potential employers. The interviewing committee consists of a human resources manager and the supervising manager of the department where you would work. At various times during the interview, the supervising manager has asked questions that made you feel uncomfortable. For example, he asked if you were married. You know this question is illegal, but you saw no harm in answering it. But then he asked how old you were. Since you started college early and graduated in two years, you are worried that you may not be considered mature enough for this position. But you have most of the other qualifications required and you are convinced you could succeed on the job. How should you answer this question?

12.8 Saying Thanks for the Interview. You've just completed an exciting employment interview, and you want the interviewer to remember you.

Your Task. Write a follow-up thank-you e-mail to Ronald T. Ranson, Human Resources Development, Electronic Data Sources, 132 Maplegrove Plaza, Montreal, QC H1L 2W4 (or a company of your choice).

12.9 Refusing to Take No for an Answer. After an excellent interview with Electronic Data Sources (or a company of your choice), you're disappointed to learn that it hired someone else. But you really want to work for the company.

Your Task. Write a follow-up e-mail to Ronald T. Ranson, Human Resources Development, Electronic Data Sources, 132 Maplegrove Plaza, Montreal, QC H1L 2W4 (or a company of your choice). Indicate that you are disappointed but still interested.

Grammar/Mechanics Review—12

The following sentences contain errors in grammar and mechanics. Below each sentence write a corrected version.

1. City officials asked the two companys directors for help in hiring local employees.

2. One store listed its Seiko Watch at eighty dollars; while its competitor listed the same watch at seventy-five dollars.

3. Here are a group of participating manufactures whom you may wish to contact regarding there webcites.

4. If we going to remain friends this personal information must be kept between you and I.

5. As soon as the merger is complete we will inform entire staffs, until then its business as usual.

6. Smart organizations can increase profit's allmost one hundred percent by keeping just five percent more of there customers.

7. Many companies' sell better at home then abroad; because they not have overseas experience.

8. The quality of the e-mails, letters memos and reports in this organization need to be improve.

9. You were charge an additional cost because of your recent purchase of new equipments.

10. The entire team of thirty-five managers were willing to proceed with the proposal for asian expansion.

11. Several copys of the sales report was sent to the CEO immediatley.

12. Stored on open shelfs in room 17 is a group of office supplys and at least seven boxes of stationary.

13. Darren Highsmith who was recently appointed Sales Manager submitted six different suggestion for increasing sales.

14. China the worlds fastest growing country will be buying personal computers at a thirty percent rate by 2010.

15. Congratulations, your finished!

Document for Revision

The following interview thank-you e-mail has faults in grammar, punctuation, spelling, wordiness, and word use. Correct the errors in strategy as well. When you finish, your instructor can show you the revised version of this e-mail.

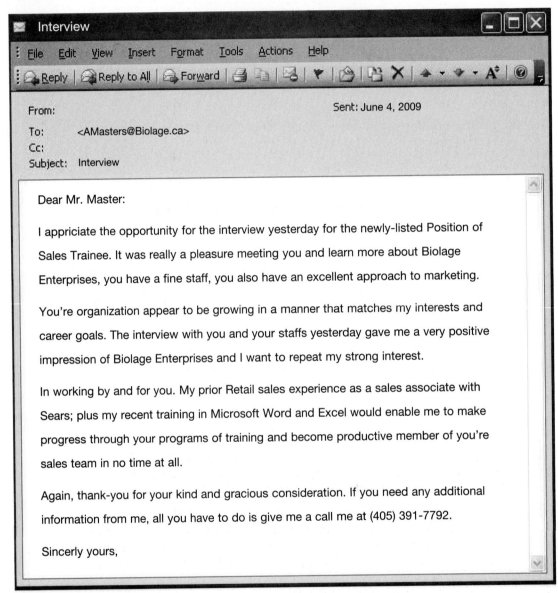

Interview

File   Edit   View   Insert   Format   Tools   Actions   Help

Reply   Reply to All   Forward

From: Sent: June 4, 2009

To: <AMasters@Biolage.ca>
Cc:
Subject: Interview

Dear Mr. Master:

I appriciate the opportunity for the interview yesterday for the newly-listed Position of Sales Trainee. It was really a pleasure meeting you and learn more about Biolage Enterprises, you have a fine staff, you also have an excellent approach to marketing.

You're organization appear to be growing in a manner that matches my interests and career goals. The interview with you and your staffs yesterday gave me a very positive impression of Biolage Enterprises and I want to repeat my strong interest.

In working by and for you. My prior Retail sales experience as a sales associate with Sears; plus my recent training in Microsoft Word and Excel would enable me to make progress through your programs of training and become productive member of you're sales team in no time at all.

Again, thank-you for your kind and gracious consideration. If you need any additional information from me, all you have to do is give me a call me at (405) 391-7792.

Sincerly yours,

Let's Talk Money: Negotiating a Salary

When to talk about salary causes many job applicants concern. Some advisors recommend bringing the issue up immediately; others suggest avoiding the topic entirely. What happens if the company asks for salary expectations in the job advertisement? The best plan is to be prepared to discuss salary when required but not to force the issue. The important thing to remember is that almost all salaries are negotiable. The following suggestions come from Michael Sheckter, MBA, operator of the Marketing Advisory, consultant in the marketing community, and frequent contributor to Workopolis.ca.[4]

Suggestion No. 1: Talk money only when requested.

If the interested company asks for salary expectations in the job advertisement, then put it in the cover letter—if not, try to hold off as long as possible. Your goal is to avoid discussing salary until you know that the interviewing company is interested. If salary comes up and you are not sure whether the job is being offered to you, it's time for you to be direct. Here are some things you could say:

Are you making me a job offer?

What salary range do you pay for positions with similar requirements?

I'm very interested in the position, and my salary would be open to discussion.

Tell me what you have in mind for the salary range.

Suggestion No. 2: Know the salary range for similar jobs in similar organizations but be aware of an amount that would motivate you.

Remember, though, that if you provide an amount that is too high you will price yourself out of the market. If the amount is too low you might be sorry. Everyone wants to make money, but salary by itself should not be a reason to take or reject a job. The important thing here is to think in terms of a wide range. Let's say you are hoping to start at between $30,000 and $40,000. To an interviewer, you might say, *I was looking for a salary in the low to the high thirties.*

Suggestion No. 3: Start by considering what you are making now.

Remember to be realistic. You probably have some idea of what the interviewing company is willing to pay for this position. You definitely know what you are getting paid in your current job. Try to find a reasonable compromise between the two and think about a salary that would motivate and reward. Keep in mind that it can be useful to suggest a range that is slightly higher than what you expect. That way you'll have some room to negotiate should it be required.

Suggestion No. 4: Consider a salary offer before reacting.

Why would anyone refuse a job offer before it's made? It happens all the time. Let's say you were hoping for a salary of $27,000. The interviewer tells you that the salary scheduled for this job is $24,000. You respond, *Oh, that's out of the question!* Before being offered the job, you have, in effect, refused it.

Suggestion No. 5: Trust that a fair and reasonable salary will be offered.

Generally, companies can't afford to offer salaries that are too low. If they do, they will lose people too easily to other opportunities that pay fairly. Be ready to bargain if offered a low starting salary.

Many salaries are negotiable. Companies are often willing to pay more for someone who interviews well and fits their culture. If the company seems right to you and you are pleased with the sound of the open position but you have been offered a low salary, say *That is somewhat lower than I had hoped but this position does sound exciting. If I were to consider this, what sorts of things could I do to quickly become more valuable to this organization?*

Another possibility is to ask for more time to think about the low offer. Tell the interviewer that this is an important decision, and you need some time to consider the offer. The next day you can call and say *I am flattered by your offer but I cannot accept because the salary is lower than I would like. Perhaps you could reconsider your offer or keep me in mind for future openings.*

Suggestion No. 6: Know your "walk away" number.

Be serious about your salary expectations, and ask yourself what you really want to get—would you be willing to walk away from a job that didn't pay your expected amount?

A good standard is to know your "walk away" number. Pick the number you would like to have, and make it realistic and reasonable—maybe they will meet it, maybe they will make a counteroffer.

Career Application

You've just passed the screening interview and have been asked to come in for a personal interview with the human resources representative and the hiring manager of a company where you are very eager to work. Although you are delighted with the company, you have promised yourself that you will not accept any position that pays less than $30,000 to start.

Your Task

- In teams of two, role-play the position of interviewer and interviewee.
- *Interviewer:* Set the interview scene. Discuss preliminaries, and then offer a salary of $29,000.
- *Interviewee:* Respond to preliminary questions and then to the salary offer of $29,000.
- Reverse roles so that the interviewee becomes the interviewer. Repeat the scenario.

Reference Guide to Document Formats

Business documents carry two kinds of messages. Verbal messages are conveyed by the words chosen to express the writer's ideas. Nonverbal messages are conveyed by the appearance of a document. If you compare an assortment of letters from various organizations, you will notice immediately that some look more attractive and more professional than others. The nonverbal message of the professional-looking documents suggests that they were sent by people who are careful, informed, intelligent, and successful. Understandably, you're more likely to take seriously documents that use attractive stationery and professional formatting techniques.

Over the years certain practices and conventions have arisen regarding the appearance and formatting of business documents. Although these conventions offer some choices (such as letter and punctuation styles), most business letters follow standardized formats. To ensure that your documents carry favourable nonverbal messages about you and your organization, you'll want to give special attention to the appearance and formatting of your letters, envelopes, e-mails memos, and fax cover sheets.

Appearance

To ensure that a message is read and valued, you need to give it a professional appearance. Two important elements in achieving a professional appearance are stationery and placement of the message on the page.

Stationery. Most organizations use high-quality stationery for business documents. This stationery is printed on paper with good weight and cotton-fibre content.

Paper is measured by weight and may range from 9 pounds (thin onionskin paper) to 32 pounds (thick card and cover stock). Most office stationery is in the 16-to-24-pound range. Lighter 16-pound paper is generally sufficient for internal documents. Heavier 20-to-24-pound paper is used for printed letterhead stationery.

Paper is also judged by its cotton-fibre content. Cotton fibre makes paper stronger, softer in texture, and less likely to yellow. Good-quality stationery contains 25 percent or more cotton fibre.

Spacing after Punctuation. In the past, typists left two spaces after end punctuation (periods, question marks, and so forth). This practice was necessary, it was thought, because typewriters did not have proportional spacing and sentences were easier to read if two spaces separated them. Fortunately, today's word processors make available the same fonts used by professional typesetters.

The question of how many spaces to leave after concluding punctuation is one of the most frequently asked questions at the Modern Language Association site <www.mla.org>. MLA experts point out that most publications today have the same spacing after a punctuation mark as between words on the same line. Influenced by the look of typeset publications (e.g., this book), many writers now leave only one space after end punctuation. As a practical matter, however, it is not wrong to use two spaces.

Letter Placement. The easiest way to place letters on the page is to use the defaults of your word processing program. The defaults are usually set for side margins of 2.5 cm. Many companies today find these margins acceptable.

If you want to adjust your margins to better balance shorter letters, use the following chart:

Words in Body of Letter	Side Margins	Blank Lines After Date
Under 200	4 to 5 cm	4 to 10
Over 200	2.5 cm	2 to 3

Experts say that a "ragged right" margin is easier to read than a justified (even) margin. You might want to turn off the justification feature of your word processing program if it automatically justifies the right margin.

Letter Parts

Professional-looking business letters are arranged in a conventional sequence with standard parts. Following is a discussion of how to use these letter parts properly. Figure A.1 illustrates the parts in a block-style letter. (See Chapter 6 for additional discussion of letters and their parts.)

Letterhead. Most business organizations use 8½-by-11-inch paper printed with a letterhead displaying their official name, street address, Web site address, e-mail address, and telephone and fax numbers. The letterhead may also include a logo and an advertising tag-line such as *Ebank: A new way to bank*.

Dateline. On letterhead paper you should place the date two blank lines below the last line of the letterhead or 5 cm from the top edge of the paper (line 13). On plain paper place the date immediately below your return address. Since the date goes on line 13, start the return address an appropriate number of lines above it. The most common dateline format is as follows: *June 9, 2006*. Don't use *th* (or *rd*) when the date is written this way. For European or military correspondence, use the following dateline format: *9 June 2006*. Notice that no commas are used.

Addressee and Delivery Notations. Delivery notations such as *FAX TRANS-MISSION, FEDERAL EXPRESS, MESSENGER DELIVERY, CONFIDENTIAL,* or *CERTIFIED MAIL* are typed in all capital letters two blank lines above the inside address.

Inside Address. Type the inside address—that is, the address of the organization or person receiving the letter—single-spaced, starting at the left margin. The number of lines between the dateline and the inside address depends on the size of the letter body, the type size (point or pitch size), and the length of the typing lines. Generally, two to ten lines are appropriate.

Be careful to duplicate the exact wording and spelling of the recipient's name and address on your documents. Usually, you can copy this information from the letterhead of the correspondence you are answering. If, for example, you are responding to *Jackson & Perkins Company*, don't address your letter to *Jackson and Perkins Corp.*

FIGURE A.1 Block and Modified Block Letter Styles

Letterhead ——————

peerless graphics
893 Dillingham Boulevard Stony Plain, AB
Phone (403) 667-8880   Fax (403) 667-8830   www.peergraph.com

↓ line 13, or 2 blank lines below letterhead

Dateline ——————

September 14, 2009

↓ 2 to 10 blank lines

Inside address ——————

Mr. T. M. Wilson, President
Visual Concept Enterprises
1256 Lumsden Avenue
Nordegg, AB T0M 3T0

↓ 1 blank line

Salutation ——————

Dear Mr. Wilson

↓ 1 blank line

Subject line ——————

SUBJECT: BLOCK LETTER STYLE

↓ 1 blank line

This letter illustrates block letter style, about which you asked. All typed lines begin at the left margin. The date is usually placed 5 cm from the top edge of the paper or two lines below the last line of the letterhead, whichever position is lower.

This letter also shows open punctuation. No colon follows the salutation, and no comma follows the complimentary close. Although this punctuation style is efficient, we find that most of our customers prefer to include punctuation after the salutation and the complimentary close.

Body ——————

If a subject line is included, it appears two lines below the salutation. The word SUBJECT is optional. Most readers will recognize a statement in this position as the subject without an identifying label. The complimentary close appears two lines below the end of the last paragraph.

↓ 1 blank line

Sincerely

Mark H. Wong

↓ 3 to 4 blank lines

Complimentary close
and signature block

Mark H. Wong
Graphics Designer

↓ 1 blank line

MHW:pil

In block-style letters, as shown above, all lines begin at the left margin. In modified block-style letters, as shown at the left, the date is centred or aligned with the complimentary close and signature block, which start at the centre. The date may also be backspaced from the right margin. Paragraphs may be blocked or indented. Mixed punctuation includes a colon after the salutation and a comma after the complimentary close. Open punctuation, shown above, omits the colon following the salutation and omits the comma following the complimentary closing.

Always be sure to include a courtesy title such as *Mr.*, *Ms.*, *Mrs.*, *Dr.*, or *Professor* before a person's name in the inside address—for both the letter and the envelope. Although many women in business today favour *Ms.*, you'll want to use whatever title the addressee prefers.

Remember that the inside address is not included for readers (who already know who and where they are). It's there to help writers accurately file a copy of the message.

In general, avoid abbreviations (such as *Ave.* or *Co.*) unless they appear in the printed letterhead of the document being answered.

Attention Line. An attention line allows you to send your message officially to an organization but to direct it to a specific individual, officer, or department. However, if you know an individual's complete name, it's always better to use it as the first line of the inside address and avoid an attention line. Here are two common formats for attention lines:

MultiMedia Enterprises
931 Calkins Road
Toronto, ON M3W 1E6

MultiMedia Enterprises
Attention: Marketing Director
931 Calkins Road
Toronto, ON M3W 1E6

ATTENTION MARKETING DIRECTOR

Attention lines may be typed in all caps or with upper- and lowercase letters. The colon following *Attention* is optional. Notice that an attention line may be placed two lines below the address block or printed as the second line of the inside address. You'll want to use the latter format if you're composing on a word processor because the address block may be copied to the envelope and the attention line will not interfere with the last-line placement of the postal code. (Mail can be sorted more easily if the postal code appears in the last line of a typed address.)

Whenever possible, use a person's name as the first line of an address instead of putting that name in an attention line. Some writers use an attention line because they fear that letters addressed to individuals at companies may be considered private. They worry that if the addressee is no longer with the company, the letter may be forwarded or not opened. Actually, unless a letter is marked "Personal" or "Confidential," it will very likely be opened as business mail.

Salutation. Place the letter greeting, or salutation, two lines below the last line of the inside address or the attention line (if used). If the letter is addressed to an individual, use that person's courtesy title and last name (*Dear Mr. Lanham*). Even if you are on a first-name basis (*Dear Leslie*), be sure to add a colon (not a comma or a semicolon) after the salutation, unless you are using open punctuation. Do not use an individual's full name in the salutation (not *Dear Mr. Leslie Lanham*) unless you are unsure of gender (*Dear Leslie Lanham*).

For letters with attention lines or those addressed to organizations, the selection of an appropriate salutation has become more difficult. Formerly, *Gentlemen* was used generically for all organizations. With increasing numbers of women in business management today, however, *Gentlemen* is outdated. Because no universally acceptable salutation has emerged as yet, you'll probably be safest with *Ladies and Gentlemen* or *Gentlemen and Ladies*.

One way to avoid the salutation dilemma is to address a document to a specific person. Another alternative is to use the simplified letter style, which conveniently omits the salutation (and the complimentary close).

Subject and Reference Lines. Although experts suggest placing the subject line one blank line below the salutation, many businesses actually place it above the salutation. Use whatever style your organization prefers. Reference lines often show policy or file numbers; they generally appear two lines above the salutation.

Body. Most business letters and memorandums are single-spaced, with double line spacing between paragraphs. Very short messages may be double-spaced with indented paragraphs.

Complimentary Close. Typed two lines below the last line of the letter, the complimentary close may be formal (*Very truly yours*) or informal (*Sincerely* or *Respectfully*). The simplified letter style omits a complimentary close.

Signature Block. In most letter styles the writer's typed name and optional identification appear three to four blank lines below the complimentary close. The combination of name, title, and organization information should be arranged to achieve a balanced look. The name and title may appear on the same line or on separate lines, depending on the length of each. Use commas to separate categories within the same line, but not to conclude a line.

Sincerely,

Jeremy M. Wood

Jeremy M. Wood, Manager
Technical Sales and Services

Respectfully,

Casandra Baker-Murillo

Casandra Baker-Murillo
Executive Vice-President

Courtesy titles (Mr., *Ms.*, *Mrs.*, or *Miss*) should be used before names that are not readily distinguishable as male or female. They should also be used before names containing only initials and international names. The title is usually placed in parentheses, but it may appear without them.

Yours truly,

Ms. K.C. Tripton

(Ms.) K. C. Tripton
Project Manager

Sincerely,

Mr. Leslie Hill

(Mr.) Leslie Hill
Public Policy Department

Some organizations include their names in the signature block. In such cases the organization name appears in all caps one blank line below the complimentary close, as shown here.

Sincerely,

LITTON COMPUTER SERVICES

Ms. Shelina A. Simpson

Ms. Shelina A. Simpson
Executive Assistant

Reference Initials. If used, the initials of the typist and writer are typed two lines below the writer's name and title. Generally, the writer's initials are capitalized and the typist's are lowercased, but this format varies.

Enclosure Notation. When an enclosure or attachment accompanies a document, a notation to that effect appears two lines below the reference initials. This notation reminds the typist to insert the enclosure in the envelope, and it reminds the recipient to look for the enclosure or attachment. The notation may be spelled out (*Enclosure, Attachment*), or it may be abbreviated (*Enc., Att.*). It may indicate the number of enclosures or attachments, and it may also identify a specific enclosure (*Enclosure: Form 1099*).

Copy Notation. If you make copies of correspondence for other individuals, you may use *cc* to indicate carbon copy, *pc* to indicate photocopy, or merely *c* for any kind of copy. A colon following the initial(s) is optional.

Second-Page Heading. When a letter extends beyond one page, use plain paper of the same quality and colour as the first page. Identify the second and succeeding pages with a heading consisting of the name of the addressee, the page number, and the date. Use either of the following two formats:

Ms. Rachel Ruiz   2   May 4, 2009

Ms. Rachel Ruiz
Page 2
May 4, 2009

Both headings appear on line 7 followed by two blank lines to separate them from the continuing text. Avoid using a second page if you have only one line or the complimentary close and signature block to fill that page.

Plain-Paper Return Address. If you prepare a personal or business letter on plain paper, place your address immediately above the date. Do not include your name; you will type (and sign) your name at the end of your letter. If your return address contains two lines, begin typing it on line 11 so that the date appears on line 13. Avoid abbreviations except for a two-letter province/territory abbreviation.

580 East Leffels Street
Dartmouth, NS B6R 2F3
December 14, 2009

Ms. Ellen Siemens
Retail Credit Department
Union National Bank
1220 Dunsfield Boulevard
Halifax, NS B4L 2E2

Dear Ms. Siemens:

For letters prepared in the block style, type the return address at the left margin. For modified block-style letters, start the return address at the centre to align with the complimentary close.

Letter Styles

Business letters are generally prepared in one of three formats. The most popular is the block style, but the simplified style has much to recommend it.

Block Style. In the block style, shown in Figure A.1, all lines begin at the left margin. This style is a favourite because it is easy to format.

Modified Block Style. The modified block style differs from block style in that the date and closing lines appear in the centre, as shown at the bottom of Figure A.1. The date may be (1) centred, (2) begun at the centre of the page (to align with the closing lines), or (3) backspaced from the right margin. The signature block—including the complimentary close, writer's name and title, or organization identification—begins at the centre. The first line of each paragraph may begin at the left margin or may be indented five or ten spaces. All other lines begin at the left margin.

Simplified Style. Introduced by the Administrative Management Society a number of years ago, the simplified letter style, shown in Figure A.2, requires little formatting. Like the block style, all lines begin at the left margin. A subject line appears in all caps two blank lines below the inside address and two blank lines above the first paragraph. The salutation and complimentary close are omitted. The signer's name and identification appear in all caps four blank lines below the last paragraph. This letter style is efficient and avoids the problem of appropriate salutations and courtesy titles.

Punctuation Styles

Two punctuation styles are commonly used for letters. *Open* punctuation, shown with the block-style letter in Figure A.1, contains no punctuation after the salutation or complimentary close. *Mixed* punctuation, shown with the modified block style letter in Figure A.1, requires a colon after the salutation and a comma after the complimentary close. Many business organizations prefer mixed punctuation, even in a block style letter.

If you choose mixed punctuation, be sure to use a colon—not a comma or semicolon—after the salutation. Even when the salutation is a first name, the colon is appropriate.

Envelopes

An envelope should be of the same quality and colour of stationery as the letter it carries. Because the envelope introduces your message and makes the first impression, you need to be especially careful in addressing it. Moreover, how you fold the letter is important.

Return Address. The return address is usually printed in the upper left corner of an envelope, as shown in Figure A.3. In large companies some form of identification (the writer's initials, name, or location) may be typed or handwritten above the company name and return address. This identification helps return the letter to the sender in case of nondelivery.

On an envelope without a printed return address, single-space the return address in the upper left corner. Beginning on line 3 on the fourth space (approximately 12 mm or ½ inch) from the left edge, type the writer's name, title, company, and mailing address.

Mailing Address. On legal-sized No. 10 envelopes (10.5 cm by 24 cm), begin the address on line 13 about 11.5 cm from the left edge, as shown in Figure A.3. For small envelopes (7.5 cm by 15 cm), begin typing on line 12 about 6.2 cm from the left edge.

FIGURE A.2 Simplified Letter Style

ABC ★ Automation Business Consultants
2682 Roefield Street
Cactus Lake, SK S0K 4L3   (306) 369-1109   ↓ line 13 or 1 blank line below letterhead

July 20, 2009   ↓ 2 to 7 blank lines

↓ 1 blank line

Identifies method of delivery —

FAX TRANSMISSION

Ms. Sara Hendricks, Manager
Western Land and Home Realty
17690 Anscombe Avenue
Porcupine Plain, SK S0E 2H1   ↓ 2 blank lines

Replaces salutation with subject line —

SUBJECT: SIMPLIFIED LETTER STYLE ↓ 2 blank lines

Leaves 2 blank lines above and below subject line —

You may be interested to learn, Ms. Hendricks, that some years ago the Administrative Management Society recommended the simplified letter format illustrated here. Notice the following efficient features:

1. All lines begin at the left margin.

2. The salutation and complimentary close are omitted.

3. A subject line in all caps appears 3 lines below the inside address and 3 lines above the first paragraph.

4. The writer's name and identification appear 5 lines (i.e., 4 blank lines) below the last paragraph.

In addition to its efficiency, this letter style is helpful in dealing with the problem of appropriate salutations. Since it has no salutation, your writers need not worry about which to choose. For many reasons we recommend this style to your staff.

↓ 4 blank lines

Omits complimentary close —

Holly Higgins

Highlights writer's name and identification with all caps —

HOLLY HIGGINS, MANAGER, OFFICE DIVISION ↓ 1 blank line

HH:tlb

Identifies copy —

c John Fox

Canada Post recommends that addresses be typed in all caps without any punctuation. This Postal Service style, shown in the small envelope in Figure A.3, was originally developed to facilitate scanning by optical character readers. Today's OCRs, however, are so sophisticated that they scan upper- and lowercase letters easily. Many companies today prefer to use the same format for the envelope as for the inside address. If the same format is used, writers can take advantage of word processing programs to "copy" the inside address to the envelope, thus saving keystrokes and reducing errors. Having the same format on both the inside address and the envelope also looks more professional and consistent. For these reasons you may choose to use the familiar upper- and lowercase combination format. But you will want to check with your organization to learn its preference.

FIGURE A.3 Envelope Formats

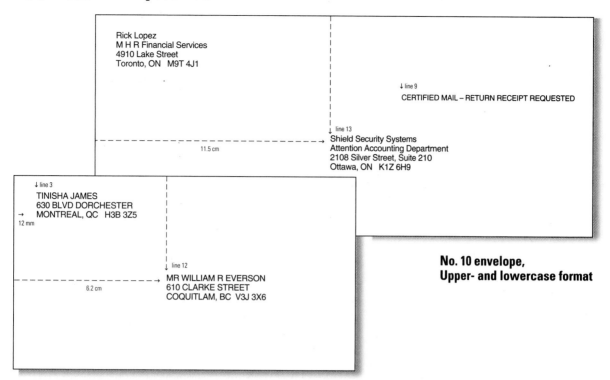

Rick Lopez
M H R Financial Services
4910 Lake Street
Toronto, ON   M9T 4J1

↓ line 9
CERTIFIED MAIL – RETURN RECEIPT REQUESTED

↓ line 13
Shield Security Systems
Attention Accounting Department
2108 Silver Street, Suite 210
Ottawa, ON   K1Z 6H9

11.5 cm

**No. 10 envelope,
Upper- and lowercase format**

↓ line 3
TINISHA JAMES
630 BLVD DORCHESTER
→   MONTREAL, QC   H3B 3Z5
12 mm

↓ line 12
MR WILLIAM R EVERSON
610 CLARKE STREET
COQUITLAM, BC V3J 3X6

6.2 cm

No. 6 ¾ envelope, uppercase format

In addressing your envelopes for delivery in North America, use the two-letter province, territory, and state abbreviations shown in Figure A.4. Notice that these abbreviations are in capital letters without periods.

Folding. The way a letter is folded and inserted into an envelope sends additional nonverbal messages about a writer's professionalism and carefulness. Most businesspeople follow the procedures shown here, which produce the least number of creases to distract readers.

For large No. 10 envelopes, begin with the letter face up. Fold slightly less than one third of the sheet toward the top, as shown in the following diagram. Then fold down the top third to within 6 to 7 mm of the bottom fold. Insert the letter into the envelope with the last fold toward the bottom of the envelope.

For small No. 8 envelopes, begin by folding the bottom up to within 6 to 7 mm of the top edge. Then fold the right third over to the left. Fold the left third to within 6 to 7 mm of the last fold. Insert the last fold into the envelope first.

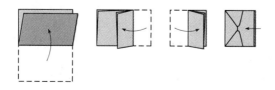

FIGURE A.4 Abbreviations of Provinces, Territories, and States

Province or Territory	Two-Letter Abbreviation	Province	Two-Letter Abbreviation
Alberta	AB	Nova Scotia	NS
British Columbia	BC	Nunavut	NU
Manitoba	MB	Ontario	ON
New Brunswick	NB	Prince Edward Island	PE
Newfoundland and		Quebec	QC
Labrador	NL	Saskatchewan	SK
Northwest Territories	NT	Yukon Territory	YT

State or Territory	Two-Letter Abbreviation	State or Territory	Two-Letter Abbreviation
Alabama	AL	Missouri	MO
Alaska	AK	Montana	MT
American Samoa	AS	Nebraska	NE
Arizona	AZ	Nevada	NV
Arkansas	AR	New Hampshire	NH
California	CA	New Jersey	NJ
Colorado	CO	New Mexico	NM
Connecticut	CT	New York	NY
Delaware	DE	North Carolina	NC
District of Columbia	DC	North Dakota	ND
Florida	FL	North Mariana Islands	MP
Georgia	GA	Ohio	OH
Guam	GU	Oklahoma	OK
Hawaii	HI	Oregon	OR
Idaho	ID	Palau	PW
Illinois	IL	Pennsylvania	PA
Indiana	IN	Puerto Rico	PR
Iowa	IA	Rhode Island	RI
Kansas	KS	South Carolina	SC
Kentucky	KY	South Dakota	SD
Louisiana	LA	Tennessee	TN
Maine	ME	Texas	TX
Marshall Islands	MH	Utah	UT
Maryland	MD	Vermont	VT
Massachusetts	MA	Virgin Islands	VI
Michigan	MI	Virginia	VA
Micronesia	FM	Washington	WA
Minnesota	MN	West Virginia	WV
Minor Outlying Islands	UM	Wisconsin	WI
Mississippi	MS	Wyoming	WY

E-Mail Messages

Because e-mail is an evolving communication medium, formatting and usage are still fluid. The following suggestions, illustrated in Figure A.5 and also in Figure 5.2 on page 86, may guide you in setting up the parts of an e-mail message. Always check, however, with your organization so that you can observe its practices.

To Line. Include the receiver's e-mail address after *To.* If the receiver's address is recorded in your address book, you just have to click on it. Be sure to enter all addresses carefully since one mistyped letter prevents delivery.

FIGURE A.5 E-Mail Message

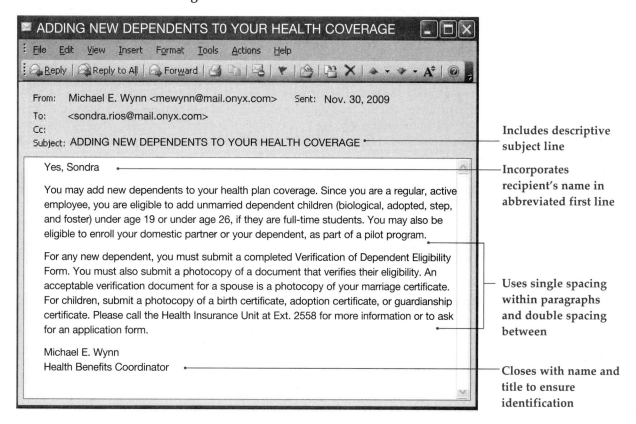

ADDING NEW DEPENDENTS T0 YOUR HEALTH COVERAGE

File   Edit   View   Insert   Format   Tools   Actions   Help

Reply | Reply to All | Forward

From: Michael E. Wynn <mewynn@mail.onyx.com>   Sent: Nov. 30, 2009
To: <sondra.rios@mail.onyx.com>
Cc:
Subject: ADDING NEW DEPENDENTS TO YOUR HEALTH COVERAGE

Yes, Sondra

You may add new dependents to your health plan coverage. Since you are a regular, active employee, you are eligible to add unmarried dependent children (biological, adopted, step, and foster) under age 19 or under age 26, if they are full-time students. You may also be eligible to enroll your domestic partner or your dependent, as part of a pilot program.

For any new dependent, you must submit a completed Verification of Dependent Eligibility Form. You must also submit a photocopy of a document that verifies their eligibility. An acceptable verification document for a spouse is a photocopy of your marriage certificate. For children, submit a photocopy of a birth certificate, adoption certificate, or guardianship certificate. Please call the Health Insurance Unit at Ext. 2558 for more information or to ask for an application form.

Michael E. Wynn
Health Benefits Coordinator

Includes descriptive subject line

Incorporates recipient's name in abbreviated first line

Uses single spacing within paragraphs and double spacing between

Closes with name and title to ensure identification

From **Line.** Most e-mail programs automatically include your name and e-mail address after *From.*

Cc and Bcc. Insert the e-mail address of anyone who is to receive a copy of the message. *Cc* stands for carbon copy or courtesy copy. Don't be tempted, though, to send needless copies just because it's so easy. *Bcc* stands for *blind carbon copy.* Some writers use *bcc* to send a copy of the message without the addressee's knowledge. Writers also use the *bcc* line for mailing lists. When a message is being sent to a number of people and their e-mail addresses should not be revealed, the *bcc* line works well to conceal the names and addresses of all receivers.

Subject. Identify the subject of the e-mail message with a brief but descriptive summary of the topic. Be sure to include enough information to be clear and compelling. Capitalize the initial letters of principal words, or capitalize the entire line if space permits.

Salutation. Include a brief greeting, if you like. Some writers use a salutation such as *Dear Selina* followed by a comma or a colon. Others are more informal with *Hi, Selina!,* or *Good morning* or *Greetings.* Some writers simulate a salutation by including the name of the receiver in an abbreviated first line, as shown in Figure A.5. Others writers treat an e-mail message like a memo and skip the salutation entirely.

Message. Cover just one topic in your message, and try to keep your total message under one screen in length. Single-space and be sure to use both upper- and lowercase letters. Double-space between paragraphs, and use graphic high-lighting (bullets, numbering) whenever you are listing three or more items.

Closing. Conclude an external message, with *Cheers* or *Best wishes*, followed by your name. If the recipient is unlikely to know you, it's not a bad idea to include your title and organization. Many e-mail users include a signature file with identifying information embellished with keyboard art. Use restraint, however, because signature files take up precious space. Writers of e-mail messages sent within organizations may omit a closing and even skip their names at the ends of messages because receivers recognize them from identification in the opening lines.

Attachment. Use the attachment window or button to select the file name of any file you wish to send with your e-mail message. You can also attach a Web page to your message.

Memos

As discussed in Chapter 5, memos deliver messages within organizations. Many offices use computer memo templates imprinted with the organization name and logo and, optionally, the department or division names, as shown in Figure A.6. Although the design and arrangement of memos vary, they usually include the basic elements of *TO, FROM, DATE,* and *SUBJECT.* Large organizations may include other identifying headings, such as *FILE NUMBER, FLOOR, EXTENSION, LOCATION,* and *DISTRIBUTION.*

If no computer template is available, memos may be typed on company letterhead or on plain paper, as shown in Figure A.7. On a full sheet of paper, start on line 13; on a half sheet, start on line 7. Double-space and type in all caps the guide words: *TO:, FROM:, DATE:, SUBJECT:*. Align all the fill-in information two spaces after the longest guide word (SUBJECT:). Leave three lines after the last line of the

FIGURE A.6 Printed Memo Forms

BANK OF MONTREAL
Mortgage Department   BMO ▲   Interoffice
Memorandum

DATE:

TO:

FROM:

SUBJECT:

PYRAMID INDUSTRIES
Internal Memorandum

TO: DATE:

FROM: FILE:

SUBJECT:

↓ line 10
MEMO

→
3 cm

DATE: February 3, 2009

TO: Dawn Stewart, Manager
Sales and Marketing   *JM*

FROM: Jay Murray, Vice-President
Operations

SUBJECT: TELEPHONE SERVICE REQUEST FORMS

↓ 2 blank lines

To speed telephone installation and improve service within the Bremerton facility, we are starting a new application procedure.

Service request forms will be available at various locations within the three buildings. When you require telephone service, obtain a request form at one of the locations that is convenient for you. Fill in the pertinent facts, obtain approval from your division head, and send the form to Brent White. Request forms are available at the following locations:

heading and begin typing the body of the memo. Like business letters, memos are single-spaced.

Memos are generally formatted with side margins of 3.5 cm (1¼ inches), or they may conform to the printed memo form. For more information about memos, see Chapter 5.

Fax Cover Sheet

Documents transmitted by fax are usually introduced by a cover sheet, such as that shown in Figure A.8 on the next page. As with memos, the format varies considerably. Important items to include are (1) the name and fax number of the receiver, (2) the name and fax number of the sender, (3) the number of pages being sent, and (4) the name, telephone number, and e-mail address of the person to notify in case of unsatisfactory transmission.

When the document being transmitted requires little explanation, you may prefer to attach an adhesive note (such as a Post-it™ fax transmittal form) instead of a full cover sheet. These notes carry essentially the same information as shown in our printed fax cover sheet. They are perfectly acceptable in most business organizations and can save considerable paper and transmission costs.

FIGURE A.8 Fax Cover Sheet

FAX TRANSMISSION

DATE: _____

FAX
TO: _____   NUMBER:_____
_____
_____

FAX
FROM:_____   NUMBER:_____
_____
_____

NUMBER OF PAGES TRANSMITTED INCLUDING THIS COVER SHEET: ___

MESSAGE:

If any part of this fax transmission is missing or not clearly received, please contact:

NAME: _____

PHONE:_____

E-MAIL:_____

Proofreading Marks

PROOFREADING MARK	DRAFT COPY	FINAL COPY
⹀ Align horizontally	TO: Rick Munoz	TO: Rick Munoz
‖ Align vertically	‖166.32	166.32
	132.45	132.45
⹀ Capitalize	Coca-cola	Coca-Cola
◡ Close up space	runs on ms–dos	runs on MS-DOS
⏋⏌ Centre	meeting at 3 p. m.	meeting at 3 p.m.
⩔ Delete	]Recommendations[	Recommendations
⩕ Insert apostrophe	in my ~~final~~ judgement	in my judgment
⩔ Insert comma	our companys product	our company's product
⩕ Insert semicolon	you will of course	you will, of course,
⯮ Insert hyphen	value therefore, we feel	value; therefore, we feel
⊙ Insert period	tax free income	tax-free income
⩔ Insert quotation mark	Ms Holly Hines	Ms. Holly Hines
	shareholders receive a	shareholders receive a
# Insert space	bonus	"bonus"
/ Lowercase (remove capitals)	wordprocessing program	word processing program
	the Vice-President	the vice-president
⊏ Move to left	HUMAN RESOURCES	Human Resources
⊐ Move to right	I. Labour costs	I. Labour costs
◯ Spell out	A. Findings of study	A. Findings of study
	aimed at (2) (depts)	aimed at two departments
¶ Start new paragraph	¶Keep the screen height	Keep the screen
	at eye level.	height at eye level.
···· Stet (don't delete)	officials talked ~~openly~~	officials talked openly
∼ Transpose	accounts recievable	accounts receivable
∿ Use boldface	Conclusions	**Conclusions**
⎯ Use italics	The Perfect Résumé	*The Perfect Résumé*
⌐ Start new line	Globex, 23 Acorn Lane	Globex
		23 Acorn Lane
⊋ Run lines together	Invoice No.	Invoice No. 122059
	122059	

C Documentation Formats

Careful writers work hard to document properly any data appearing in reports or messages for many reasons. Citing sources strengthens a writer's argument, as you learned in Chapter 10. Acknowledging sources also shields writers from charges of plagiarism. Moreover, good references help readers pursue further research. Fortunately, word processing programs have taken much of the pain out of documenting data, particularly for footnotes and endnotes.

Source and Content Notes

Before we discuss specific documentation formats, you should know the difference between source notes and content notes. Source notes identify quotations, paraphrased passages, and author references. They lead readers to the sources of cited information, and they must follow a consistent format. Content notes, on the other hand, enable writers to add comments, explain information not directly related to the text, or refer readers to other sections of a report.

Two Documentation Methods for Source Notes

For years researchers have struggled to develop the perfect documentation system—one that is efficient for the writer and crystal-clear to the reader. Most of these systems can be grouped into two methods: the footnote/endnote method and the parenthetic method.

Footnote/Endnote Method. Writers using footnotes or endnotes insert a small superscript (raised) figure into the text close to the place where a reference is mentioned. This number leads the reader to a footnote at the bottom of the page or to an endnote at the end of the report. Footnotes or endnotes contain a complete description of the source document. In this book we have used the endnote method. We chose this style because it least disrupts the text. Most of the individual citation formats in this book follow the traditional style suggested in *The Chicago Manual of Style*, 15th ed. (Chicago: The University of Chicago Press, 2002). Here are some of the most frequently used endnotes, styled in accordance with the *Chicago Manual*. They are numbered here with full-sized numbers; your word processor, however, may show endnotes with superscript figures. Either form is acceptable.

Book, One Author
1. Sara White, *Profiting in the Knowledge Age: A Canadian Guide to the Future* (Toronto: McKnight Publishing, 2001), 25.

Book, Many Authors
2. Manny Colver, Dan Smith, and Jeremy Devport, *Careers in the 21st Century* (Scarborough, ON: ITP Nelson, 2000), 356–358.

Academic Journal Article

3. John Drovich, "Peace in the Middle East," *Canadian Journal of International Studies* 19, no. 5 (2001): 23–45.

Monthly Magazine Article

4. Bill Safer, "Future Leadership," *Canadian Management*, April 2002, 45.

Newspaper Article

5. Trisha Khan, "Beyond 2000: Working in the Next Century," *Winnipeg Free Press*, August 22, 2001, B3.

Government Publication

6. Human Resources Development Canada, *How to Find a Job* (Ottawa: Supply and Services Canada, 2000), 30.

Online Services

7. Loblaw Companies Ltd., *Great Stores Start With...: 2004 Annual Report*, http://www.loblaw.com/en/inv_ar.html#, p. 14 (accessed May 23, 2005).

Interview

8. Geoffrey H. Wilson (senior vice-president, Investor Relations and Public Affairs, Loblaw Companies Ltd.), personal interview, May 25, 2005.

In referring to a previously mentioned footnote, cite the page number along with the author's last name or a shortened form of the title if no author is given. The Latin forms *ibid., op. cit.,* and *et al.* are rarely seen in business reports today. A portion of a business report using the endnote method for source citation is found in Figure C.1 on the next page.

Parenthetic Method. Many writers of scholarly works prefer to use a parenthetic style to cite references. In this method a reference to the author appears in parentheses close to the place where it is mentioned in the text. Some parenthetic styles show the author's last name and date of publication (for example, *Cook 2000*), while others show the author's last name and page cited (for example, *Cook 24*). One of the most well-known parenthetic systems is the Modern Language Association (MLA) format. To provide guidance in preparing your academic and business papers, we'll focus on the MLA format.

Which Method for Business? Students frequently ask, "But what documentation system is most used in business?" Actually no one method dominates. Many businesses have developed their own hybrid systems. These companies generally supply guidelines illustrating their in-house style to employees. Before starting any research project on the job, you'll want to inquire about your organization's preferred documentation style. You can also look in your company's files for examples of previous reports.

MLA Style—Modern Language Association

The MLA citation style uses parenthetic author references in the text. These in-text citations guide the reader to a bibliography called "Works Cited." Following are selected characteristics of the MLA style. For more information, consult Joseph Gibaldi, *MLA Handbook for Writers of Research Papers*, 6th ed. (New York: The Modern Language Association of America, 2003).

FIGURE C.1 Portion of Report Page Showing *Chicago Manual of Style* Endnote Method

These changes are introducing challenges to companies operating both in Canada and abroad. Obviously, all of these employees need specific business and technology skills, but they also need to be aware of, and be sensitive to, the cultures in which they are living and working.[1] The Bank of Montreal has targeted several of these areas in which to enhance services. Chinese-Canadian business has increased 400 percent in the last five years.[2]

Women are increasing their role as both customer and worker. By the year 2003 women are expected to compose 47 percent of the labour force in Canada, as compared with 27 percent in 1961.[3] However, women hold only about 6 percent of the top management positions in organizations in the industrialized world.[4]

Companies that focus on diversity are improving their bottom line. Recently, Federal Express was named in *The Financial Post* as one the 100 best companies to work for in Canada. Canadian Pacific Forest Products received recognition for ensuring that selection committees had diverse membership, for their development of antiharassment policies, and for other diversity initiatives.[5]

Notes

1. Brenda Lynn, "Diversity in the Workplace: Why We Should Care," *CMA Management Accounting Magazine* 70, no. 5 (June 2000): 9–12.

2. Richard Sommer, "Firms Gain Competitive Strength from Diversity (Says Report by Conference Board of Canada)," *Financial Post,* 9 May 2001, 31.

3. British Columbia, Ministry of Education, Skills and Training, *The Impact of Demographic Change* (Victoria: Ministry of Education, Skills, and Training, 2002), 35.

4. R. J. Burke and C. A. McKeen, "Do Women at the Top Make a Difference? Gender Proportions and the Experiences of Managerial and Professional Women," *Human Relations* 49, no. 8 (2002): 1093–1104.

5. British Columbia, 36.

In-Text Citations

Within the text the author's last name and relevant page reference appear in parentheses, such as "(Chartrand 310)." In-text citations should be placed close to the reference they cite. Notice that no separating comma appears. If the author's name is mentioned in the text, cite only the page number in parentheses. If you don't know the author's name (e.g., when quoting from a Web site or blog), use the title of the Web site section or blog entry you took the information from in your in-text citation. Your goal is to avoid interrupting the flow of your writing. Thus, you should strive to place the parenthetical reference where a pause would naturally occur, but as near as possible to the material documented. Note the following examples:

Author's Name in Text

Peters also notes that stress could be a contributing factor in the health problems reported thus far (135).

Author's Name Unknown

One Web site goes so far as to claim that new communication technologies such as BlackBerrys and multi-purpose cell phones will soon make in-person conversations "a thing of the past" ("Talking Not Cool").

Author's Name in Reference

The study was first published in 1958 (Peters 127–135).

Authors' Names in Text

Others, like Bergstrom and Voorhees (243–251), support a competing theory.

Authors' Names in Reference

Others support a competing theory (e.g., Bergstrom and Voorhees 243–251).

When citing films, television programs, or electronic references, MLA style recommends that you include in the text, rather than in a parenthetical reference, the name of the person or organization that begins the corresponding entry in the works-cited list.

Electronic Source with Author

William J. Kennedy's <u>Bits and Bites</u> discusses new computer technologies in the context of the digital telecommunications revolution. (In the "Works Cited" list, the reader would find a complete reference under the author's name.)

Electronic Source Without Author

More companies today are using data mining to unlock hidden value in their data. The data mining program "TargetSource," described at the Tener Solutions Group Web site, helps organizations predict consumer behaviour. (In the "Works Cited" list, the reader would find a complete reference under "Tener Solutions Group," the organization that owns the Web site.)

Works Cited

In-text citations lead the reader to complete bibliographical citations in the "Works Cited." This alphabetical listing may contain all works consulted or only those mentioned in the text. Check with your instructor or editor to learn what method is preferred. Below are selected guidelines summarizing important elements of the MLA format for "Works Cited," as shown in Figure C.2 (page 304).

- **Hanging indented style.** Indent the second and succeeding line for each item. Single-space within entries and double-space between.
- **Book and Web site titles.** Underline the titles of books and use "headline style" for capitalization. This means that the initial letters of all main words are capitalized:

Lewe, Glenda, & Carol D. MacLeod. <u>Step into the World of Workplace Learning: A Collection of Authentic Workplace Materials</u>. Scarborough, ON: Nelson Thomson Learning, 2001.

"ACE Aviation to take minority stake in merged U.S. airline." <u>CBC.ca</u>. 2005. Retrieved 23 May 2005 <www.cbc.ca/story/business/national/2005/05/19/merger-050519.html>.

- **Magazine titles.** For the titles of magazine articles, include the date of publication but omit volume and issue numbers:

Lee, Mary M. "Investing in International Relationships." <u>Business Monthly</u> 18 Feb. 2000.

FIGURE C.2   Model MLA Bibliography of Sample References

Works Cited

Online annual report — Air Canada. <u>2004 Annual Report.</u> Retrieved 26 May 2005 <http://www.aircanada.com/en/about/investor/index.html#reports>.

Magazine article — Beresford, Marcia. "The Shift in Profit." <u>Maclean's</u> 24 Oct. 2001: 25–26.

Government publication — British Columbia Ministry of Education, Skills and Training, <u>The Impact of Demographic Change.</u> Victoria: Ministry of Education, Skills and Training, 2002.

Company Web site, no author — "Clementine@work." <u>SPSS Web Site.</u> Retrieved 7 Sept. 2005. <http://www.spss.com/customer/clem_stories/>.

Newspaper article, no author — "Globalization Often Means That the Fast Track Leads Overseas." <u>The Globe and Mail</u>, 16 June 2002: A10.

Online research database magazine article, where "CBCA Current Affairs" — Jahl, Andrew. "PowerPoint of No Return." <u>Canadian Business</u>. 24 Nov. 2003: 14–15. CBCA Current Affairs. George Brown College Library. Retrieved 27 May 2005.

Newspaper article, one author — Lancaster, Hal. "When Taking a Tip from a Job Network, Proceed with Caution." <u>The Wall Street Journal</u>, 7 Feb. 2002: B1.

Online newspaper article — Mark, John. "Feds Provide Summary of New Privacy Legislation for Internet Users." 5 June 2002 <u>globe and mail.com</u>. Retrieved 9 June 2005 <http://www.globeandmail.com/servlet/story/RTGAM.20020605.privacy/National>.

Web site, no author — "Message Treatment." <u>Communication, Culture and Media Studies</u> Web site. Retrieved 23 May 2005 <www.cultsock.ndirect.co.uk/MUHome/cshtml/>.

Online magazine article — Murdry, Henry. "Consumers Still Driving the Economy." <u>Marketing News Online</u>, 31 Aug. 2001. Retrieved 1 Sept. 2005 <http://www.canadianmarketingmagazine.ca/consumers.story>.

Brochure — Pinnacle Security Services. <u>What Employers Should Know About Employees</u>, 2nd ed. Toronto: Pinnacle Information Centre, 2002.

Interview — Rivers, John. Personal interview. 16 May 2005.

Book, two authors — Rosen, Richard, and Ethel Montgomery. <u>How to Make a Buck and Still Be a Decent Human Being</u>. New York: HarperCollins, 1998.

Journal article with volume and issue numbers — Weathers, Nicholas. "Key Trends in Systems Development." <u>Journal of Information Management</u> 3.2 (2000): 5–20.

- **Journal articles.** For journal articles follow the same format as for magazine articles except include the volume number, issue number (if needed), and the year of publication inside parentheses:

  Green, Deidre. "A Textbook Case for Online Searching," <u>CMAJ: Canadian Medical Association Journal</u> 164:7 (2001). ["164:7" indicates volume 164, issue 7.]

- **Italics and underscoring.** MLA style recommends underscoring book, magazine, and journal titles because underscores are easier to read than italics. Italics, however, are preferred in many organizations. Check with your instructor or organization for the preferred style.

Electronic References

The objective in citing sources, whether print publications or electronic publications, is to provide enough information that your reader can locate your sources. In addition to the information provided for all print sources (e.g., author's name if available, title, date of publication, etc.), a citation for an electronic source requires at least two other kinds of information. First, you must provide the date when you accessed the source. Second, you must provide the source's electronic address between angle brackets (e.g., <www.cbc.ca>). The electronic address (or URL) is the final part of an electronic source citation.

Although MLA style does not suggest including the word "Retrieved" before the access date, we include it to distinguish the retrieval date from the publication date. Figure C.2 illustrates the electronic and other formats for many different kinds of references. The MLA also posts some helpful guidelines for documenting electronic sources at its Web site <www.mla.org>; follow the prompts to "Documenting Sources from the World Wide Web."

The MLA makes the following recommendations for citing electronic sources:

- Give the same information for electronic sources as you would if you were citing a print publication (e.g., author name, title, page number).

- Give all relevant dates. Because electronic sources can change or move, cite the date the document was produced (if available) as well as the date you accessed the information. Do not use any punctuation to separate the date you received the information and the URL. If the electronic publication is or was available in print form (that is, as a book or in a journal), include the original print publication date before the other dates.

- Include the electronic address or universal resource locator (URL) where you found your information. Provide entire URLs in angle brackets (<, >), being sure to break lines only after a slash, dot, or hyphen. Never add a hyphen to mark a break in the address.

- Download and print any citation information for future reference.

Article in an Online Journal

Chrisman, Laura, and Laurence Phillips. "Postcolonial Studies and the British Academy." <u>Jouvert</u> 3:3. (1999). Retrieved 10 June 2001 <http://social. chass.ncsu.edu/jouvert/v3i3/chrisph/htm>.

Brown, Ronnie R. "Photographs That Should Have Been Taken." <u>Room of One's Own</u> 18:2 (Summer 1995). Retrieved 26 May 2002 <http://www.islandnet.com/ Room/enter/poetry/photos.htm>.

Article in an Online Newspaper or on a Newswire

These sites change very frequently—in some cases daily—so it is a good idea to download or record URL and citation information immediately.

Scarth, Deborah. "Many Top University Students Use Tutors to Keep an Edge." <u>Globe and Mail Online</u>. 4 June 2000. Retrieved 5 Oct. 2000 <http://www. globeandmail.com/dailyglobe2/150/learning/Many-top-university-students-use-tutors-to-keep-an-edge+.shtm>.

"Canada's Unemployment Rate Dips." <u>CBC News Online</u>. 4 June 2000. Retrieved 5 Aug. 2000 <http://www.cbcnews.cbc.ca/cgi-bin/templates/view.cgi?/news/ 1999/06/04/unemploy990604>.

Article in an Online Magazine

Caragata, Warren. "Guide to Y2K." <u>Maclean's Online</u>. 19 Apr. 2000. Retrieved 5 June 2000 <http://www.macleans.ca/pub-doc/1999/04/19/Cover/4998.html>.

Professional or Personal Web Site

List the publication information in the following order: the name of the creator of the site, the title of the site (underlined), a description (for example, *Home page*, neither underlined nor italicized nor enclosed in quotation marks), the date you accessed the information, and the electronic address. If some of this information is unavailable, cite whatever is available.

Canadiantire.ca. Investor Relations page. Retrieved 28 May 2005 <www.canadiantire.ca>.

Ellison, Sara. Sara's Home Page. Sarah's Astronomy Stuff. Retrieved 29 July 2005 <http://orca.phys.uvic.ca/~sara/>.

Online Book

Many books are now available electronically, either independently or as part of a scholarly project. Follow the general recommendations for citing books in print, but include the additional information as required for electronic citations.

If it is available, give the name of the author first; if not, give the name of the editor, translator, or compiler, followed by a period and then the appropriate abbreviation (*ed.*, *trans.*, or *comp.*). Next give the title of the work (underlined), the name of the editor, translator, or compiler (if relevant), the publication information, the date you accessed the information, and the address. The publication information will vary depending on whether the text has been previously published in print form. If it has not been previously published, give the date it was published electronically and the name of any associated organization or university. If it has been previously published in print form, include, if available, the city of publication, the name of the publisher and the year of publication, followed by the date of electronic publication, and the name of any associated organization or university. In either case, complete your citation with the date you accessed the information and the electronic address.

Montgomery, Lucy Maud. Anne of Green Gables. 1908. Retrieved 30 May 2001 <http://www.literature.org/authors/montgomery-lucy-maud/anne-of-green-gables/>.

Dewey, John. Democracy and Education. London: Macmillan, 1916. 22 Nov. 1995. Retrieved 5 June 2001 <http://www.ilt.columbia.edu/academic/texts/dewey/d_e/contents.html>.

Scholarly Project or Information Services

Information on a wide variety of topics is available through scholarly projects or in information services. If you are using information taken from these sources, cite the title of the project or information service first (underlined), followed by the name of the editor (if available), any relevant and available electronic publication information (for example, version number, date of electronic publication or most recent update, and name of any sponsoring institution or organization), the date you accessed the information, and the network address.

The Orlando Project: An Integrated History of Women's Writing in the British Isles. 1998. Department of English, University of Alberta. 1998. Retrieved 25 April 2000 <http://www.ualberta.ca/ORLANDO/>.

"South Yorkshire." Encyclopedia Britannica Online. 26 May 2001 <http://members.eb.com/bol/topic?eu=70678&sctn=1>.

Other Electronic Sources. The citations for other electronic sources will follow the recommendations for print versions with some additional required information.

Be sure to include the type of document you are citing (for example, transcript, online posting, or e-mail) between the date of publication and the date you accessed the information. End your citation with the date you accessed the information and the network address.

Television/Radio

Mansbridge, Peter. "Sears Saga." The National. CBC-TV. 4 June 2001. Transcript. 5 June 2001 <http://www.tv.cbc.ca/national/trans/current.html>.

E-Mail Communication

Pen Canada. "Your Inquiries to PEN." E-mail to author. 3 July 2005.

Online Posting

Murley, Susan. "Technical Writing." Online posting. 2 May 2000. MLA Grad List. 3 May 2000 <e-grad@nwe.ufl.edu>.

Material from an Online Research Database

Online services such as ProQuest and LexisNexis provide a variety of databases that your college library will have. Give the name of the service before the date you accessed the information. Indicate the method by which you retrieved the information. For example, if you used a keyword search, write "keyword" (neither in quotation marks nor underlined) at the end of your citation, followed by a colon and the keyword you used to find your information.

Golden, Anne. "Do Our Foreign Investment Laws Still Have Legs?" The Globe and Mail. 1 Dec. 2004: A23. CBCA Current Affairs. Retrieved 2 March 2005. Keyword: Noranda and Minmetals.

APA Style—American Psychological Association

Popular in the social and physical sciences, the American Psychological Association (APA) documentation style uses parenthetic citations. That is, each author reference is shown in parentheses when cited in the text. Below are selected features of the APA style. For more information see the *Publication Manual of the American Psychological Association*, 5th Edition (Washington, DC: American Psychological Association, 2001).

In-Text Citation

In-text citations consist of the author's last name, year of publication, and pertinent page number(s). These items appear in parentheses usually at the end of a clause or end of a sentence in which material is cited. This parenthetic citation, as shown in the following illustration, directs readers to a reference list at the end of the report where complete bibliographic information is recorded.

The strategy of chicken king Don Tyson was to expand aggressively into other "center-of-the-plate" proteins, such as pork, fish, and turkey (Berss, 2000, p. 64).

Bibliography

All reference sources are alphabetized in a bibliography entitled "References." Below are selected guidelines summarizing important elements of the APA bibliographic format:

- Include authors' names with the last name first followed by initials, such as **Smith, M. A.** First and middle names are not used.
- Show the date of publication in parentheses, such as **Smith, M. A. (2001)**.
- Italicize the titles of books and use "sentence-style" (sometimes called *down style*) capitalization. This means that only the first word of a title, proper nouns, or the first word after an internal colon is capitalized. Book titles are followed by the place of publication and publisher's name, such as **Smith, M. A. (2001).** *Communication for managers.* **Elmsford, NY: Pergamon Press.**
- Type the titles of magazine and journal articles without italics or quotation marks. Use sentence-style capitalization for article titles. However, italicize the names of magazines and journals and capitalize the initial letters of all important words. Also italicize the volume number, such as **Cheung, H. K., & Burn, J. M. (1994). Distributing global information systems resources in multinational companies—a contingency model.** *Journal of Global Information Management,* **2(3), 14–27.** ["2(3), 14–27" indicates volume 2, issue 3, pages 14–27.]
- Space only once following periods and colons.
- Do not include personal communications (such as interviews, telephone conversations, e-mail, and messages from nonarchived discussion groups and online forums) in the reference list, since they are not retrievable.

Electronic References

When print information is available, APA suggests placing it first followed by online information. For example, a newspaper article: **Schellhardt, T. D. (1999, March 4). In a factory schedule, where does religion fit in?** *The Wall Street Journal,* **pp. B1, B12. Retrieved March 5, 1999, from http://interactive.wsj.com** For additional discussion and examples, visit the APA Web site <**www.apastyle.org/ elecref.html**>.

Figure C.3, on the next page, shows the format of an APA Reference List.

FIGURE C.3 Model APA Bibliography Sample References

References

Air Canada. (2004). *2004 annual report*. Retrieved May 26, 2005, from http://www .aircanada.com/en/about/investor/index.html#reports

Berss, M. (2000, October 24). Protein man. *Forbes, 154,* 64–66.

Globalization often means that the fast track leads overseas. (1999, June 16). *The Financial Post,* p. A10.

Jahl, A. (2003, November 24). PowerPoint of no return. *Canadian Business,* 14–15. Retrieved May 27, 2005, from CBCA Current Affairs, George Brown College Library.

Lancaster, H. (1998, February 7). When taking a tip from a job network, proceed with caution. *The Wall Street Journal,* p. B1.

Markoff, J. (1999, June 5). Voluntary rules proposed to help ensure privacy for Internet users. *The New York Times.* Retrieved June 9, 2005, from http://www.nytimes .com/ library/cyber/week/y05dat.html

Murphy, H. L. (1998, August 31). Saturn's orbit still high with consumers. *Marketing News Online.* Retrieved September 1, 2004, from http://www.ama.org/pubs/ mn/0818n1.htm

Pinkerton Investigation Services. (1998). *The employer's guide to investigation services* (3rd ed.) [Brochure]. Atlanta, GA: Pinkerton Information Center.

Rose, R. C., & Garrett, E. M. (1998). *How to make a buck and still be a decent human being.* New York: HarperCollins.

Statistics Canada. (1995). *A portrait of persons with disabilities: Target groups project.* Ottawa, ON: Department of Industry, Science and Technology.

Transmission models—criticism. (2005). *Communication, Culture and Media Studies.* Retrieved 23 May 2005 from http://www.cultshock.ndirect.co.uk/MUHome/cshtml/

Wetherbee, J. C., Vitalari, N. P., & Milner, A. (1998). Key trends in systems development in Europe and North America. *Journal of Global Information Management, 3*(2), 5–20.

Online annual report

Magazine article

Newspaper article, no author

Online research database magazine article

Newspaper article,

Online newspaper article

Online magazine article

Brochure

Book, two authors

Government publication

Web site, no author

Journal article with volume and issue numbers

Grammar/Mechanics Handbook

Because many students need a review of basic grammar and mechanics, we provide a number of resources below. The Grammar/Mechanics Handbook consists of four parts:

- **Grammar/Mechanics Diagnostic Test.** This 65-point test shows your strengths and weaknesses in eight areas of grammar and mechanics.
- **Grammar/Mechanics Profile.** The G/M Profile presents specific areas in which you need remedial instruction or review.
- **Grammar Review with Checkup and Editing Exercises.** A concise set of guidelines reviews basic principles of grammar, punctuation, capitalization, and number style. The review also provides checkup and quiz exercises that help you with the principles of grammar and test your comprehension. The guidelines not only provide a study guide for review but also serve as a reference manual throughout the writing course. The grammar review can be used for classroom-centred instruction or for self-guided learning.
- **Confusing Words and Frequently Misspelled Words.** A selected list of confusing words, along with a list of 160 frequently misspelled words, completes the Grammar/Mechanics Handbook.

The first step in your systematic review of grammar and mechanics involves completing a diagnostic test.

Grammar/Mechanics Diagnostic Test

Name _____

This diagnostic test is intended to reveal your strengths and weaknesses in using the following:

plural nouns	adjectives	punctuation
possessive nouns	adverbs	capitalization style
pronouns	prepositions	number style
verbs	conjunctions	

The test is organized into sections corresponding to these categories. In sections A–H, each sentence is either correct or has one error related to the category under which it is listed. If a sentence is correct, write *C*. If it has an error, underline the error and write the correct form in the space provided. Use ink to record your answers. When you finish, check your answers with your instructor and fill out the Grammar/Mechanics Profile at the end of the test.

A. Plural Nouns

Example: Two <u>branchs</u> of the tree were broken during the storm.

branches _____

1. Lawyers from many different citys in Canada were in court today. _____
2. Students in history class discussed the many heros of World War II. _____
3. Since the late 1990s, most companys have begun to send bills to their clients via the Internet. _____
4. I earned two A's and three B's on last semester's report card. _____
5. The manager asked all secretaries to work on the next four Saturdays. _____

B. Possessive Nouns

6. We sincerely hope that the jurys judgment reflects the stories of all the witnesses. _____
7. In a little over two months time, the analysts had finished three reports for the president. _____
8. Mr. Franklins staff is responsible for all accounts of customers purchasing electronics parts. _____
9. At the next supervisors meeting, we will discuss benefits for employees. _____
10. Three months ago several employees in the sales department complained of Mrs. Kwons smoking. _____

C. Pronouns

Example: Whom did you ask to replace Tom and <u>I</u>?

me _____

11. My manager and myself sent copies of the contract to whoever needed them. _____
12. Some of the work for Mr. Gagne and I had to be given to Mark and him. _____
13. Although its motor was damaged, the car started for the mechanic and me. _____
14. Just between you and me, only you and I know that she will be transferred. _____
15. My friend and I applied for employment at Reynolds, Inc., because of their excellent employee benefits. _____

D. Verb Agreement

Example: The list of arrangements <u>have</u> to be approved by Tim and her.

has _____

16. The keyboard, printer, and monitor costs less than I expected. _____
17. A description of the property, together with several other legal documents, were submitted by my lawyer. _____
18. There was only two enclosures and the letter in the envelope. _____
19. Neither the manager nor the employees in the office think the solution is fair. _____
20. Because of the holiday, our committee prefer to delay its action. _____

E. Verb Mood, Voice, and Tense

21. If I was able to fill your order immediately, I certainly would. _____
22. To operate the machine, first open the CD caddy and then you insert the CD. _____
23. If I could chose any city, I would select Vancouver. _____
24. Please lie the baby carefully into its crib. _____
25. The auditors have went over these accounts carefully, and they have found no mistakes. _____

F. Adjectives and Adverbs

_____ 26. Until we have a more clearer picture of the episode, we shall proceed cautiously.

_____ 27. For about a week their newly repaired copier worked just beautiful.

_____ 28. The new prime minister had a coast to coast campaign.

_____ 29. Mr. Snyder only has two days before he must complete the end-of-the-year report.

_____ 30. The architects submitted there drawings in a last-minute attempt to beat the deadline.

G. Prepositions and Conjunctions

_____ 31. Can you tell me where the meeting is scheduled at?

_____ 32. It seems like we have been taking this test forever.

_____ 33. Our investigation shows that the distribution department is more efficient then the sales department.

_____ 34. Business letters should be concise, correct, and written clearly.

_____ 35. Do you know where this shipment is going to?

H. Commas

For each of the following sentences, insert any necessary commas. Count the number of commas that you added. Write that number in the space provided. All punctuation must be correct to receive credit for the sentence. If a sentence requires no punctuation, write C.

1 _____ **Example:** In fact, all students will complete the program by April 30.

_____ 36. For example management decides how orders assignments and responsibilities are given to employees.

_____ 37. Your order Mrs. Tahan will be sent from Toronto Ontario on July 10.

_____ 38. When you need service on your equipment we will be happy to help you Mr. Hamel.

_____ 39. Kevin Long who is the project manager at Techdata suggested that I call you.

_____ 40. You have purchased from us often and your payments in the past have always been prompt.

I. Commas and Semicolons 1

Add commas and semicolons to the following sentences. In the space provided, write the number of punctuation marks that you added.

_____ 41. The salesperson submitted her report however she did not indicate what time period it covered.

_____ 42. Some interest payments may be tax deductible bonus payments are not.

_____ 43. We are opening a branch office in Kelowna and hope to serve all your needs from that office by the middle of January.

_____ 44. As suggested by the committee we must first get enough funding then we may consider expansion.

_____ 45. When you do research for a report consider the many library sources available such as books periodicals government publications and databases.

Grammar/Mechanics Handbook

J. Commas and Semicolons 2

46. After our office manager had the printer repaired it jammed again within the first week.   _____
47. Our experienced courteous staff has been trained to anticipate your every need.   _____
48. In view of the new law that went into effect April 1 our current insurance must be increased however we cannot immediately afford it.   _____
49. According to our latest contract your agency will supervise our graphic arts and purchase our media time.   _____
50. As you know Mrs. Laurendeau we aim for long-term business relationships not quick profits.   _____

K. Other Punctuation

Each of the following sentences may require dashes, colons, question marks, quotation marks, periods, and underscores, as well as commas and semicolons. Add the appropriate punctuation to each sentence. Then, in the space provided, write the total number of marks that you added.

Example: Price service and reliability these are our prime concerns.   3 _____

51. The following members of the department helped on Saturday Kim Carlos Dan and Sylvia.   _____
52. Mr. Danner, Miss Reed, and Mrs. Rossi usually arrived at the office by 8 30 a.m.   _____
53. Three of our top managers Tim, Marcy, and Asad received cash bonuses.   _____
54. Did the vice-president really say "All employees may take Friday off   _____
55. We are trying to locate an edition of Maclean's that carried an article entitled E-mail Beats Office Politics   _____

L. Capitalization

For each of the following sentences, circle any letter that should be capitalized. In the space provided, write the number of circles that you marked.

Example: vice-president mark daniels created a procedure for sending orders from the number 4 warehouse.   5 _____

56. although english was his first language, he also spoke spanish and could read french.   _____
57. on a trip throughout canada, uncle henry visited the the city of vancouver.   _____
58. karen enrolled in classes in history, german, and sociology.   _____
59. the business manager and the vice-president each received a new macintosh computer.   _____
60. jane lee, the president of kendrick, inc., will speak to our conference in the spring.   _____

M. Number Style

Decide whether the numbers in the following sentences should be written as words or as figures. Each sentence either is correct or has one error. If it is correct, write C. If it has an error, underline it and write the correct form in the space provided.

Example: The bank had 5 branches in three suburbs.   **five** _____

61. More than 2,000,000 people have visited the Parliament Buildings in the past five years.
62. Of the 35 letters sent out, only three were returned.
63. We set aside forty dollars for petty cash, but by December 1 our fund was all gone.
64. The meeting is scheduled for May 5th at 3 p.m.
65. In the past 20 years, nearly 15 percent of the population changed residences at least once.

Grammar/Mechanics Profile

In the spaces at the right, place a check mark to indicate the number of correct answers you had in each category of the Grammar/Mechanics Diagnostic Test.

		Number Correct*				
		5	4	3	2	1
1–5	Plural Nouns	____	____	____	____	____
6–10	Possessive Nouns	____	____	____	____	____
11–15	Pronouns	____	____	____	____	____
16–20	Verb Agreement	____	____	____	____	____
21–25	Verb Mood, Voice, and Tense	____	____	____	____	____
26–30	Adjectives and Adverbs	____	____	____	____	____
31–35	Prepositions and Conjunctions	____	____	____	____	____
36–40	Commas	____	____	____	____	____
41–45	Commas and Semicolons 1	____	____	____	____	____
46–50	Commas and Semicolons 2	____	____	____	____	____
51–55	Other Punctuation	____	____	____	____	____
56–60	Capitalization	____	____	____	____	____
61–65	Number Style	____	____	____	____	____

*Note: 5 = have excellent skills; 4 = need light review; 3 = need careful review; 2 = need to study rules; 1 = need serious study and follow-up reinforcement.

Grammar Review

Parts of Speech (1.01)

1.01 Functions. English has eight parts of speech. Knowing the functions of the parts of speech helps writers better understand how words are used and how sentences are formed.

a. *Nouns.* Name persons, places, things, qualities, concepts, and activities (for example, *Kevin, Montreal, computer, joy, work, banking*).
b. *Pronouns.* Substitute for nouns (for example, *he, she, it, they*).
c. *Verbs.* Show the action of a subject or join the subject to words that describe it (for example, *walk, heard, is, was jumping*).
d. *Adjectives.* Describe or limit nouns and pronouns and often answer the questions what kind? how many? and which one? (for example, *fast sale, ten items, good manager*).
e. *Adverbs.* Describe or limit verbs, adjectives, or other adverbs and frequently answer the questions when? how? where? or to what extent? (for example, *tomorrow, rapidly, here, very*).

f. *Prepositions.* Join nouns or pronouns to other words in sentences (for example, *desk **in** the office, ticket **for** me, letter **to** you*).

g. *Conjunctions.* Connect words or groups of words (for example, *you **and** I, Marc **or** Nikola*).

h. *Interjections.* Express strong feelings (for example, *Wow! Oh!*).

Nouns (1.02–1.06)

Nouns name persons, places, things, qualities, concepts, and activities. Nouns may be classified into a number of categories.

1.02 Concrete and Abstract. Concrete nouns name specific objects that can be seen, heard, felt, tasted, or smelled. Examples of concrete nouns are *telephone, dollar, IBM,* and *grape.* Abstract nouns name generalized ideas such as qualities or concepts that are not easily pictured. *Emotion, power,* and *tension* are typical examples of abstract nouns.

Business writing is most effective when mostly concrete nouns are used. It's clearer to write *We need to sell more books* than to write *We need to increase our profitability.* Chapter 4 provides practice in developing skill in the use of concrete words.

1.03 Proper and Common. Proper nouns name specific persons, places, or things and are always capitalized *(Nortel, Chicago, Dinah).* All other nouns are common nouns and begin with lowercase letters *(company, city, student).* Rules for capitalization are presented in sections 3.01–3.16.

1.04 Singular and Plural. Singular nouns name one item; plural nouns name more than one. From a practical view, writers seldom have difficulty with singular nouns. They may need help, however, with the formation and spelling of plural nouns.

1.05 Guidelines for Forming Noun Plurals

a. Add *s* to most nouns *(chair, chairs; mortgage, mortgages; Monday, Mondays).*

b. Add *es* to nouns ending in *s, x, z, ch,* or *sh* *(bench, benches; boss, bosses; box, boxes; Schultz, Schultzes).*

c. Change the spelling in irregular noun plurals *(man, men; foot, feet; mouse, mice; child, children).*

d. Add *s* to nouns that end in *y* when *y* is preceded by a vowel *(attorney, attorneys; valley, valleys; journey, journeys).*

e. Drop the *y* and add *ies* to nouns ending in *y* when *y* is preceded by a consonant *(company, companies; city, cities; secretary, secretaries).*

f. Add *s* to the principal word in most compound expressions *(editors in chief, fathers-in-law, runners-up).*

g. Add *s* to most numerals, letters of the alphabet, words referred to as words, degrees, and abbreviations *(5s, 1990s, Bs, ands, CAs, yrs.).* Note that metric abbreviations take neither a period nor an *s* to make them plural *(20 km).*

h. Add *'s* only to clarify letters of the alphabet that might be misread, such as *A's, I's, M's,* and *U's* and *i's, p's,* and *q's.* An expression such as *c.o.d.s* requires no apostrophe because it would not easily be misread.

1.06 Collective Nouns. Nouns such as *staff, faculty, committee, group,* and *herd* refer to a collection of people, animals, or objects. Collective nouns may be considered singular or plural depending on their action. See section 1.10i for a discussion of collective nouns and their agreement with verbs.

Grammar Review

Review Exercise A—Nouns

In the space provided for each item, write *a* or *b* to complete the following statements accurately. When you finish, compare your responses with those provided. Answers are provided for odd-numbered items. Your instructor has the remaining answers. For each item on which you need review, consult the numbered principle shown in parentheses.

_____   1. Nearly all (a) editor in chiefs, (b) editors in chief demand standard punctuation.
_____   2. Several (a) attorneys, (b) attornies worked on the case together.
_____   3. Please write to the (a) Davis's, (b) Davises about the missing contract.
_____   4. The new shopping centre has space for nine additional (a) companys, (b) companies.
_____   5. That accounting firm employs two (a) secretaries, (b) secretarys.
_____   6. Four of the wooden (a) benches, (b) benchs must be repaired.
_____   7. The home was constructed with many (a) chimneys, (b) chimnies.
_____   8. Tours of the new college campus are made only on (a) Tuesdays, (b) Tuesday's.
_____   9. We asked the (a) Jones's, (b) Joneses to contribute to the fundraising drive.
_____   10. Both my (a) sister-in-laws, (b) sisters-in-law agreed to attend the party.
_____   11. There are too many (a) ands, (b) and's in that sentence.
_____   12. Three (a) mouses, (b) mice were seen near the garbage cans.
_____   13. This office is unusually quiet on (a) Sundays, (b) Sunday's.
_____   14. Several (a) boxs, (b) boxes were missing from the warehouse.
_____   15. Two major (a) countries, (b) countrys will participate in trade negotiations.
_____   16. I have two (a) a's (b) as in my surname.
_____   17. The (a) board of directors, (b) boards of directors of all the major companies participated in the surveys.
_____   18. In their letter, the (a) Metzes, (b) Metzs said they intended to purchase the property.
_____   19. When we ship our goods, we are careful to include all (a) bill of sales, (b) bills of sale.
_____   20. Over the holidays many (a) turkies, (b) turkeys were consumed.

1. b (1.05f) 3. b (1.05b) 5. a (1.05e) 7. a (1.05d) 9. b (1.05b) 11. a (1.05g) 13. a (1.05a) 15. a (1.05e) 17. b (1.05f) 19. b (1.05f) (Only odd-numbered answers are provided. Consult your instructor for the others.)

Grammar/Mechanics Checkup—1

Nouns

Review sections 1.01–1.06 above. Then study each of the following statements. Underline any mistakes and write a correction in the space provided. Record the appropriate Handbook section and letter that illustrates the principle involved. If a sentence is correct, write C. When you finish, compare your responses with those provided in the answer key on page 372. If your answers differ, carefully study again the principles shown in parentheses.

companies   (1.05e)   **Example:**   Two surveys revealed that many <u>companys</u> will move to the new industrial park.

_____   1. Several attornies worked on the three cases simultaneously.
_____   2. Counter business is higher on Saturday's, but telephone business is greater on Sundays.

Grammar/Mechanics Handbook

3. Some of the citys in Kevin's report offer excellent opportunities. _____
4. Frozen chickens and turkies are kept in the company's lockers. _____
5. All secretaries were asked to check supplies and other inventorys. _____
6. Only the Nashs and the Lopezes brought their entire families. _____
7. In the 1980s profits grew rapidly; in the 1990's investments lagged. _____
8. Both editor in chiefs demanded excellent proofreading skills. _____
9. Luxury residential complexs are part of the architect's plan. _____
10. Trustees in three municipalitys are likely to approve increased school taxes. _____
11. The instructor was surprised to find three Jennifer's in one class. _____
12. Andre sent descriptions of two valleys in France to us via the Internet. _____
13. How many copies of the statements showing your assets and liabilitys did you make? _____
14. My monitor makes it difficult to distinguish between o's and a's. _____
15. Both runner-ups complained about the winner's behaviour. _____

Pronouns (1.07–1.09)

Pronouns substitute for nouns. They are classified by case.

1.07 Case. Pronouns function in three cases, as shown in the following chart.

Nominative Case (used for subjects of verbs and subject complements)	Objective Case (used for objects of prepositions and objects of verbs)	Possessive Case (used to show possession)
I	me	my, mine
we	us	our, ours
you	you	your, yours
he	him	his
she	her	her, hers
it	it	its
they	them	their, theirs
who, whoever	whom, whomever	whose

1.08 Guidelines for Selecting Pronoun Case

a. Pronouns that serve as subjects of verbs must be in the nominative case:

   He and I (not *Him* and *me*) decided to apply for the jobs.

b. Pronouns that follow linking verbs (such as *am, is, are, was, were, be, being, been*) and that re-name the words to which they refer must be in the nominative case.

   It must have been she (not *her*) who placed the order. (The nominative-case pronoun *she* follows the linking verb *been* and re-names *It*.)

   If it was he (not *him*) who called, I have his number. (The nominative-case pronoun *he* follows the linking verb *was* and re-names *It*.)

c. Pronouns that serve as objects of verbs or objects of prepositions must be in the objective case:

   Mr. Laporte asked them to complete the proposal. (The pronoun *them* is the object of the verb *asked*.)

   All computer printouts are sent to him. (The pronoun *him* is the object of the preposition *to*.)

Just between you and me, profits are falling. (The pronoun *me* is one of the objects of the preposition *between*.)

d. Pronouns that show ownership must be in the possessive case. Possessive pronouns (such as *hers, yours, ours, theirs,* and *its*) require no apostrophes:

We found my diskette, but yours (not *your's*) may be lost.

All parts of the machine, including its (not *it's*) motor, were examined.

The house and its (not *it's*) contents will be auctioned.

Don't confuse possessive pronouns and contractions. Contractions are shortened forms of subject-verb phrases (such as *it's* for *it is, there's* for *there is,* and *they're* for *they are*).

e. When a pronoun appears in combination with a noun or another pronoun, ignore the extra noun or pronoun and its conjunction. In this way pronoun case becomes more obvious:

The manager promoted Jasper and me (not *I*). (Ignore *Jasper and.*)

f. In statements of comparison, mentally finish the comparative by adding the implied missing words:

Next year I hope to earn as much as she. (The verb *earns* is implied here: *as much as she earns.*)

g. Pronouns must be in the same case as the words they replace or re-name. When pronouns are used with appositives, ignore the appositive:

A new contract was signed by us (not *we*) employees. (Temporarily ignore the appositive *employees* in selecting the pronoun.)

We (not *us*) citizens have formed our own organization. (Temporarily ignore the appositive *citizens* in selecting the pronoun.)

h. Pronouns ending in *self* should be used only when they refer to previously mentioned nouns or pronouns:

The CEO herself answered the telephone.

Robert and I (not *myself*) are in charge of the campaign.

i. Use objective-case pronouns as objects of the prepositions *between, but, like,* and *except:*

Everyone but John and him (not *he*) qualified for the bonus.

Employees like Miss Gallucci and her (not *she*) are hard to replace.

j. Use *who* or *whoever* for nominative-case constructions and *whom* or *whomever* for objective-case constructions. In making the correct choice, it's sometimes helpful to substitute *he* for *who* or *whoever* and *him* for *whom* or *whomever*:

For whom was this book ordered? (This book was ordered for him/whom?)

Who did you say would drop by? (*Who/he ... would drop by?*)

Deliver the package to whoever opens the door. (In this sentence the clause *whoever opens the door* functions as the object of the preposition *to*. Within the clause itself *whoever* is the subject of the verb *opens*. Again, substitution of *he* might be helpful: *He/Whoever opens the door.*)

Grammar/Mechanics Handbook

1.09 Guidelines for Making Pronouns Agree with Their Antecedents.
Pronouns must agree with the words to which they refer (their antecedents) in gender and in number.

a. Use masculine pronouns to refer to masculine antecedents, feminine pronouns to refer to feminine antecedents, and neutral pronouns to refer to antecedents without gender:

The woman opened her office door. (Feminine gender applies.)

A man sat at his desk. (Masculine gender applies.)

This computer and its programs fit our needs. (Neutral gender applies.)

b. Use singular pronouns to refer to singular antecedents. Common-gender pronouns (such as *him* or *his*) traditionally have been used when the gender of the antecedent is unknown. Business writers construct sentences to avoid the need for common-gender pronouns. See Chapter 2 for additional discussion of common-gender pronouns and inclusive language. Study these examples for alternatives to the use of common-gender pronouns:

Each student must submit a report on Monday.

All students must submit their reports on Monday.

Each student must submit his or her report on Monday. (This alternative is least acceptable, since it is wordy and calls attention to itself.)

c. Use singular pronouns to refer to singular indefinite subjects and plural pronouns for plural indefinite subjects. Words such as *anyone, something,* and *anybody* are considered indefinite because they refer to no specific person or object. Some indefinite pronouns are always singular; others are always plural.

Always Singular			**Always Plural**
anybody	everyone	somebody	both
anyone	everything	someone	few
anything	neither		many
each	nobody		several
either	no one		

Somebody in the group of touring women left her (not *their*) purse in the museum.

Either of the companies has the right to exercise its (not *their*) option to sell shares.

d. Use singular pronouns to refer to collective nouns and organization names:

The engineering staff is moving its (not *their*) facilities on Friday. (The singular pronoun *its* agrees with the collective noun *staff* because the members of staff function as a single unit.)

Jones, Cohen, & James, Inc., has (not *have*) cancelled its (not *their*) contract with us. (The singular pronoun *its* agrees with *Jones, Cohen, & James, Inc.*, because the members of the organization are operating as a single unit.)

e. Use a plural pronoun to refer to two antecedents joined by *and*, whether the antecedents are singular or plural:

Our company president and our vice-president will be submitting their expenses shortly.

f. Ignore phrases—introduced by expressions such as *together with*, *as well as*, and *in addition to*—that separate a pronoun from its antecedent:

> One of our managers, along with several salespeople, is planning his retirement. (If you wish to emphasize both subjects equally, join them with *and*: One of our managers and several salespeople are planning their retirements.)

g. When antecedents are joined by *or* or *nor*, make the pronoun agree with the antecedent closest to it.

> Neither Jackie nor Kim wanted her (not *their*) desk moved.

Review Exercise B—Pronouns

In the space provided for each item, write *a*, *b*, or *c* to complete the statement accurately. When you finish, compare your responses with those provided. For each item on which you need review, consult the numbered principle shown in parentheses.

1. Mr. Behrens and (a) I, (b) myself will be visiting sales personnel in Toronto next week.
2. Joel promised that he would call; was it (a) him, (b) he who left the message?
3. Much preparation for the seminar was made by Mrs. Willmar and (a) I, (b) me before the brochures were sent out.
4. The Employee Benefits Committee can be proud of (a) its, (b) their achievements.
5. A number of inquiries were addressed to Jonelle and (a) I, (b) me, (c) myself.
6. (a) Who, (b) Whom did you say the letter was addressed to?
7. When you visit the bank, inquire about (a) its, (b) their savings program.
8. Copies of all reports are to be reviewed by Mr. Khan and (a) I, (b) me, (c) myself.
9. One of the female applicants forgot to sign (a) her, (b) their application.
10. Both the printer and (a) it's, (b) its cover are missing.
11. I can work as fast as (a) him, (b) he on any project.
12. Just between you and (a) I, (b) me, Johnson is planning to quit next week.
13. Give the supplies to (a) whoever, (b) whomever ordered them.
14. (a) Us, (b) We employees are getting a new benefits package.
15. On her return from Mexico, Mrs. Lamas, along with many other passengers, had to open (a) her, (b) their luggage for inspection.
16. Either Jason or Raymond will have (a) his, (b) their work reviewed next week.
17. Any woman who becomes a member of this organization will have (a) her, (b) their own e-mail address.
18. We are certain that (a) our's, (b) ours is the smallest wristwatch available.
19. Everyone has completed the reports except Danica and (a) he, (b) him.
20. Lack of work disturbs Mr. Jin as much as (a) I, (b) me.

1. a (1.08h) 3. b (1.08c) 5. b (1.08c, 1.08e, 1.08h) 7. a (1.09d) 9. a (1.09b) 11. b (1.08f) 13. a (1.08j) 15. a (1.09f) 17. a (1.09b) 19. b (1.08i)

Grammar/Mechanics Checkup—2

Pronouns

Review sections 1.07-1.09 above. Then study each of the following statements. In the space provided, write the word that completes the statement correctly and the number of the Handbook principle illustrated. When you finish, compare your responses with those provided in the answer key on page 372. If your responses differ, carefully study again the principles in parentheses.

Example: The Benefits Committee will be submitting (its, their) report soon.   <u>**its**</u>   (1.09d)

1. I was expecting the manager to call. Was it (he, him) who left the message? _____
2. Every one of the members of the men's soccer team had to move (his car, their cars) before the game could begin. _____
3. A serious disagreement between management and (he, him) made him quit the job. _____
4. Does anyone in the office know for (who, whom) this stationery was ordered? _____
5. It looks as if (her's, hers) is the only report that has no grammatical errors. _____
6. Ms. Simmons asked my colleague and (I, me, myself) to help her complete the work. _____
7. My friend and (I, me, myself) were also asked to work on Saturday. _____
8. Both printers were sent for repairs, but (yours, your's) will be returned shortly. _____
9. Give the budget figures to (whoever, whomever) asked for them. _____
10. Everyone except the teacher and (I, me, myself) attended the party. _____
11. No one knows that problem better than (he, him, himself). _____
12. Information about profits was sent to (we, us) shareholders. _____
13. If anyone in the group has lost (their, her) ticket, she should see the tour director. _____
14. Neither the glamour nor the excitement of the position had lost (its, it's, their) appeal. _____
15. Any new subscriber may cancel (their, his or her) subscription within the first month. _____

Cumulative Editing Quiz 1

Use proofreading marks (see Appendix B) to correct errors in the following sentences. All errors must be corrected to receive credit for the sentence. Check with your instructor for the answers.

Example: Nicholas and ~~him~~ *he* made all ~~there~~ *their* money in the 1990's.

1. Just between you and I, who do you think would make the best manager?

2. Either Sari or me is responsible for correcting all errors in news bulletins.

3. Several attornies asked that there cases be postponed.

4. One of the secretarys warned Sharif and I to get the names of all students registered for the course.

5. The committee sent there decision to the president and I last week.

6. Who should Angela or me call to verify the three bills received today?

7. Several of we employees complained that it's keyboard made the new computer difficult to use.

8. All the CEO's agreed that the low interest rates of the early 2000's could not continue.

9. Every customer has a right to expect there inquirys to be treated courteously.

10. You may send you're contribution to Eric or myself or to whomever is listed as your representative.

Verbs (1.10-1.15)

Verbs show the action of a subject or join the subject to words that describe it.

1.10 Guidelines for Agreement with Subjects. One of the most troublesome areas in English is subject-verb agreement. Consider the following guidelines for making verbs agree with subjects.

a. A singular subject requires a singular verb:

    The stock market opens at 10 a.m. (The singular verb *opens* agrees with the singular subject *market*.)

    He doesn't (not *don't*) work on Saturday.

b. A plural subject requires a plural verb:

    Several items seem (not *seems*) to be missing.

c. A verb agrees with its subject regardless of prepositional phrases that may separate the subject from the verb:

    This list of management objectives is extensive. (The singular verb *is* agrees with the singular subject *list*.)

    Every one of the letters shows (not *show*) proper form.

d. A verb agrees with its subject regardless of separating phrases introduced by *as well as, in addition to, such as, including, together with,* and similar expressions:

    An important memo, together with several letters, was misplaced. (The singular verb *was* agrees with the singular subject *memo*.)

    The president as well as several other top-level executives approves of our proposal. (The singular verb *approves* agrees with the subject *president*.)

e. A verb agrees with its subject regardless of the location of the subject:

    Here is one of the letters about which you asked. (The verb *is* agrees with its subject *one*, even though it precedes *one*. The adverb *here* cannot function as a subject.)

    There are many problems yet to be resolved. (The verb *are* agrees with the subject *problems*. The adverb *there* cannot function as a subject.)

    In the next office are several printers. (In this inverted sentence the verb *are* must agree with the subject *printers*.)

f. Subjects joined by *and* require a plural verb:

    Analyzing the reader and organizing a strategy are the first steps in letter writing. (The plural verb *are* agrees with the two subjects, *analyzing* and *organizing*.)

    The tone and the wording of the letter were persuasive. (The plural verb *were* agrees with the two subjects, *tone* and *wording*.)

g. Subjects joined by *or* or *nor* may require singular or plural verbs. Make the verb agree with the closer subject:

    Neither the memos nor the report is ready. (The singular verb *is* agrees with *report*, the closer of the two subjects.)

h. The following indefinite pronouns are singular and require singular verbs: *anyone, anybody, anything, each, either, every, everyone, everybody, everything, many, neither, nobody, nothing, someone, somebody,* and *something:*

Either of the alternatives that you present is acceptable. (The verb *is* agrees with the singular subject *either.*)

i. Collective nouns may take singular or plural verbs, depending on whether the members of the group are operating as a unit or individually:

Our management team is united in its goal.

The faculty are sharply divided on the tuition issue. (Although acceptable, this sentence sounds better recast: *The faculty members are sharply divided on the tuition issue.*)

j. Organization names and titles of publications, although they may appear to be plural, are singular and require singular verbs:

Deme, Sokolov, and Horne, Inc., has (not *have*) hired a marketing consultant.

Thousands of Investment Tips is (not *are*) again on the bestseller list.

1.11 Voice. Voice is that property of verbs that shows whether the subject of the verb acts or is acted upon. Active-voice verbs direct action from the subject toward the object of the verb. Passive-voice verbs direct action toward the subject.

Active voice: Our employees write excellent letters.
Passive voice: Excellent letters are written by our employees.

Business writing that emphasizes active-voice verbs is generally preferred because it is specific and forceful. However, passive-voice constructions can help a writer be tactful. Strategies for effective use of active- and passive-voice verbs are presented in Chapter 3.

1.12 Mood. Three verb moods express the attitude or thought of the speaker or writer toward a subject: (1) the **indicative** mood expresses a fact; (2) the **imperative** mood expresses a command; and (3) the **subjunctive** mood expresses a doubt, a conjecture, or a suggestion.

Indicative: I am looking for a job.
Imperative: Begin your job search with the want ads.
Subjunctive: I wish I were working.

Only the subjunctive mood creates problems for most speakers and writers. The most common use of subjunctive mood occurs in clauses including *if* or *wish.* In such clauses substitute the subjunctive verb *were* for the indicative verb *was:*

If he were (not *was*) in my position, he would understand.

Mr. Dworski acts as if he were (not *was*) the boss.

I wish I were (not *was*) able to ship your order.

The subjunctive mood may be used to maintain goodwill while conveying negative information. The sentence *I wish I were able to ship your order* sounds more pleasing to a customer than *I cannot ship your order,* although, for all practical purposes, the two sentences convey the same negative message.

1.13 Tense. Verbs show the time of an action by their tense. Speakers and writers can use six tenses to show the time of sentence action; for example:

Present tense:	I work; he works.
Past tense:	I worked; she worked.
Future tense:	I will work; he will work.
Present perfect tense:	I have worked; he has worked.
Past perfect tense:	I had worked; she had worked.
Future perfect tense:	I will have worked; he will have worked.

1.14 Guidelines for Verb Tense

a. Use present tense for statements that, although they may be introduced by past-tense verbs, continue to be true:

What did you say his name is? (Use the present tense *is* if his name has not changed.)

b. Avoid unnecessary shifts in verb tenses:

The manager saw (not *sees*) a great deal of work yet to be completed and remained to do it herself.

Although unnecessary shifts in verb tense are to be avoided, not all the verbs within one sentence have to be in the same tense; for example:

She said (past tense) that she likes (present tense) to work late.

1.15 Irregular Verbs. Irregular verbs cause difficulty for some writers and speakers. Unlike regular verbs, irregular verbs do not form the past tense and past participle by adding *-ed* to the present form. Here is a partial list of selected troublesome irregular verbs. Consult a dictionary if you are in doubt about a verb form.

Troublesome Irregular Verbs

Present	Past	Past Participle *(always use helping verbs)*
begin	began	begun
break	broke	broken
choose	chose	chosen
come	came	come
drink	drank	drunk
go	went	gone
lay (to place)	laid	laid
lie (to rest)	lay	lain
ring	rang	rung
see	saw	seen
write	wrote	written

a. *Use only past-tense verbs to express past tense.* Notice that no helping verbs are used to indicate simple past tense:

The auditors went (not *have went*) over our books carefully.

He came (not *come*) to see us yesterday.

b. *Use past participle forms for actions completed before the present time.* Notice that past participle forms require helping verbs:

Steve had gone (not *went*) before we called. (The past participle *gone* is used with the helping verb *had*.)

c. *Avoid inconsistent shifts in subject, voice, and mood.* Pay particular attention to this problem area, for undesirable shifts are often characteristic of student writing.

Inconsistent:	When Mrs. Moscovitch read the report, the error was found. (The first clause is in the active voice; the second, passive.)
Improved:	When Mrs. Moscovitch read the report, she found the error. (Both clauses are in the active voice.)
Inconsistent:	The clerk should first conduct an inventory. Then supplies should be reordered. (The first sentence is in the active voice; the second, passive.)
Improved:	The clerk should first conduct an inventory. Then he or she should order supplies. (Both sentences are in the active voice.)
Inconsistent:	All workers must wear security badges, and you must also sign a daily time card. (This sentence contains an inconsistent shift in subject from all workers in first clause to you in second clause.)
Improved:	All workers must wear security badges, and they must also sign a daily time card.
Inconsistent:	Begin the transaction by opening an account; then you enter the customer's name. (This sentence contains an inconsistent shift from the imperative mood in first clause to the indicative mood in second clause.)
Improved:	Begin the transaction by opening an account; then enter the customer's name. (Both clauses are now in the indicative mood.)

Review Exercise C—Verbs

In the space provided for each item, write *a* or *b* to complete the statement accurately. When you finish, compare your responses with those provided. For each item on which you need review, consult the numbered principle shown in parentheses.

1. A list of payroll deductions for our employees (a) was, (b) were sent to the personnel manager. _____
2. There (a) is, (b) are a customer service engineer and two salespeople waiting to see you. _____
3. Increased computer use and more complex automated systems (a) is, (b) are found in business today. _____
4. Crews, Meliotes, and Bauve, Inc., (a) has, (b) have opened an office in Montreal. _____
5. Yesterday Mrs. Phillips (a) choose, (b) chose a new office on the second floor. _____
6. The man who called said that his name (a) is, (b) was Johnson. _____
7. The journal Office Computing and Networks (a) is, (b) are beginning a campaign to increase readership. _____
8. Either of the flight times (a) appears, (b) appear to fit my proposed itinerary. _____
9. If you had (a) saw, (b) seen the rough draft, you would better appreciate the final copy. _____
10. Across from our office (a) is, (b) are the parking structure and the information office. _____

11. Although we have (a) began, (b) begun to replace outmoded equipment, the pace is slow.
12. Specific training as well as lots of experience (a) is, (b) are important for that position.
13. Inflation and increased job opportunities (a) is, (b) are resulting in increased numbers of working women.
14. Neither the organizing nor the staffing of the program (a) has been, (b) have been completed.
15. If I (a) was, (b) were you, I would ask for a raise.
16. If you had (a) wrote, (b) written last week, we could have sent a brochure.
17. The equipment that you ordered (a) is, (b) are packed and will be shipped Friday.
18. One of the reasons that sales have declined in recent years (a) is, (b) are lack of effective advertising.
19. Either of the proposed laws (a) is, (b) are going to affect our business negatively.
20. Bankruptcy statutes (a) requires, (b) require that a failed company pay its debts to secured creditors first.

1. a (1.10c) 3. b (1.10f) 5. b (1.15a) 7. a (1.10j) 9. b (1.15b) 11. b (1.15b) 13. b (1.10f) 15. b (1.12) 17. a (1.10a) 19. a (1.10h)

Review Exercise D—Verbs

In the following sentence pairs, choose the one that illustrates consistency in use of subject, voice, and mood. Write *a* or *b* in the space provided. When you finish, compare your responses with those provided. For each item on which you need review, consult the numbered principle shown in parentheses.

1. (a) You need more than a knowledge of equipment; one also must be able to interact well with people.
   (b) You need more than a knowledge of equipment; you also must be able to interact well with people.
2. (a) Maurice and Jon were eager to continue, but Bob wanted to quit.
   (b) Maurice and Jon were eager to continue, but Bob wants to quit.
3. (a) The salesperson should consult the price list; then you can give an accurate quote to a customer.
   (b) The salesperson should consult the price list; then he or she can give an accurate quote to a customer.
4. (a) Read all the instructions first; then you install the printer program.
   (b) Read all the instructions first, and then install the printer program.
5. (a) She was an enthusiastic manager who always had a smile for everyone.
   (b) She was an enthusiastic manager who always has a smile for everyone.

1. b (1.15c) 3. b (1.15c) 5. a (1.14b)

Grammar/Mechanics Checkup—3

Verbs

Review sections 1.10–1.15 above. Then study each of the following statements. Underline any verbs that are used incorrectly. In the space provided, write the correct form (or *C* if correct) and the number of the Handbook principle illustrated.

When you finish, compare your responses with those provided in the answer key on page 372. If your responses differ, carefully study again the principles in parentheses.

Example: Our inventory of raw materials <u>were</u> presented as collateral for a short-   **was**   **(1.10c)**
term loan.

1. Located across town is a research institute and our product-testing facility.   _____
2. Can you tell me whether a current list with all customers' names and   _____
addresses have been sent to marketing?
3. The credit union, along with 20 other large national banks, offer a variety of   _____
savings plans.
4. Neither the plans that this bank offers nor the service by the tellers are   _____
impressive.
5. Locating a bank and selecting a savings/chequing plan often require consid-   _____
erable research and study.
6. The budget analyst wants to know whether the Equipment Committee are   _____
ready to recommend a printer.
7. Either of the printers that the committee selects is acceptable to the budget   _____
analyst.
8. If Mr. Tutchone had chose the Maximizer Plus savings plan, his money   _____
would have earned maximum interest.
9. Although the applications have laid there for two weeks, they may still be   _____
submitted.
10. Nadia acts as if she was the manager.   _____
11. One of the reasons that our Nunavut sales branches have been so costly are   _____
the high cost of living.

In the space provided, write the letter of the sentence that illustrates consistency in subject, voice, and mood.
12. (a) If you will read the instructions, the answer can be found.   _____
    (b) If you will read the instructions, you will find the answer.
13. (a) All employees must fill out application forms; only then will you be   _____
insured.
    (b) All employees must fill out application forms; only then will they be
insured.
14. (a) First, take an inventory of equipment; then, order supplies.   _____
    (b) First, take an inventory of equipment; then, supplies must be ordered.
15. (a) Select a savings plan that suits your needs; deposits may be made   _____
immediately.
    (b) Select a savings plan that suits your needs; begin making deposits
immediately.

Cumulative Editing Quiz 2

Use proofreading marks (see Appendix B) to correct errors in the following sentences. All errors must be corrected to receive credit for the sentence. Check with your instructor for the answers.

1. My partner and myself must investigate all deposits to that account.

2. If I was you, I would ask whomever is in charge for their opinion.

3. The faculty agree that it's first concern is educating students.

4. The book and it's cover was printed in Japan.

5. Waiting to see you is a sales representative and a job applicant.

6. Every employee could have picked up his ballot if he had went to the cafeteria.

7. Your choice of mutual funds are reduced by this plan and it's restrictions.

8. My uncle and her come to visit my parents and myself last night.

9. According to both editor in chiefs, the tone and wording of all our letters needs revision.

10. The Davis'es said they were unconcerned with the up's and down's of the stock market.

Adjectives and Adverbs (1.16-1.17)

Adjectives describe or limit nouns and pronouns. They often answer the questions what kind? how many? or which one? Adverbs describe or limit verbs, adjectives, or other adverbs. They often answer the questions when? how? where? or to what extent?

1.16 Forms. Most adjectives and adverbs have three forms, or degrees: **positive, comparative,** and **superlative.**

	Positive	**Comparative**	**Superlative**
Adjective:	clear	clearer	clearest
Adverb:	clearly	more clearly	most clearly

Some adjectives and adverbs have irregular forms:

	Positive	**Comparative**	**Superlative**
Adjective:	good	better	best
	bad	worse	worst
Adverb:	well	better	best

Adjectives and adverbs composed of two or more syllables are usually compared by the use of *more* and *most*; for example:

The Payroll Department is more efficient than the Shipping Department.

Payroll is the most efficient department in our organization.

1.17 Guidelines for Use

a. Use the comparative degree of the adjective or adverb to compare two persons or things; use the superlative degree to compare three or more:

Of the two letters, which is better (not *best*)?

Of all the plans, we like this one best (not *better*).

b. Do not create a double comparative or superlative by using *-er* with *more* or *-est* with *most*:

His explanation couldn't have been clearer (not *more clearer*).

c. A linking verb (*is, are, look, seem, feel, sound, appear,* and so forth) may introduce a word that describes the verb's subject. In this case be certain to use an adjective, not an adverb:

The characters on the monitor look bright (not *brightly*). (Use the adjective *bright* because it follows the linking verb *look* and modifies the noun *characters*. It answers the question *What kind of characters?*)

Grammar/Mechanics Handbook

The company's letter made the customer feel bad (not *badly*). (The adjective *bad* follows the linking verb *feel* and describes the noun *customer*.)

d. Use adverbs, not adjectives, to describe or limit the action of verbs:

The business is running smoothly (not *smooth*). (Use the adverb *smoothly* to describe the action of the verb *is running*. *Smoothly* tells how the business is running.)

Don't take his remark personally (not *personal*). (The adverb *personally* describes the action of the verb take.)

e. Two or more adjectives that are joined to create a compound modifier before a noun should be hyphenated:

The four-year-old child was tired.

Our agency is planning a coast-to-coast campaign.

Hyphenate a compound modifier following a noun only if your dictionary shows the hyphen(s):

Our speaker is very well-known. (Include the hyphen because most dictionaries do.)

The tired child was four years old. (Omit the hyphens because the expression follows the word it describes, *child*, and because dictionaries do not indicate hyphens.)

f. Keep adjectives and adverbs close to the words that they modify:

She asked for a cup of hot coffee (not a *hot cup of coffee*).

Patty had only two days of vacation left (not *Patty only had two days*).

Students may sit in the first five rows (not *in the five first rows*).

He has saved almost enough money for the trip (not *He has almost saved*).

g. Don't confuse the adverb *there* with the possessive pronoun *their* or the contraction *they're*:

Put the documents there. (The adverb *there* means "at that place or at that point.")

There are two reasons for the change. (*There* is used as filler preceding a linking verb.)

We already have their specifications. (The possessive pronoun *their* shows ownership.)

They're coming to inspect today. (The contraction *they're* is a shortened form of *they are*.)

Review Exercise E—Adjectives and Adverbs

In the space provided for each item, write *a*, *b*, or *c* to complete the statement accurately. If two sentences are shown, select (a) or (b) to indicate the one expressed more effectively. When you finish, compare your responses with those provided. For each item on which you need review, consult the numbered principle shown in parentheses.

1. After the interview, Kyoko looked (a) calm, (b) calmly. _____
2. If you had been more (a) careful, (b) carefuler, the box might not have broken. _____
3. Because a new manager was hired, the advertising campaign is running very (a) smooth, (b) smoothly. _____

4. To avoid a (a) face to face, (b) face-to-face argument, she wrote a letter.
5. Bayani completed the employment test (a) satisfactorily, (b) satisfactory.
6. I felt (a) bad, (b) badly that he was not promoted.
7. Which is the (a) more, (b) most dependable of the two models?
8. Can you determine exactly what (a) there, (b) their, (c) they're company wants us to do?
9. Of all the copiers we tested, this one is the (a) easier, (b) easiest to operate.
10. (a) Mr. Aldron almost was ready to accept the offer.
    (b) Mr. Aldron was almost ready to accept the offer.
11. (a) We only thought that it would take two hours for the test.
    (b) We thought that it would take only two hours for the test.
12. (a) Please bring me a glass of cold water.
    (b) Please bring me a cold glass of water.
13. (a) The committee decided to retain the last ten tickets.
    (b) The committee decided to retain the ten last tickets.
14. New owners will receive a (a) 60-day, (b) 60 day trial period.
15. The time passed (a) quicker, (b) more quickly than we expected.
16. We offer a (a) money back, (b) money-back guarantee.
17. Today the financial news is (a) worse, (b) worst than yesterday.
18. Please don't take his comments (a) personal, (b) personally.
19. You must check the document (a) page by page, (b) page-by-page.
20. (a) We try to file only necessary paperwork.
    (b) We only try to file necessary paperwork.

---

1. a (1.17c) 3. b (1.17d) 5. a (1.17d) 7. a (1.17a) 9. b (1.17a) 11. b (1.17f) 13. a (1.17f) 15. b (1.17d) 17. a (1.17a) 19. a (1.17e)

Grammar/Mechanics Checkup—4

Adjectives and Adverbs

Review sections 1.16 and 1.17 above. Then study each of the following statements. Underline any inappropriate forms. In the space provided, write the correct form (or C if correct) and the number of the Handbook principle illustrated. You may need to consult your dictionary for current practice regarding some compound adjectives. When you finish, compare your responses with those provided in the answer key on page 372. If your answers differ, carefully study again the principles in parentheses.

**live-and-let-live
(1.17e)**

Example: He was one of those individuals with a live and let live attitude.

1. Most of our long time customers have credit card accounts.
2. Many subscribers considered the $50 per year charge to be fair.
3. Other subscribers complained that $50 per year was too much.
4. The Internet supplied the answer so quick that we were all amazed.
5. He only had $5 in his pocket.
6. Some experts predict that double digit inflation may return.
7. Jeremy found a once in a lifetime opportunity.
8. Although the car was four years old, it was in good condition.
9. Of the two colours, which is best for a website background?
10. Professor Candace Carbone is well known in her field.
11. Channel 12 presents up to the minute news broadcasts.
12. Lower tax brackets would lessen the after tax yield of some bonds.

13. The conclusion drawn from the statistics couldn't have been more clearer. _____
14. You have a fifty fifty chance of winning the coin toss. _____
15. If you feel badly about the business deal, contact your manager. _____

Prepositions (1.18)

Prepositions are connecting words that join nouns or pronouns to other words in a sentence. The words *about, at, from, in,* and *to* are examples of prepositions.

1.18 Guidelines for Use

a. Include necessary prepositions:

What type of software do you need? (Not *What type software.*)

I graduated from high school two years ago. (Not *I graduated high school.*)

b. Omit unnecessary prepositions:

Where is the meeting? (Not *Where is the meeting at?*)

Both printers work well. (Not *Both of the printers.*)

Where are you going? (Not *Where are you going to?*)

c. Avoid the overuse of prepositional phrases:

Weak: We have received your application for credit at our branch in the Halifax area.
Improved: We have received your credit application at our Halifax branch.

d. Repeat the preposition before the second of two related elements:

Applicants use the résumé effectively by summarizing their most important experiences and by relating their education to the jobs sought.

e. Include the second preposition when two prepositions modify a single object:

George's appreciation of and aptitude for computers led to a promising career.

Conjunctions (1.19)

Conjunctions connect words, phrases, and clauses. They act as signals, indicating when a thought is being added, contrasted, or altered. Coordinate conjunctions (such as *and, or, but*) and other words that act as connectors (such as *however, therefore, when, as*) tell the reader or listener in what direction a thought is heading. They're like road signs signalling what's ahead.

1.19 Guidelines for Use

a. Use coordinating conjunctions to connect only sentence elements that are parallel or balanced.

Weak: His report was correct and written in a concise manner.
Improved: His report was correct and concise.

Weak: Management has the capacity to increase funds, or reduction can be achieved through various policies.
Improved: Management has the capacity to increase or reduce funds through various policies.

b. Do not use the word *like* as a conjunction:

It seems as if (not *like*) this day will never end.

c. Avoid using *when* or *where* inappropriately. A common writing fault occurs in sentences with clauses introduced by *is when* and *is where*. Written English ordinarily requires a noun (or a group of words functioning as a noun) following the linking verb *is*. Instead of acting as conjunctions in these constructions, the words *where* and *when* function as adverbs, creating faulty grammatical equations (adverbs cannot complete equations set up by linking verbs). To avoid the problem, revise the sentence, eliminating *is when* or *is where*.

Weak: A bullish market is when prices are rising in the stock market.
Improved: A bullish market is created when prices are rising in the stock market.

Weak: A flowchart is when you make a diagram showing the step-by-step progression of a procedure.
Improved: A flowchart is a diagram showing the step-by-step progression of a procedure.

Weak: Word processing is where you use a computer and software to write.
Improved: Word processing involves the use of a computer and software to write.

A similar faulty construction occurs in the expression *I hate when*. English requires nouns, noun clauses, or pronouns to act as objects of verbs, not adverbs.

Weak: I hate when we're asked to work overtime.
Improved: I hate it when we're asked to work overtime.
Improved: I hate being asked to work overtime.

d. Don't confuse the adverb *then* with the conjunction *than*. *Then* means "at that time"; *than* indicates the second element in a comparison:

We would rather remodel than (not *then*) move.

First, the equipment is turned on; then (not *than*) the program is loaded.

Review Exercise F—Prepositions and Conjunctions

In the space provided for each item, write *a* or *b* to indicate the sentence that is expressed more effectively. When you finish, compare your responses with those provided. For each item on which you need review, consult the numbered principle shown in parentheses.

1. (a) Do you know where this shipment is being sent?
   (b) Do you know where this shipment is being sent to?
2. (a) She was not aware of nor interested in the company insurance plan.
   (b) She was not aware nor interested in the company insurance plan.
3. (a) Mr. Samuels graduated college last June.
   (b) Mr. Samuels graduated from college last June.
4. (a) "Flextime" is when employees arrive and depart at varying times.
   (b) "Flextime" is a method of scheduling work in which employees arrive and depart at varying times.
5. (a) Both employees enjoyed setting their own hours.
   (b) Both of the employees enjoyed setting their own hours.
6. (a) I hate when the tape sticks in my VCR.
   (b) I hate it when the tape sticks in my VCR.
7. (a) What style of typeface should we use?
   (b) What style typeface should we use?
8. (a) Business letters should be concise, correct, and written clearly.
   (b) Business letters should be concise, correct, and clear.

Grammar/Mechanics Handbook

9. (a) Mediation in a labour dispute occurs when a neutral person helps union and management reach an agreement.
   (b) Mediation in a labour dispute is where a neutral person helps union and management reach an agreement. _____

10. (a) It looks as if the plant will open in early January.
    (b) It looks like the plant will open in early January. _____

11. (a) We expect to finish up the work soon.
    (b) We expect to finish the work soon. _____

12. (a) At the beginning of the program in the fall of the year at the central office, we experienced staffing difficulties. _____
    (b) When the program began last fall, the central office experienced staffing difficulties.

13. (a) Your client may respond by letter or a telephone call may be made. _____
    (b) Your client may respond by letter or by telephone.

14. (a) A résumé is when you make a written presentation of your education and experience for a prospective employer. _____
    (b) A résumé is a written presentation of your education and experience for a prospective employer.

15. (a) Stacy exhibited both an awareness of and talent for developing innovations. _____
    (b) Stacy exhibited both an awareness and talent for developing innovations.

16. (a) This course is harder then I expected.
    (b) This course is harder than I expected. _____

17. (a) An ombudsman is an individual hired by management to investigate and resolve employee complaints. _____
    (b) An ombudsman is when management hires an individual to investigate and resolve employee complaints.

18. (a) I'm uncertain where to take this document to.
    (b) I'm uncertain where to take this document. _____

19. (a) By including accurate data and by writing clearly, you will produce effective memos. _____
    (b) By including accurate data and writing clearly, you will produce effective memos.

20. (a) We need computer operators who can load software, monitor networks, and files must be duplicated. _____
    (b) We need computer operators who can load software, monitor networks, and duplicate files.

1. a (1.18b) 3. b (1.18a) 5. a (1.18b) 7. a (1.18a) 9. a (1.19c) 11. b (1.18b) 13. b (1.19a) 15. a (1.18e) 17. a (1.19c) 19. a (1.18d)

Grammar/Mechanics Checkup—5

Prepositions and Conjunctions

Review sections 1.18 and 1.19 above. Then study each of the following statements. Write *a* or *b* to indicate the sentence in which the idea is expressed more effectively. Also record the number of the Handbook principle illustrated. When you finish, compare your responses with those provided in the answer key on page 372. If your answers differ, carefully study again the principles shown in parentheses.

Example: (a) Raoul will graduate college this spring.   **b** _____ (1.18a)
             (b) Raoul will graduate from college this spring.

1. (a) DataTech enjoyed greater profits this year then it expected.
   (b) DataTech enjoyed greater profits this year than it expected.
2. (a) I hate it when we have to work overtime.
   (b) I hate when we have to work overtime.
3. (a) Dr. Simon has a great interest and appreciation for the study of robotics.
   (b) Dr. Simon has a great interest in and appreciation for the study of robotics.
4. (a) Gross profit is where you calculate the difference between total sales and the cost of goods sold.
   (b) Gross profit is the difference between total sales and the cost of goods sold.
5. (a) We advertise to increase the frequency of product use, to introduce complementary products, and to enhance our corporate image.
   (b) We advertise to have our products used more often, when we have complementary products to introduce, and we are interested in making our corporation look better to the public.
6. (a) What type printer do you prefer?
   (b) What type of printer do you prefer?
7. (a) Where are you going to?
   (b) Where are you going?
8. (a) The sale of our Halifax office last year should improve this year's profits.
   (b) The sale of our office in Halifax during last year should improve the profits for this year.
9. (a) Do you know where the meeting is at?
   (b) Do you know where the meeting is?
10. (a) The cooling-off rule is a provincial government rule that protects consumers from making unwise purchases at home.
    (b) The cooling-off rule is where the provincial government has made a rule that protects consumers from making unwise purchases at home.
11. (a) Meetings can be more meaningful if the agenda is stuck to, the time frame is followed, and if someone keeps follow-up notes.
    (b) Meetings can be more meaningful if you stick to the agenda, follow the time frame, and keep follow-up notes.
12. (a) They printed the newsletter on yellow paper like we asked them to do.
    (b) They printed the newsletter on yellow paper as we asked them to do.
13. (a) A code of ethics is a set of rules indicating appropriate standards of behaviour.
    (b) A code of ethics is where a set of rules indicates appropriate standards of behaviour.
14. (a) We need an individual with an understanding and serious interest in black-and-white photography.
    (b) We need an individual with an understanding of and serious interest in black-and-white photography.
15. (a) The most dangerous situation is when employees ignore the safety rules.
    (b) The most dangerous situation occurs when employees ignore the safety rules.

Cumulative Editing Quiz 3

Use proofreading marks (see Appendix B) to correct errors in the following sentences. All errors must be corrected to receive credit for the sentence. Check with your instructor for the answers.

1. If Treena types faster then her, shouldn't Treena be hired?

2. We felt badly that Mark's home was not chose for the tour.

3. Neither the company nor the workers is pleased at how slow the talks seems to be progressing.

4. Just between you and I, it's better not to take his remarks personally.

5. After completing there floor by floor inventory, managers will deliver there reports to Mr. Quinn and I.

6. If the telephone was working, Jean and myself could have completed our calls.

7. Powerful software and new hardware allows us to send the newsletter to whomever is currently listed in our database.

8. The thirteen year old girl and her mother was shopping for a graduation dress yesterday.

9. We begun the work two years ago, but personnel and equipment has been especially difficult to obtain.

10. Today's weather is worst then yesterday's.

Punctuation Review

Commas 1 (2.01–2.04)

2.01 Series. Commas are used to separate three or more equal elements (words, phrases, or short clauses) in a series. To ensure separation of the last two elements, careful writers always use a comma before the conjunction in a series:

> Business letters usually contain a dateline, address, salutation, body, and closing. (This series contains words.)

> The job of an ombudsman is to examine employee complaints, resolve disagreements between management and employees, and ensure fair treatment. (This series contains phrases).

> Trainees complete basic keyboarding tasks, technicians revise complex documents, and editors proofread completed projects. (This series contains short clauses.)

2.02 Direct Address. Commas are used to set off the names of individuals being addressed:

> Your inquiry, Mrs. Johnson, has been referred to me.

> We genuinely hope that we may serve you, Mr. Lee.

2.03 Parenthetical Expressions. Skilled writers use parenthetical words, phrases, and clauses to guide the reader from one thought to the next. When these expressions interrupt the flow of a sentence and are unnecessary for its grammatical completeness, they should be set off with commas. Examples of commonly used parenthetical expressions follow:

all things considered	however	needless to say
as a matter of fact	in addition	nevertheless
as a result	incidentally	no doubt
as a rule	in fact	of course
at the same time	in my opinion	on the contrary
consequently	in the first place	on the other hand
for example	in the meantime	therefore
furthermore	moreover	under the circumstances

Punctuation Review

As a matter of fact, I wrote to you just yesterday. (Phrase used at the beginning of a sentence.)

We will, in the meantime, send you a replacement order. (Phrase used in the middle of a sentence.)

Your satisfaction is our first concern, needless to say. (Phrase used at the end of a sentence.)

Do not use commas if the expression is necessary for the completeness of the sentence:

Tamara had no doubt that she would finish the report. (Omit commas because the expression is necessary for the completeness of the sentence.)

2.04 Dates, Addresses, and Geographical Items. When dates, addresses, and geographical items contain more than one element, the second and succeeding elements are normally set off by commas.

a. Dates:

The conference was held February 6 at our home office. (No comma is needed for one element.)

The conference was held February 6, 2009, at our home office. (Two commas set off the second element.)

The conference was held Tuesday, February 6, 2009, at our home office. (Commas set off the second and third elements.)

In February 2001 the conference was held. (This alternate style omitting commas is acceptable if only the month and year are written.)

b. Addresses:

The letter addressed to Mr. Jim W. Ellman, 600 Novella St., Red Deer, AB T0B 2P3, should be sent today. (Commas are used between all elements except the province and postal code, which in this special instance are considered a single unit.)

c. Geographical items:

She moved from Windsor, Ontario, to Truro, Nova Scotia. (Commas set off the province—unless it appears at the end of the sentence, in which case only one comma is used.)

In separating cities from provinces or territories and days from years, many writers remember the initial comma but forget the final one, as in the examples that follow:

The package from Edmonton, Alberta{,} was lost.

We opened June 1, 1995{,} and have grown steadily since.

Review Exercise G—Commas 1

Insert necessary commas in the following sentences. In the space provided, write the number of commas that you add. Write *C* if no commas are needed. When you finish, compare your responses with those provided. For each item on which you need review, consult the numbered principle shown in parentheses.

1. As a rule we do not provide complimentary tickets.
2. You may be certain Mr. Kirchoff that your policy will be issued immediately.
3. I have no doubt that your calculations are correct.

4. The safety hazard on the contrary can be greatly reduced if workers wear rubber gloves. _____

5. Every official TV newscaster radio broadcaster and newspaper reporter had access to the media room. _____

6. Deltech's main offices are located in Vancouver British Columbia and Regina Saskatchewan. _____

7. The employees who are eligible for promotions are Terry Evelyn Maneesh Rosanna and Yves. _____

8. During the warranty period of course you are protected from any parts or service charges. _____

9. Many of our customers include architects engineers lawyers and others who are interested in database management programs. _____

10. I wonder Ms. Stevens if you would send my letter of recommendation as soon as possible. _____

11. The new book explains how to choose appropriate legal protection for ideas trade secrets copyrights patents and restrictive agreements. _____

12. The factory is scheduled to be moved to 2250 North Main Street Belleville Ontario L4A 1T2 within two years. _____

13. You may however prefer to correspond directly with the manufacturer in Hong Kong. _____

14. Are there any alternatives in addition to those that we have already considered? _____

15. The rally has been scheduled for Monday January 14 in the football stadium. _____

16. A cheque for the full amount will be sent directly to your home Mr. Ivanic. _____

17. Goodstone Tire & Rubber for example recalled 400,000 steel-belted radial tires because some tires failed their rigorous tests. _____

18. Alex agreed to unlock the office open the mail and check all the equipment in my absence. _____

19. In the meantime thank you for whatever assistance you are able to furnish. _____

20. Research facilities were moved from Montreal Quebec to Fredericton New Brunswick. _____

---

1. rule, (2.03) 3. C (2.03) 5. newscaster, radio broadcaster, (2.01) 7. Terry, Evelyn, Maneesh, Rosanna, (2.01) 9. architects, engineers, lawyers, (2.01) 11. ideas, trade secrets, copyrights, patents, (2.01) 13. may, however, (2.03) 15. Monday, January 14, (2.04a) 17. Rubber, for example, (2.03) 19. meantime, (2.03)

Grammar/Mechanics Checkup—6

Commas 1

Review sections 2.01–2.04 above. Then study each of the following statements and insert necessary commas. In the space provided, write the number of commas that you add; write *0* if no commas are needed. Also record the number of the Handbook principle illustrated. When you finish, compare your responses with those in the answer key on page 372. If your answers differ, carefully study again the principles shown in parentheses.

Example: In this class students learn to write clear and concise business letters⋀ memos⋀ and reports.   <u>2</u>   (2.01)

1. We do not as a rule allow employees to take time off for dental appointments. _____
2. You may be sure Ms. Schwartz that your car will be ready by 4 p.m. _____
3. Anyone who is reliable hard-working and honest should be very successful. _____

_____ 4. A conference on sales motivation is scheduled for May 5 at the Plainsview Hotel beginning at 2 p.m.

_____ 5. As a matter of fact I just called your office this morning.

_____ 6. We are relocating our distribution centre from Calgary Alberta to Sherbrooke Quebec.

_____ 7. In the meantime please continue to send your orders to the regional office.

_____ 8. The last meeting recorded in the minutes was on February 4 2001 in Windsor.

_____ 9. Ms. Horne Mr. Hae Mrs. Andorra and Mr. Baker are our new representatives.

_____ 10. The package mailed to Ms. Leslie Holmes 3430 Larkspur Lane Regina Saskatchewan S5L 2E2 arrived three weeks after it was mailed.

_____ 11. The manager feels needless to say that the support of all employees is critical.

_____ 12. Eric was assigned three jobs: checking supplies replacing inventories and distributing delivered goods.

_____ 13. We will work diligently to retain your business Mr. Fuhai.

_____ 14. The vice-president feels however that all sales representatives need training.

_____ 15. The name selected for a product should be right for that product and should stress its major attributes.

Commas 2 (2.05–2.09)

2.05 Independent Clauses. An independent clause is a group of words that has a subject and a verb and that could stand as a complete sentence. When two such clauses are joined by *and, or, nor,* or *but,* use a comma before the conjunction:

> We can ship your merchandise July 12, but we must have your payment first.

> Net income before taxes is calculated, and this total is then combined with income from operations.

Notice that each independent clause in the preceding two examples could stand alone as a complete sentence. Do not use a comma unless each group of words is a complete thought (that is, has its own subject and verb).

> Net income before taxes is calculated and is then combined with income from operations. (No comma is needed because no subject follows *and*.)

2.06 Dependent Clauses. Dependent clauses do not make sense by themselves; for their meaning they depend on independent clauses.

a. *Introductory clauses.* When a dependent clause comes before an independent clause, it is followed by a comma. Such clauses are often introduced by *when, if,* and *as:*

> When your request came, we responded immediately.

> As I mentioned earlier, Sandra James is the manager.

b. *Terminal clauses.* If a dependent clause falls at the end of a sentence, use a comma only if the dependent clause is an afterthought:

> The meeting has been rescheduled for October 23, if this date meets with your approval. (Comma used because dependent clause is an afterthought.)

> We responded immediately when we received your request. (No comma is needed.)

c. *Essential versus nonessential clauses.* If a dependent clause provides information that is unneeded for the grammatical completeness of a sentence, use

Grammar/Mechanics Handbook

commas to set it off. In determining whether such a clause is essential or nonessential, ask yourself whether the reader needs the information contained in the clause to identify the word it explains:

Our district sales manager, who just returned from France, prepared this report. (This construction assumes that there is only one district sales manager. Since the sales manager is clearly identified, the dependent clause is not essential and requires commas.)

The salesperson who just returned from France prepared this report. (The dependent clause in this sentence is necessary to identify which salesperson prepared the report. Therefore, use no commas.)

The position of assistant sales manager, which we discussed with you last week, is still open. (Careful writers use *which* to introduce nonessential clauses. Commas are also necessary.)

The position that we discussed with you last week is still open. (Careful writers use *that* to introduce essential clauses. No commas are used.)

2.07 Phrases. A phrase is a group of related words that lacks both a subject and a verb. When a phrase precedes a main clause, many writers place a comma after the phrase *only if* the phrase contains a verb form or has five or more words:

Beginning November 1, Royal Bank will offer two new combination chequing/savings plans. (A comma follows this introductory phrase because the phrase contains the verb form *Beginning*.)

To promote their plan, we will conduct an extensive direct mail advertising campaign. (A comma follows this introductory phrase because the phrase contains the verb form *To promote*.)

In a period of only one year, we were able to improve our market share by 30 percent. (A comma follows the introductory phrase—actually two prepositional phrases—because its total length exceeds five words.)

In 1999 our organization installed a multi-user system that could transfer programs easily. (No comma needed after the short introductory phrase.)

2.08 Two or More Adjectives. Use a comma to separate two or more adjectives that equally describe a noun. A good way to test the need for a comma is this: mentally insert the word *and* between the adjectives. If the resulting phrase sounds natural, a comma is used to show the omission of *and*:

We're looking for a flexible, bug-free operating system. (Use a comma to separate *versatile* and *bug-free* because they independently describe *operating system*. *And* has been omitted.)

Our experienced, courteous staff is ready to serve you. (Use a comma to separate *experienced* and *courteous* because they independently describe *staff*. *And* has been omitted.)

It was difficult to refuse the sincere young telephone caller. (No commas are needed between *sincere* and *young* because *and* has not been omitted.)

2.09 Appositives. Words that re-name or explain preceding nouns or pronouns are called appositives. An appositive that provides information not essential to the identification of the word it describes should be set off by commas:

Rozmin Kamani, the project director for Sperling's, worked with our architect. (The appositive, *the project director for Sperling's*, adds nonessential information. Commas set it off.)

Review Exercise H—Commas 2

Insert only necessary commas in the following sentences. In the space provided, indicate the number of commas that you add for each sentence. If a sentence requires no commas, write C. When you finish, compare your responses with those provided. For each item on which you need review, consult the numbered principle shown in parentheses.

_____C_____ 1. A corporation must be registered in the province in which it does business and it must operate within the laws of that province.

_____C_____ 2. The manager made a point-by-point explanation of the distribution dilemma and then presented his plan to solve the problem.

_____1_____ 3. If you will study the cost analysis, you will see that our company offers the best system at the lowest price.

_____C_____ 4. Molly Epperson who collected the greatest number of sales points was awarded the bonus trip to Hawaii.

_____C_____ 5. The salesperson who collects the greatest number of sales points will be awarded the bonus trip to Hawaii.

_____1_____ 6. To promote goodwill and to generate international trade, we are opening offices in Southeast Asia and in Europe.

_____1_____ 7. On the basis of these findings, I recommend that we retain Raine Jada as our counsel.

_____C_____ 8. Mary Lam is a dedicated hard-working employee for our company.

_____C_____ 9. The bright young student who worked for us last summer will be able to return this summer.

_____1_____ 10. When you return the completed form, we will be able to process your application.

_____C_____ 11. We will be able to process your application when you return the completed form.

_____C_____ 12. The employees who have been with us over ten years automatically receive additional insurance benefits.

_____1_____ 13. Knowing that you wanted this merchandise immediately, I sent it by Express Parcel Services.

_____C_____ 14. The business office has no air conditioning and is very warm in the summer.

_____C_____ 15. International competition nearly ruined the Canadian shoe industry but the textile industry remains strong.

_____2_____ 16. Joyce D'Agostino, our newly promoted office manager, has made a number of good suggestions.

_____1_____ 17. For the benefit of employees recently hired, we are offering a two-hour seminar about employee benefit programs.

_____C_____ 18. Please bring your suggestions and those of Mr. Maisonneuve when you attend our meeting next month.

_____C_____ 19. The meeting has been rescheduled for September 30 if this date meets with your approval.

_____C_____ 20. Some of the problems that you outline in your recent memo could be fixed through more strict purchasing procedures.

---

1. business, (2.05) 3. analysis, (2.06a) 5. C (2.06c) 7. findings, (2.07) 9. C (2.08) 11. C (2.06b) 13. immediately, (2.07) 15. industry, (2.05) 17. hired, (2.07) 19. September 30, (2.06b)

Commas 2

Review sections 2.05–2.09 above. Then study each of the following statements and insert necessary commas. In the space provided write the number of commas that you add; write *0* if no commas are needed. Also record the number of the Handbook principle(s) illustrated. When you finish, compare your responses with those provided in the answer key on page 372. If your answers differ, carefully study again the principles shown in parentheses.

Example: When businesses encounter financial problems, they often lay off employees.   1   2.06a

1. As stated in the warranty, this printer is guaranteed for one year.   1
2. Today's profits come from products on the market and tomorrow's profits come from products still in production.   c
3. Companies introduce new products in one part of the country and then watch how the product sells in that area.   c
4. One large automobile manufacturer which must remain nameless wants all customers to receive a free gift when they purchase a car.   c
5. The imaginative talented agency opened its offices April 22 in Cambridge.
6. The sales associate who earns the highest number of recognition points this year will be honoured with a bonus vacation trip.
7. Ian Sims our sales manager in the North Bay area will present the new sales campaign at the June meeting.
8. Our new product has many qualities that appeal to buyers but it also has one significant weakness.
9. Although they have different technical characteristics and vary considerably in price and quality two or more of a firm's products may be seen by shoppers as almost the same.
10. To motivate future buyers we are offering a cash refund of $25.

Review of Commas 1 and 2

11. When you receive the application please fill it out and return it before Monday January 3.
12. On the other hand we are very interested in hiring hard-working reliable individuals.
13. In March we expect to open a new branch in Bragg Creek which is an area of large growth.
14. As we discussed on the telephone the ceremony is scheduled for Thursday June 9 at 3 p.m.
15. Dr. Adams teaches the morning classes and Ms. Miori is responsible for evening sections.

Commas 3 (2.10-2.15)

2.10 Degrees and Abbreviations. Degrees following individuals' names are set off by commas. Abbreviations such as *Jr.* and *Sr.* are also set off by commas unless the individual referred to prefers to omit the commas:

Anne G. Turner, M.B.A., joined the firm.

Michael Migliano, Jr., and Michael Migliano, Sr., work as a team.

Anthony A. Gensler Jr. wrote the report. (The individual referred to prefers to omit commas.)

The abbreviations *Inc.* and *Ltd.* are set off by commas only if a company's legal name has a comma just before this kind of abbreviation. To determine a company's practice, consult its stationery or a directory listing:

Firestone and Blythe, Inc., is based in Canada. (Notice that two commas are used.)

Computers Inc. is extending its franchise system. (The company's legal name does not include a comma before *Inc.*)

2.11 Omitted Words. A comma is used to show the omission of words that are understood:

On Monday we received 15 applications; on Friday, only 3. (Comma shows the omission of *we received.*)

2.12 Contrasting Statements. Commas are used to set off contrasting or opposing expressions. These expressions are often introduced by such words as *not, never, but,* and *yet*:

The consultant recommended CD storage, not tape storage, for our operations.

Our budget for the year is reduced, yet adequate.

The greater the effort, the greater the reward.

If increased emphasis is desired, use dashes instead of commas, as in *Only the sum of $100 — not $1000 — was paid on this account.*

2.13 Clarity. Commas are used to separate words repeated for emphasis. Commas are also used to separate words that may be misread if not separated:

The building is a long, long way from completion.

Whatever is, is right.

No matter what, you know we support you.

2.14 Quotations and Appended Questions
  a. A comma is used to separate a short quotation from the rest of a sentence. If the quotation is divided into two parts, two commas are used:

The manager asked, "Shouldn't the managers control the specialists?"

"Not if the specialists," replied Xiang, "have unique information."

  b. A comma is used to separate a question appended (added) to a statement:

You will confirm the shipment, won't you?

2.15 Comma Overuse. Do not use commas needlessly. For example, commas should not be inserted merely because you might drop your voice or pause if you were speaking the sentence:

One of the reasons for expanding our operations in the Atlantic region is{,} that we anticipate increased sales in that area. (Do not insert a needless comma before a clause.)

I am looking for an article entitled{,} "State-of-the-Art Communications." (Do not insert a needless comma after the word *entitled.*)

Grammar/Mechanics Handbook

A number of food and nonfood items are carried in convenience stores such as{,} 7-Eleven and Stop-N-Go. (Do not insert a needless comma after *such as*.)

We have{,} at this time{,} an adequate supply of parts. (Do not insert needless commas around prepositional phrases.)

Review Exercise I—Commas 3

Insert only necessary commas in the following sentences. Remove unnecessary commas with the delete sign (✐). In the space provided, indicate the number of commas inserted or deleted in each sentence. If a sentence requires no changes, write C. When you finish, compare your responses with those provided. For each item on which you need review, consult the numbered principle shown in parentheses.

1. We expected Charles Bedford not Krystina Rudko to conduct the meeting. _____
2. Brian said "We simply must have a bigger budget to start this project." _____
3. "We simply must have" said Brian "a bigger budget to start this project." _____
4. In August customers opened at least 50 new accounts; in September, only about 20. _____
5. You returned the merchandise last month didn't you? _____
6. Employees will now be expected to contribute more to their own retirement funds. _____
7. The better our advertising and recruiting the stronger our personnel pool will be. _____
8. Mrs. Delgado investigated selling her shares not her real estate to raise the necessary cash. _____
9. "On the contrary" said Ms. Mercer "we will continue our present marketing strategies." _____
10. Our company will expand into surprising new areas such as, women's apparel and fast foods. _____
11. What we need is more not fewer suggestions for improvement. _____
12. Randall Clark B.Comm. and Jonathon Georges M.B.A. joined the firm. _____
13. "Canada is now entering" said CEO Saunders "the Knowledge Age." _____
14. One of the reasons that we are inquiring about the publisher of the software is, that we are concerned whether that publisher will give us a discount. _____
15. The talk by D. A. Spindler Ph.D. was particularly difficult to follow because of his technical vocabulary. _____
16. The month before a similar problem occurred in distribution. _____
17. We are very fortunate to have, at our disposal, the services of excellent professionals. _____
18. No matter what you can count on us for support. _____
19. Mary Sandoval was named legislative counsel; Jacy Freeman executive adviser. _____
20. The data you are seeking can be found in an article entitled, "The Fastest Growing Game in Computers." _____

---

1. Bedford, Rudko, (2.12) 3. have," said Brian, (2.14a) 5. month, (2.14b) 7. recruiting, (2.12) 9. contrary," Mercer, (2.14a) 11. more, not fewer, (2.12) 13. entering," Saunders, (2.14a) 15. Spindler, Ph.D., (2.10) 17. have at our disposal (2.15) 19. Freeman, (2.11)

Punctuation Review

Commas 3

Review sections 2.10–2.15 above. Then study each of the following statements and insert necessary commas. In the space provided write the number of commas that you add; write *0* if no commas are needed. Also record the number of the Handbook principle(s) illustrated. When you finish, compare your responses with those provided in the answer key on page 372. If your answers differ, carefully study the principles again shown in parentheses.

2 _____ (2.12) **Example:** It was Lucia Bosano ͙ not Melinda Ho ͙ who was given the Kirkland account.

_____ 1. "The choice of a good name" said President Etienne "cannot be overestimated."
_____ 2. Hanna H. Cox Ph.D. and Katherine Meridian M.B.A. were hired as consultants.
_____ 3. Their August 15 order was shipped on Monday wasn't it?
_____ 4. The Web is useful in providing customer service such as online catalogue information and proof of shipping dates.
_____ 5. The bigger the investment the greater the profit.

Review Commas 1, 2, 3

_____ 6. As you requested your order for cartridges file folders and copy paper will be sent immediately.
_____ 7. We think however that you should re-examine your website and that you should consider changing it.
_____ 8. Within the next eight-week period we hope to hire Mina Vidal who is currently CEO of a small consulting firm.
_____ 9. Our convention will attract more participants if it is held in a resort location such as Collingwood the Laurentians or Banff.
_____ 10. If everyone who applied for the position were interviewed we would be very busy organizing interviews.
_____ 11. In the past ten years we have employed over 30 well-qualified individuals many of whom have selected banking as their career.
_____ 12. Kimberly Johansson who spoke to our class last week is the author of a book entitled Writing Winning Résumés.
_____ 13. A recent study of productivity that was conducted by authoritative researchers revealed that Canadian workers are more productive than workers in Europe or Japan.
_____ 14. The report concluded that Canada's productivity did not depend on bigger companies more robots or even brainier managers.
_____ 15. As a matter of fact the report said that Canada's productivity resulted from unprotected hands-off competition.

Cumulative Editing Quiz 4

Use proofreading marks (see Appendix B) to correct errors and omissions in the following sentences. All errors must be corrected to receive credit for the sentence. Check with your instructor for the answers.

1. Business documents must be written clear, to ensure that readers understand the message quick.

2. Needless to say the safety of our employees have always been most important to the president and I.

3. Agriculture Canada which provide disaster loans are setting up an office in Miami Manitoba.

4. Many entrepreneurs who want to expand there markets, have choosen to advertise heavy.

5. Our committee have agreed on a benefits package but management have been slow to respond.

6. Although the business was founded in the 1970's its real expansion took place in the 1990s.

7. According to the contract either the dealer or the distributor are responsible for repair of the product.

8. Next June, Lamont and Jones, Inc., are moving their headquarters to Calgary Alberta.

9. Our company is looking for intelligent, articulate, young, people who has a desire to grow with an expanding organization.

10. As you are aware each member of the jury were asked to avoid talking about the case.

Semicolons (2.16)

2.16 Independent Clauses, Series, Introductory Expressions

a. *Independent clauses with conjunctive adverbs.* Use a semicolon before a conjunctive adverb that separates two independent clauses. Some of the most common conjunctive adverbs are *therefore, consequently, however,* and *moreover:*

Business letters should sound conversational; therefore, familiar words and contractions are often used.

The bank closes its doors at 3 p.m.; however, the ABM is open 24 hours a day.

Notice that the word following a semicolon is not capitalized (unless, of course, that word is a proper noun).

b. *Independent clauses without conjunctive adverbs.* Use a semicolon to separate closely related independent clauses when no conjunctive adverb is used:

Some interest payments are tax deductible; bonus payments are not.

Jonas typed the report; Maria edited it for clarity and correctness.

Use a semicolon in compound sentences, not in complex sentences:

After one week the paper feeder jammed; we tried different kinds of paper. (Use a semicolon in a compound sentence.)

After one week the paper feeder jammed, although we tried different kinds of paper. (Use a comma in a complex sentence. Do not use a semicolon after *jammed.*)

The semicolon is very effective for joining two closely related thoughts. Don't use it, however, unless the ideas are truly related.

c. *Series with internal commas.* Use semicolons to separate items in a series when one or more of the items contains internal commas:

Delegates from Brandon, Manitoba; Lethbridge, Alberta; and North Bay, Ontario, attended the conference.

The speakers were Katrina Lang, manager, Riko Enterprises; Henry Holtz, vice-president, Trendex, Inc.; and Margaret Slater, personnel director, West Coast Productions.

d. *Introductory expressions.* Use a semicolon when an introductory expression such as *namely, for instance, that is,* or *for example* introduces a list following an independent clause:

Switching to computerized billing are several local companies; namely, Ryson Electronics, Miller Vending Services, and Blaque Advertising.

The author of a report should consider many sources; for example, books, periodicals, databases, and newspapers.

Colons (2.17–2.19)

2.17 Listed Items

a. *With colon.* Use a colon after a complete thought that introduces a formal list of items. A formal list is often preceded by such words and phrases as *these, thus, the following,* and *as follows.* A colon is also used when words and phrases like these are implied but not stated:

Additional costs in selling a house involve the following: title examination fee, title insurance costs, and closing fee. (Use a colon when a complete thought introduces a formal list.)

Collective bargaining focuses on several key issues: cost-of-living adjustments, benefits, job security, and hours of work. (The introduction of the list is implied in the preceding clause.)

b. *Without colon.* Do not use a colon when the list immediately follows a *to be* verb or a preposition:

The employees who should receive a bonus are James Sachi, Ramona Speers, and Rose Paquet. (No colon is used after the verb *are*.)

We expect to consider equipment for Accounting, Legal Services, and Payroll. (No colon is used after the preposition *for*.)

2.18 Quotations. Use a colon to introduce long one-sentence quotations and quotations of two or more sentences:

Our consultant said: "This system can support up to 32 users. It can be used for decision support, computer-aided design, and software development operations at the same time."

2.19 Salutations. Use a colon after the salutation of a business letter:

Gentlemen:

Dear Ms. Tsang:

Dear Odin:

Grammar/Mechanics Handbook

Review Exercise J—Semicolons, Colons

In the following sentences, add semicolons, colons, and necessary commas. For each sentence, indicate the number of punctuation marks that you add. If a sentence requires no punctuation, write C. When you finish, compare your responses with those provided. For each item on which you need review, consult the numbered principle(s) shown in parentheses.

1. A strike in Montreal has delayed shipments of parts consequently our production has fallen behind schedule. _____

2. Our branch in Burnaby specializes in industrial real estate our branch in Island Lakes concentrates on residential real estate. _____

3. The sedan version of the automobile is available in these colours Olympic red metallic silver and Aztec gold. _____

4. If I can assist the new manager please call me however I will be gone from June 10 through June 15. _____

5. The individuals who should receive copies of this announcement are Jeff Doogan Alicia Green and Kim Wong. _____

6. We would hope of course to send personal letters to all potential buyers but we have not yet decided just how to do this. _____

7. Many of our potential customers are in southern British Columbia therefore our promotional effort will be strongest in that area. _____

8. Since the first of the year we have received inquiries from one lawyer two accountants and one analyst. _____

9. Three dates have been reserved for initial interviews January 15 February 1 and February 12. _____

10. Several staff members are near the top of their salary ranges and we must review their jobs. _____

11. Several staff members are near the top of their salary ranges we must review their jobs. _____

12. Several staff members are near the top of their salary ranges therefore we must review their jobs. _____

13. If you open an account within two weeks you will receive a free cookbook moreover your first 500 cheques will be printed at no cost to you. _____

14. Monthly reports from the following departments are missing Legal Department Human Resources Department and Engineering Department. _____

15. Monthly reports are missing from the Legal Department Human Resources Department and Engineering Department. _____

16. Since you became director of that division sales have tripled therefore I am recommending you for a bonus. _____

17. The convention committee is considering Dartmouth Nova Scotia Moncton New Brunswick and Charlottetown Prince Edward Island. _____

18. The following large companies allow employees access to their personnel files Nortel Corel Corp. and Ford Canada. _____

19. Sylvie first asked about salary next she inquired about benefits. _____

20. Sylvie first asked about the salary and she next inquired about benefits. _____

---

1. parts; consequently, (2.16a) 3. colours: Olympic red, metallic silver, (2.01, 2.17a) 5. Doogan, Alicia Green, (2.01, 2.17b) 7. British Columbia; therefore, (2.16a) 9. interviews: January 15, February 1, (2.01, 2.17a) 11. ranges; (2.16b) 13. weeks, cookbook; moreover, (2.06a, 2.16a) 15. Department, Human Resources Department, (2.01, 2.17b) 17. Dartmouth, Nova Scotia; Moncton, New Brunswick; Charlottetown, (2.16c) 19. salary; (2.16b)

Semicolons and Colons

Review sections 2.16–2.19 above. Then study each of the following statements. Insert any necessary punctuation. Use the delete symbol to omit unnecessary punctuation. In the space provided, indicate the number of changes you made and record the number of the Handbook principle(s) illustrated. (When you replace one punctuation mark with another, count it as one change.) If you make no changes, write *0*. This exercise concentrates on semicolon and colon use, but you will also be responsible for correct comma use. When you finish, compare your responses with those shown in the answer key on page 372. If your responses differ, carefully study again the specific principles shown in parentheses.

2 _____ **(2.16a)** **Example:** The job of Mr. Wellworth is to make sure that his company has enough cash to meet its obligations moreover he is responsible for locating credit when needed.

_____ 1. Short-term financing refers to a period of under one year long-term financing on the other hand refers to a period of ten years or more.

_____ 2. Cash resulting from product sales does not arrive until December therefore our cash flow becomes critical in October and November.

_____ 3. We must discuss short-term financing during the following months September October and November.

_____ 4. Large corporations that offer huge amounts of trade credit are, automobile dealers, utility companies, oil companies, and computer hardware manufacturers.

_____ 5. Although some firms rarely, if ever, need to borrow short-term money many businesses find that they need a lot of credit to pay for production and sales costs.

_____ 6. A grocery store probably requires no short-term credit, a greeting card manufacturer however typically would need a lot of short-term credit.

_____ 7. We offer three basic types of credit: loans promissory notes and floating lines of credit.

_____ 8. Speakers at the conference on credit include the following businesspeople Mary Ann Mahan financial manager Ritchie Industries Terry L. Buchanan comptroller International Bank and Edmée Cavalier operations Business Bank of Canada.

_____ 9. The prime interest rate is set by the Bank of Canada and this rate goes up or down as the cost of money to the bank itself fluctuates.

_____ 10. Most banks are in business to lend money to commercial customers for example retailers service companies manufacturers and construction firms.

_____ 11. Avionics, Inc. which is a small electronics firm with a solid credit rating recently applied for a loan however the Federal Business Development Bank refused the loan application because the risk was too great.

_____ 12. When Avionics, Inc., was refused by the Federal Business Development Bank its financial managers submitted applications to the following Worldwide Investments, Dominion Securities, and Mid Mountain Group.

_____ 13. The cost of financing capital investments at the present time is very high therefore Avionics' managers may elect to delay certain expansion projects.

14. If interest rates reach as high as 18 percent the cost of borrowing becomes _____
    too expensive consequently many businesses are forced to change or leave
    projects that require financing.
15. Several investors decided to pool their resources then they could find attrac- _____
    tive investments.

Apostrophes (2.20–2.22)

2.20 Basic Rule. The apostrophe is used to show ownership, origin, authorship, or measurement.

Ownership:	We are looking for Dmitri's keys.
Origin:	At the president's suggestion, we doubled the order.
Authorship:	The accountant's annual report was questioned.
Measurement:	In two years' time we expect to reach our goal.

a. *Ownership words not ending in* **s**. To place the apostrophe correctly, you must first determine whether the ownership word is singular or plural. If the ownership word is singular, add an apostrophe and an *s* to the ownership word.

the employee's file	(the file of a single employee)
a member's address	(the address of a single member)
a year's time	(the time of a single year)
a month's notice	(notice of a single month)
the company's building	(the building of a single company)

b. *Ownership words ending in* **s**. If the ownership word is plural, usually add only an apostrophe:

several employees' files	(files of several employees)
ten members' addresses	(addresses of ten members)
five years' time	(time of five years)
several months' notice	(notice of several months)
many companies' buildings	(buildings of many companies)

A few singular nouns that end in *s* are pronounced with an extra syllable when they become possessive. To these words, add '*s*.

my boss's desk
the waitress's table
the actress's costume

Use no apostrophe if a noun is merely plural, not possessive:

All the sales representatives, as well as the secretaries and managers, had their names and telephone numbers listed in the directory. (Nobody is owning anything in this sentence).

2.21 Names. The writer may choose either traditional or popular style in making singular names possessive. The traditional style uses the apostrophe plus an *s*, while the popular style uses just the apostrophe. Note that only with singular names does this option exist.

Traditional style	**Popular style**
Russ's computer	Russ' computer
Mr. Jones's car	Mr. Jones' car
Mrs. Morris's desk	Mrs. Morris' desk
Ms. Horowitz's job	Ms. Horowitz' job

The possessive form of plural names is consistent: the *Joneses'* car, the *Horowitzes'* home, the *Morrises'* daughter.

2.22 Gerunds. Use *'s* to make a noun possessive when it precedes a gerund, a verb form used as a noun:

> Mr. Smith's smoking prompted a new office policy. (Mr. Smith is possessive because it modifies the gerund *smoking*.)

> It was Britta's careful proofreading that revealed the discrepancy.

Review Exercise K—Apostrophes

Insert necessary apostrophes in the following sentences. In the space provided for each sentence, indicate the number of apostrophes that you added. If none were added, write C. When you finish, compare your responses with those provided. For each item on which you need review, consult the numbered principle shown in parentheses.

1. Your account should have been credited with six months interest.
2. If you go to the third floor, you will find Mr. Londons office.
3. All the employees personnel folders must be updated.
4. In a little over a year's time, that firm was able to double its sales.
5. The Harrises daughter lived in Whitehorse for two years.
6. An inventors patent protects his or her rights for several years.
7. Both companies headquarters will be moved within the next six months.
8. That position requires at least two years experience.
9. All the students arrived on time; therefore, the teachers started the test promptly at noon.
10. All secretaries workstations were equipped with terminals.
11. The package of electronics parts arrived safely despite two weeks delay.
12. Many nurses believe that nurses uniforms should be colourful and bright.
13. According to Mr. Cortez latest proposal, all employees would receive an additional holiday.
14. Many of our members names and addresses must be checked.
15. His supervisor had to correct Jacks financial reports.
16. We believe that this firms service is much better than that firms.
17. Mr. Schur estimated that he spent a years profits in reorganizing his staff.
18. After paying six months rent, we were given a receipt.
19. The contract is not valid without Ms. Harris signature.
20. Mr. Smiths signature was required on that contract.

1. months' (2.20b) 3. employees' (2.20b) 5. Harrises' (2.21) 7. companies' (2.20b) 9. C (2.20b) 11. weeks' (2.20b) 13. Cortez' [or Cortez's] (2.21) 15. Jack's (2.21) 17. year's (2.20a) 19. Harris' [or Harris's] (2.21)

Grammar/Mechanics Checkup—10

Apostrophes

Review sections 2.20–2.22 above. Then study each of the following statements. Underline any inappropriate form. Write a correction in the space provided, and record the number of the Handbook principle(s) illustrated. If a sentence is correct, write C. When you finish, compare your responses with those in the answer key on page 373. If your answers differ, carefully study again the principles shown in parentheses.

Example: In just two <u>years</u> time, the accountants and managers devised an entirely new system.   years'   (2.20b)

1. Two supervisors said that Mr. Faulkners work was excellent.   _____
2. In less than a years time, the offices of both lawyers were moved.   _____
3. None of the employees in our Electronics Department had taken more than   _____
   two weeks vacation.
4. All the secretaries agreed that Ms. Lanhams suggestions were practical.   _____
5. After you obtain your boss approval, send the application to Human   _____
   Resources.
6. We tried to sit in our favourite server section, but all her tables were filled. _____
7. Despite Kaspar grumbling, his wife selected two bonds and three stocks for   _____
   her investments.
8. The apartment owner requires two months rent in advance from all applicants.   _____
9. Four companies buildings were damaged in the fire.   _____
10. In one months time we hope to be able to complete all the address files.   _____
11. One secretaries desk will have to be moved to make way for the computer.   _____
12. Several sellers permits were issued for two years.   _____
13. Marks salary was somewhat higher than David.   _____
14. Latikas job in accounts receivable ends in two months.   _____

Cumulative Editing Quiz 5

Use proofreading marks (see Appendix B) to correct errors and omissions in the following sentences. All errors must be corrected to receive credit for the sentence. Check with your instructor for the answers.

1. The three C's of credit are the following character capacity and capital.

2. We hope that we will not have to sell the property however that may be our only option.

3. As soon as the supervisor and her can check this weeks sales they will place an order.

4. Any of the auditors are authorized to proceed with an independent action however only the CEO can alter the councils directives.

5. Although reluctant technicians sometimes must demonstrate there computer software skills.

6. On April 6 1998 we opened the new employee computer centre.

7. A list of maintenance procedures and recommendations are in the owners manual.

8. The Morrises son lived in London Ontario however there daughter lived in Saint John New Brunswick.

9. Employment interviews were held in Winnipeg Manitoba Calgary Alberta and Victoria British Columbia.

10. Mr. Lees determination courage and sincerity are admirable however his methods was often questioned.

Other Punctuation (2.23-2.29)

2.23 Periods

a. *Ends of sentences.* Use a period at the end of a statement, command, indirect question, or polite request. Although a polite request may have the same structure as a question, it ends with a period:

Corporate legal departments demand precise skills from their workforce. (End a statement with a period.)

Get the latest data by reading current periodicals. (End a command with a period.)

Mr. Rand wondered whether we had sent any follow-up literature. (End an indirect question with a period.)

Would you please re-examine my account and determine the current balance. (A polite request suggests an action rather than a verbal response.)

b. *Abbreviations and initials.* Use periods after initials and after many abbreviations.

R. M. Johnson	c.o.d.	Ms.
M.D.	a.m.	Mr.
Inc.	i.e.	Mrs.

Use just one period when an abbreviation falls at the end of a sentence:

Guests began arriving at 5:30 p.m.

2.24 Question Marks. Direct questions are followed by question marks:

Did you send your proposal to Datatronix, Inc.?

Statements with questions added are punctuated with question marks.

We have completed the proposal, haven't we?

2.25 Exclamation Points. Use an exclamation point after a word, phrase, or clause expressing strong emotion. In business writing, however, exclamation points should be used sparingly:

Incredible! The entire network is down.

2.26 Dashes. The dash (constructed at a keyboard by striking the hyphen key twice in succession) is a legitimate and effective mark of punctuation when used according to accepted conventions. As an emphatic punctuation mark, however, the dash loses effectiveness when overused.

a. *Parenthetical elements.* Within a sentence, a parenthetical element is usually set off by commas. If, however, the parenthetical element itself contains internal commas, use dashes (or parentheses) to set it off:

Three top salespeople—Tom Judkins, Morgan Templeton, and Mary Yashimoto—received bonuses.

b. *Sentence interruptions.* Use a dash to show an interruption or abrupt change of thought:

News of the dramatic merger—no one believed it at first—shook the financial world.

Ship the materials Monday—no, we must have them sooner.

Sentences with abrupt changes of thought or with appended afterthoughts can usually be improved through rewriting.

c. *Summarizing statements.* Use a dash (not a colon) to separate an introductory list from a summarizing statement:

Sorting, merging, and computing—these are tasks that our data processing programs must perform.

2.27 Parentheses. One means of setting off nonessential sentence elements involves the use of parentheses. Nonessential sentence elements may be punctuated in one of three ways: (1) with commas, to make the lightest possible break in the normal flow of a sentence; (2) with dashes, to emphasize the enclosed material; and (3) with parentheses, to de-emphasize the enclosed material. Parentheses are frequently used to punctuate sentences with directions, explanations, questions, and references added for extra detail:

The cost analysis (which appears on page 8 of the report) indicates that the copy machine should be leased.

Units are lightweight (approximately 500 g) and come with a leather case and operating instructions.

The IBM laser printer (have you heard about it?) will be demonstrated for us next week.

A parenthetical sentence that is not embedded within another sentence should be capitalized and end-punctuated:

The Model 20 has stronger construction. (You may order a Model 20 brochure by circling 304 on the reader service card.)

2.28 Quotation Marks

a. *Direct quotations.* Use double quotation marks to enclose the exact words of a speaker or writer:

"Keep in mind," Mrs. Fontaine said, "that you'll have to justify the cost of automating our office."

The boss said that automation was inevitable. (No quotation marks are needed because the exact words are not quoted.)

b. *Quotations within quotations.* Use single quotation marks (apostrophes on the typewriter) to enclose quoted passages within quoted passages:

In her speech, Ms. Deckman remarked, "I believe it was the poet Robert Frost who said, 'All the fun's in how you say a thing.'"

c. *Short expressions.* Slang, words used in a special sense, and words following *stamped* or *marked* are often enclosed within quotation marks:

Rafael described the damaged shipment as "gross." (Quotation marks enclose slang.)

Students often have trouble spelling the word "separate." (Quotation marks enclose words used in a special sense.)

Jobs were divided into two categories: most stressful and least stressful. The jobs in the "most stressful" list involved high risk or responsibility. (Quotation marks enclose words used in a special sense.)

The envelope marked "Confidential" was put aside. (Quotation marks enclose words following *marked*.)

In the four preceding sentences, the words enclosed within quotation marks could instead be set in italics, if italics are available.

d. **Definitions.** Double quotation marks are used to enclose definitions. The word or expression being defined should be underscored or set in italics:

The term *penetration pricing* is defined as "the practice of introducing a product to the market at a low price."

e. **Titles.** Use double quotation marks to enclose titles of literary and artistic works such as magazine and newspaper articles, chapters of books, movies, television shows, poems, lectures, and songs. Names of major publications—such as books, magazines, pamphlets, and newspapers—are set in italics (or underscored) or typed in capital letters.

Particularly helpful was the chapter in Smith's EFFECTIVE WRITING TECHNIQUES entitled "Right Brain, Write Well!"

John's article, "E-mail Blunders," appeared in *The Toronto Star*; however, we could not locate it in a local library.

f. **Additional considerations.** Periods and commas are always placed inside closing quotation marks. Semicolons and colons, on the other hand, are always placed outside quotation marks:

Mrs. Levesque said, "I could not find the article entitled 'Cell Phone Etiquette.'"

The president asked for "absolute security": all written messages were to be destroyed.

Question marks and exclamation points may go inside or outside closing quotation marks, as determined by the form of the quotation:

Sales Manager Motega said, "Who placed the order?" (The quotation is a question.)

When did the sales manager say, "Who placed the order?" (Both the incorporating sentence and the quotation are questions.)

Did the sales manager say, "Narwinder placed the order"? (The incorporating sentence asks question; the quotation does not.)

"In the future," shouted Bob, "ask me first!" (The quotation is an exclamation.)

2.29 Brackets. Within quotations, square brackets are used by the quoting writer to enclose his or her own inserted remarks to correct, illustrate, or explain:

June Cardillo said, "CRTC [Canadian Radio-television and Telecommunications Commission] has been one of the most widely criticized agencies of the federal government."

Review Exercise L—Other Punctuation

Insert necessary punctuation in the following sentences. In the space provided for each item, indicate the number of punctuation marks that you added. Count sets of parentheses and dashes as two marks. Emphasis or de-emphasis will be indicated for some parenthetical elements. When you finish, compare your responses with those provided. For each item on which you need review, consult the numbered principle shown in parentheses.

1. Will you please stop payment on Cheque No. 233   _____
2. (Emphasize.) Your order of October 16 will be on its way you have my word   _____
   by October 20.
3. Mr Sirakides, Mrs Sylvester, and Miss Sidhu have not yet responded   _____
4. Wanda Penner asked if the order had been sent c o d (cash on delivery).   _____
5. Interviews have been scheduled for 3:15 pm, 4 pm, and 4:45 pm   _____
6. (De-emphasize.) Three knowledgeable individuals the plant manager, the   _____
   construction engineer, and the construction supervisor all expressed concern
   about soil settlement.
7. Fantastic The value of our shares just rose 10 points on the stock market   _____
8. The word de facto means existing in fact regardless of the legal situation.   _____
9. (De-emphasize.) Although the appliance now comes in limited colours   _____
   brown, beige, and ivory, we expect to see new colours available in the next
   production run.
10. Was it the manager who said "What can't be altered must be endured   _____
11. The stock exchange went crazy over the news of the takeover.   _____
12. Because the envelope was marked Personal, we did not open it.   _____
13. Price, service, and reliability these are our prime considerations in equipment   _____
    selection.
14. The letter carrier said Would you believe that this package was marked   _____
    Fragile
15. (Emphasize.) Three branch managers Kelly Cardinal, Stan Meyers, and Ivan   _____
    Sergo will be promoted.
16. (De-emphasize.) The difference between portable and transportable com-   _____
    puters see Figure 4 for weight comparisons may be considerable.
17. All the folders marked Current Files should be sent to Human Resources.   _____
18. I am trying to find the edition of Canadian Business that carried an article   _____
    entitled The Future Without Shock.
19. Martha Simon MD and Gail Nemire RN were hired by Healthnet, Inc   _____
20. The computer salesperson said This innovative, state-of-the-art laptop sells   _____
    for a fraction of the cost of big-name computers.

---

1. 233. (2.23a) 3. Mr. Mrs. responded. (2.23a, 2.23b) 5. p.m. p.m. p.m. (2.23b) 7. Fantastic! market! (2.25) 9. (brown ivory) (2.27) 11. "crazy" (2.28c) 13. reliability— (2.26c) 15. managers— Sergo— (2.26a) 17. "Current Files" (2.28c) 19. Simon, M.D., Nemire, R.N., Inc. (2.23b)

Grammar/Mechanics Checkup—11

Other Punctuation

Although this checkup concentrates on sections 2.23–2.29 above, you may also refer to other punctuation principles. Insert any necessary punctuation. In the space provided, indicate the number of changes you make and record the number of the Handbook principle(s) illustrated. Count each mark separately; for example, a set of parentheses counts as 2. If you make no changes, write *0*. When you finish, compare your responses with those provided in the answer key on page 373. If your responses differ, carefully study again the specific principles shown in parentheses.

Example: The use of cereal products is highest in certain provinces (Manitoba, Saskatchewan, Alberta, and Newfoundland), but this food trend is spreading to other parts of the country.

_____ 1. (Emphasize.) The convention planning committee has invited three managers Yu Wong, Frank Behr, and Yvette Sosa to make presentations.

_____ 2. Would you please Miss Fundy use your computer to recalculate these totals.

_____ 3. (De-emphasize.) A second set of demographic variables see Figure 13 on page 432 includes nationality, religion, and race.

_____ 4. Because the word recommendation is frequently misspelled we are adding it to our company style book.

_____ 5. Recruiting, hiring, and training these are three important functions of a human resources officer.

_____ 6. The office manager asked, Who placed an order for two dozen printer cartridges

_____ 7. Have any of the research assistants been able to locate the article entitled How Tax Reform Will Affect You

_____ 8. (Emphasize.) The biggest oil-producing provinces Alberta, Newfoundland, and Ontario are experiencing significant tax cuts.

_____ 9. Have you sent invitations to Mr Kieran E Manning, Miss Kathy Tanguay, and Ms Petra Bonaventura?

_____ 10. Dr. Y. W. Yellin wrote the chapter entitled Trading on the Options Market that appeared in a book called Securities Markets.

_____ 11. James said, "I'll be right over" however he has not appeared yet.

_____ 12. In business the word liability may be defined as any legal obligation requiring payment in the future.

_____ 13. Because the work was scheduled to be completed June 10 we found it necessary to hire temporary workers to work June 8 and 9.

_____ 14. Did any c o d shipments arrive today

_____ 15. Hooray I have finished this checkup haven't I

Grammar/Mechanics Checkup—12

Punctuation Review

Review sections 1.19 and 2.01–2.29. Study the groups of sentences below. In the space provided, write the letter of the one that is correctly punctuated. When you finish, compare your responses with those in the answer key on page 373. If your responses differ, carefully study again the principles in parentheses.

_____ 1. a. Our accounting team makes a point of analyzing your business operations, and getting to know what's working for you and what's not.

           b. We are dedicated to understanding your business needs over the long term, and taking an active role when it comes to creating solutions.

           c. We understand that you may be downsizing or moving into new markets, and we want to help you make a seamless transition.

_____ 2. a. If you are growing, or connecting to new markets, our team will help you accomplish your goals with minimal interruptions.

           b. When you look at our organization chart, you will find the customer at the top.

           c. Although we offer each customer a dedicated customer account team we also provide professional general services.

_____ 3. a. The competition is changing; therefore, we have to deliver our products and services more efficiently.

    b. Although delivery systems are changing; the essence of banking remains the same.

    c. Banks will continue to be available around the corner, and also with the click of a mouse.

4. a. One of the reasons we are decreasing the number of our ABMs, is that two-thirds of the bank's customers depend on tellers for transactions. _____

    b. We are looking for an article entitled, "Online Banking."

    c. Banks are at this time competing with new rivals that can provide extensive financial services.

5. a. We care deeply about the environment; but we also care about safety and good customer service. _____

    b. The president worked with environmental concerns; the vice-president focused on customer support.

    c. Our website increases our productivity, it also improves customer service.

6. a. Employees who will be receiving salary increases are: Terri, Mark, Rob, and Géza. _____

    b. The following employees are eligible for bonuses: Robin, Olivia, Bill, and Jorge.

    c. Our consulting firm is proud to offer services for: website design, market analysis, e-commerce, and hosting.

7. a. All secretaries' computers were equipped with Excel. _____

    b. Both lawyers statements confused the judge.

    c. Some members names and addresses must be re-keyed.

8. a. Our committee considered convention sites in Regina, Saskatchewan, Charlottetown, Prince Edward Island; and Banff, Alberta. _____

    b. Alizar was from Humbolt, Saskatchewan; Josh was from The Pas, Manitoba, and Rachel was from Whitehorse, Yukon.

    c. The following engineers were approved: J. W. Ellis, civil; Dr. Thomas Lu, structural; and W. R. Proudlove, mechanical.

9. a. The package from Albany, New York was never delivered. _____

    b. We have scheduled an inspection tour on Tuesday, March 5, at 4 p.m.

    c. Send the cheque to M. E. Williams, 320 Summit Ridge, Elizabethtown, Ontario K6T 1A9 before the last mail pickup.

10. a. The best plan of action in my opinion, is a straightforward approach. _____

    b. Under the circumstances we could not have hoped for better results.

    c. Our department will, in the meantime, reduce its services.

11. a. If you demand reliable, competent service, you should come to us. _____

    b. We could not resist buying cookies from the enthusiastic, young Girl Guide.

    c. Our highly trained technicians, with years of experience are always available to evaluate and improve your network environment.

12. a. We guarantee same-day, not next-day, service. _____

    b. Our departmental budget requests are considerably reduced yet adequate.

    c. The nominating committee selected Todd Shimoyama, not Suzette Chase as its representative.

13. a. Their wealthy uncle left $1 million to be distributed to Hayden, Carlotta, and Susanna. _____

    b. Their wealthy uncle left $1 million to be distributed to Hayden, Carlotta and Susanna.

    c. Our agency will maintain and upgrade your computers, printers, copiers and fax machines.

14. a. Beginning June 1, we will service many top vendors, including: _____ Compaq, Hewlett Packard, IBM, Dell and Mita.

b. To promote our new business we are offering a 10 percent discount.

c. In a period of only one month, we gained 150 new customers.

15. a. We specialize in network design, however we also offer troubleshooting and consulting.

b. We realize that downtime is not an option; therefore, you can count on us for reliable, competent service.

c. Our factory-trained and certified technicians perform repairs at your location, or in our own repair depot for products under warranty and out of warranty.

Cumulative Editing Quiz 6

Use proofreading marks (see Appendix B) to correct errors and omissions in the following sentences. All errors must be corrected to receive credit for the sentence. Check with your instructor for the answers.

1. Although the envelope was marked Confidential the vice-presidents assistant thought it should be opened.

2. Would you please send my order c.o.d?

3. To be eligible for an apartment you must pay two months rent in advance.

4. We wanted to use Russ computer, but forgot to ask for permission.

5. Wasnt it Jeff Singh not Eileen Lee who requested a 14 day leave.

6. Miss. Judith L. Beam is the employee who the employees council elected as their representative.

7. The Leader Post our local newspaper featured an article entitled The Worlds Most Expensive Memo.

8. As soon as my manager or myself can verify Ricks totals we will call you, in the meantime you must continue to pay out funds.

9. Just inside the entrance, is the receptionists desk and a complete directory of all departments'.

10. Exports from small companys has increased thereby affecting this countrys trade balance positively.

Style and Usage

Capitalization (3.01-3.16)

Capitalization is used to distinguish important words. However, writers are not free to capitalize all words they consider important. Rules or guidelines governing capitalization style have been established through custom and use. Mastering these guidelines will make your writing more readable and more understandable.

3.01 Proper Nouns. Capitalize proper nouns, including the specific names of persons, places, schools, streets, parks, buildings, religions, holidays, months, agreements, programs, services, and so forth. Do not capitalize common nouns that make only general references.

Proper Nouns	Common Nouns
Michael DeNiro	a salesperson in electronics

Germany, Japan	major trading partners of Canada
George Brown College	a community college
Assiniboine Park	a park in the city
Phoenix Room, Delta Inn	a meeting room in the hotel
Catholicism, Buddhism	two religions
Canada Day, New Year's Day	two holidays
Priority Post	a special package delivery service
Lions Gate Bridge	a bridge
Consumer Protection Act	a law to protect consumers
Winnipeg Chamber of Commerce	a chamber of commerce
Digby Municipal Airport	a municipal airport

3.02 Proper Adjectives. Capitalize most adjectives that are derived from proper nouns:

Greek symbol	British thermal unit
Roman numeral	Norwegian ship
Shakespearean drama	Inuit land claims

Do not capitalize adjectives that, although originally derived from proper nouns, have become common adjectives through usage. Consult your dictionary when in doubt:

italic type	diesel engine
pasteurized milk	cheddar cheese

3.03 Geographic Locations. Capitalize the names of specific places such as cities, states, mountains, valleys, lakes, rivers, oceans, and geographic regions:

Iqaluit	Lake Ontario
Rocky Mountains	Arctic Ocean
Cape Breton Island	James Bay
the East Coast	the Pacific Northwest

3.04 Organization Names. Capitalize the principal words in the names of all business, civic, educational, governmental, labour, military, charitable, political, professional, religious, and social organizations:

Inland Steel Company	The Rainbow Society
Toronto Stock Exchange	Securities and Exchange Commission
United Way	Psychological Association of Manitoba
Child and Family Services	Mennonite Brethren Bible College
Board of Directors, Teachers' Credit Union	

Capitalize *the* only when it is part of the official name of an organization, as printed on the organization's stationery.

I read about her promotion in *The Globe and Mail*.
However, the *National Post* didn't mention it.

3.05 Academic Courses and Degrees. Capitalize particular academic degrees and course titles. Do not capitalize references to general academic degrees and subject areas:

Professor Bernadette Ordian, Ph.D., will teach Accounting 221 next fall.

Beth Snyder, who holds bachelor's and master's degrees, teaches marketing classes.

René enrolled in classes in history, business English, and management.

a. Capitalize personal and business titles when they precede names:

Vice-President Ames	Uncle Edward
Board Chairman Frazier	Councillor Hebert
Member of Parliament Ronald Fontaine	Sales Manager Klein
Professor McLean	Dr. Myra Rosner

b. Capitalize titles in addresses, salutations, and closing lines:

Mr. Juan deSanto	Very truly yours,
Director of Purchasing	
Space Systems, Inc.	Clara J. Smith
Richmond, BC V3L 4A6	Supervisor, Marketing

c. Capitalize titles of high government rank or religious office, whether they precede a name, follow a name, or replace a name.

the Prime Minister of Canada	Gaston Pelletier, Senator
the Premier's office	the Speaker of the House of Commons
J. W. Ross, Minister of Finance	an audience with the Pope
the Lieutenant-Governor of	
British Columbia	

d. Do not capitalize most common titles following names:

The speech was delivered by Wayne Hsu, president, Inter-Tel Canada.

Lois Herndon, chief executive officer, signed the order.

e. Do not capitalize common titles appearing alone:

Please speak to the supervisor or to the office manager.

Neither the president nor the vice-president was asked.

However, when the title of an official appears in that organization's minutes, bylaws, or other official document, it may be capitalized.

f. Do not capitalize titles when they are followed by appositives naming specific individuals:

We must consult our director of research, Ronald E. Weston, before responding.

g. Do not capitalize family titles used with possessive pronouns:

my mother	our aunt	your father	his cousin

h. Capitalize titles of close relatives used without pronouns:

Both Mother and Father must sign the contract.

3.07 Numbered and Lettered Items. Capitalize nouns followed by numbers or letters (except in page, paragraph, line, and verse references):

Flight 34, Gate 12	Plan No. 2
Volume I, Part 3	Warehouse 33-A
Invoice No. 55489	Figure 8.3
Model A5673	Serial No. C22865404-2
Rural Route 10	page 6, line 5

3.08 Points of the Compass. Capitalize *north, south, east, west,* and their derivatives when they represent specific geographical regions. Do not capitalize the points of the compass when they are used in directions or in general references.

Specific Regions	General References
from the South	heading north on the highway
living in the North	west of the city
Easterners, Westerners	western Ontario, southern Saskatchewan
going to the Middle East	the northern part of Canada
from the East Coast	the east side of the street

3.09 Departments, Divisions, and Committees. Capitalize the names of departments, divisions, or committees within your own organization. Outside your organization capitalize only specific department, division, or committee names:

The inquiry was addressed to the Legal Department in our Consumer Products Division.

John was appointed to the Employee Benefits Committee.

Send your résumé to their human resources division.

A planning committee will be named shortly.

3.10 Governmental Terms. Do not capitalize the words *federal, government, nation,* or *province* unless they are part of a specific title:

Unless federal support can be secured, the state project will be abandoned.

The Provincial Employees' Pension Fund is looking for secure investments.

3.11 Product Names. Capitalize product names only when they refer to trademarked items. Except in advertising, common names following manufacturers' names are not capitalized:

Dictaphone	Apple computer
Kleenex	X-Acto knife
Q-Tip	3M diskettes
Levi's jeans	Sony Walkman
Teflon pan	Canon camera

3.12 Literary Titles. Capitalize the principal words in the titles of books, magazines, newspapers, articles, movies, plays, songs, poems, and reports. Do not capitalize articles (*a, an, the*), short conjunctions (*and, but, or, nor*), and prepositions of fewer than five (some say four) letters (*in, to, by, for,* etc.) unless they begin or end the title:

Jackson's *What Job Is for You?* (Capitalize book titles.)

Gant's "Software for the Executive Suite" (Capitalize principal words in article titles.)

"Performance Standards to Go By" (Capitalize article titles.)

"The Improvement of Fuel Economy with Alternative Motors" (Capitalize report titles.)

3.13 Beginning Words. In addition to capitalizing the first word of a complete sentence, capitalize the first word in a quoted sentence, independent phrase, item in an enumerated list, and formal rule or principle following a colon:

The business manager said, "All purchases must have requisitions." (Capitalize first word in a quoted sentence.)

Yes, if you agree. (Capitalize an independent phrase.)

Some of the duties of the position are as follows:

1. Editing and formatting Word files

2. Receiving and routing telephone calls

3. Verifying records, reports, and applications (Capitalize items in an enumerated list.)

One rule has been established through the company: No smoking is allowed in open offices. (Capitalize a rule following a colon.)

3.14 Planets and Celestial Bodies. Capitalize the names of celestial bodies such as Mars, Saturn, and Neptune. Do not capitalize the terms *earth, sun,* or *moon* unless they appear in a context with other celestial bodies:

Where on earth did you find that manual typewriter?

Venus and Mars are the closest planets to Earth.

3.15 Ethnic References. Capitalize terms that refer to a particular culture, language, or race:

Asian	Hebrew
Celtic	Indian
Latino	Japanese
Persian	Judeo-Christian

3.16 Seasons. Do not capitalize seasons:

In the fall it appeared that winter and spring sales would increase.

Review Exercise M—Capitalization

In the following sentences, correct any errors in capitalization that you find. Circle any lowercase letter that should be changed to a capital letter. Draw a slash (/) through a capital letter that you wish to change to a lowercase letter. In the space provided, indicate the total number of changes you have made in each sentence. If you make no changes, write *0*. When you finish, compare your responses with those provided. For each item on which you need review, consult the numbered principle shown in parentheses.

5   (3.06d, 3.09)   **Example:** Bill McAdams, currently Assistant Manager in our Personnel department, will be promoted to Manager of the Employee Services division.

1. The pensions act, passed in 1949, established the present system of social security.
2. Our company will soon be moving its operations to the west coast.
3. Marilyn Hunter, m.b.a., received her bachelor's degree from McGill university in montreal.
4. The President of Datatronics, Inc., delivered a speech entitled "Taking off into the future."
5. Please ask your Aunt and your Uncle if they will come to the Lawyer's office at 5 p.m.
6. Your reservations are for flight 32 on air canada leaving from gate 14 at 2:35 p.m.
7. Once we establish an organizing committee, arrangements can be made to rent holmby hall.

8. Bob was enrolled in history, spanish, business communications, and physical education courses. _____

9. Either the President or the Vice-President of the company will make the decision about purchasing xerox copiers. _____

10. Rules for hiring and firing Employees are given on page 7, line 24, of the Contract. _____

11. Some individuals feel that canadian management does not have the sense of loyalty to their employees that japanese management has. _____

12. Where on Earth can we find better workers than Robots? _____

13. The minister of finance said, "we must encourage our domestic producers to compete internationally." _____

14. After crossing the lions gate bridge, we drove to Southern British Columbia for our vacation. _____

15. All marketing representatives of our company will meet in the empire room of the red lion motor inn. _____

16. Richard Elkins, ph.d., has been named director of research for spaceage strategies, inc. _____

17. The special keyboard for the IBM Computer must contain greek symbols for Engineering equations. _____

18. After she received a master's degree in electrical engineering, Joanne Dudley was hired to work in our product development department. _____

19. In the Fall our organization will move its corporate headquarters to the franklin building in downtown vancouver. _____

20. Dean Amador has one cardinal rule: always be punctual. _____

---

1. Pensions Act (3.01) 3. M.B.A. University Montreal (3.01, 3.05) 5. aunt uncle lawyer's (3.06e, 3.06g) 7. Holmby Hall (3.01) 9. president vice-president Xerox (3.06e, 3.11) 11. Canadian Japanese (3.02) 13. Minister Finance We (3.06c, 3.13) 15. Empire Room Red Lion Motor Inn (3.01) 17. computer Greek engineering (3.01, 3.02, 3.11) 19. fall Franklin Building Vancouver (3.01, 3.16)

Grammar/Mechanics Checkup—13

Capitalization

Review sections 3.01–3.16 above. Then study each of the following statements. Circle any lowercase letter that should be capitalized. Draw a slash (/) through any capital letter that you wish to change to lowercase. Indicate in the space provided the number of changes you made in each sentence and record the number of the Handbook principle(s) illustrated. If you made no changes, write 0. When you finish, compare your responses with those provided in the answer key on page 373. If your responses differ, carefully study again the principles in parentheses.

Example: After consulting our Attorneys for Legal advice, Vice-President Fontaine signed the Contract.   4   (3.01, 3.06a)

1. All canadian passengers from Flight 402 must pass through Customs Inspection at Gate 17 upon arrival at Pearson international airport. _____

2. Personal tax rates for japanese citizens are low by International standards; rates for japanese corporations are high, according to Iwao Nakatani, an Economics Professor at Osaka university. _____

3. All Investors would be wise to remember the first rule of the Stock Market: What goes up must come down. _____

4. Abel enrolled in courses in History, Sociology, Spanish, and Computer Science. _____

5. Did you see the *Maclean's* article entitled "Careers in horticulture are nothing to sneeze at"?

6. Although I recommend Minex Printers sold under the brand name MPLazerJet, you may purchase any Printers you choose.

7. According to a Federal Government report, any development of Provincial waterways must receive an environmental assessment.

8. The prime minister of canada said, "this country continues to encourage Foreign investment."

9. The Comptroller of Ramjet International reported to the President and the Board of Directors that the canada revenue agency was beginning an investigation of their Company.

10. My Mother, who lives near Plum Coulee, reports that protection from the Sun's rays is particularly important when travelling to the South.

11. Our Managing Editor met with Leslie Hawkins, Manager of the Advertising Sales Department, to plan an Ad Campaign for our special issue.

12. Next winter, Editor in Chief Mercredi plans an article detailing the astounding performance of the australian dollar.

13. To reach Terrasse-Vaudreuil park, which is located on an Island in the St. Lawrence River, tourists pass over the vanier bridge.

14. On page 6 of the catalogue you will see that the computer science department is offering a number of courses in programming.

15. Please consult figure 3.2 in chapter 5 for statistics Canada figures regarding non-english-speaking residents.

Cumulative Editing Quiz 7

Use proofreading marks (see Appendix B) to correct errors and omissions in the following sentences. All errors must be corrected to receive credit for the sentence. Check with your instructor for the answers.

1. The Manager thinks that you attending the three day seminar is a good idea, however we must find a replacement.

2. We heard that professor watson invited edward peters, president of micropro, inc. to speak to our business law class.

3. Carla Jones a new systems programmer in our accounting department will start monday.

4. After year's of downsizing and restructuring canada has now become one of the worlds most efficient manufacturers.

5. When our company specialized in asian imports our main office was on the west coast.

6. Company's like amway discovered that there unique door to door selling methods was very successful in japan.

7. If you had given your sony camera to she or I before you got on the roller coaster it might have stayed dry.

8. Tracy recently finished a bachelors degree in accounting, consequently she is submitting many résumé's to companys across the country.

9. The Lopezs moved from Edmonton Alberta to Vancouver British Columbia when mr lopez enrolled at the university of british columbia.

10. When we open our office in montreal we will need employees whom are fluent in english and french.

Number Style (4.01–4.13)

Usage and custom determine whether numbers are expressed in the form of figures (for example, *5, 9*) or in the form of words (for example, *five, nine*). Numbers expressed as figures are shorter and more easily understood, yet numbers expressed as words are necessary in certain instances. The following guidelines are observed in expressing numbers in written sentences. Numbers that appear on business forms—such as invoices, monthly statements, and purchase orders—are always expressed as figures.

4.01 General Rules

a. The numbers one through ten are generally written as words. Numbers above ten are written as figures:

   The bank had a total of nine branch offices in three suburbs.

   All 58 employees received benefits in the three categories shown.

   A shipment of 45,000 light bulbs was sent from two warehouses.

b. Numbers that begin sentences are written as words. If a number beginning a sentence involves more than two words, however, the sentence should be written so that the number does not fall at the beginning.

   Fifteen different options were available in the annuity programs.

   A total of 156 companies participated in the promotion (not *One hundred fifty-six companies participated in the promotion*).

4.02 Money.
Sums of money $1 or greater are expressed as figures. If a sum is a whole dollar amount, omit the decimal and zeros (whether or not the amount appears in a sentence with additional fractional dollar amounts):

   We budgeted $30 for blank CDs, but the actual cost was $37.96.

   On the invoice were items for $6.10, $8, $33.95, and $75.

   Sums less than $1 are written as figures that are followed by the word *cents*:

   By shopping carefully, we can save 15 cents per blank CD.

4.03 Dates.
In dates, numbers that appear after the name of the month are written as cardinal figures (*1, 2, 3,* etc.). Those that stand alone or appear before the name of a month are written as ordinal figures (*1st, 2nd, 3nd,* etc.). Some writers use the space-saving *2d* and *3d* instead of *2nd* and *3rd.*

   The Personnel Practices Committee will meet May 7.

   On the 5th day of February and again on the 25th, we placed orders.

In domestic business documents, dates generally take the following form: *January 4, 2009.* An alternative form, used primarily in military and foreign correspondence, begins with the day of the month and omits the comma: *4 January 2009.*

4.04 Clock Time.
Figures are used when clock time is expressed with *a.m.* or *p.m.* Omit the colon and zeros in referring to whole hours. When exact clock time is expressed with the contraction *o'clock*, either figures or words may be used:

   Mail deliveries are made at 11 a.m. and 3:30 p.m.

   At four (or 4) o'clock employees begin to leave.

a. Except for the number one, house numbers are expressed in figures:

540 Elm Street   17802 Parliament Avenue

One Desmeurons Boulevard   2 Highland Street

b. Street names containing numbers ten or lower are written entirely as words. For street names involving numbers greater than ten, figures are used. Both are expressed using ordinal form (*-st, -nd, -th*):

330 Third Street   3440 Seventh Avenue

256 42nd Street   1390 11th Avenue

If a compass direction (*North, South, East, West*) separates a house number from a street number, however, do not use the ordinal form.

6945 East 32 Avenue   4903 West 103 Street

c. Telephone numbers are expressed with figures. When used, the area code is placed in parentheses preceding the telephone number:

Please call us at (818) 347-0551 to place an order.

Mr. Sui asked you to call (619) 554-8923, Ext. 245, after 10 a.m.

4.06 Related Numbers. Numbers are related when they refer to similar items in a category within the same reference. All related numbers should be expressed as the largest number is expressed. Thus if the largest number is greater than ten, all the numbers should be expressed in figures:

Only 5 of the original 25 applicants completed the processing. (Related numbers require figures.)

The two plans affected 34 employees working in three sites. (Unrelated numbers use figures and words.)

Petro-Canada operated 86 rigs, of which 6 were rented. (Related numbers require figures.)

The company hired three accountants, one customer service representative, and nine sales representatives. (Related numbers under ten use words.)

4.07 Consecutive Numbers. When two numbers appear consecutively and both modify a following noun, generally express the first number in words and the second in figures. If, however, the first number cannot be expressed in one or two words, put it in figures also (*120 34-cent stamps*). Do not use commas to separate the figures.

Historians divided the era into four 25-year periods. (Use word form for the first number and figure form for the second.)

We ordered twelve 30-page colour brochures. (Use word form for the first number and figure form for the second.)

Did the manager request 150 100-watt bulbs? (Use figure form for the first number since it would require more than two words.)

4.08 Periods of Time. Periods of time are generally expressed in word form. However, figures may be used to emphasize business concepts such as discount rates, interest rates, warranty periods, credit terms, loan or contract periods, and payment terms:

This business was incorporated over fifty years ago. (Use words for a period of time.)

Any purchaser may cancel a contract within 72 hours. (Use figures to explain a business concept.)

The warranty period is 5 years. (Use figures for a business concept.)

Cash discounts are given for payment within 30 days. (Use figures for a business concept.)

4.09 Ages. Ages are generally expressed in word form unless the age appears immediately after a name or is expressed in exact years and months:

At the age of twenty-one, Elizabeth inherited the business.

Wanda Unger, 37, was named acting president.

At the age of 4 years and 7 months, the child was adopted.

4.10 Round Numbers. Round numbers are estimates. They may be expressed in word or figure form, although figure form is shorter and easier to comprehend:

About 600 (or *six hundred*) stock options were sold.

It is estimated that 1000 (or *one thousand*) people will attend.

For ease of reading, round numbers in the millions or billions should be expressed with a combination of figures and words:

At least 1.5 million readers subscribe to the ten top magazines.

Deposits in money market accounts totalled more than $115 billion.

4.11 Weights and Measurements. Weights and measurements are expressed with figures:

The new deposit slip measures 5 by 15 cm.

Her new suitcase weighed only 1.2 kg.

Regina is 750 kilometres from Calgary.

4.12 Fractions. Simple fractions are expressed as words. Complex fractions may be written either as figures or as a combination of figures and words:

Over two thirds of the shareholders voted.

This microcomputer will execute the command in 1 millionth of a second. (Combination of words and numbers is easier to comprehend.)

She purchased a one-fifth share in the business. (Note that fractions used as adjectives require hyphens.)

4.13 Percentages and Decimals. Percentages are expressed with figures that are followed by the word *percent*. The percent sign (%) is used only on business forms or in statistical presentations:

We had hoped for a 7 percent interest rate, but we received a loan at 8 percent.

Over 50 percent of the residents supported the plan.

Decimals are expressed with figures. If a decimal expression does not contain a whole number (an integer) and does not begin with a zero, a zero should be placed before the decimal point:

The actuarial charts show that 1.74 out of 1,000 people will die in any given year.

Style and Usage

Inspector Norris found the setting to be .005 centimetres off. (Decimal begins with a zero and does not require a zero before the decimal point.)

Considerable savings will grow if the unit production cost is reduced by 0.1 percent. (A zero is placed before a decimal that neither contains a whole number nor begins with a zero).

Quick Chart—Expression of Numbers

Use Words	Use Figures
Numbers ten and under	Numbers 11 and over
Numbers at beginning of sentence	Money
Periods of time	Dates
Ages	Addresses and telephone numbers
Fractions	Weights and measurements
	Percentages and decimals

Review Exercise N—Number Style

Circle *a* or *b* to indicate the preferred number style. Assume that these numbers appear in business correspondence. When you finish, compare your responses with those provided. For each item on which you need review, consult the numbered principle shown in parentheses.

_____	1.	(a) 2 alternatives	(b)	two alternatives
_____	2.	(a) Seventh Avenue	(b)	7th Avenue
_____	3.	(a) sixty sales reps	(b)	60 sales reps
_____	4.	(a) November ninth	(b)	November 9
_____	5.	(a) forty dollars	(b)	$40
_____	6.	(a) on the 23d of May	(b)	on the twenty-third of May
_____	7.	(a) at 2:00 p.m.	(b)	at 2 p.m.
_____	8.	(a) 4 two-hundred-page books	(b)	four 200-page books
_____	9.	(a) at least 15 years ago	(b)	at least fifteen years ago
_____	10.	(a) 1,000,000 viewers	(b)	1 million viewers
_____	11.	(a) twelve cents	(b)	12 cents
_____	12.	(a) a sixty-day warranty	(b)	a 60-day warranty
_____	13.	(a) ten percent interest rate	(b)	10 percent interest rate
_____	14.	(a) 4/5 of the voters	(b)	four-fifths of the voters
_____	15.	(a) the rug measures two by four metres	(b)	the rug measures 2 by 4 metres
_____	16.	(a) about five hundred people attended	(b)	about 500 people attended
_____	17.	(a) at eight o'clock	(b)	at 8 o'clock
_____	18.	(a) located at 1 Broadway Boulevard	(b)	located at One Broadway Boulevard
_____	19.	(a) three computers for twelve people	(b)	three computers for 12 people
_____	20.	(a) 4 out of every 100 licences	(b)	four out of every 100 licences

1. b (4.01a) 3. b (4.01a) 5. b (4.02) 7. b (4.04) 9. b (4.08) 11. b (4.02) 13. b (4.13) 15. b (4.11) 17. a or b (4.04) 19. b (4.06)

Number Style

Review sections 4.01–4.13 above. Then study each of the following pairs. Assume that these expressions appear in the context of letters, reports, or e-mails. Write *a* or *b* in the space provided to indicate the preferred number style and record the number of the Handbook principle illustrated. When you finish, compare your response with those in the answer key on page 373. If your responses differ, carefully study again the principles in parentheses.

Example: (a) six investments (b) 6 investments   a _____ (4.01a)

1. (a) sixteen credit cards	(b) 16 credit cards	_____
2. (a) Fifth Avenue	(b) 5th Avenue	_____
3. (a) 34 newspapers	(b) thirty-four newspapers	_____
4. (a) July eighth	(b) July 8	_____
5. (a) twenty dollars	(b) $20	_____
6. (a) on the 15th of June	(b) on the fifteenth of June	_____
7. (a) at 4:00 p.m.	(b) at 4 p.m.	_____
8. (a) 3 200-page reports	(b) three 200-page reports	_____
9. (a) over 18 years ago	(b) over eighteen years ago	_____
10. (a) 2,000,000 people	(b) 2 million people	_____
11. (a) fifteen cents	(b) 15 cents	_____
12. (a) a thirty-day warranty	(b) a 30-day warranty	_____
13. (a) 2/3 of the e-mails	(b) two-thirds of the e-mails	_____
14. (a) two telephones for 15 employees	(b) 2 telephones for 15 employees	_____
15. (a) 6 of the 130 letters	(b) six of the 130 letters	

Cumulative Editing Quiz 8

Use proofreading marks (see Appendix B) to correct errors and omissions in the following sentences. All errors must be corrected to receive credit for the sentence. Check with your instructor for the answers.

1. The prime minister of Canada recommended a 30 day break in the united nations peace negotiations.

2. Please meet at my lawyers office at four p.m. on May 10th to sign our papers.

3. A Retail Store at 405 7th avenue had sales of over one million dollars last year.

4. Every new employee must receive their permit to park in lot 5-A or there car will be towed.

5. Mr thompson left three million dollars to be divided among his 4 children rachel, timothy, rebecca and kevin.

6. Most companys can boost profits almost one hundred percent by retaining only 5% more of there current customers.

7. Although the bill for coffee and doughnuts were only three dollars and forty cents Pavel and myself had trouble paying it.

8. Only six of the 19 employees, who filled out survey forms, would have went to hawaii as their vacation choice.

9. Danielles report is more easier to read then david because her's was better organized and had good headings.

10. At mcdonald's we devoured 4 big macs 3 orders of french fries and 5 coca colas for lunch.

Confusing Words

accede:	to agree or consent	device:	invention or mechanism
exceed:	over a limit	devise:	to design or arrange
accept:	to receive	disburse:	to pay out
except:	to exclude; (*prep.*) but	disperse:	to scatter widely
advice:	suggestion, opinion	elicit:	to draw out
advise:	to counsel or recommend	illicit:	unlawful
affect:	to influence	every day:	each single day
effect:	(*n.*) outcome, result; (*v.*) to bring about, to create	everyday:	ordinary
		farther:	a greater distance
		further:	additional
all ready:	prepared	formally:	in a formal manner
already:	by this time	formerly:	in the past
all right:	satisfactory	hole:	an opening
alright:	(unacceptable variant spelling)	whole:	complete
		imply:	to suggest indirectly
altar:	structure for worship	infer:	to reach a conclusion
alter:	to change	liable:	legally responsible
appraise:	to estimate	libel:	damaging written statement
apprise:	to inform		
assure:	to promise	loose:	not fastened
ensure:	to make certain	lose:	to misplace
insure:	to protect from loss	miner:	person working in a mine
capital:	(*n.*) city that is seat of government; wealth of an individual; (*adj.*) chief	minor:	a lesser item; person under age
		patience:	calm perseverance
capitol:	building that houses state or national lawmakers	patients:	people receiving medical treatment
		personal:	private, individual
cereal:	breakfast food	personnel:	employees
serial:	arranged in sequence	precede:	to go before
cite:	to quote; to summon	proceed:	to continue
site:	location	precedence:	priority
sight:	a view; to see	precedents:	events used as an example
complement:	that which completes	principal:	(*n.*) capital sum; school official; (*adj.*) chief
compliment:	to praise or flatter		
conscience:	regard for fairness	principle:	rule of action
conscious:	aware	stationary:	immovable
council:	governing body	stationery:	writing material
counsel:	to give advice; advice	than:	conjunction showing comparison
desert:	arid land; to abandon		
dessert:	sweet food	then:	adverb meaning "at that time"

their:	possessive form of they	*waiver:*	abandonment of a claim
there:	at that place or point	*waver:*	to shake or fluctuate
they're:	contraction of they are		
to:	a preposition; the sign of the infinitive		
too:	an adverb meaning "also" or "to an excessive extent"		
two:	a number		

160 Frequently Misspelled Words

absence	desirable	independent	prominent
accommodate	destroy	indispensable	qualify
achieve	development	interrupt	quantity
acknowledgment	disappoint	irrelevant	questionnaire
across	dissatisfied	itinerary	receipt
adequate	division	judgment	receive
advisable	efficient	knowledge	recognize
analyze	embarrass	legitimate	recommendation
annually	emphasis	library	referred
appointment	emphasize	licence	regarding
argument	employee	maintenance	remittance
automatically	envelope	manageable	representative
bankruptcy	equipped	manufacturer	restaurant
becoming	especially	mileage	schedule
beneficial	evidently	miscellaneous	secretary
budget	exaggerate	mortgage	separate
business	excellent	necessary	similar
calendar	exempt	nevertheless	sincerely
cancelled	existence	ninety	software
catalogue	extraordinary	ninth	succeed
changeable	familiar	noticeable	sufficient
column	fascinate	occasionally	supervisor
committee	feasible	occurred	surprise
congratulate	February	offered	tenant
conscience	fiscal	omission	therefore
conscious	foreign	omitted	thorough
consecutive	forty	opportunity	though
consensus	fourth	opposite	through
consistent	friend	ordinarily	truly
control	genuine	paid	undoubtedly
convenient	government	pamphlet	unnecessarily
correspondence	grammar	permanent	usable
courteous	grateful	permitted	usage
criticize	guarantee	pleasant	using
decision	harass	practical	usually
deductible	height	prevalent	valuable
defendant	hoping	privilege	volume
definitely	immediate	probably	weekday
dependent	incidentally	procedure	writing
describe	incredible	profited	yield

Confusing Words

Key to Grammar/ Mechanics Checkups

Checkup 1
1. attorneys (1.05d) 2. Saturdays (1.05a) 3. cities (1.05e) 4. turkeys (1.05d) 5. inventories (1.05e) 6. Nashes (1.05b) 7. 1990s (1.05g) 8. editors in chief (1.05f) 9. complexes (1.05b) 10. municipalities (1.05e) 11. Jennifers (1.05a) 12. C (1.05d) 13. liabilities (1.05e) 14. C (1.05h) 15. runners-up (1.05f)

Checkup 2
1. he (1.08b) 2. his car (1.09b) 3. him (1.08c) 4. whom (1.08j) 5. hers (1.08d) 6. me (1.08c) 7. I (1.08a) 8. yours (1.08d) 9. whoever (1.08j) 10. me (1.08i) 11. he (1.08f) 12. us (1.08g) 13. her (1.09c) 14. its (1.09g) 15. his or her (1.09b)

Checkup 3
1. *are* for *is* (1.10e) 2. *has* for *have* (1.10c) 3. *offers* for *offer* (1.10d) 4. *is* for *are* (1.10g) 5. C (1.10f) 6. *is* for *are* (1.10i) 7. C (1.10h) 8. *chosen* for *chose* (1.15) 9. *lain* for *laid* (1.15) 10. *were* for *was* (1.12) 11. *is* for *are* (1.10c) 12. b (1.15c) 13. b (1.15c) 14. a (1.15c) 15. b (1.15c)

Checkup 4
1. long-time (1.17e) 2. $50-per-year (1.17e) 3. C (1.17e) 4. quickly (1.17d) 5. had only (1.17f) 6. double-digit (1.17e) 7. once-in-a-lifetime (1.17e) 8. C (1.17e) 9. better (1.17a) 10. well-known (1.17e) 11. up-to-the-minute (1.17e) 12. after-tax (1.17e) 13. couldn't have been clearer (1.17b) 14. fifty-fifty (1.17e) 15. feel bad (1.17c)

Checkup 5
1. b (1.19d) 2. a (1.19c) 3. b (1.18e) 4. b (1.19c) 5. a (1.19a) 6. b (1.18a) 7. b (1. 18b) 8. a (1.18c) 9. b (1.18b) 10. a (1.19c) 11. b (1.19a) 12. b (1.19b) 13. a (1.19c) 14. b (1.18e) 15. b (1.19c)

Checkup 6
1. (2) not, as a rule, (2.03) 2. (2) sure, Schwartz, (2.02) 3. (2) reliable, hard-working, (2.01) 4. (0) 5. (1) fact, (2.03) 6. (3) Calgary, Alberta, Sherbrooke, (2.04c) 7. (1) meantime, (2.03) 8. (2) February 4, 2001, (2.04a) 9. (3) Horne, Hae, Andorra, (2.01) 10. (4) Holmes, Lane, Regina, Saskatchewan S5L 2E2, (2.04b) 11. (2) feels, needless to say, (2.03) 12. (2) supplies, replacing inventories, (2.01) 13. (1) business, (2.02) 14. (2) feels, however, (2.03) 15. 0

Checkup 7
1. (1) warranty, (2.06a) 2. (1) market, (2.05) 3. (0) (2.05) 4. (2) manufacturer, nameless, (2.06c) 5. (1) imaginative, (2.08) 6. (0) (2.06c) 7. (2) Sims, area, (2.09) 8. (1) buyers, (2.05) 9. (1) quality, (2.06a) 10. (1) buyers, (2.07) 11. (2) application, Monday, (2.04a, 2.06a) 12. (2) hand, hard-working, (2.03, 2.08) 13. (1) Creek, (2.06c) 14. (3) telephone, Thursday, 9, (2.04a, 2.06a) 15. (1) classes, (2.05)

Checkup 8
1. (2) name," Etienne, (2.14a) 2. (4) Cox, Ph.D., Meridian, M.B.A., (2.10) 3. (1) Monday, (2.14b) 4. (0) (2.15) 5. (1) investment, (2.12) 6. (3) requested, cartridges, folders, (2.01, 2.06a) 7. (2) think, however, (2.03) 8. (2) period, Vidal, (2.06c, 2.07) 9. (2) Collingwood, Laurentians, (2.01, 2.15) 10. (1) interviewed, (2.06a) 11. (2) years, individuals, (2.07, 2.09) 12. (2) Johansson, week, (2.06c, 2.15) 13. (0) (2.15) 14. (2) companies, robots, (2.01) 15. (2) fact, unprotected, (2.03, 2.08)

Checkup 9
1. (3) year; long-term financing, hand, (2.03, 2.16b) 2. (2) December; therefore, (2.16a) 3. (3) months: September, October, (2.01, 2.17a) 4. (1) include [omit comma] (2.17b) 5. (1) money, (2.06a) 6. (3) short-term credit; manufacturer, however, (2.03, 2.16b) 7. (2) loans, notes, (2.01, 2.17a) 8. (9) businesspeople: Mahan, manager, Industries; Buchanan, comptroller, Bank; Cavalier, operations, (2.16c, 2.17a) 9. (1) Canada, (2.05) 10. (5) customers; example, retailers, companies, manufacturers, (2.01, 2.16d) 11. (4) Inc., rating, loan; however, (2.03, 2.06c, 2.16a) 12. (2) Bank, following: (2.06a, 2.17a) 13. (2) high; therefore, (2.16a) 14. (3) percent, expensive; consequently, (2.06a, 2.16a) 15. (1) resources; (2.16b)

Checkup 10

1. Faulkner's (2.20a) 2. year's (2.20a) 3. weeks' (2.20b) 4. Lanham's (2.21) 5. boss's (2.20b) 6. server's (2.20a) 7. Kaspar's (2.22) 8. months' (2.20b) 9. companies' (2.20b) 10. month's (2.20a) 11. secretary's (2.20a) 12. sellers' (2.20b) 13. Mark's, David's (2.20a) 15. Latika's (2.20a)

Checkup 11

1. (2) managers—Yu Sosa—to (2.26a) 2. (3) please, Fundy, totals. (2.02, 2.23a) 3. (2) (see 432) (2.27) 4. (3) "recommendation" misspelled, (2.06a, 2.28c) 5. (1) training—these (2.26c) 6. (3) "Who cartridges?" (2.28f) 7. (3) "How You"? (2.28e, 2.28f) 8. (2) provinces—Alberta Ontario—are (2.26a) 9. (3) Mr. E. Ms. (2.23b, 2.24) 10. (3) "Trading Market" *Securities Markets* (2.28e) 11. (2) over"; however, (2.16, 2.28f) 12. (3) *liability* "any future." (2.28d) 13. (1) 10; (2.06a) 14. (4) c.o.d. today? (2.23b, 2.24) 15. (3) Hooray! checkup, I? (2.14b, 2.24, 2.25)

Checkup 12

1. c (2.05) 2. b (2.06) 3. a (2.16a) 4. c (2.15) 5. b (2.16b) 6. b (2.17a) 7. a (2.20b) 8. c (2.16c) 9. b (2.04a) 10. c (2.03) 11. a (2.08) 12. a (2.12) 13. a (2.01) 14. c (2.07) 15. b (2.16a)

Checkup 13

1. (5) Canadian customs inspection International Airport (3.01, 3.02, 3.07) 2. (6) Japanese international Japanese economics professor University (3.01, 3.02, 3.04, 3.06d) 3. (3) investors stock market (3.01, 3.13) 4. (4) history sociology computer science (3.05) 5. (5) Horticulture Are Nothing Sneeze At (3.12) 6. (2) printers printers (3.11) 7. (3) federal government provincial (3.10) 8. (5) Prime Minister Canada This foreign (3.01, 3.06c, 3.13) 9. (8) comptroller president board directors Canada Revenue Agency company (3.01, 3.04, 3.06c) 10. (2) mother sun's (3.03, 3.06g, 3.08, 3.14) 11. (5) managing editor manager ad campaign (3.01, 3.06d, 3.06e, 3.09) 12. (1) Australian (3.02, 3.06a, 3.16) 13. (4) Park island Vanier Bridge (3.01, 3.03) 14. (3) Computer Science Department (3.05, 3.07, 3.09) 15. (4) Figure Chapter Statistics English (3.02, 3.04, 3.07)

Checkup 14

1. b (4.01a) 2. a (4.05b) 3. a (4.01a) 4. b (4.03) 5. b (4.02) 6. a (4.03) 7. b (4.04) 8. b (4.07) 9. b (4.08) 10. b (4.10) 11. b (4.02) 12. b (4.08) 13. b (4.12) 14. a (4.06) 15. a (4.06)

Notes

Chapter 1

1. Rick Spence, "Seven Trends That Could Make or Break Your Business," *Profit*, May 2005, http://www.profitguide.com (accessed April 26, 2005).

2. Statistics Canada predicts that by 2017, visible minorities will in fact be the majority of the population in major centres such as Toronto, Vancouver, and Montreal. See Statistics Canada, *The Daily*, March 22, 2005, http://www.statcan.ca/Daily/English/050322/d050322b.htm.

3. Anne Papmehl, "Remote Access," *CMA Management*, 75, no. 3 (May 2001): 11.

4. Ray Birdwhistell, *Kinesics and Context* (Philadelphia: University of Pennsylvania Press, 1970).

5. E. T. Hall, *The Hidden Dimension* (Garden City, NY: Doubleday, 1966), 107–122.

6. Catherine Bell, "Prime Impressions Corporate Training," "Prime Impressions Telecoaching," http://www.prime-impressions.com (accessed April 26, 2005).

7. Norman McGuinness and Nigel Campbell, "Selling Machinery to China: Chinese Perceptions of Strategies and Relationships," *Journal of International Business Studies* 22, no. 3 (1991): 187.

8. Statistics Canada, CANSIM, Matrices 6367 (estimates), 6900 (projections), http://www.statcan.ca/english/Pgdb/People/Population/demo23c.htm; and Matrix 3472, available www.statcan.ca/english/Pgdb/People/Labour/labor05.htm (accessed April 23, 2002).

9. Virginia Galt, "Western Union Remakes Canadian Image: Profits from Overseas Hiring, Staff Diversity," *The Globe and Mail*, November 23, 2004, B1.

10. Lee Gardenswartz and Anita Rowe, "Helping Managers Solve Cultural Conflicts," *Managing Diversity*, August 1996, http://www.jalmc.org/hlp-mgr.htm (accessed April 23, 2002).

11. Pete Engardio, "Hmm. Could Use a Little More Snake," *BusinessWeek*, March 15, 1993, 53.

Chapter 2

1. John DeGoey, personal interview, April 28, 2005.

2. Editorial Staff, "Canadian CEOs Are Big on Communication," *CMA Management*, 74, no. 9 (November 2000): 8.

3. Don Tapscott, "R U N2 It?" *Enroute* Magazine, October 2003, 35–36.

4. Kevin Marron, "Instant Messaging Comes of Age," *The Globe and Mail*, November 1, 2001, B30.

5. Earl N. Harbert, "Knowing Your Audience," in *The Handbook of Executive Communication*, ed. John L. Digaetani (Homewood, IL: Dow Jones/Irwin, 1986), 17.

Chapter 3

1. Shelly Chagnon, personal interview, April 28, 2005.

2. Nicholas Russell, "Russell's Rules for Good Writing," *Canadian Association of Newspaper Editors*, May 4, 1996, http://www.cane.ca/english/me_res_russell.htm (accessed May 2, 2001).

3. Maryann V. Piotrowski, *Effective Business Writing* (New York: Harper Perennial, 1996), 12.

Chapter 4

1. Stephanie Mikelbrencis, personal interview, May 24, 2005.

2. Chan Tran, "Signs of Status Even in E-mail," *Workforce* 80, no. 6 (June 2001): 18.

Chapter 5

1. Peter Schneider, personal interview, May 1, 2005.

2. "Canadians Lead the World in Internet Use," *Canadian Press*, May 28, 2001.

3. Editors, "We've Got (Lots of) Mail," *School Library Journal* 46, no. 12 (December 2000): 44.

4. Statistics Canada, "Perspectives on Labour and Income," *Working with Computers* 13, no. 2 (Summer 2001).

5. Nova Scotia Human Rights Commission, "Rights on Religion or Creed," http://www.gov.ns.ca/humanrights/rights/religionorcreed.htm (accessed April 27, 2005).

6. Editors. "'Surfeillance' in the Workplace," *Worklife Report*; 12(4) (2000): 13.

7. Ibid.

8. Ibid.

9. Chris Wood and Brenda Branswell, "Do You Know Who's Watching You?" *Maclean's*, February 19, 2001.

Chapter 6

1. Reg Pirie, "The Lost Art of Business Letter Writing," *CanadaOne Magazine*, June 1999, http://www.canadaone.com/ezine/june99/letters.html (accessed April 29, 2005).

2. Marcia Mascolini, "Another Look at Teaching the External Negative Message," *The Bulletin of the Association of Business Communication*, June 1994, 46.

3. Pamela Gilbert, "Two Words That Can Help a Business Thrive," *The Wall Street Journal*, December 30, 1996, A12.

4. Canadian Business for Social Responsibility, "Definition of Key Terms," *GoodCompany: Guidelines for Corporate Social Performance*, http://www.cbsr.bc.ca/files/GoodCompany-SummaryDocument.pdf (accessed May 1, 2005).

Chapter 7

1. Jose Ribau, personal interview, April 29, 2005.

2. Editors, Doing Business in Canada website, Section 2.7, http://www.dbic.com/guide/tm2-7.html (accessed January 10, 2002).

3. Neil Morton, "Some Like It Cold," *Canadian Business*, September 1997, 99.

4. Canadian Fitness and Lifestyle Research Institute, "2002 Physical Activity Monitor," http://www.cflri.ca/cflri/pa/surveys/2002survey/2002survey.html (accessed November 3, 2005).

5. Government of Canada, Public Service Commission, Recourse Branch, "Workplace Conflict? Making the Right Choice," July 2000.

6. Statistics Canada, "Sources of Workplace Stress," *The Daily*, June 25, 2003, http://www.statcan.ca/Daily/English/030625/d030625c.htm (accessed April 21, 2005).

7. Bernard Morrow and Lauren M. Bernardi, "Resolving Workplace Disputes," *Canadian Manager*, 24, no. 1 (Spring 1999): 17.

8. Nora Wood, "Singled Out," *Incentive*, July 1998, 20–23.

Chapter 8

1. Maria Duncan, personal interview, April 28, 2005.

2. Mohan R. Limaye, "Further Conceptualization of Explanations in Negative Messages," *Business Communication Quarterly*, June 1997, 46.

3. Elizabeth M. Dorn, "Case Method Instruction in the Business Writing Classroom," *Business Communication Quarterly*, March 1999, 51–52.

4. Michael Granberry, "Lingerie Chain Fined $100 000 for Gift Certificates," *Los Angeles Times*, November 14, 1992, D3.

5. Tyler Hamilton, "Price Snafu Stings Web Retailer," *The Toronto Star*, November 17, 2000, C01.

6. Based on Robert D. Ramsey, "Social Skills for Supervisors," *Supervision*, January 1997, 5–7; Marjorie Brody, "Test Your Manners I.Q.," *Successful Meetings*, September 1999, 145-146; and Edith Helmich, "Business Etiquette for a Technological Age," http://www.hightechcareers.com/doc799/how-to799.html (accessed December 8, 1999).

Chapter 9

1. Heather Jack, personal interview, May 12, 2005.

Chapter 10

1. Orna Spira, personal interview, May 27, 2005.

2. Shearlean Duke, "E-mail: Essential in Media Relations, But No Replacement for Face-to-Face Communication," *Public Relations Quarterly* (Winter 2001): 19; and Lisa M. Flaherty, Kevin J. Pearce, and Rebecca B. Rubin, "Internet and Face-to-Face Communication: Not Functional Alternatives," *Communication Quarterly* (Summer 1998): 250.

3. Aimee L. Drolet and Michael W. Morris, "Rapport in Conflict Resolution: Accounting for How Face-to-Face Contact Fosters Mutual Cooperation in Mixed-Motive Conflicts," *Journal of Experimental Social Psychology* (January 2000): 26.

4. Jean Miculka, *Speaking for Success* (Cincinnati: South-Western, 1999), 19.

5. Miculka, *Speaking*, 127.

6. "Fire Up Your Phone Skills," *Successful Meetings*, November 2000, 30.

7. Winston Fletcher, "How to Make Sure It's a Good Call," *Management Today*, February 2000, 34.

8. "Did You Know That ...," *Boardroom Reports*, August 15, 1992.

9. Elizabeth Guilday, "Voicemail Like a Pro," *Training & Development*, October 2000, 68.

Chapter 11

1. Christine Shreves, personal interview, May 20, 2005.

2. Interview by author, January 21, 1997.

3. "Consider Adding a Keyword Summary," *Royal Bank of Canada*, http://www.royalbank.com/fastforward/apply_res.html (accessed December 1, 2001).

4. Harriet M. Augustin, "The Written Job Search: A Comparison of the Traditional and a Nontraditional Approach," *The Bulletin of the Association for Business Communication*, September 1991, 13.

5. Judith Schroer, "Seek a Job With a Little Help From Your Friends," *USA Today*, November 19, 1990, B1.

Chapter 12

1. Michael Stern, "Dear Sir: You Are An Oaf ...," *Canadian Business*, April 1998, 38.

2. Caryl Rae Krannich and Ronald L. Krannich, *Dynamite Answers to Interview Questions* (Manassas Park, VA: Impact Publications, 1994), 46.

3. Julia Lawlor, "Networking Opens More Doors to Jobs," *USA Today*, November 19, 1990, B7.

4. Michael Shekter, "How to State Your Salary Expectations," http://www.workopolis.ca (accessed September 21, 2001).

Index

Information reports, 189, 195, 196–197
Information response letters, 112–114
Initials, 352
Inside address, 286
Instant messaging, 26–27
insure, ensure, assure, 370
Interest, building, 139
Interjections, 315
Internal communication, 80–81
Internet
    career search on, 20, 236–237
    personal use of, 105–106
Interviews, 193, 264–276
    actions to avoid, 269
    chronological, 265
    closing, 272–274
    fear, 267
    follow-up letters, 274–276
    get acquainted questions, 269–270
    group, 265
    hiring/placement, 264–265
    illegal questions, 272–273
    investigating company before, 265–266
    money questions, 272
    nonverbal messages during, 267
    one-on-one, 265
    preparation for, 265–266
    question about experience/accomplishments, 270
    questions, 268–273
    questions about future, 270–271
    steps (recruiter's perspective), 268
    uncomfortable questions, 271
In-text citations, 302–303, 307
Introductory clauses, 338
Introductory expressions, 346
Introductory words, 65–66
Irregular verbs, 324–325
Italics, 304

Jargon, 66
Job application forms, 276
Job interviews. *See* Interviews
Job market, hidden, 262–263
Job search techniques
    electronic, 20, 236–237
    traditional, 236
JobsEtc.ca, 236
Journal articles, 304
Justification reports, 196, 197, 199–200

Keywords, for résumés, 246–247

Language
    inclusive, 29–30
    positive, 29
    sexist, 30
Lead-ins, 65–66
Letter parts, 286–290
Letter placement, 286
Letter styles, 287, 290–291
Letterhead, 286
Letters, 26, 27
    bad news, 164–184
    body of, 111
    claim requests, 111–112, 139–140, 141
    closings, 111, 114, 118
    complaint, 139–140
    cover, 249–254
    customer claim responses, 114–118
    follow-up, 274–276
    formatting, 110
    good news in, 116
    goodwill messages, 120
    information requests, 110
    information response, 112–114
    openings, 109, 111–112, 114
    of recommendation, 118–121
    of response, 123
    routine, 108–133
    sales, 143–150
    thank you, 122–123
    See also Document formats
liable, libel, 370
Listed items, 346
Listening skills
    development of, 5–7
    with diverse audiences, 14
Lists, in e-mails, 90–91
Literary titles, 361

Magazine titles, 303
Mailing address, 291–293
Main idea
    in e-mails, 82–83
    placement of, 45–46
Management, layers of, 3
Margins, 286
Masculine pronouns, 30
Meaning, transmission of, 4
Measurements, 367
Mechanics, emphasis through, 49
Meetings
    face-to-face, 26
    minutes of, 196, 201–202